THE DEVIL IN DREAMLAND

Catholic Faith
UFOs
the Occult
and the End of the
Supernatural

URSULA BIELSKI

GADARENE PRESS

ISBN 13: 979-8-218-49322-6

Cover design image:
The Fallen Angel by Alexandre Cabanel
Printed in the United States of America

That all may look up at the stars
and see God.

I am convinced these 'things' are spooked by us, that they see an image of something that they want to be, that they know what we are, in respect to identity, but that we as humans do not know who we represent.

-Jo Tagliarini, Psychotherapist

In dealing with the mystery of UFOs, we are not on the lunatic fringe of theology…. We are in defensive warfare at a major point of assault on humanity.

-David Allen Lewis, *UFO: End Time Delusion*

The natural person does not accept the things of the Spirit of God, for they are folly to him, and he cannot understand them because they are spiritually discerned.

-1 Corinthians 2:14

CONTENTS

PREFACE 9

ANOTHER WORLD 17

OF THE AIR 25

STORIES FROM THE SKY 33

NINETEEN FORTY-SEVEN 43

THE BEAST AND THE GRAY 57

THE WIZARD OF PASADENA 63

SHADY CRUSADE 69

CALLED 85

MEN IN THE NIGHT 95

A LITTLE TOO FAMILIAR (PART 1) 109

SPIRITED AWAY 127

THE DAYS OF NOAH 143

A LITTLE TOO FAMILIAR (PART 2) 151

AS ABOVE, SO BELOW 159

SPIRITUALISTS, SKIN WALKERS AND SPACE X 173

A LITTLE TOO FAMILIAR (PART 3) 183

THE SUMMONERS 191

THE DEEP END 209

AWOL FOR THE ANTICHRIST 225

JUST HERE FOR THE SOULS 233

ABOVE ALL OTHER 241

WONDROUS THINGS 247

UNDER THEIR SKIN 277

THE POSTER CHILD 285

OF UNKNOWN ORIGIN 293

TREKKIES IN THE VATICAN 307

EPILOGUE 339

ACKNOWLEDGEMENTS 349

INDEX 351

NOTES 367

PREFACE

In the summer of 1990, between undergraduate terms at Benedictine University near Chicago, I asked my then boyfriend, Jim, if he wanted to take a road trip to Wisconsin. Located about two hours north of the Illinois border, on a bluff above the town of Wonewoc, is a nineteenth-century Spiritualist camp founded by psychic mediums. As a student of American religion—and someone destined for a lifetime of work in paranormal research— this was (and still is) my idea of fun.

Jim agreed readily, and a few days later we drove north through the lush June landscape to the camp. Once there, we checked in and were assigned one of the historic but dilapidated whitewashed cabins original to the site. Inside, we discovered the furnishings sparse, the floor bare. A sign taped to the sink warned the water was unsafe to drink, and the only lock on the door was an eye hook. The rickety metal frame beds appeared original to the structure, and the only wall decoration was a black velvet painting of "Chief White Feather" who, the registrar said, served as the "spirit guide" watching over our cabin.

Despite my fascination with the history and mystery of the place, I found it somehow unnerving. In the evening, fellow campers gathered in the camp chapel to sing songs accompanied by organ music, in between attempts to communicate with the dead. I had come here to join those sessions, but something I couldn't put a finger on kept me, throughout our stay, at arm's length. I guess you could say that, at one of the nation's oldest Spiritualist camps, I was spooked.

Jim was too, and so we decided to keep to ourselves. We ventured into town and spent a few hours at a local tavern, drinking water glasses filled with Pabst Blue Ribbon. Afterwards, we returned to the edge of the camp to watch the sunset from the bluff overlooking the town. Some local kids below called up, "Wooooo!"--imitating, I guess, the sound of ghosts. (I found out later that locals refer to the camp "Spook Hill.")

Walking back to our cabin, we passed the camp café called the Flying Saucer, its name hand-painted on the sign. At the time I didn't understand the connection between Spiritualism and UFOs, and this would mark my first exposure to the link between extraterrestrials and the spirit world--the latter a subject I would study for the next thirty-five years. It would take almost that long before I came to realize how deep—and dark—this connection really was.

In the past I have engaged in what many people popularly now refer to as "ghost hunting." But mostly I'm an historian and folklorist of the supernatural. I study religion, belief and experience.

I'm also a Catholic.

As such, when I (like so many people these days) obsessively read and watch and generally devour all I can find about experiences with UFO and extraterrestrials, I find a very troubling phenomenon unfolding. What I see are great minds—theologians, apologists, academics—abandoning their faith, little by little (or maybe a lot faster) for what is, in their minds, a glittering alternative: the prospect that their childhood dreams of alien contact may actually be coming true.

As they support the so-called extraterrestrial hypothesis (ETH)—the belief in intelligent alien life—scholars and theologians (and their trusting followers) seem to also be accepting the deeply occult origins of the entire UFO phenomenon. For while congressional hearings and mainstream journalists have been addressing what ufologists call a "nuts and bolts" question of UFOs and extraterrestrial life (i.e. are spacecraft piloted by physical beings visiting earth?), the true nature of UFOs is not that easy— and far from benign. And if one wants to meet these alien beings, one *must* employ esoteric tools to make it happen.

It's the exact same story that played out around seance tables a century and a half ago, as Enlightened seekers demanded voices, raps and the manifestation of spirits as proof of an invisible realm.

Today, believers are summoning "spacecraft," meditating to receive "downloads" from "extraterrestrials," and asking AI chatbots to write magical rituals. The terms are different, but the tale as old as time: human beings defying God's law to grasp something forbidden.

I know a bit about how this all works. After the cultural explosion of "hobby ghost hunting" at the dawn of the 2000s, I found myself lured into a new kind of parapsychology. It was far from the academic work I had begun as an eighteen-year old undergraduate student assisting a psychology-major friend of mine on field research into reported hauntings, poltergeists and other parapsychological "spontaneous phenomena." It also differed from the careful, quiet, methodical research and investigation I had done alone in graduate school and beyond, working as an independent chronicler of the supernatural. This new type of paranormal research was sloppy, dramatic and, most of all, unapologetically occult, with only one real goal: real-time, two-way communication with spirits via mediums, psychics, recorders, "ghost box" radios or, in fact, by any means necessary.

In the end this work took me to a very dark place. And I didn't get there alone. As we'll see later in this book, a horde of Vatican approved scholars and clerics – priests, monsignors, bishops and at least two popes – seemed to rubber stamp what I and others were doing, all in the name of science. As a result, many devout colleagues joined me in gleefully throwing Deuteronomy 18 (and other scriptural commands) to the wind.

In the end, I learned my lesson – the hard way. Five years ago, I walked away from the occult methodologies I had come to rely on in my work. Why? Because I'd come to realize something most of my fellows—those still actively researching remote viewing, telepathy, psychokinesis and, most popularly, spirit communication--apparently don't wish to accept: that there is no way one can engage in the study of these subjects and also save one's soul.

Shell-shocked by a real spiritual battle from which I'd emerged, I decided to investigate the "harmless" field of UFO research.

What I discovered is a world more steeped in the occult than any tarot card-reading, crystal-carrying psychic witch I'd encountered in my long career (there were many). I found, in fact, that the study of UFOs draws one into a world and history filled with channeling, seances, black magic and every other subcategory of the New Age.

As I devoured the literature on encounters with purported UFOs and extraterrestrials, I also found, in case after case, that the "evidence" left behind by these beings—burns, scratches, bruises, unexplained pregnancies, poltergeist activity, radio and phone communications, and (most maliciously) dark turns in personalities and relationships—was often identical to the evidence left after encounters with the demonic.

I further discovered that, despite the claims presented of "nuts and bolts" craft and "alien bodies," there was zero scientific evidence of anything not frankly terrestrial. What there *was* a lot of was cash. That and seemingly endless servings of "alphabet soup": those three-to-five-letter acronym government agencies and their smoke and mirror committees, all part of some vast, unspoken operation.

I wasn't the only one who saw through the dark and devilish underpinnings of the UFO enigma. The alarm was sounding throughout evangelical and other Protestant communities everywhere. These weren't spacemen in spaceships, the preachers and pastors were saying, but an old Enemy dressed in the latest fashion, a disguise *du jour*. The end game, of course, is what it's always been: to erase God. To transform the great Unknown into a world that has nothing to do with Him—or with the age-old spiritual battle between His children and the devil.

But while many Christian faithful are issuing a warning against the occult—especially regarding the UFO enigma—many Catholic scholars are, disturbingly, embracing it.

Beloved lay Catholic scholar Jimmy Akin–who hosts extended podcasts in which he presents "both sides" of the theological argument for and against such topics as remote viewing, channeling and spirit communication—frequently employs hermeneutical gymnastics so to make it "just fine" for Catholics to partake of occult fare. He's taken lately to promoting the extraterrestrial hypothesis, positing abominable possibilities like multiple incarnations of Jesus (and multiple mothers of Jesus), as well as suggesting that some of those Jesuses might not be born of a male and female, because the ETs' biology may be different than our own.[1]

Paul Thigpen, who literally wrote the book on the Catholic Church and UFOs (*Extraterrestrials and the Catholic Faith*), giddily assures us that the idea of aliens is no problem for members of the Church, even claiming—without any real evidence—that various saints, including the beloved Saint Padre Pio, endorsed the idea. Like others, he also has failed to inform his trusting followers of the outrageously occult roots and activities of both UFO experiencers and the ufologists who seek them.

Even secular UFO believers continue to embrace the teachings of the late Vatican official and theologian Monsignor Corrado Balducci. Though he worked as an exorcist and fervently believed in the devil and the spiritual battle between good and evil, Balducci reassured the faithful that there is nothing demonic about the UFO phenomenon, choosing to willfully ignore its long connection to the occult and the often overtly anti-Christian tenets taught by "extraterrestrials."

Diana Pasulka, an historian of religion and professed Catholic who has become no less than an icon in ufology (the study of the UFO phenomenon) meanwhile tells us that she doesn't quite know why, but that anyone who wants to study UFOs must engage in occult methods to do so. She also has a record of regaling secular UFO believers with theories that Catholic saints' visits from angels, the stigmata of St. Francis of Assisi and the Miracle of the Sun at Fatima, Portugal in 1917 were just like UFO encounters, something backed up by her mentor and friend, Jaque Vallée.

Vallée—arguably the most knowledgeable and respected of all ufologists—was the model for Steven Spielberg's character of the French scientist in the film *Close Encounters of the Third Kind.* He is often embraced by God-believers, because he was one of the first researchers to suggest that UFOs (and the things we call "extraterrestrials") are not physical beings from out in space but interdimensional ones involved in some kind of massive deception of humanity.

But Vallée isn't saying, as many Christians think he is, that ETs are demons, or even that they are spiritual. Vallée is an agnostic at best, and "interdimensional" is the new "material" for him and his millions of followers, fans and proteges—including Catholics like Pasulka. And yet, while visiting Vallée at his California condo, Pasulka noticed the iconic ufologist's bookshelves were brimming with volumes about angels and demons.

In the secular UFO world, there's one hard and fast rule. I call it "ABG," or Anything But God. Anything is believable today, as long as God isn't behind it. So when UFOs are the subject, anything else goes. Aliens created us. We are living in an alien-controlled computer simulation. Aliens are inseminating humans to create a terrestrial army. ETs burn, bite, scratch, bruise and batter humans—that's proof they exist. In the new secular UFO religion, people can summon spacecraft, have long telepathic conversations with extraterrestrial beings, and—did I mention?—the Miracle of the Sun at Fatima, Portugal in 1917 was a UFO.

So when Chris Bledsoe, an uber-popular experiencer of today, has encounters with an ethereal "Lady" who gives him mysterious messages for the world about an imminent New Age headed by the Divine Feminine, it's totally fine, and he's considered a "hero." But Marian apparitions approved by the Catholic Church? That's nonsense for gullible fools.

In the middle of my writing this book, a far greater one was published. *Only Man Bears His Image* by Daniel O'Connor—a philosopher and theology professor (and actual devout Catholic)—is a must-read for any Catholic who has gone gleefully down the road behind the approved "professional Catholics" (as O'Connor calls them): those lay Catholic theologians, Vatican scholars and even popes who want to be both UFO-believers and defenders of the faith.

This book is not his book. I make almost no attempt to theologically prove that UFOs and extraterrestrials cannot exist in a Christian world. They cannot and do not exist, and I urge you to seek out O'Connor's book to school yourself in the plentiful evidence for that fact. You'll soon find that *any attempt* to theologically allow for intelligent ET life quickly leads down heretical and even abominable paths. Sadly, numerous Catholic scholars are more than willing to travel them, and to lead their fans down those roads, too. Roads that lead right into the arms of the Deceiver.

Mr. O'Connor and I share the same mission, but this book you are now reading presents the case against alien belief from my own perspective, which is (I think) a unique one: that of not only a womb to tomb, believing, loving, faithful Catholic but a Catholic with a long history of experience in paranormal research (particularly ghost, haunting and possession research) as well as American religion, history and supernatural folklore.

To be clear, however, I'm not the only Catholic voice with a background in the occult and parapsychology. I mentioned specifically Jimmy Akin, who is well known as both a Catholic theologian and a paranormal researcher. His voice is so much louder than mine. So many people trust him. He could do so much more good than I can. But like so many others, he wants too much for the untrue things to be true.

While it deeply troubles me to see my own Catholic brothers and sisters foolishly accepting an insidious deception, it also saddens me to observe secular and atheist ufologists marveling at a world they don't understand—the spiritual world—, seeing their struggle to comprehend something our "Enlightened" culture has given neither the knowledge to recognize nor the vocabulary to articulate. They don't know how the devil works, how the angels and saints work, or how—in fact—God Himself works. They think the creatures they encounter and "insights" they cull from an ayahuasca trip are brushes with extraterrestrials; that technology schematics "downloaded" during mind-to-mind communication with "aliens" are for a greater good; or that healing from a being of light identifying as an ancient goddess is part of a new, awakened "interdimensional" (but ultimately materialistic) world that's at the door.

But it's all, as you'll see, a lie.

At long last, and after taking a lot of people down my own wrong road with my spirit research methodologies, I knew I had to choose again, now that I was confronting the question of UFOs. Was I was going to be a scientist who'd seek knowledge "by any means necessary?" Or was I was going to choose God?

I chose God.

I hope this book helps to show you why I made that choice, and why the Catholic Church must lead every human being to do the same.

And urgently.

Ursula Bielski

Chicago

July 2024

ANOTHER WORLD

When I'd gone on to graduate school in the 1990s to study nineteenth-century religious history, my professor—who would become a dear friend and mentor—invited a few of us students to visit various churches around Chicago over the course of several months. The purpose was to experience the different ways people worship, and to observe the various elements that contribute to their services. One of the highlights of these visits was the day we sat in on a "mass" of the Liberal Catholic Church.

The organization's name is a little confusing, because the church actually appears quite conservative on its face but encourages liberty of belief and spiritual and religious exploration. Its founders aimed to mesh French Catholic foundations with the principles of the French Revolution, but they were also obsessed with Eastern religious thought. What emerged was a sort of New Age version of the Anglican Church—but with all the Catholic "bells and whistles." During the service we attended, the priest (I think he may have been a bishop) and a number of sacristans were heavily vested, and they changed vestments during the liturgy. There was a prolific use of incense and chanting. I would later discover that this hyper-ritualistic liturgical form of worship has its roots largely in the work of a man named Charles Leadbetter.

Leadbetter was a Protestant minister and a clairvoyant: someone who claims to see beings and objects invisible to the eye. In liturgies of the Old Catholic Church—a sect of which he was consecrated a priest in 1916—, Leadbetter clairvoyantly made a striking observation: the more ritual that occurred, the more sacramentals like candles and incense were used, and the more singing and chanting that was done, the more angelic, ethereal beings gathered around the altar.[2] It followed for him that all of the "trappings" of Catholicism that had been attacked by Martin Luther and his followers were actually pivotal in the efficacy of worship.

Leadbeater would become a prominent figure in the Theosophical Society, a spiritual movement founded in the late nineteenth century. Drawn to the teachings of Theosophy, Leadbeater found himself diving deeper and deeper into the esoteric world.

In addition to contributing paranormal insight to Theosophy's founders and followers, Leadbeater was an accomplished writer, publishing numerous books on an array of esoteric subjects, linking the spiritual with science in much of his work.. Topics like reincarnation, karma, and mystical symbolism formed the core of his literary contributions, and the concept of chakras owes its current popularity to him. Through his writings, Leadbeater aimed to disseminate Theosophical teachings while offering practical guidance for individuals seeking spiritual growth and enlightenment.

Despite his popularity, Leadbeater's teachings—and the man—were not without controversy. Certain aspects of his life became the subject of scrutiny and criticism, such as allegations of inappropriate conduct with young boys under his Theosophical mentorship. It was proven that he regularly recommended masturbation to boys who were struggling with sexual urges, but others claimed he would personally assist them in carrying out these recommendations.

The accusations tainted Leadbetter's reputation and led to his resignation from the Theosophical Society in 1906. Despite the controversies, he continued to explore the realms of spirituality and metaphysics independently, and many followed his advancements in esoteric thought long after the scandal had spoiled his standing.

Although his anti-Christian Theosophical leanings and work would pull back later to embrace much of the

Christianity he'd left behind, Leadbetter was one of an army of Victorian thinkers drawn like moths to their flame: the charismatic spiritual leader Helena Blavatsky, who literally wrote the book(s) on the sort of seeking out and summoning of otherworldly contact that Leadbetter was observing, he believed, as a result of prayer, ritual and sacramentals.

"Madame" Blavatsky they called her, and as the mind behind Theosophy she was largely responsible for breaking down, with the help of the Spiritualist movement, the Western Christian opposition to occultism and the dismantling of Western belief in one God. She despised the Catholic Church above all Christian denominations, and she loathed the Christian idea of a personal and singular spiritual authority, urging an understanding of the divine as something quite different indeed.

A Russian-born dreamer, Blavatsky exhibited paranormal gifts as a child, including clairvoyance and clairaudience. She was reportedly seen by her Orthodox family as demonically possessed; her sister would claim that Helena had at one point undergone an exorcism. But though the priest had doused her with "enough holy water to float a ship," the ritual didn't work; even after it, she continued to speak to mysterious entities that no one else could see. [3]

After fleeing her husband soon after their 1848 marriage, Blavatsky began her life of literally incredible adventures. She said she'd fought side-by-side with Italian revolutionaries, lived among the native tribes of Canada, and studied with Tibetan mystics—even though Europeans were not allowed in the region at the time. She recalled her hours studying with mysterious Masters in Tibet who were not quite physical, not quite spiritual beings. She'd learned, she said, to talk to the dead.

And to extraterrestrials.

Exploiting the nineteenth century boom of interest in the afterlife—and in speaking to those in it—she hawked herself as a Spiritualist medium, drawing ever-increasing crowds to her seances. But it wasn't she herself contacting the dead, Blavatsky insisted. It was her spirit guides, the Masters.

In 1875, Blavatsky founded her "unsectarian body of seekers after Truth" and, five years later, moved her operations to India. But in 1885, the prestigious Society for Psychical Research, comprised of Cambridge intellectuals, investigated Blavatsky's claims and pronounced her a fraud. The denouncement meant little to the masses who had become Blavatsky's idolators—spread, now, around the world. Blavatsky's influence would grow to become among the biggest of the age, and it's an influence that goes on and on today, including in today's ufology.

In 1888, Blavatsky published *The Secret Doctrine*. The book detailed what she called the seven root races of humanity, which represent stages of human evolution. The first race is that of invisible, sky-dwelling jellyfish. The second, also ethereal, is called hyperborean. The third race consists of a type of lemur who had eyes in the back of its head. These beings lived on a continent called Lemuria, somewhere in the Pacific Ocean. The fourth race consisted of the people of Atlantis. We are the fifth. According to Blavatsky, there are two more races to come.

Blavatsky's conceptions of the celestial realms—which she gleaned from her mysterious Eastern Masters—formed an early version of today's pop culture sensation, the "ancient astronaut theory." In fact, it was part of Theosophy's creed that some of the denizens of the worlds beyond not only existed but even visited our planet. A key element in this line of thought was the belief that these teachers would meet with us in some kind of quasi-physical, quasi-spiritual form, an idea we'll see rampant among contemporary UFO believers.

Blavatsky argued that these celestial entities were like gardeners looking after the humanity that had taken root on planet Earth, and it's here we find the concept that ETs might not just be visitors to our world but cultivators of it or even the very creators of humanity. With these ideas came the inevitable theory that these beings also had some stake in the state and future of the human race. Whoever they were, or wherever they came from, it was argued that our own reaching out would pave the way for these beings in their journeys here. It followed that, the more we reached out, the sooner and the more frequently they would come. And so, from the beginning, the attempt to contact UFOs and extraterrestrials had its roots entwined with Spiritualism: the determination to contact (by occult means) beings from an interacting but invisible world.

Theosophy also spawned the idea that all religions on our little planet were either inspired or directly developed by these cosmic helpers in order to benefit humanity by the virtues they taught. In a multifaceted cosmos, each of the religious faiths was a puzzle piece in a larger, divine, universal truth. Theosophy further asserted that each of these faiths had been established by teachers who came to this Earth to enlighten humanity. Blavatsky insisted that, from Buddha to Jesus and beyond, one could behold a long line of these Masters who had been sent to our planet to help raise humanity's awareness of its own divinity: the root of today's "Christ consciousness" gospel of personal autonomy and "god-ness."

The planet Venus is central to Theosophy. Blavatsky believed a civilization there had begun hundreds of millions of years before mankind's. Moreover, she claimed that the god which governs the Earth—"Sanat Kumara"—came here from Venus. Blavatsky believed that Venus was home to the bringers of light, of knowledge, and that these beings would deliver an era of enlightenment, a New Age, to humanity.

The name Venus means "light bearer," and the Latin name for Venus is "Lucifer." So you could say these beings of Blavatsky's were claiming to come from Lucifer and be correct, at least linguistically.

At least.

This fact has not been lost on many Christian scholars, who believe the whole New Age is one big, bad joke—and one that's not the least bit funny. In fact, it's from Theosophy that we get the belief that Lucifer was the "good guy," and that he was trying to enlighten mankind: Genesis turned on its head. Even St. Paul called Satan the "god of this world" (2 Corinthians 4:4), a maybe not-so-strange parallel to Blavatsky's "god of the Earth," a being named Sanat Kumara. In fact, we'll see a bit later that some alien visitors have given names identical to or very similar to the names of known demons/gods.

A long line of Christian scholars has written about the willing demonization of Theosophy's believers and of the intellectually Luciferian ideals of Theosophy. These claims may sound like those of "Bible-thumping" Christians, but it's indisputable that the goals of Theosophy include not only talking to demons but becoming human vessels for them (though Theosophists, not recognizing God, have always denied that the brilliant spiritual beings they call the "Masters" are the demons they are).

The late Harvard psychologist John Mack remains inarguably one of the most prominent and influential of all ufologists. He maintained that human-alien contact is "unequivocally spiritual" and that it "involves some sort of powerful encounter with, or immersion in, divine light." [4]

In his book, *UFO Religions and Abduction Spiritualities*, historian of religion Christopher Partridge affirms Mack's observation but makes an important clarification:

> [It] is hard to avoid the fact that the 'enhanced spirituality' typical of abductees is consistent with the Eastern-influenced New Age spirituality that has emerged in the West, particularly since the 1960s, much of which can be traced back to theosophical thought. [It is] part of a stream of alternative spirituality which is indebted implicitly to Theosophy and explicitly to ideas found within the Indian religious tradition. [5]

Partridge reminds us of four tenets of Theosophy abundant in UFO and alien contact narratives, as noted by another researcher, Andrew Rawlinson. *First*, human beings are primarily consciousness-based rather than physical beings. *Second*, human beings can transform consciousness by spiritual practice. *Third*, teachers known as Masters or gurus have achieved transcendence by such practice. *Fourth*, these Masters can assist humans in transforming their own consciousness, and this is done through some kind of transmission of initiatory knowledge.[6]

Partridge rightly asserts that these tenets can be found in UFO religions and abduction spiritualities, as can a host of other beliefs popular within the New Age network: e.g. reincarnation, chakras, past lives, future lives, psychic therapy, oneness with the Earth, channeling, astral travel, and so on.[7] I would go much further to say that UFO belief and experience are no less than *infested* with these beliefs, with a reminder that infestation is a spiritual phenomenon— and not a good one.

As influential as she was, the sensation that was Blavatsky likely wouldn't have happened on the scale it did without the stage being set for her emergence.

And set it was.

Emmanuel Swedenborg was an eighteenth-century Swedish scientist, theologian, philosopher, and mystic best known for his religious writings, particularly his accounts of personal spiritual experiences and interactions with the unseen realm. Many readers of Swedenborg's works have noticed intriguing parallels between his descriptions of cosmic phenomena and the modern-day concept of unidentified flying objects. Some scholars and UFO enthusiasts speculate that Swedenborg may have encountered UFOs during his intense spiritual experiences.

Swedenborg detailed his spiritual journeys in a book, *Heaven and Hell*, which describes his encounters with various angelic beings and otherworldly landscapes during his visits to other planets, moons, and stars, and he shares vivid descriptions of their geography, climates and inhabitants. During one of these cosmological adventures, Swedenborg saw a great flying city on the planet Jupiter, describing a massive structure with shining lights and windows, suspended in the air and capable of lightning-fast movement.

Swedenborg also encountered beings on other planets who possessed advanced technologies and knowledge far beyond what was known in his time, including propulsion systems that allowed them to effortlessly navigate through space. Swedenborg compared their vehicles to chariots or carriages which emitted bright lights and made no sound while in motion (descriptors common to most modern UFO craft sightings). Despite the parallels, it's important to note that Swedenborg himself never explicitly referred to his unusual "travels" as UFO or extraterrestrial encounters. He interpreted his experiences as visions granted to him by divine intervention, stating that his primary intention was to convey spiritual truths and promote a deeper understanding of the nature of Heaven, Hell and the human soul.

While some enthusiasts find the similarities between Swedenborg's writings and UFO phenomena intriguing, others argue that these correlations are merely coincidences and his writings an example of the strong influence of science fiction on the popular imagination. The popular imagination was indeed ignited by Swedenborg's claims, and if Blavatsky would be the mother of the New Age, he was the undeniable father. As the nineteenth century came to a close, their love child was about to arrive.

In a UFO.

OF THE AIR

It's a common misconception among those outside the ufology world that the notion of unidentified flying objects began around the time of the so-called "Roswell Incident" in the 1940s, which we'll look at in detail shortly. It's understandable why this might be the case, since Roswell and a few other events of that era stand out as watershed moments: moments that first brought the whole concept of craft of unknown origin to our collective consciousness. Yes, the events in the New Mexico desert (or non-events, some claim) were triggering ones, but it wasn't the first time in history that strange craft were seen in the skies. In fact, we can find a surprising abundance of unusual flying objects throughout recorded history, with isolated incidents occurring very long ago indeed.

Several cave paintings found in Val Camonica depict mysterious flying objects resembling modern-day UFOs. These paintings, believed to date back to 20,000 BC, show humanoid figures alongside saucer-like objects in the sky, sparking speculation about possible extraterrestrial encounters in prehistoric times.

Sumerian clay tablets dating back to 2000 BC contain references to celestial beings and gods descending from the sky. These accounts, recorded in ancient cuneiform script, mention encounters with beings who arrived in shining vessels, leading some to interpret them as, in fact, early UFO sightings or interactions with advanced extraterrestrial races.

During the reign of Pharaoh Akhenaten in ancient Egypt (1347-1338 BC), several striking reliefs and carvings depict the pharaoh and his family receiving offerings from winged, disk-like objects. These peculiar representations have been widely debated, with interpretations ranging from ritual symbolism to actual evidence of ancient alien visitations.

In 312 A.D, during the Battle of Saxa Rubra between the Roman Emperor Constantine and his rival, Maxentius, both armies reportedly observed a "great luminous object" in the sky. According to historical accounts, this object emitted beams of light and hovered over the battlefield, leading to interpretations of both divine intervention and extraterrestrial involvement.

On April 14, 1561, an extraordinary celestial occurrence took place in Nuremberg, Germany when witnesses reported seeing a clash of objects in the sky, along with a variety of celestial shapes, smoke, and a dark spinning orb. Multiple accounts were documented, including in woodcut illustrations, leading to debates about possible spiritual or even extraterrestrial encounters.

Given the limited historical documentation and the interpretative nature of these events, it's a challenge to draw any definitive conclusions about UFO sightings from 20,000 BC to 1800. But the world would get up close and personal with the idea of UFOs beginning in the nineteenth century, when the first so-called "UFO flap" (the lingo for a surge of sightings) played out, peppering American newspapers with reports not only of unusual flying craft, but also their supposed occupants.

It's crucial to note that all of these sightings happened before the invention of the airplane. The only real flying vehicle that these "experiencers" (to use a ufological term) would have been familiar with was the hot air balloon, and later the more experimental zeppelin-style craft commonly referred to as an "airship." It was for this reason that many of these unknown objects, especially those witnessed during the late 1890s, were often dubbed as such. Not everyone, however, thought these interlopers were humans in air-filled balloons.

One of the more interesting cases from the nineteenth century (and one fairly well documented for the time) is the 1864 James Lumley sighting. This incident included eyewitnesses on the ground, and a full account of the event was published in several newspapers. The sighting occurred in September, up in the mountainous terrain of Montana, in a place called the Cadotte Pass.

A local fur trapper by the name of James Lumley was busy hunting up some hoped-for bounty in the mountains when he just happened to look up and see what he later described as a "bright, luminous body in the heavens." [8] The object zoomed across the sky and headed eastward. According to Mr. Lumley's account, he was staring at this UFO when it suddenly split apart into multiple different craft that shot off in every direction. Poor Lumley didn't know what to make of all this, but many later sightings would parallel this early experience, and a number of recent researchers have theorized that this "decoupling" of objects—a frequent part of modern sightings—is perhaps scout craft being sent forth from a "mother ship."

Seconds after the objects split apart, Lumley both "heard and felt" a thunderous boom, as a shockwave of tremors rippled through the mountain pass. This was immediately followed by a rapid gust of tornado-force wind that seemed to be coming from the same direction as the sound. One of the split-off objects slammed into the Earth, creating a loud explosion, followed by a great whoosh. The surrounding air, Lumley remembered, was filled with the unmistakable stench of sulfur. This particular scent would be reported in many future encounters; it's also one frequently reported in demonic encounters[9].

The story gets stranger, because the next day this intrepid trapper went to investigate. He was shocked at what he saw. There appeared to be a huge gash in the ground, and it led all the way to what seemed to be a crash site. He followed the trail of debris and discovered a strange object sticking out of the ground. Lumley wasn't an astronomer and likely not well versed in meteors and comets, but even he quickly figured it was some sort of giant rock that had fallen from the sky. It was only upon closer inspection that he changed his mind.

As he examined the specimen up close, Lumley could see that the rock appeared artificial in its construction. It had several "compartments" and what appeared to be "hieroglyphics" etched into the surface. The surrounding debris included shards of what Lumley described as glass, as well as a pool of liquid that seemed to have seeped out of the damaged hull of the craft.

Interestingly, and in stark contrast with more modern times, the media seemed to take Lumley at his word. One journalist with the Missouri *Democrat* remarked, "Strange as this story appears, Mr. Lumley relates it with so much sincerity that we are forced to accept it as true. But the same writer—apparently now a true believer—then goes on to speculate that perhaps this visitor and its brethren might one day return . . . and not be friendly. [10]

It was roughly a decade later, in 1878, that a "flying saucer" encounter took place. The sighting occurred in the skies over northern Texas, when a local farmer by the name of John Martin looked up and saw the sun blocked out by what he described as a large saucer. From his vantage point on the ground, the object initially appeared to be about the size of an orange but increased in size as it rapidly approached his position. The fact that whatever this was zoomed across the sky at such a high velocity would seem to rule out any conventional airship.[11]

A few years later, in 1884, there appeared in the press yet another tale of an alleged UFO crash.[12] This one played out in the vicinity of Benkelman, Nebraska. Some cowboys working a local ranch were busy rounding up cattle when they happened to notice a commotion up above their heads. They saw what appeared to be a "blazing streak of light" emanating from a cylinder-shaped airship. They watched as this object slammed into the ground and tumbled into a ravine across the way.

Curiosity getting the better of them, they rode off to try and get a better look at whatever had fallen from the skies. Reaching the impact site the pair found wreckage surrounding the crater where the craft had hit. They cautiously picked up parts of the debris and were amazed to find that, although the material was very light, it was incredibly tough. More than half a century later debris in the alleged Roswell, New Mexico crash would be described in the same way.

After an initial bustle of interest, things died down, and the ranchers went back to work. One of them, who had not only handled debris from the craft but had tried to get close to the object itself, developed some kind of strange sickness. His face erupted in blisters, and his hair took on a burned appearance, leading later researchers to speculate that he had suffered radiation poisoning. [13]

So, what happened to this crashed craft? Did the nineteenth-century version of the Men in Black (of which more later) come and retrieve it?

Not exactly.

According to local reports, the wreckage was washed away in a bad rainstorm. Several onlookers who had come to view the strange sight were caught in a torrential downpour during their visit. Most retreated to shelter, but a few of the more curious souls continued their vigil over the downed craft. To their amazement, once the water made contact with the material, it melted into a gelatinous substance that was then washed away by the rain.

These early incidents were strange but also few and far between. It wasn't until 1896 that a veritable wave—or "flap"—of sightings erupted. One of the most thought provoking was the one reported in the vicinity of Lodi, California on November 25, 1896.

Two men—Camille Spooner and Colonel H. G. Shaw—were heading down the road by way of horse and buggy when they spotted a cylindrical object floating above a local body of water. They later reported the sighting to the Stockton *Evening Mail,* claiming they had also witnessed several of the craft's pilots roaming around on the ground.. [14]

These entities were described as humanoid in appearance—but clearly *not* human. They were tall and slim, with large, bald heads and oddly oversized feet. The beings were covered in what the witnesses described as "fine fuzz," and they also reportedly spoke in an unintelligible warble. The witnesses further claimed that the entities were utilizing some kind of breathing apparatus, consisting of a nozzle held in the mouth and attached to a bag fitted to the being's body.

The most alarming part of this story, however, occurred toward the end of the encounter when—in what seems to have been one of the earliest known "abduction" attempts—one of the beings tried to make away with Camille and the colonel. The latter was the first to be picked up bodily by one of the visitors, but the being was described as struggling under the strain and was unable to hold him. After a short effort, the beings retreated to the ship and departed.

More strange sightings followed this one, but by December of 1896 this particular wave had come to an end. A new and perhaps even more disturbing one would start up again the very next year. During the course of 1897, multiple sightings were reported in Nebraska, Kansas, Illinois, Michigan, Iowa, Ohio, Indiana and Texas.

It was in a small Texas town called Aurora, however, that perhaps the most infamous of all the airship flaps occurred. There, in April of 1897, a strange craft was seen hovering over the town square before it drifted to overshadow the homestead of a certain Judge J. S. Proctor. It then slammed into his windmill and shattered into multiple pieces of debris midair, raining down on his property. Among this wreckage was found the "pilot" of the craft.. [15]

It was dead.

According to witnesses, it was obvious that the dead aviator was not a fellow earthling. One newspaper quoted a certain T. J. Weems who claimed to be part of the U. S Signal Service. Weems offered his suggestion that the occupant of the craft was, perhaps, a Martian. Though the being couldn't be questioned, it did have some paperwork on its person which contained strange, indecipherable writing, also described as "hieroglyphics" by witnesses.[16]

It was the *Dallas Morning News* that first shared the news, reporting that a full-blown funeral would be held for the occupant of the craft on April eighteenth. The Fort Worth *Register* then later picked up the story, reporting that "(t)he pilot, who was not an inhabitant of this world, was given proper Christian burial at the Aurora Cemetery."

The tombstone placed on the alien pilot's grave has been missing since at least 1973. That year, a local journalist by the name of Bill Case personally went to the site and took notes on what he saw, claiming that he saw the stone that had been placed on the grave by the townspeople. He described it as sporting an engraving of a classic flying saucer, complete with portholes around the edges. Sadly, it was likely his story on the incident—and the tombstone—that led to the marker's theft soon after.

Today, a large rock marks the site many believe to be the grave of the "extraterrestrial." Visitors make pilgrimage to the cemetery throughout the year and place memorabilia on the grave: small efforts to remember and keep alive the day the universe came down, they say, to this sleepy town. As for the body of the pilot, according to legend it's still buried somewhere in that little cemetery in Texas. The cemetery and the authorities, however, have denied all requests to dig in the area.

STORIES FROM THE SKY

Ten years after the first sightings of the modern UFO era had morphed into a bona fide extraterrestrial epidemic Carl Jung published a small but significant volume summing up his take on it all. Being Jung, of course, he pronounced it to be all in the mind.

In *Flying Saucers: A Modern Myth of Things Seen in the Sky* Jung wrote of a world gravely disturbed by its own dark, destructive nature, as evidenced by all that had taken place in the first half of that shocking twentieth century. To escape it, the collective consciousness of earthlings, he said, was looking for both an escape from who they'd become and for a chance to do it over (and better) next time.

Of course, those earthlings looked up.

It was just what they'd done for millennia: looking to the heavens when the terrestrial had failed them. But by the time the flying saucers came, what humanity was looking up for wasn't spiritual salvation anymore. It was the hard salvation of science and technology. After all, God was "dead," and it was now up to humanity to work out its own salvation. And, as biblical scholar David Laughlin has phrased it, "Perhaps the grass was greener on the other side of the galaxy."

By the time Jung penned his observations, an assortment of imaginative minds had already begun to muse about where that salvation might come from. They weren't, of course, Christian or even Deist minds, and so from the beginning, beginning science fiction had at its starting point the abandonment of God. It would prove a crucial truth as the ET era rolled out, as the genre would seem to both inform and reflect much of the modern UFO era and its intricate web of myth and experience.

The ferocious religious fervor of science fiction pioneer H.G. Wells has been well documented. But the bestselling author of both science fiction and scientific theory was no Christian or Buddhist or even Theosophist.

He was a Darwinist.

Abandoning Christianity after encountering the Theory of Evolution at school, Wells would spend the remainder of his life spreading Darwin's gospel, which he'd learned at the feet of Darwin's best pupil, T.H. Huxley. From the work of Darwin, Wells and Huxley—and the many men of science they influenced—rose a new religion of Science: a faith that worshipped science as the god and savior of the human race.

The impact of Wells' work on Western thought and culture would be difficult to overestimate. Not only were his science fiction novels like *War of the Worlds* and *The Shape of Things to Come* phenomenal bestsellers, but his scientific works and historical treatises reached huge audiences as well. His Darwinist *Outline of History*, published in 1920, would sell millions of copies and is today considered a pivotally influential text crucial for understanding Wells' intellectual era—and those to come.

Scholar Jerry Bergman tells us, however, that it was with his belief in eugenics that Wells "out-Darwined" even Darwin,[17] laying out a program for perfecting humanity in his book, *Anticipations*. The aim of the program was to take control of evolution, so that humankind would not fall victim to the very "laws" that had raised Man to the pinnacle of Darwinian development.

In the book, Wells proposed wholesale "mercy killings" of inferior specimens of humanity, and he wrote of mankind's need to aspire to "an ideal that will make killing worth the while." Along with the disabled, the elderly and the mentally ill, the racially impure would also have to go: the "swarms of blacks, and brown, and dirty-white, and yellow people."

Wells also encouraged less-than-perfect people to take their own lives, suggesting that they would readily do so given a little encouragement. Wells further recommended immediate death for anyone convicted of a serious crime. It's likely his plan was also influenced—and at least supported by—one of the many women he bedded during the infamous "free love" escapades of his marriage: Margaret Sanger, founder of Planned Parenthood and advocate of unfettered sexual exploration, contraception and abortion.

In both his fiction and nonfiction, Wells was famous for predicting the future—sometimes eerily. He predicted that many Christians would abandon their faith and later turn to Spiritualism, witchcraft and other esoteric faiths. He predicted in 1933 that a second world war would begin in 1940—just months off the mark.

Fascinatingly for us, he also predicted a current of thought (some say conspiracy theory) underlying much of today's ufology: the idea that the Catholic Church has long known the truth about the place of man in space but has kept it covered up to safeguard its own power. Darwin believed that closely-guarded secret to be the reality of evolution. Today's UFO believers posit that the Church—and other authorities—are hiding the "truth" that extraterrestrials created us.

Wells despised all Christians, but he especially hated Catholics—a fact ruthlessly exposed by numerous Catholic scholars, most notably Hilaire Belloc, who publicly thrashed him on numerous occasions. In 1943, when Wells was 77, a largely anti-Catholic press published the American issue of his *Crux Ansata: An Indictment of the Roman Catholic Church*, in which Wells rhetorically suggested the bombing of Rome. Strangely, the book (and Wells' anger) was incited by Pope Pius the XII's alleged participation in—or at least *laissez faire* attitude towards—the Nazis (a notion that has since been shown to be false). [18]

It's odd, because Wells was obviously anti-Semitic in addition to being anti-Christian.[19] With the Darwinian and eugenics-infused thought and work of Wells and his tutors central to the Nazi regime, it's a bit weird that the Nazis upset

Wells at all. Weren't they just enforcing his eugenical "ideal" and hastening the end of his most hated religions by getting rid of not only Jews and Catholics but all of the "swarms" of people of color as was well?

Born in Wisconsin in the summer of 1910, Raymond Palmer had a passion for storytelling from a young age. [20] As an adult, he would find fame publishing a magazine called *Amazing Stories*, a periodical whose impact on modern Western Culture cannot be overstated. From its inception in 1926, the pulp fiction periodical captured the imaginations of countless individuals, igniting a passion for science fiction and fantasy literature and inspiring generations of the future to literally reach for the stars, not only in astrophysics but virtually every other realm of research.

Many renowned authors would credit the magazine as their gateway into the world of speculative fiction. Influential figures such as Isaac Asimov, Ray Bradbury and Arthur C. Clarke would all acknowledge the profound impact *Amazing Stories* had on their careers. The magazine's content pushed the boundaries of creativity and opened up new avenues of storytelling, propelling these writers to pen their own tales of extraterrestrial life and boundless technological vistas, leading eventually to projects like the *Star Wars* and *Close Encounters* films, the world of *Star Trek* and beyond.

At a young age, Jet Propulsion Laboratory founder and rocketeering icon Jack Parsons became captivated by the stories featured in the magazine; its tales of space exploration, time travel, and alien civilizations captured his young mind and instilled in him a sense of wonder and curiosity about the possibilities of science and technology. [21] With his friend, Edward Foreman, Parsons began experimenting with rocketry in his teenage years, inspired by the ideas presented in *Amazing Stories*.

As Parsons delved deeper into rocketry, he was drawn to the writings of British author and inventor, E. E. Smith. Smith's tales in *Amazing Stories,* such as the influential series "Skylark" and "Lensman," presented futuristic technologies and intergalactic adventures. These tales further fueled Parsons' already burgeoning fascination with space exploration and fueled his ambition to contribute to the development of rocket technology.

Amazing Stories also played a significant role in Parsons' interest in the occult. The magazine occasionally featured stories involving magic, ancient civilizations and mysticism. These themes resonated with Parsons, who began exploring occult philosophies, eventually becoming a devoted follower of Aleister Crowley, the notorious British occultist. Parsons' fascination with the occult, combined with his scientific pursuits, created a unique amalgamation of interests that set him apart from his contemporaries. (We'll be learning a lot more about Parsons' and Crowley's activities and their relation to the theme of this book shortly.)

Ray Palmer was hired in 1938 as editor of *Amazing Stories*. By then, he had already come under a decidedly esoteric influence and was well-versed in the occult. In the early 1930s he had discovered an obscure religious manuscript called the Ohaspe bible. The document was supposedly channeled by a dentist named John Ballou Newbrough, who claimed it was a group of new revelations about a god who was both masculine and feminine. Readers called it a combination (or mess, depending on their opinion) of the ideas of Eastern and Judeo-Christian religions. Newbrough wrote it by sitting at a typewriter and waiting for his fingers to become enrobed in light. Then he would start typing, with no knowledge or direction of what was being typed, a method known in the occult as "automatic writing." The Ohaspe bible captivated Palmer, and he became convinced that its teachings held profound wisdom and insight. He even went on to republish it himself, adding copious notes.

During Palmer's tenure at *Amazing Stories*, he introduced the world to the so-called "Shaver Mystery," a controversial series of stories penned by Richard S. Shaver that was believed by some to be fact, not fiction. Shaver wrote of encounters with underground civilizations and painted a dark and mysterious picture of the world beneath our feet. We'll see the impact (some say evidence) of his claims in current-day reports of underground alien bases and communities a bit later in this book.

Palmer's decision to publish Shaver's stories ignited a cultural phenomenon, attracting both passionate supporters and vocal critics. Some saw him as a visionary, exploring uncharted territories within the genre. Others dismissed him as a fringe figure, delving too deep into fantastical and nonsensical realms, and with too many occult overtones. In fact, Palmer would go on to found numerous occult publications. After the famed Kenneth Arnold UFO sightings (which we'll visit shortly), Palmer founded the influential *FATE* magazine in response to the sensation the sightings caused. Arnold appeared on the cover of the first issue, and *FATE* would become a beacon and outlet for generations interested in—and experienced in—unexplained phenomena and occult practice of every kind.

Even as a boy, Arthur C. Clarke imagined a future in which science would be triumph as savior of mankind and man be recognized as a race of gods. It should be no surprise, then, that Clarke would emerge as the star pupil of the school of A*mazing Stori*es.

Clarke's staggeringly influential book, *Childhood's End*—called by many the very best of the more than 100 he wrote—stands as a masterful synthesis of the sci fi dreams of *Amazing Stories* and the Gnostic vision of Theosophy. Indeed, it would be difficult to overestimate its influence on not only modern writing and filmmaking but scientific inquiry itself—and, of course, ufology.

At one point in the book, Clarke describes a technology by which viewers can watch on a screen as just about any point in history plays out. It's seen as a wonderful gift, because it destroys false beliefs about religion and renders every creed meaningless and instantly powerless:

> Though it had always been obvious to any rational mind that all the world's religious writings could not be true, the shock was nevertheless profound. Here was a revelation that no one

could doubt or deny: here, seen by some unknown magic of Overlord science, were the true beginnings of all the world's great faiths. Most of them were noble and inspiring—but that was not enough. Within a few days, all mankind's multitudinous messiahs had lost their divinity. Beneath the fierce and passionless light of truth, faiths that had sustained millions for twice a thousand years vanished like the morning dew. All the good and all the evil they had wrought were swept suddenly into the past and could touch the minds of men no more. Humanity had lost its ancient gods: now it was old enough to have no need for new ones.[22]

John Wright has extensively addressed the overt anti-Christianity in Clarke's work, particularly *Childhood's End.*[23] Like New Agers, many UFO believers and, indeed, the very spiritual and even ritualistic followers of the technology gods (we'll meet some shortly), it's not all religions that, for Clarke, stand in the way of humanity's technological and evolutionary advancement.

Only Christianity.

Indeed, in *Out from the Silent Planet*, the Christian apologist C.S. Lewis wondered, "What if it is good for us not to venture into space?" Clarke answered readily:

> What if science can take the place of religion? What if evolution, the striving ever upward, can replace these primitive superstitions, and offer a transcendence that is real? What if it is not only good, but necessary, for us to venture into space? What if that venture is the source of our salvation . . . ? Well, even if they look like devils, what if the meeting were …. wondrous![24]

We'll see Clarke's lack of concern for what spiritual team the ETs are on running through contemporary ufology and technology. After all, if there is a God, Lucifer was the good guy. Or if there's no God—or if man is his own god—what does it matter?

Travis Perry, a Christian science fiction writer, has also written about the treatment of Christianity in sci fi.[25] His observations have shown that, while there's no "unified front" in science fiction regarding the future of Christianity, a majority of sci fi stories do portray that future in one of three distinct ways:

> 1)along with all other human religion, it doesn't exist at all in the future, 2) religion exists, but Christianity doesn't. 3) Christianity exists, but it's the faith of a tiny minority and essentially insignificant.[26]

Though he says he wouldn't overstate it (or accuse *most* of the writers of doing it on purpose as "deliberate propagandists"), Perry does suggest a certain degree of propaganda inherent in the representations, clarifying:

> I'm not claiming that science fiction by itself is responsible for a general cultural turning away from all religion and Christianity in particular–but it seems reasonable to me to conclude science fiction has contributed to this effect.

Obviously, if the most important and influential sci fi writers (like Clarke) *have* dumped on Christianity through deliberate propaganda, that's a significant point to consider, even if it's not blanketly intended by all or even most of the genre's authors.

It's especially significant when we see the influence of sci fi on scientific inquiry itself—and its offspring, ufology. In a later chapter, we'll look more closely as promised at Jack Parsons, one of the undisputed pioneers of space travel, who was so deeply influenced by *Amazing Stories*, as were so many future pioneers in science and technology. I don't think anyone would doubt that our current generation of scientists has been exponentially influenced by sci fi. (One only has to reference the long-standing and accurate stereotype of the superhero-and-Star Trek/Star Wars-obsessed science and tech geek we've all met a thousand times.)

I must point out here that, while atheism and New Age beliefs have been the most common religious influences on sci fi, Christianity and even the Catholic Church specifically have also influenced the genre to a lesser extent—and not always in a good way. Jules Verne was a longtime Catholic, though he seemed to sway into Deism later in life. Ray Bradbury credited his life's work to God, though he said he was influenced by many religions, called himself mostly Buddhist in practice and said Jesus was, essentially, one of many great guys. In a later chapter, when we examine the public response of the Catholic Church to the extraterrestrial question, we'll discover a bizarre sub-genre of science fiction which one commentor has dubbed "Jesuits in Space." Believe it or not, a classification was, in fact, needed to categorize the growing number of novels featuring members of the famously science-minded order and their cosmological adventures.

We could be here all year talking about the influence of science fiction and its authors' religious beliefs on popular thought, science and culture. We could spend hours, for example, discussing Ursula K. Le Guin's *Earthsea* trilogy (what one Christian commentator has described as a "full-scale assault on what she perceived as religion's destructive preoccupation with living forever" [27]). We could spend a day looking at the cultural climate panic monster created in large part by the Whitley Strieber-inspired film, *The Day After Tomorrow* (elements of which he claims to have received from the mysterious alien "Visitors" who have shared his life for decades). Or we could talk about the path from Robert E. Howard's 1929 story, *The Shadow Kingdom* to the current religious-level belief of many today in demonic reptilian extraterrestrial overlords. Suffice it to say that, like so many threads in this story, this one will turn up again and again in the pages ahead.

What must be remembered for our purposes is that a strong, pulsing vein of anti-Christian thought has run through many of the most influential and popular science fiction works, *particularly those focused on space exploration, extraterrestrials and humanity's place in the cosmos.* These works have undoubtedly influenced not only the stories of successive generations of writers but science and culture's very perceptions of Christianity and its place in our cosmological future.

Before we leave this topic for now, we should briefly recognize another major literary genre and its connection to our subject, because horror fiction as well as sci fi has been profoundly influenced by the ideas of Theosophy. H.P. Lovecraft was inarguably one of the most overarching influences on the genre, and scholars agree that the teachings and taxonomy of the Theosophical spirit world joined with traditional horror influences to form Lovecraft's phenomenally popular style of "weird fiction." His stories often have a whole lot to do with the non-terrestrial, and his singular character, Cthulhu, has inspired an army of fan fiction writers, all of them enthralled by the many-tentacled descendent of cosmological evil. Cthulhu and his cohorts lie in wait on planet Earth, biding time until the moment is right to rise up and take over the world.

In Lovecraft, then, we see the idea (evocative of Wells) of the alien as not only enemy but enemy that's already here, a la *War of the Worlds*. As cultural and political historian Dan Nexon has observed, rather than bringing enlightenment and evolution, those Theosophical "mystical energy beings coming through that portal . . . are going to eat your brains." [28] This view of the universe formed Lovecraft's unique "religion" of *cosmicism*: an atheistic materialism with a firm focus on the terrifying nature of the cosmos and the minute place of humanity in it. This idea of a dark, vicious, godless universe populated with hateful aliens with an evil plan would go largely underground in the early UFO era, surfacing powerfully again in later UFO theory.

NINETEEN FORTY-SEVEN

As 1947 dawned, the United States should have been quite confident of its position in the world. The nation had just come out on the winning side of the Second World War. Not only that, the U.S. had displayed its clear dominance over not only its enemies but potential enemies as well by detonating two nuclear bombs over Japan. America's growing rival, the Soviet Union, wouldn't achieve this capability until 1949. In 1947, then, the United States was inarguably the ruling nation of planet Earth.

Yet right when the U. S government was at the top of the mountain, highly superior visitors—more advanced than anything America could conceive of—supposedly dropped down for a visit. On the tails of Earthly victory, a wave of strange, seemingly otherworldly craft began to appear in American skies. Unknown to anyone at the time, the wave would prove unstoppable.

On June 24th, a pilot by the name of Kenneth Arnold was traveling over the peaks of Mount Rainer on America's West Coast when he just happened to look up and see a group of shiny, metallic objects shoot across the horizon. They were flying some 9500 feet in the air at what Arnold estimated to be 1500 miles per hour.

The following day, June 25th, Arnold sat down and gave his first round of interviews. Simply describing what he had seen – not a flying saucer but a delta-winged triangular craft—, he at first left the speculation to others. It was only in a later interview, on July 7th, that the pilot began to openly suggest that, just perhaps, the craft he had witnessed was not of this world. The very next day, July 8th, 1947, would become no less than the most explosive day in UFO history.

On that day, Walter Haut, the public information officer at the U.S. military's Roswell, New Mexico airbase, issued a statement indicating that the army had a "flying disc" in its possession. The statement was reinforced later that day when it was distributed by the Associated Press. The statement read:

> The many rumors regarding the flying disc became a reality yesterday when the intelligence office of the 509th Bomb group of the Eighth Air Force, Roswell Army Airfield, was fortunate enough to gain possession of a disc through the cooperation of one of the local ranchers and the sheriff's office of Chaves County. The flying object landed on a ranch near Roswell sometime last week. Not having phone facilities, the rancher stored the disc until such time as he was able to contact the sheriff's office, who in turn notified Maj. Jesse A. Marcel of the 509th Bomb Group Intelligence Office.[29]

And so the door was opened.

It was a really big door, and the public's response was to eagerly rush in, filled with intense interest and curiosity. That door, however, was slammed shut the very next day when, on July 9th, Haut retracted his words, directing all newspapers to follow suit and retract and deny the flying saucer story.

They did.

Across the nation and the world, papers ran retractions and sedate new headlines. "Excitement not justified," they said; the alleged flying saucer was just a "weather balloon." [30] People accepted what they were told, and this would be the end of the Roswell story for decades.

It wasn't until the late 1970s that UFO researchers would revive interest in Roswell. The puzzle pieces of the past would then be put together once again, and a startling, seemingly covered-up story would emerge: the story of what the rancher had really found scattered across his property on that soon-to-be-infamous day so long ago.

Mac Brazel wasn't sure what to make of the material, but he gathered the largest pieces together and held on to them until he could notify the authorities. He eventually loaded up his truck with some of the stuff and made his way to the local sheriff in Roswell. It was the sheriff that directed Brazel to contact the air base. He was then put in contact with one Major Jesse Marcel. Marcel took a look at the debris.

Marcel later recalled that the material looked not even remotely like anything he had ever seen. This was saying something; Marcel was a veteran officer and should have been able to identify conventional aircraft—and a good number of experimental ones—, yet this material had him drawing a complete blank. Marcel later brought some of the material back to his own home, where he demonstrated the unusual tenacity of the debris to his wife and son, Jesse Jr. The boy would later recall the material as not only exceedingly strong but with some sort of internal, structural memory. It had the capacity to bounce back into shape even after being bent, scratched or burned. No matter what he and his dad did to the material, it always quickly returned to its original state.

Major Marcel returned to base and informed the base commander Colonel William C. "Butch" Blanchard of his findings. It was Blanchard who then directed press officer Walter Haut to retract his original statement to the press and issue a decidedly changed one. There was no "flying saucer," no mysterious disc. This would be the story, and they were going to stick to it.

Haut kept these orders secret until decades later, when UFO researcher Stanton Friedman tracked him down and convinced him to share the truth of what had happened in New Mexico in 1947. [31] Haut went on the record with Friedman to state that anyone who worked at the base could very easily tell the difference between a weather balloon and a wrecked spacecraft.

It was apparently only after the higher ups in DC got wind of what was happening that concerted action was taken to kill the story. Friedman in his research had also managed to track down a certain colonel based out of Fort Worth, Texas, by the name of Thomas Jefferson DuBose. It was Colonel DuBose who shared what he claimed was the true rationale for a cover up: The government feared that a war-weary public would not be able to handle what had really happened. It was, as he told Friedman, "just too much" for the public to digest what he called "this flying saucer business." .

It, according to the cover-up story, the base meteorologist—a man named Irving Newton—who came up with the fake "debris" from the alleged weather balloon. After Marcel's briefing, he went to the base and picked up from Newton a load of balsa wood, tin foil and other innocuous material related to the mundane use of weather balloons. This box of tinfoil junk would be famously spread out before reporters and their cameramen, with Marcel dumbly grinning over them. Following orders, Marcel was forced to basically shoot himself in the foot, since it made him look entirely incompetent as a commanding officer to have to say that he somehow confused a weather balloon with a spacecraft. The shame of being the fall guy—as well as his memory of what the army had truly uncovered—would haunt him, they say, the rest of his days.

Walter Haut was also particularly appalled by what had happened but he chalked it up to the sentiment of the times. He told Friedman that, back in those days, you just did what you were told and didn't ask questions.

According to Friedman's interview subjects, it wasn't until after the media frenzy had died down that the military really went to business actually recovering the wreckage. It took some time, but they found the main crash site, which was located near Mac Brazel's ranch. Yet though Brazel's land was littered with debris, it was not where the craft had initially hit the ground. The main chunk had split apart from the rest on impact and had reportedly slammed into the ground a short distance away.

The hardest part of the story, witnesses would state decades later, wasn't the part about the strange material the craft was made of, or that it didn't seem to be of any known earthly material at all.

The hardest part was the bodies.

Friedman's interviewees told him that at least two dead aliens were recovered along with the wreckage. Some said one more was found that was still alive.

The military cordoned off a huge circumference around the area. Soldiers were ordered to go crawling the desert floor on their hands and knees, picking out of the scruff and sand the tiniest bits of debris. They worked, hot, dazed and exhausted, until the place was absolutely spotless and there was no evidence that anything—known or unknown—had ever been there.

Those many years later, as he sought out the witnesses to what would become known as the Roswell Incident, Friedman came into contact with a long-retired funeral director by the name of Glenn Dennis. Dennis informed Friedman that he had been working out of Roswell when the incident had occurred. He claimed that, during the summer of 1947, the Army had suddenly approached him and requested several small caskets. He had no idea what the caskets were needed for, but as a funeral director it wasn't his job to ask questions.

Not long after, Dennis learned of something strange brewing at the base hospital, and he tried to get inside to see what the commotion was all about. Troops blocked his entrance, telling him in no uncertain terms to go home. But later, an army nurse who worked at the facility would confide in him.

The nurse told Dennis she'd been present during the autopsy of two non-human bodies—bodies with brownish-grey skin and large, hairless heads. The nurse was highly disturbed by what she had seen, and although she had likely been sworn to secrecy, she obviously could not help but talk about what she had witnessed. Dennis would later lose contact with the young nurse, and despite attempts, couldn't find her again. He attempted to write letters to her, but the letters came back postmarked as "deceased."

In 1994, congressman Steven Schiff kicked the hornet's nest by merely asking the General Accounting Office (GAO) to take a peek at the financial records from this period in Roswell's history. It was supposedly this inquiry that led the Air Force to compile a new report on the incident, in which a cover up was finally admitted. Yet according to this report, which was dubbed "Roswell Case Closed, " it wasn't alien ships and extraterrestrial pilots that the military had covered up, but rather a top-secret research outfit called "Project Mogul." This project used special high-altitude balloons to monitor potential nuclear testing in Russia.

This version of events sought to explain not only the debris found but also the origin of the supposed alien bodies. This was due to the project's use of test dummies, whose charred countenances after falling back to Earth were said to have looked rather disturbing to the untrained eye.

Despite all the smoke and mirrors, efforts by the GAO to get to the bottom of certain documents ultimately failed, and for a simple reason: Most of them were missing.

The fact that a whole ream of documents from 1947 magically disappeared was, of course, very suspicious. Some used the word "outrageous." Perhaps it was this sense of outrage that prompted a military veteran by the name of Philip J. Corso to come forward. In 1997, shortly after the Pentagon declared the Roswell case closed, Corso emerged with his own version of events, and he most certainly begged to differ.. [32]

According to Corso, he first became involved with the Roswell Incident shortly after it occurred. He was stationed at Wright Patterson Air Force base as a major in 1947 when, one afternoon, an alarmed corporal rushed up to him, clearly distressed. The corporal had apparently snuck a peek into some cargo that had just been flown in from Roswell, and he was scared to death at what he'd seen. Even though it was breaking the rules, the corporal took Corso to see the cargo for himself. It was a "dead alien" from the recently recovered Roswell crash.

Corso was stunned. He immediately thumbed through the top-secret memo that came with the crate. It was here that he learned what he wasn't supposed to know: The creature was an extraterrestrial from a downed spacecraft that had crash-landed just outside of Roswell.

Corso was in shock but determined to do his duty. He put the lid back on and told the corporal, "You never saw this, and you tell no one."

Corso agreed and was, indeed, in on the conspiracy for many years. He was eventually placed in charge of special access projects, clandestinely gifting various contractors with materials from the wreckage to see what they could make of it.

The alleged efforts to reverse engineer the Roswell craft would later come out in Corso's book *The Day After Roswell*. Yes, he was part of the secret, but towards the end of his life, Corso had apparently grown weary of keeping his silence and decided to come forward.

It was shortly after he owned up to what had really happened at Roswell—and confessed to how he had played a part in it— that Corso himself perished. Although he was an old man, the death was untimely. Preparations were being made for Corso to give sworn testimony before a congressional hearing. That hearing never happened, due to Corso's abrupt passing from what was officially called a heart attack.

If that congressional hearing had been held, Corso would almost certainly have given explosive testimony as to the role of the U.S. in recovering crashed alien craft, and he would have likely detailed how he headed Research and Development projects that were tasked with reverse engineering the technology. He had already claimed in his book that many of the technological advancements that we enjoy today, such as computers, surgical lasers, and even night vision goggles are all derivatives of technology recovered from the Roswell crash. He further claimed that the Strategic Defense Initiative (known as "Star Wars") was created not only to combat incoming nuclear warheads but to deal with alien spacecraft.

Corso, as extraordinary as his claims might have been, was what you'd call "an unimpeachable witness." As a veteran of the army and of military intelligence, his credentials were rock solid. If Philip J. Corso was not telling us the truth, one could only conclude that his man had gone insane in his twilight years, or that he had decided to make up a big lie just before he died.

Or maybe it was something else?

In 2011, journalist Annie Jacobsen released a book called *Area 51*, a thick tome tracing the "uncensored" history of the mysterious desert development and test site operated by the U.S. military. [33] She doesn't deny that something crashed at Roswell in 1947. She also doesn't deny there were bodies in the craft that came down. But it wasn't, she concludes, a spacecraft. And the passengers were neither aliens nor test dummies. After interviewing dozens of former and current military and state and federal agents, as well as civilians, Jacobsen came away with maybe the strangest theory of all about Roswell.

According to Jacobsen, after World War II the Russians had expanded on the achievements of a group of former Nazi engineers led by Walter and Reimar Horten, who had been developing disk-shaped craft capable of evading radar detection. Later, the U.S. would use the technology to create the F-117 Stealth and other highly advanced planes at Area 51.

At the same time, Russia was deeply disturbed by the development of the atom bomb. Worried about its own inability to yet match such power, the Soviets instead decided to threaten the U.S. with another kind of power.

Mass hysteria.

According to Jacobsen's informant, in the summer of 1947 Stalin sent a "flying disk" into U.S. airspace from a "mothership" stationed over Alaska. Aboard the craft were small beings, but they weren't extraterrestrials. They were children or little people who had been genetically altered by Nazi scientist Josef Mengele. After the crash, two of them were found alive. Their large heads and bulbous eyes shocked all who saw them, though none could talk about it.

Jacobsen's source explained that he'd seen the bodies—and the remains of the craft—at Area 51 in 1951, when they were returned to Nevada after being studied at Wright Patterson AFB in Ohio. When he saw them in 1951, the children or little people were on some kind of life support. As for the "hieroglyphics" on the craft described by past witnesses, Jacobsen's source said it was actually Russian writing.

Many have attacked Jacobsen's book, especially her single-source revelation on Roswell. But she defends that conclusion and that source, reminding us that these engineers had such a top-tier clearance they could neither ask questions about the debris or the bodies nor discuss them, even with each other, during or after their work with them. That had been the case with other witnesses, too. No one was told what the craft was, or who the beings were, and they couldn't talk to each other about the possibilities.

With the Air Force immediately quashing the UFO story in the papers, it's likely that many witnesses would have assumed it to be, in fact, an alien coverup. After all, isn't that honestly less crazy-sounding then the prospect of *children engineered by Nazis to look like aliens?* Or that Russia had dared to enter the airspace of a country that had recently almost blown Japan off the map? Wasn't it, too, less panic-inducing than revealing to the world the fact that Russia had aircraft with not only hover technology but which could also evade radar detection?

Today, many ufologists and their followers believe that Jacobsen's conclusions about Roswell are just too crazy. Less crazy, they say, is their own, unshakeable belief that it was aliens.

A middle road is one traversed before his death by the late Michael Heiser in the documentary film, *Aliens and Demons*. He believed that, if there was a crash at Roswell, it was not an alien one. It was an experimental one belonging to the United States, and the "pilots" on board were likely deformed children or small adults, possibly suffering from Crouzon syndrome or another physical abnormality presenting with large heads or protruding eyes. We know such "disposable human beings" were regularly used in experimentation—and likely still are. The cruelty of our government, I recall Heiser remarking, must always be considered.

And never underestimated.

Before we leave Roswell, we must consider one more theory about it, and also a very different one. It's the theory that there was no crash at all in that New Mexican desert in that summer of 1947.

In fact, I've encountered in my research more than one theorist who believes the "crash material" and/or "bodies" removed from that legendary site were not from a crash. Rather, they were placed there or dropped there. This theory posits that entities created the materials as part of their own interdimensional or spiritual psyop to make it look like aliens had crashed their spaceship. Others believe that yes, the materials were placed—but that the government planted them, though toward the same end.

In recent years, NASA scientist Tim Taylor reportedly took religious historian Diana Pasulka to another "crash" site in the New Mexico desert which is known to insiders as the "donation" or "gifting" site, because extraterrestrial entities have dropped exotic materials to earth there. [34] Not long after they met, Taylor took Pasulka to the location to show it to her, insisting that she be blindfolded on the car drive there. At the site they found, she said, two pieces of metallic material, including one that looked "like frog skin," that she "can't explain."

The modern UFO era began when a mild-mannered pilot named Kenneth Arnold happened to look over and see a squadron of shiny craft hurtling through the skies. The Roswell Incident—whatever it may have been or not been—was the next explosive salvo. The U.S. government tried to bury the story and had, for the most part, succeeded. Roswell was all but forgotten when the tale was dug up decades later by, among others, a long-retired veteran who'd seen it all.

Or so he said.

Today, we've found ourselves in the middle of a flood of whistleblower reports on the entire UFO enigma. At the same time, we have rock-solid evidence of intense and ruthless disinformation campaigns, such as that of the infamous Doty-Bennewitz case, which we'll visit a bit later. We know we've been lied to in the past by government officials, and on a grand scale. And so today, when "whistleblowers" say they're uncovering the covered-up, we have to question their honesty, just as we have to question the true "unimpeachability" of the Roswell witnesses. With many crying "psyop" in answer to their alleged confessions, who is to be believed? Might even long-ago "witnesses" like Corso been part of some other government line having nothing to do with extraterrestrials?

The most famous whistleblower of the contemporary UFO craze is former military intelligence agent David Grusch. In 2023 Grusch testified before Congress regarding the truth of a multi-decade research and development project centered on UFOs, known today as Unidentified Anomalous Phenomena (UAP) (the government's new term for UFO/ET phenomena). [35] He claimed under oath that it was all real. In addition to verifying an alien craft retrieval and reverse engineering program, he even seemed to refer to extraterrestrials, speaking about "biological nonhuman entities" (NHEs) that had been recovered from UFO crash sites.

Seemed to.

Because Grusch didn't overtly state that they were intelligent biological nonhuman entities, and he didn't say he himself saw them, or saw their craft, or saw anything. But lots of people had told him about it, he insisted.

Of course, Americans had questions after Grusch's testimony: two big ones. Number one, why would these super-advanced craft crash so often? And number two, how in the world could the U.S. government keep such a thing secret for so long?

Perhaps, as some skeptics are claiming, the "crashes" haven't been real at all. Perhaps they've been staged as part of either some other unknown government psyop for some unknown reason, or perhaps they've been staged by someone—or something—else.

As for the incredulity at the ability of the government to keep the secret? The fact is the Roswell crash *has not been kept secret*. Far from being a secret, the Roswell crash is the most well-known event in UFO history. Roswell, if anything—*is an open secret*. And this has just added fuel to the fire of those who believe it's just one big fake out—or psyop—to cover up something completely different, and perhaps infinitely more sinister.

We'll look at Roswell again later, when we examine some very *terrestrial* information about the case as we address the physical aspects of the UFO/ET phenomenon. For now we'll take away what I think is an indisputable fact about not only this fundamental 1947 case but UFOs in general: As Michael Heiser commented of the Roswell story, "Somebody wants this myth to live."

There have been a number, now, of deathbed confessions from high up officials who have contributed to "disclosure" of the open secret of Roswell. This includes the signed statement of Walter Haut—which was directed to be opened only after his death—, testifying that what he believed he saw was a spacecraft and extraterrestrial pilots.

Though UFO believers called him a "patriot" and "brave" when he came forward, UFO whistleblower David Grusch has, for the wider world of Americans, become a laughingstock for his "nondisclosure disclosure" and "non-witness witness testimony" and what many experts even call dirty, lying body language.[36] As one *New York Magazine* headline proclaimed of Grusch, "'The UFO Whistleblower is Back with More Crazy Claims.'" .

We'll see as this story rolls out that the "extraterrestrials" themselves seem to use the ridicule factor as our a valuable tool. What's generally called the "absurdity" of UFO/ET experience has been present in many of the actual UFO/UAP and alien encounters themselves, from the earliest, nineteenth century "spacecraft" encounters and even further back. Some ufologists believe that the absurdity is not just an unfortunate aspect of the UFO experience but a deliberate element of it. That is to say: Whoever is creating these experiences is adding elements of the absurd on purpose, presumably as a surefire way to defuse their power to convince others of their reality.

In the end, and without knowing who's lying and what premises are true, we're forced to draw conclusions. We're forced to make a choice. Some choose to believe in the crash at Roswell. In the spacecraft. In the bodies. In the whole UFO phenomenon as extraterrestrial.

And some choose not to believe.

As we progress in our examination, we'll explore the belief factor among certain officials in the military intelligence community over the course of this modern extraterrestrial era. In particular, we'll look at the specific belief of an enigmatic group who, from the beginning, believed something very specific about UFOs and ETs: that they are not visitors from other planets but, rather, intruders from another reality.

It's a sketchy tale at best, and a lot of that sketchiness comes from the group's connection—though indirectly—to one of the most . . . well, *absurd* groups of people in modern history: the followers of the so-called "wickedest man in the world."

Aleister Crowley.

THE BEAST AND THE GRAY

Just before the pandemic officially hit, I found myself very sick. I thought it was the typical winter flu that makes the rounds starting in October each year and going through the winter months. It was late January of 2020. I had the worst headache, and nothing but nothing would take it away. I found out later that many others had had a similar illness that winter, and many of us came to believe we'd had COVID-19 before it grabbed the headlines here in the U.S. At any rate, it was during that time that I started watching a lot of YouTube channels that focused on religion and spirituality, especially regarding the occult. And it was during this time that, for the first time, I really began to learn about the life of Aleister Crowley.

As someone involved since high school in the study of secret societies, religious history and parapsychology, I knew the name well, but I had never taken any real dive into what Crowley actually did. I knew he was into what he called "sex magick [sic]" and drugs, and that he fancied himself some kind of great occult master. I used to talk about Crowley on the ghost tours I hosted in Chicago, because there's a little tavern in Lincoln Park which some claim was a meeting place for a chapter of some 1920s Crowleyan club. But I didn't know anything specific.

It was during the winter of 2020 that I learned about a lot of the things that Crowley did. In particular, I learned about *the one big thing* he did—in his infamous house in Scotland—and the *other big thing he did*—right here in the United States. Later, I would come to learn about a pair of very influential American occultists who counted themselves among his followers. Above all, I would learn about the connection of all of it to UFOs.

It may be a ridiculous understatement, but Aleister Crowley lived a rather strange life, a life which ended on December 1st, 1947. As we've learned, this was the same year the modern-day UFO era began. Crowley was born in 1875 in Leamington, England. The son of a wealthy brewer, he inherited a vast fortune while still in his early 20s. Having turned against his Christian upbringing, and with his every care met—at least at first—, he spent the majority of his time probing the depths of the occult.

In 1898, after leaving Cambridge University, Crowley was initiated into the Order of the Golden Dawn, which included Bram Stoker and W.B. Yeats as members. Crowley soon found himself on the outs with many of his esoteric associates, who believed sobriety and self-control were crucial to the practice of arcane rituals. Crowley, however, loved drinking and drugs and, moreover, had a voracious sexual appetite, seeking out sex with women, men and, eventually, even animals. He would later write poetry about engaging in sex acts with his lover's infant daughter. His followers hotly debate whether these entries were descriptors of real events or products of his foul mind.

Crowley wrote that his first mystical experience had taken place during a homosexual encounter; the act, he claimed, had summoned some kind of deity. This belief led him to what would become an obsessive pursuit of spiritual growth through sex and the practice of "sex magick" to facilitate it.

In just a few short years, Crowley had burned bridge after bridge, because he did not care for rules, boundaries or any institution or person that told him what to do. In particular, Crowley tussled with the poet W. B. Yeats. Rumors flew that Crowley was using black magic on the poet, and some said Yeats responded with his own. Crowley was forever embroiled in some kind of conflict; even among freaks of the forbidden, he didn't fit in.

And so, in 1900, Crowley left it all behind and bought a house on the shores of Scotland's Loch Ness. He was just 25 years old. The place was called Boleskine Manor, an old hunting lodge, and Crowley chose it for a specific purpose. He planned to hunker down in the remote fortress and attempt one of the most ambitious and dangerous rituals known in the occult world: the Abramelin. The ritual would take six months and result, he hoped, in the summoning of Crowley's "holy guardian angel." In occultism, that's not a God-given protector but one's "higher self." The ritual includes evoking the 12 Kings and Dukes of Hell—including Satan, Leviathan and Belial—in order to bind them. Many experts in Crowley's life believe he originally meant well: to bring these demons under his control and force them to do good.

That's not what happened.

Before beginning the ritual, Crowley sharpened his skills as an occultist, engaging in all manner of ritual practice. He reportedly summoned a number of angels, demons and other beings while "warming up" for the big one. (In fact, some have posited that the legendary Loch Ness Monster was conjured up by Crowley during his time in the house.)

After much preparation, Crowley began the Abramelin. But after months of rituals, during which he claimed to see— according to plan—demonic beings assembling at Boleskine, Crowley was called away from the house by the Golden Dawn. A schism had broken out in the organization, and Crowley was needed at once. Without ending the ritual, he left. Crowley had summoned demons—and left the door open wide.

Some have wondered if the unfinished ritual at Boleskine was the reason Crowley's life took such a deep dive into evil in the years that followed. As we'll see, some also believe the impact of Crowley's unfinished ritual would even impact the whole world.

It was on his honeymoon in 1904 that Crowley finally

claimed to have successfully contacted his holy guardian angel. Over a period of three days, an entity who called itself "Aiwass" dictated *The Book of the Law*, which would serve as the foundation of a full-blown religion. It included a motto that would underly countless Luciferian and Satanic religions and organizations to come:

Do what thou wilt shall be the whole of the law.

Crowley later relocated to the East Coast of the United States. One favorite retreat was Esopus Island, located on the Hudson River. Here, Crowley reportedly camped for 40 days and 40 nights, engaging in all manner of rituals and incantations. But it was in his own apartment in New York City that the aspiring magus performed one of his biggest "magick" tricks—when he reportedly summoned a strange, diminutive being which he called "LAM." LAM appeared to Crowley while he was performing a ritual known as the Amalantrah Working, a ritual meant to open a portal between the seen and unseen worlds.

Crowley was so enthralled by this character that, in one of his many altered states, he drew up a sketch of the being: a sketch which would later appear on the cover of Crowley's commentary on *The Voice of the Silence,* a book written earlier by our friend, Madame Blavatsky. The sketch, drawn many decades before the modern UFO era, looks astonishingly similar to the entity of UFO lore known as a "gray alien." Alistair Crowley's LAM has that same bulbous, inverted teardrop-shaped head, large eyes, diminutive holes for a nose and a slit for a mouth.

Crowley did not refer to the entity as an extraterrestrial, of course, since such terms were not in vogue at the time. He called LAM a "preternatural intelligence." (Interestingly, since many current UFO researchers—and even some government officials—have taken to using the term "non-human intelligence"(NHI) in referring to the beings encountered in UFO/UAP experiences.)

Famously, Crowley remarked of the many entities he encountered in his supernatural travels, "Today they call them angels and demons; tomorrow they'll call them something else."

Call them demons, interdimensional beings, Crowley's preferred "preternatural intelligences"—or whatever you wish to call them. But Crowley in his later life was dedicated to making contact with them.

And so, too, was his most apt American pupil.

THE WIZARD OF PASADENA

If you recognize the name Jack Parsons, you likely have some familiarity with the aeronautic wizardry of California's Jet Propulsion Laboratory, which Parsons was instrumental in founding. Indeed, some have joked that the iconic acronym of JPL really stands for "Jack Parsons Laboratory," since he played such a pivotal role in shaping it into what it would ultimately become.

Born on October 2nd, 1914 as Marvel Whiteside Parsons, Jack led a privileged life prior to his public service. He was a bit of a whiz kid growing up, dabbling in science experiments from a young age. Parsons' professional career can be traced back to the 1930s, when he was hired on as a chemical engineer for the Guggenheim Aeronautical Laboratory, under the umbrella of the California Institute of Technology (Caltech). It was after he became associated with Caltech that the U.S. Army became interested in his unique skillset for use in the development of what was then termed "jet assisted aircraft."

Rockets.

The term "jet" was often interchangeable with "rocket" in those days, since the latter sounded a bit too sci-fi for the tastes of the top military brass. Parsons, though a noted eccentric, was viewed as a valuable contributor to the field. And he certainly wasn't the only scientist known for unusual behavior.

Fellow Caltech alum Theodore von Karman, for example, claimed he had an ancestor who had successfully created a "golem": a mythical, animated creature from Jewish folklore. Robert Oppenheimer was also known for his eccentricities, including a fascination with Eastern religion, famously quoting lines from the *Bhagavad Gita* when the first atomic bombs were being tested. The eccentricities of Parsons, then, were initially humored about as well as anyone else's in the field.

At first.

It's all taken as a big lark by most, but JPL was founded on Halloween night, 1936, one of the many occult "circumstances" that surrounded its inception and operation. Unlike the founding date, other facts can't be so easily dismissed. It was in 1938, just a couple of years into the lab's existence, that Parsons began attending gatherings of Aleister Crowley's Ordo Templi Orientis in Los Angeles, a group of followers of Crowley's Thelema religion. Parsons quickly distinguished himself as a keen protégé, and some believed Parsons might eventually even succeed Crowley himself.

Parsons, in turn, adored Crowley. When he wrote to him, he began the letters with *Most Beloved Father,* and signed them *Thy Beloved Son, Jack.*

Fittingly, among his esoteric peers Parsons was a bit of a star. His good looks and rogue swagger led some to call him the "James Dean of the occult." Even Crowley had to admit an admiration for his student though he worried about the young man's reckless nature.

Parsons had set up what served as an OTO satellite headquarters in a large house in Pasadena. Anyone could move into this sort of Luciferian boarding house. There was reportedly only one rule for tenants: one couldn't believe in God.

It was here that all manner of strange goings on and wild parties would be reported. On occasion, alarmed

neighbors called the police, but the charming Parsons (with a smile and a wave of his credentials) was typically able to brush off any inquiries.

It was while operating this depraved hostel that Parsons met an aspiring writer and fellow occultist named L. Ron Hubbard, future founder of the Church of Scientology. Later, some would claim that Hubbard, who was a Naval officer himself, was really a spy for a federal agency, who'd sent him to gather intelligence on Parsons. Whatever the case may have been, Hubbard decided to join in with what was happening at Parsons' unholy B&B.

Hubbard and Parsons became fast, close friends. After some

minor occult misadventures, they decided to embark upon some major conjuring. The aim was to bring about the birth of an immaculately-conceived "moonchild" or Antichrist, the demon goddess Crowley called "Babalon [*sic*)."[37]

First, however, Parsons insisted he needed a kind of mystical muse he referred to as an elemental. Specifically, he sought out a "female magical partner with red hair and green eyes." The pair attempted to summon this "woman" by conducting "sex magick" rituals in the Nevada desert. [38] (Legend has it these sessions were held in the vicinity of the later Area 51.) Parsons would masturbate while Hubbard recited incantations designed to manifest Parsons' ethereal mate. Parsons would write that the pair had returned to Pasadena to find a woman at the door: a woman named Marjorie Cameron.

Cameron was an Iowa farm girl who'd moved to California to pursue her artistic and spiritual interests. She would later become a cult figure in the local alternative scene. Her meeting with Crowley's Pasadena pupils stirred something deep within the young dreamer, and she soon became embroiled in the Thelemic lifestyle of the commune, via Parsons and Hubbard.

This unholy trinity began to engage in sex magick through an extensive ritual called the "Babalon Working." Much like Crowley's earlier New York ritual that had, he claimed, manifested LAM, Parson's ritual was designed to manifest a collection of interdimensional entities, including the moonchild Antichrist Babalon, essentially to bring about the end of Judeo-Christian civilization. Part of the process involved the so-called "Enochian calls" that had been used by the mystic and seer of the Middle Ages, John Dee, which he'd devised while in a state of intense meditation.

Crowley didn't approve of these activities, and he warned his American students of the danger of engaging in them. Of course, prior to Parsons banging on the interdimensional gates, Crowley himself had supposedly opened his own rift in time and space by his summoning of LAM. While he'd had a jolly good time with LAM, he'd learned from that experience (and from the mess he'd made at Boleskine), to responsibly close a spiritual door when he was done with it. It was the irresponsibility of Jack Parsons, then, that an older and wiser Crowley apparently feared.

But Parsons didn't listen. In January of 1946, he began the Babalon Working.

Parsons seemed to achieve some success in the ritual as it progressed. He wrote in his diary that at one point a brownish yellow light came through an interior doorway of the Pasadena house, and that he was struck by an invisible something that knocked a candle out of his hand.

But Parsons apparently grew bored of the ritual, and he and Cameron turned their attention to more worldly affairs. They began a racket of buying and selling yachts to wealthy patrons. It was while this pair was distracted by these dealings that Hubbard and Parson's then wife—Betty—withdrew a large amount of Jack's cash and fled to Florida. [39] Parsons later had Hubbard arrested, but not before putting a spell on his boat. He eventually reclaimed some of his cash, but Hubbard would keep Betty, and together they would found the Church of Scientology.

Jack Parsons died suddenly and violently in a fiery lab explosion in 1952, some say without ever closing that door he'd opened through the Babalon Working. Following his death, another UFO flap broke out in the United States: the bizarre DC flap of 1952 during which UFOs swarmed the nation's capital. Today, one of the biggest conspiracy theories in ufology claims that Parsons' 1946 ritual did, indeed, open a portal for interdimensional entities to enter our world: entities in the guise of "spacecraft" and "extraterrestrials.

The idea that the Babalon Working was responsible for the modern UFO surge seems to have originated with Scientologist Peter Moon and his co-author Preston Nichols, who penned the *Montauk Project* and a number of related books. The books are classified as science fiction, but many believe the stories of secret underground mind control experiments at Long Island's Montauk Point (one of Crowley's American haunts) to be true, and many "witnesses" to the experiments have emerged since, claiming they recalled memories of abuse while under hypnosis.

Moon believed that Hubbard was sent into Parson's Pasadena compound by the government to infiltrate it, and Moon (a reported Scientologist himself) apparently saw Hubbard as a sort of white knight fighting against the black magicians Parsons and Crowley. Incidentally, the Montauk Project legend reportedly inspired the wildly popular streaming program, *Stranger Things.*

As bizarre as it may seem, many decades after Parsons' death, the theory of a connection between the Babalon Working and UFOs would gain traction after the emergence of what seemed to be an evidential story. The story was chronicled by paranormal journalist Nick Redfern, who developed it after getting a very hot—and almost unbelievable—tip from a Christian scholar and fellow ufologist.

It's a story of government agents, rockets, aliens and the occult . . . including no less than human sacrifice.

The story of the Collins Elite.

SHADY CRUSADE

According to the story, the name "Collins Elite" began as a lark. One of the members of the group hailed from the old Quaker town of Collins in Upstate New York. This guy had once mentioned to the other members something about his hometown being known only for folks that made cheese. Someone then cracked a joke about how, since he hailed from the "cheese town" of Collins yet didn't make cheese, he must be elite. The name stuck.

In his controversial book, *Final Events,* paranormal journalist Nick Redfern broke the saga of this covert association of fundamentalist Christian government agents who'd allegedly been watching the modern UFO enigma (and Parsons' and Crowley's involvement in it) from the start. They'd had their work cut out for them, for along with his bothersome occult activity, Jack Parsons was suspected, as Crowley had been, of engaging in espionage. What's most interesting in all of this, however, was that Duke and his colleagues claimed to know something others did not: that Jack Parsons was an associate of Kenneth Arnold, the pilot whose sightings in the summer of 1947 are credited with igniting the modern UFO era.

Duke told Redfern that, after the outbreak of the UFO plague in 1947, Parsons was sat down by the government and asked some pretty serious questions about it. Reportedly, he either offered or concurred that the craft being witnessed were likely entering into our reality by way of an interdimensional portal. But that wasn't all. Parsons also claimed he'd opened it himself through the Babalon Working.

On July 17, 1952, shortly after this alleged admission, Parsons would turn up dead by way of the tragic lab accident. That D.C. UFO flap would follow, running two straight days from July 19th through July 20th.

Was the "accident" in the lab the result of one of Parsons' crazy rituals? Had the mad rocketeer and black magician just opened that interdimensional rift a little wider, killing himself in the process? It seems that was just what some government agents may have surmised.

Duke further informed Redfern that it was just weeks after Jack Parsons perished that the Collins Elite officially came together. They were a loose association of government agents tasked with getting to the bottom of the UFO outbreak and its ties to the occult. Far different than popular ideas about no-nonsense "G Men," the group was reportedly comprised of passionate fundamentalist Christians. As they pondered all that had transpired and dug deeper into the mystery, the group slowly began to piece together a strange puzzle: one that connected what appeared to be extraterrestrial visitors with supernatural forces from an old, familiar source:

The Bible.

Before we get into this truly wild tale, let's set the stage, because Jack Parsons and Aleister Crowley weren't the only fringe-y things on the government's radar after World War II.

In 1927, American botanist J.B. Rhine founded the first parapsychology laboratory at Duke University in Durham, North Carolina. In 1922, while working on his doctoral degree at the University of Chicago, Rhine and his wife, fellow botany doctoral student Louisa, had been deeply impressed by a lecture given by Arthur Conan Doyle on the topic of scientific proof of the afterlife.[40] Obsessed with the possibility of such proof, Rhine eventually turned to the study of psychology and moved to Duke to work under well-known paranormal researcher William McDougall. There, in the late 1920s, Rhine began putting into motion the founding of a new branch of science.

Rhine wanted to isolate and study what he felt were the scientifically pursuable aspects of the paranormal: human abilities he would call *telepathy, clairvoyance, precognition* and *psychokinesis*. These abilities had really taken center stage in the latter half of the nineteenth Century with the explosion of Spiritualism, when prominent thinkers of the day—including scientists—had gathered around séance tables with believers.

Many great minds had become convinced there was something strange going on, but many also wondered if the amazing things mediums were demonstrating—knowing things that couldn't be known, seeing things that were far away, moving things without visible human effort—could be credited to human agency and not discarnate entities. Rhine believed these things might be studied under strict scientific conditions, unlike so-called "spontaneous phenomena" such as experiences of ghosts, hauntings and other unpredictable events of human experience

It was putting a lab coat on a whole host of activities that are eschewed by the Church, but by then the tidal wave of Spiritualism had already obliterated most Western associations of paranormal activity with the diabolical. In fact, most Spiritualists had been Christians; a good number were even Protestant ministers.

It was puzzlement, though, rather than rapping spirits that haunted the movement's skeptics, like George Templeton Strong, disturbed by Spiritualism's popularity in that "enlightened nineteenth century," calling the whole movement "a strange chapter in the history of human credulity." [41] Still, although fraud would make the gullible easy prey for the movement, the promise of evidence of immortality inspired the rational minds of the age's most respected thinkers and kept that "enlightened nineteenth century" utterly enchanted.

In fact, it was the nineteenth-century fanaticism with empirical science—not spirituality—that made Spiritualism seem so promising. Ironically materialistic, its increasing reliance on materialization of spirits prompted disgust in metaphysicians like Ralph Waldo Emerson, because Spiritualists rejected supernaturalism, trumpeted the inviolability of natural law, demanded external facts rather than intuition, and threw their faith behind the progressive development of natural knowledge.

This weird marriage of the mechanical and the spiritual was an easy one for many Americans, who in the century before Spiritualism's fervor had marveled at inventions of innovators like

Benjamin Franklin. As historian Werner Sollors recognized, Spiritualism was actually a sacralization of empiricism, an attempt to "find transcendental meaning in graphite pencils and gaslight…batteries, locomotives, and the telegraph itself." [42]

The telegraph.

It was this single invention that opened wide the doors to Spiritualist possibility. For if real-time communication could be accomplished across thousands of miles of space, why not communication to other realms, where the dearly beloved reportedly reside? It shouldn't be surprising, then, that the spirit of Benjamin Franklin made frequent appearances at many séances, thrilling mediums and sitters in his role of "heavenly inventor" of modern spirit communication.

With spiritual advocates like Franklin, earthbound proselytizers like Davis and Doyle, and the support of a generous portion of the literary and philosophical giants of the age, Spiritualism won over a conservatively estimated 1.5 million Americans who had rejected orthodox Christianity in the belief that life had only so many questions, all of which humanity— innovative, rational and clever—was quite capable of answering. Taking their regular places in séance parlors and Spiritualist churches, they sought evidence of the unknown in the form of ectoplasmic hands and trivial information from the great beyond.

And so by the early decades of the twentieth century, Spiritualism's somewhat monstrous empiricism had brought the occult into the laboratory, and there was definitely some weird stuff going on there—at least by normal American standards of the 1930s: demonstrations of what seemed to be extrasensory perception, clairvoyance and psychokinesis. Still, the government didn't seem too interested in the happenings at Rhine's lab. That is, until everything changed with the Second World War.

Everything.

As the 1950s dawned, U.S. agencies found themselves actively investigating paranormal phenomena and abilities. There was one mission: Control and power must be kept at any cost, and every ability and resource must be tapped and exploited to that end.. [43]

In 1952, the Army enlisted Duke University to help discover whether dogs demonstrate extrasensory perception (ESP). One project had dogs locating underwater explosives in California. Though early results seemed a bit promising, program was later deemed a total failure.

Around the same time, the Department of Defense sent Henry "Andrija" Puharich out to find mushrooms rumored to foster psychic ability. Puharich was, at the same time, spending much of his time looking into the reality of faith healing for the Atomic Energy Commission, and he would later dive deeply into psychokinesis (PK) research.

Interest in paranormal abilities and occult science skyrocketed after a woman named Nina Kulagina became a Russian sensation. Claiming to be able to influence objects with her mind, she appeared on television in the early 1960s, dazzling viewers by moving objects without touching them. The demonstrations so scared the U.S. Department of Defense that it delivered a report on what the agency called the "Soviet psychoenergetic threat," warning that a so-called "ESP gap" could seriously undermine American readiness to battle Russia's psychic warriors.

In fact, in his book, *UFO Chronicles of the Soviet* Union, Jaques Vallée recalls how a Soviet scientist told him:

> We're ahead of you in the study of the paranormal because the Western churches killed all your witches in the name of their dogma…. You only have yourselves to blame if you have fewer gifted psychics. You've eliminated their genes from the gene pool.[44]

Hugh Ross, an astrophysicist and Christian, shared that, during a secular speaking engagement in Russia, a full quarter of the scientists in the audience verbally and physically reacted to his entrance into the room, screaming assaults at Jesus Christ or physically drawing their bodies into the fetal position, leading him to believe that many of the nation's top astrophysicists were literally demonically possessed. [45]

Many paranormal-centered programs emerged in the years that followed those early forays, but there was one that captured a lot of interest—and sank a lot of government money. That was the infamous program of research into what's known as "remote viewing." [46]

Remote viewing is a scientific term for clairvoyance: the paranormal seeing of things at a distance. But it's *targeted* clairvoyance. The DoD hired professed psychics for the program, but it also sought to train others to exhibit paranormal or *psi* abilities for military applications. The program was supposed to be about finding weapons stashes and other things of military importance, but one of the most enthusiastic among its operatives was Major Ed Dames, who was more interested in psychically searching for UFOs and the Ark of the Covenant, and plenty of tax dollars went into his rogue efforts.

This was the strange government world the Collins Elite would have found themselves in when they formed to look into the occult aspects of the UFO flap, the hijinks of Parsons and company, and the dabbling of agencies in the realms of nonhuman contact.

Journalist Nick Redfern made contact with alleged Collins Elite member "Richard Duke" through an American UFO researcher and Anglican priest named Ray Boeche, who he interviewed in January of 2007. Intrigued by Boeche's mention of a sort of covert "anti-demon" government UFO task force, Redfern listened as Boeche revealed how, in 1991, two men claiming to be employed by the DoD had contacted him to ask for help. They told Boeche that the government had been trying to contact "non-human entities," and he soon realized the men were referring to extraterrestrials. As a man of God and an active investigator for the well-known, worldwide Mutual UFO Network (MUFON) investigative organization. Boeche was just the guy they were looking for.

The men were both Christians, and they had become deeply concerned about the direction the research was going in the hands of their superiors. They told Boeche that, just a few weeks after Jack Parsons' death, a small group of government employees, who later called themselves the Collins Elite, had been put together to explore the possibility of whether UFOs were entwined with the occult.

At first, the Collins Elite theorized that the UFOs—and the experiences of the early Contactees of the 1950s (who we'll meet in the next chapter)—were not real at all. With the growing knowledge of just how involved the nation's foes were in "psychotronic" warfare, wasn't it more likely that some Russian psychics were planting "experiences" and "memories" of UFOs and ETs?

In the process of their research, however, the men had come to a horrifying realization. No, these experiences of ETs and their craft weren't part of some covert psychic war. But these entities weren't extraterrestrials either.

They were demons.

Moreover, the governmental research into their nature had taken quite a turn from the kind of ESP, telekinesis and clairvoyance experiments that people of the early twentieth Century had associated with university laboratories, parapsychologists and "scientific" settings. In fact, the research was following the example of someone the government had been interested in decades before, and it was encompassing

> the use of . . . 'satanic rituals/ritual magic along the lines of that espoused by Aleister Crowley, including human sacrifices. [47]

Just to be sure you caught that: The DoD agents told Ray Boeche that the government was employing human sacrifice in UFO research.

The men cited a number of strange events that had led to their realization of what they'd been dealing with. Encounters with the entities and messages from them, they explained, always started out with seeming kindness and generosity but ended—every time— with bad luck, illness or other dark turns. Some government workers, they said, had even perished.

As evidence of their claims, the men shared with Boeche three shocking photographs of dead people who had reportedly been killed during "psychotronic weapons experiments," presumably during attempts to work with or implement the methods of these "extraterrestrial" entities. The first photograph showed a white male, allegedly killed "by remotely-induced cardiac arrest." The second, a white female white killed by "remotely transmitting and creating head trauma equivalent to crushing the right anterior portion of her skull." The third photo showed a white male killed by "remotely controlled suffocation.". [48]

The men further told Boeche that they had also observed subjects attacked with remotely transmitted "pain, paralysis, burns and other tissue damage, and acute coronary thrombosis."

As we've seen from following the sensational stories in the news the past year or so, the Collins Elite was apparently not alone in believing the government was dealing with something decidedly *not* from outer space. Lue Elizondo, who (apparently falsely) claimed to be the former director of the Pentagon's UFO task force known as the Advanced Aerospace Threat Identification Program (AATIP) and one of the primary "faces" of the most recent UFO disclosure wave, told the world that officials in the Pentagon *in recent years* have also believed in the demonic nature of the UFO phenomenon and that at least one official told him the study of it should be dropped like a hot potato.[49]

His claims seemed to line up with information in the so-called "Collins Report"—excerpts from which Duke shared with Redfern during their meetings. The report summed up the group's dire findings, and with it members began debriefing members of Congress and agency officials, delivering their urgent wake-up call and pleading for an end to the government's occult research and programs involving the entities. That's reportedly when the Collins Elite became more than just a sort of after-hours G-Man Bible study. It started getting black money (though not a lot), and it started to grow.

According to Redfern, the Collins Elite had come to believe that the government, in pursuing its occult programs, had opened such a wide door to the demonic that it would take a massive counteroffensive to push it back to where it had come from. Members had shared a two-pronged proposal for this: One,

Mosaic Law should be established as the law of the United States; two, the government should stage a fake Second Coming of Christ—with the help of holography and projections in the skies—to get people to follow it.

A prominent conspiracy theory in UFO circles seems evocative of this claim. "Project Blue Beam" was first detailed in 1994 by conspiracy theorists online, and it involved an alleged plan to stage a global "religious" event using holographic projections to dupe the international public. But Project Blue Beam's alleged intent was to create a One World Government—not to drive away the devil and his minions. Governments would project into the sky images of and messages from Jesus, Buddha, Mohammed— whichever one fit the population below. Each religious icon would deliver the same message: Religion is over. Follow the one world leader.

Some summaries of Project Blue Beam include the simulation of an imminent alien invasion using, again, holography to create three dimensional projections of "spacecraft" and "aliens" to scare folks into doing whatever the authorities told them. Some believe the avalanche of UFO sightings in the past years shows the program has now begun.

Richard Duke left the Collins Elite at the dawn of 1961. He and his family had begun to suffer strange illnesses, and he began to feel the UFOs were somehow watching him. Duke told the group his reasons and walked away.

Since his claims—and those of Boeche's two men— were first published by Redfern, many have tried to prove or disprove the existence of the Collins Elite. Opening portals, consulting demonological texts… if it was real, a lot of work had been done on the project. And funding had to have been a part of it. Redfern assumed where there was funding there had to have been some sort of body that had been put together—and some record of it. He searched through every channel and agency to find evidence of the group, without success. But Redfern says he believes in its existence, because both he and Ray Boeche met numerous separate members of the group, whose stories line up

Still, some have ventured that the group was a fake: yet another psyop intended to make the UFO enigma seem like a crazy Christian conspiracy, taint the UFO question with absurdity or send ufologists (like Boeche) running after artificial breadcrumbs.

In 2023, prior to the scheduled Congressional hearing on UFOs, an unknown source "leaked" to news agencies an extensive 177-page "report" outlining a "history" of governmental research and encounters with UAPs and "extraterrestrials."[50] Along with "evidence" that the government has been successfully researching and developing things like zero gravity and materialization of objects, the dossier also includes information about the Collins Elite. Most ufologists seem to believe the dossier is a mix of authentic and hoaxed or dis-information, so it's up to the reader to assess which parts are which, if the reader concurs with that opinion.

Included in the dossier are extracts from the 1998 "Collins Report" that Nick Redfern received from "Richard Duke," the member of the Collins Elite with whom he met. Here is that section in full, and note that, among other things, it describes not a crash but a "fall" of "unusual" materials in New Mexico in 1947:

> (PUBLIC DOMAIN) - 11 March 1998 — Author Nick Redfern claims a source who was put into contact with him from AFOSI states a group of current and former IC personnel who believed UAP were demonic in origin called the 'Collins Elite' published a lengthy document summarizing their beliefs. The report is not published but extracts are; they state the following: 'STAC Reports (I to XI) describe the fall, collection, analysis and present whereabouts of unusual fabrics, foils, parchments, chemical residuals and biological material found at found locations in Lincoln County, New Mexico between 3 and 13 July 1947.

> The report mentions the Collins Elite met at the Loftus Boat on 23 May 1997 and that the Collins Elite was unable to convince CIA S&T at 'PTC' of viability of sharing with the

> Collis Elite the 'completed NORTH files on NM discoveries of 1947…S&T at PTC are aware of our briefing from STAC on their

files but are reluctant to share NORTH material due to security issues that developed from the Nebraska debacle.'

'STAC remain committed to advancement to media and population of both Mogul and extra-terra scenarios for NM fallings and discoveries and are troubled by Collins Elite wishing to advance THE THEORY to media and population. This writer privately engaged STAC Markale in conversation on 17 June 1997 and provided him with an amended copy of *New Mexico Origins: Parsons, Hubbard and Babalon Working*. Markale remains convinced that if placed into public forum knowledge of THE THEORY will irreversibly and negatively affect global social order.

This writer privately explained to Markale that Collins Elite initiatives prepared to ensure a reasonably acceptable transition of the perceived true nature of the Lincoln County discoveries to public and media, as well as a reasonable long-term acceptance of THE THEORY can still proceed with limited social disorder if handled correctly. Markale is not convinced and speaks for the STAC membership.

Presently STAC-5 is privately sympathetic to the position of Collins Elite; he reiterates the position of CANDLE on 4 May 1991 that STAC is now "in too deep" with its attempts to reverse-control the situation and prevent enemy infiltration and deception beyond present levels."

This writer sees that disagreement on our part with STAC is unlikely to inflame situation beyond present levels due to STAC's genuine sympathy with difficulties created for everyone by recent developments. STAC-5 informs this writer STAC totally rejects notion that Collins Elite's Learning the Way paper that theorizes radically indoctrinating population with belief and faith — and revelation to media and population of true nature of Lincoln County discoveries — can halt enemy infiltration.

This writer remains greatly troubled by STAC decision to continue its relationship with contractors Jamison and Wylie who — according to STAC-5 — are still convinced that the PARSONS TECHNIQUE can assist in holding off the deception, infiltration and final invasion. This writer adheres to Collins Elite conclusion based on a reading of the original STAC Reports (I to XI) that any attempt to follow the path of Parsons will only result in a catastrophe of the type warned about in Parsons, von Karman and Goddard: *A Door Unlocked.*

STAC-5 understands this but consistently feels the need to reiterate that situation has gone too far for STAC to back down. STAC-5 also informs that WPAFB sources have had some success using the PARSONS TECHNIQUE in achieving spontaneous brief laboratory manifestation of materials very similar to two of those that "fell" at Lincoln County, NM in 1947. STAC-5 is of opinion that if long-term manifestation and stability of materials can be achieved and precise originating point of materials can be determined then this will assist NASA-TZER mission to answer the critical questions posed in our 1991 briefing to STAC, Entry Points — And How Do We Keep Them Closed? Until final outcome of STAC, NASA-TZER and WPAFB research in this area is known this writer recommends that Collins Elite continues to focus attention on planned disclosure to public of THE THEORY if STAC, NASA-TZER and WPAFB attempts to "close the door" are not satisfactory. This writer concludes that if this hypothetical stage is reached disclosure and intense indoctrination of faith and values at planetary level to radically and rapidly alter current population mindset is the only alternative that may prove successful in thwarting plans of enemy.

This writer considers the disclosure to media and population of the Lincoln County fabrics, foils, parchments, chemical residuals and biological material to be crucial and integral in terms of revealing the "Trojan Horse" aspect of THE THEORY. STAC-5 understands this too and agrees that only if present attempts by NASA-TZER and WPAFB-1T to prevent widespread infiltration and enemy deception fail that revelation, explanation of the 'Trojan Horse' aspect of the Lincoln County fallings and indoctrination may be only viable alternatives.

This writer is encouraged by confident comments from STAC-5 that if present and near-future operations fail to achieve success STAC and Collins Elite would provide a united front that would allow THE THEORY to be presented publicly and quickly and in a way that was acceptable to STAC. For that reason and likelihood that enemy infiltration will not be thwarted by STAC and NASA-TZER methods [deleted] has prepared a unique briefing paper on the Lincoln County Trojans in the event that immediate and emergency dissemination of facts to media and population is required. [51]

The dossier also included information that seemed to verify that the rituals and even human sacrifice mentioned in the Collins Report may have actually happened, referencing very dark things that had occurred as part of a covert CIA project named MKOFTEN, though without any specific details.

In Gordon Thomas' book, *Secrets and Lies*, the author writes that Sidley Gottlieb, the CIA's "Poisoner in Chief" and head of the agency's Technical Services Branch, was the founder and driving force behind MKOFTEN. Gottlieb had previously headed the notorious MKULTRA mind-control project, administering LSD and other mind-bending drugs to literally destroy the minds of test subjects in the interest of governmental power. [52]

Gottlieb's ruthless quest for military domination through mind control at any cost distinguished him throughout his career. With MKOFTEN he sought to "explore the world of black magic" and "harness the forces of darkness." To this end, he and his team sought out witches and warlocks, Satanists, psychics, mediums, astrologers, clairvoyants and other occult practitioners. As for the alleged human sacrifice, we may scoff at the idea of such a thing as part of a government project, but knowing what some extreme occult practitioners (and under the direction of Gottlieb) would be capable of—and the potential financial rewards offered by Gottlieb's agency funding—who really knows what went on?

In 1972, the Collins Elite and MOKOFTEN's staff began exchanging information after the former shared with the latter a case in which a man named Paul Garratt had died and, in a claimed near-death experience, seen demonic aliens and flying saucers capturing other human souls at the moment of death. Later, when MKOFTEN began working with world famous witch Sybil Leek, the project operatives told the Collins Elite that Leek independently volunteered her belief that the UFO phenomenon was tied to the occult.

Later, Leek went into a trance a meeting of members of both projects. The Collins Elite was hoping she'd deliver, through her spirit world contacts, more information about this soul-sucking mission of the "aliens." During the trance, a demonic voice informed them all that the alien/UFO ruse was just the latest in a long line of hoaxes by the demonic, and that Earth was just a "farm" where souls are harvested to obtain energy for the demonic to feed on.

And so one man's "near death experience" and a celebrity witch's trance-induced ramblings led to one of the biggest and most frightening conspiracy theories in modern ufology: that UFOs and ETs are harvesting human souls for food.

So what can we take away from a dramatic, truly incredible story that, as Michael Heiser commented, "rises or falls on secret informants?"[53]

Personally, I think we know all about the Collins Elite that we need to. I think we know that the meat of the story is true. Unless someone scattered a whole lot of breadcrumbs throughout the history of government agency projects, there are too many instances where the claims of the Collins Elite and Boeche's DoD mystery men appear elsewhere. We know that modern governments—including, most definitely, the U.S.—have verifiable histories of indulging in the occult, attempting to use its tools and methods for war, surveillance and control. We also know that many—most? all?—of these attempts have ended up scrubbed. We also know that a lot of the people involved had all sorts of tragic, unhealthy and weird things befall them, including remote viewers like Ed Dames and the rest of the motley crew of psychics, spoon benders and witches who've been part of the government's secret programs over the years.

I think it's clear that many evangelical Christians working around these projects would have come to a similar conclusion as that reported by the so-called Collins Elite: that the whole thing wasn't science.

It was evil.

Did people die? Did the group really want to launch a new Mosaic-type government to combat the wave of evil to be ushered in by these entities? Was there a plan to simulate the Second

Coming of Jesus with holography? Because these were all claims of the men who met with Redfern.

I don't know. But the tale of the Collins Elite is just one more place where we find some old, disturbing names come up in yet another new time and arena.

The name of Aleister Crowley.

And the name of the devil.

CALLED

Even as the Collins Elite was being formed, a whole host of messianic-style UFO experiencers was beginning to come forward. The early 1950s was the start of a movement in which folks remembered as the first "contactees" emerged with a fantastic, shared claim: They had been contacted by interstellar, enlightened beings who they called "space brothers." The most pivotal players in this strange new game were the "Four Georges": four highly unusual and influential men named (presumably coincidentally) George.

It was in that same fateful year of 1947, right around the time of Kenneth Arnold's flying saucers and the supposed Roswell crash, that something inspired George Van Tassel to drop everything and invest all of his time into a remote Mojave Desert wasteland known as Giant Rock. It's called as much because of the large rock outcropping that stands as the centerpiece of the property. Known as the largest freestanding rock in North America, this monument does indeed stand out, and Van Tassel had intentions of turning the place into a combination air strip and tourist attraction when he first encountered otherworldly entities there in 1951.

George would tell how, one fine day, he was stretched out on the desert floor, in a state of intense meditation, when he was allegedly beamed up by an alien spaceship hovering high above the Earth. Van Tassel explained that he wasn't physically taken by these aliens; it was his "astral form." On board the craft, he was introduced to a veritable council of aliens, the "Council of Seven Lights," to be exact. This council informed Tassel that they it been monitoring humanity for some time, and its members were very much alarmed at how "self-destructive" human beings had become.

. This was, of course, the dawn of the nuclear age. 1945 had made it brutally clear that destruction of the whole Earth was now just a button push away, and Van Tassel must have been deeply disturbed that even extraterrestrials had noticed mankind's recent dark developments.

Van Tassel's communion with these otherworldly visitors was not a one-off. They continued, and on one occasion he claimed to have another human witness to the ETs. Van Tassel said that a certain Reverend Robert Short was on hand during one of the meditation sessions at Giant Rock. Short would later report exactly what he saw, claiming that both he and Van Tassel were spoken to via a sort of channeling between themselves and the visitors. These apparent communications were achieved through actively channeling the speaking entities. The entities would speak to the minds and through the bodies of the two men, and the message was always the same: *Human aggression had reached dangerous levels.*

Though at the time few apparently saw the similarity, what was transpiring in the 1947 desert was very similar to the mediumship and channeling that had gone on for decades during the heyday of the Spiritualist movement and in Theosophical circles. Nevertheless, George Van Tassel continued to receive his messages, and he took many notes on the arts of the messages directly related to him.

The notes turned into his own periodical, the *Proceedings of the College of Universal Wisdom.* In its pages Van Tassel would expound upon the various personalities of the "space brothers" he had encountered and the nature of the messages they had delivered. Of particular note were those of an alleged ET leader who Van Tassel called "Ashtar," who issued a warning to the governments of Earth, suggesting that if earthlings didn't stop fighting wars, the solar system would have to be secured by outside forces.

Ashtar told Van Tassel to send this message directly to none other than the United States Air Force, and that's precisely what he did, mailing a detailed letter to the intelligence office at Wright

Patterson Air Force Base in Dayton, Ohio.

The folks at Wright Patterson didn't know quite what to make of Van Tassel, but they were sure to have gone on to keep tabs on him. As we've learned, the Air Force was by the early 1950s no stranger to reports of UFO encounters. But it wasn't just Van Tassel's odd claims that sent up red flags with the intelligence office. Unknown to Van Tassel, a California local had previously suggested in his own letter that oddball George might be working for the Soviet Union.

It's never been proven that Van Tassel was a spy, but considering the Cold War tensions of the times, such an angle had to be considered. Who was this guy spouting propaganda against the U.S. government? Was he a lackey of the Russians? Was he in contact with otherworldly entities as he claimed? Or was he simply out of his ever-loving mind?

On top of Van Tassel, other Contactees were popping up on the U.S. radar, and it wouldn't be long before intelligence agents would have their hands full.

Enter George Number 2.

George Adamski was a Polish immigrant who claimed, with several others, to have seen an alien spacecraft in the skies over a remote stretch of the Mojave Desert in southern California. The object came closer, but a squadron of military jets showed up and apparently "chased" the craft away. Before they could, however, a smaller "silver disc" disembarked from the cigar-shaped craft. The disc seemed to land in the distance, and Adamski pursued it. He supposedly took several photos of the craft.

A little later into this encounter, Adamski encountered one of the pilots of the craft. He described the being as humanoid in appearance and short in stature, around 5 feet tall and with long hair. This detail was perhaps a bit unusual for the 1950s, but other than this, the entity looked fairly similar to the average human being.

According to Adamski, he acquainted himself with the entity by extending his hand in the standard human gesture of greeting. The being grabbed hold of his hand as if to give him a handshake in traditional human fashion. What happened next, however, was far from customary—at least in any Earthly culture.

As soon as he made physical contact with the entity, Adamski would recall, his mind was flooded with a series of mental images. He learned through these mental pictures that the visitor's name was "Orthon" and that he hailed from the planet Venus.

Venus.

Once again, alien visitors were evoking an earlier period of occult exploration. Just as nineteenth Century Theosophical gurus had claimed to be in contact with enlightened Venusian "masters," Adamski was now connecting with, apparently, some version of these earlier Theosophical visitors.

It's important to point out, however, that in Adamski's time the conditions on Venus were yet unknown. He would have had no idea that Venus has a hellishly hot climate, unsurvivable by any known beings. (Less forgivable are those who currently claim to be in contact with Venusians, but more on that later.) Still, despite the (then) possibility that Orthon might have been from Venus, most of Adamski's critics—and probably his associates as well—thought he was either crazy or lying.

In fact, it might not have been poor old Adamski that was doing the lying, but the alien visitor. UFO lore is full of encounters in which supposed ETs have fed hapless humans a whole host of provably false and deceptive information. The Collins Elite and far less religious critics—Jaques Vallée, John Keel, and many others—would come to believe, for a wide variety of reasons, that those behind the UFO phenomenon were indeed engaged in an active and massive deception.

Nonetheless, Adamski claimed that Orthon and his brethren lived a good life on Venus, had a high moral standard, and were even "God-fearing" in their mentality. In fact, they were much better than humans in every way.

This alleged moral superiority of ETs to humans would prove a crucial element in the study of human encounters with UFOs. It's an idea that, like all modern thought, is inextricably wrapped up in the Theory of Evolution. With its origins in the "ascended masters" of Theosophy, the idea of other beings as unquestionably morally superior to Man would inform much of the later response to UFOs and ETs, as well as the idea that mankind can be led out of its bumbling misery into the cosmically evolutionary daylight, if only it can find its way out of the harness of Judeo-Christian belief.

At any rate, after establishing his moral authority, Orthon gave the typical ET speech, decrying humans as rotten, war-mongering ruiners of our planet. It was an early extraterrestrial speech on environmentalism that would develop into later 21st century ETs' climate change warnings, of which more later.

One of the most interesting things about Adamski, who died in 1966, is that his film and photos of UFOs have never been fully discredited, though they've been called a lot of not-so-nice-things by a lot of people. Most notably, they've been called "too good to be true," since—contrary to the typically fuzzy and out of focus UFO photographs—they are unusually crystal clear. And while many are obvious fakes, some of the photos have never really been debunked or disproven. On the contrary, one of the last video sequences he filmed, in the Spring of 1965, has been thoroughly examined and has, apparently, withstood efforts to dismiss it as fake.

The footage was examined by an optical physicist by the name of William T. Sherwood, who had previously worked as a consultant for Kodak when he began to look at Adamski's films. He put the footage through a series of rigorous tests, determining that it did, indeed, depict some sort of craft hovering through in the air. The image had not been superimposed on the film, and it wasn't some sort of optical illusion. The same sequence was also scrutinized by an aeronautics engineer by the name of Leonard Cramp. Cramp pointed out that, despite the clarity of most of the footage, the object seemed to take on the kind of fuzziness common to images and film of UFOs. He hypothesized that the effect might have resulted from the gravitational propulsion of the craft, which would make the light around it appear bent and distorted.

One of the most vocal of all modern UFO researchers also weighed in on the Adamski footage. Nick

Pope, formerly employed by the British Ministry of Defense, went on record to state that—despite his rather wild contactee claims—there seemed to be something very real in what Adamski had captured on film, stating his belief that,. even if some of his claims are nonsensical, others were legitimate.

Others were not so kind.

As believers and skeptics were poring over the evidence, something else was happening: something perhaps even stranger than Adamski's photos. Others were starting to see the same kinds of UFOs Adamski was taking pictures of. Almost immediately, secular critics posited this to be popular culture influencing public perceptions. However, we'll look a bit later at how, in cases of the demonic, there is often a "mimicry" element involved. That is, the entities seem to create experiences, objects and images that people want or expect to encounter.

One of the most troubling aspects of the Adamski story was a character in his life who he called "Uncle Sid." Many researchers don't believe Uncle Sid ever existed, though Adamski claimed they'd known one another since Adamski's childhood and that the figure, moreover, had encouraged Adamski's mother to send him to Tibet to be educated.

A number of Theosophists came to believe that Uncle Sid was one of the space brothers who had come to Earth before Orthon's appearance to be sure Adamski received the necessary occult training to prepare him for his cosmic mission on Earth.

Reportedly, our friends the Collins Elite had not failed to take note of what had been occurring in California. The group had since added George Adamski to their "watch" list, and it wouldn't be long before yet another George would set off their collective alarm.

George Number Three was George Hunt Williamson, and he is an exceptionally strange character in the generally bizarre history of the original Contactees. Not only did he claim to communicate with ETs, but he would later suddenly and inexplicably disappear. This wasn't, as you might guess, an early case of alien abduction. Rather, he changed his name, altered his background, and stopped talking about UFOs.

For the Collins Elite, Williamson's claims were particularly troublesome. George Van Tassel didn't appear to have done all that much to invite his contact with ETs. Adamski had been a lot shadier, what with his involvement in Theosophical pursuits and the financial gain with which they seemed entwined. All of that was questionable, but it was also rather foreign to the reportedly fundamentalist Christians who made up the Collins Elite. Adamski had also been using methods of EVP (Electronic Voice Phenomenon) research to talk to his aliens, but this wasn't seen by most as an occult methodology at the time, of which more later in this book.

Williamson was different. Though Williamson would use EVP as well (he often spoke to aliens using a short-wave radio, a la today's "ghost boxes" used in paranormal investigation), Williamson was primarily contacting his aliens through a method all too familiar to government agents—and most other Americans at the time.

A Ouija board.

Williamson was an academic teaching at the University of Arizona when the Kenneth Arnold-inspired flying saucer craze was in full swing, but in 1951 he was fired for poor performance. It might have been because his attention was decidedly elsewhere: Williamson had become fascinated with UFOs and extraterrestrials. He devoured whatever books on them he could find, including *Star Guests*, written by a rogue and upstart named William Dudley Pelley.

When the two first met Pelley had recently been sprung from prison, having been jailed for his antiwar activities in the 1940s.

Pelley's ideas had a profound impact on Williamson, leading him to become involved in the production of the monthly journal of an organization Pelley had founded. Fascinated by both the occult and flying saucers, Williamson embarked on a quest to contact extraterrestrial intelligences as his new mentor claimed to have done. To that end, he used a homemade Ouija board and engaged in channeling, attempting to establish communication with beings from outer space. He traveled to the compound of George Adamski with his wife, Betty, and another couple that had been at the inaugural Ouija session that first, fateful evening, when the foursome decided to try their hand at ET communication.

Williamson's channeling experiences were truly inexplicable. He would speak in different voices, one after the other, claiming to be communicating with various extraterrestrial entities. In 1954, Williamson published his own book, *The Saucers Speak*, which details his methodologies and the messages he received while employing them. In the book, readers learned of his friendships with Actar of the planet Mercury, Agfa of Uranus, Ankar-22 of the planet Jupiter and others.

The success of Williamson's Ouija group led to bad blood between them and Adamski, who had by then become nothing less than a cult leader in California, attracting much media interest in his messages. Despite the falling out, Williamson continued to channel, collect EVP and employ the Ouija board to keep up his relationships with his space brother contacts, and he continued to write about the increasing body of knowledge he received. His books, steeped in Theosophy and informed by the incessant stream of voices from "space," would prove extremely influential on future UFO believers.

Williamson had been told by his space friends that they had founded Judaism and Christianity, and that extraterrestrials had disguised themselves in the personages of pretty much every key player in the Bible. They were the performers of biblical miracles, the teachers of humanity, the builders of Earthly civilization: all ideas seen later in the pirated "work" of Erich von Däniken and central to today's wildly popular "ancient astronaut" view of everything.[54]

Williamson (or his space brothers) also influenced another contemporary, Frances Swan, who claimed to be in contact with some of the same aliens Williamson had named in his first book, including "Affa" and "Ponnar." According to the story, Swan—a Maine farm woman—attracted the attention of a retired Real Admiral, who managed to have a pair of Naval intelligence officers sent out to investigate. While in a trance, Swan reportedly gave answers to technical questions she couldn't have understood. She claimed it was extraterrestrials answering the questions.

Swan then told one of the officers, a commander, that the ETs wanted to speak directly through him, and he proceeded to successfully use automatic writing to record their answers. During the visit, the ETs also agreed to show the officers a spaceship, telling them to go to the window, where one allegedly appeared.

Famed abductee Betty Hill (who we'll meet shortly in this book) would later write that Swan refused a meeting with her and her husband, fellow abductee Barney Hill, because (Swan said) the Hills had been taken by "bad" aliens. Swan said her aliens were good ones.

The Fourth George of the Contactees was a London cabdriver named George King, and he's a whole other kettle of fish. We'll look at his story—and his influence—in a later chapter, because the UFO religion he founded is still in full swing, and it's wilder today than ever.

The end of the 1950s early Contactee movement was far from the end of contact. It would continue, with bells on, and we'll meet many other small-c contactees ahead. But while these early types of classic contact would continue—and while some very famous contactees were still to come—things were going to start escalating, and other kinds of much darker encounters were about to begin.

MEN IN THE NIGHT

Throughout the modern UFO era, aliens have frequently sent out, it seems, their own damage control crew following their appearances to humans. Rife have been the reports of mysterious men in dark suits showing up to the homes of UFO experiencers, usually to warn them against talking about what they've seen. These characters generally give no names, though typically hinting that they work for the government. They come in pairs or groups of three, drive dark cars, and sometimes exhibit strange behaviors, such as walking oddly or being confused about how to eat food.

The earliest case of such a visit by the now notorious "Men in Black" (MIB) in the annals of modern ufology came on the heels of the so-called Maury Island UFO Incident, which was reported the same summer as the alleged UFO crash at Roswell, New Mexico, and which was said to have taken place three days before the monumental Kenneth Arnold sighting at Mount Ranier. Though the Maury Island case has been largely dismissed as a hoax, the MIB motif stuck around, to appear again and again and again in future ufological cases.

According to Harold Dahl's original report, he was on a boat doing conservation work on the Puget Sound along the shoreline of Washington State's Maury Island on June 27, 1947, when he saw six "donut-shaped" objects in the sky above him, about a mile up. As he watched, one of them fell what he estimated to be about 1500 feet and then released some kind of debris. Some of the metallic objects hit the boat, striking Dahl's son and killing his dog.

The next day, Dahl received a visit from a man wearing a black suit. Saying he wanted to talk, Dahl accompanied him to a dinner in town. The man described to Dahl every detail of what Dahl had witnessed the day before, though no one but Dahl's son and his supervisor had seen the craft. The mystery man then warned Dahl to keep quiet about what he'd seen; otherwise, terrible things would happen.

Later, Dahl and his supervisor would purportedly admit to hoaxing the incident. The pair had approached a Chicago magazine—one of Ray Palmer's, in fact—hoping to sell the story, but its editors contacted Kenneth Arnold to help them fact check it. He in turn called intelligence officers to look into the claims. Bizarrely, the investigating officers' plane caught fire and crashed, and both of the agents were killed.

But it wasn't until the 1956 publication of Gray Barker's book, *They Knew Too Much About Flying Saucers*, that the MIB motif was really solidified, when Barker conjoined the stranger in black of the Maury Island tale with a classic Contactee case of the era. [55]

The case of Albert Bender.

The Bridgeport, Connecticut area from that city northwest to Monroe is known as a sort of hotspot of paranormal activity. It's one of those meccas for those interested in the strange. A place like Sonoma, or Mount Shasta.

Bridgeport was the hometown of Ed and Lorraine Warren, the infamous husband-and-wife ghostbusting team who inspired the *Conjuring* film franchise. They set up housekeeping in this nearby Monroe, and with it their famed New England Society for Psychic Research and its Occult Museum. Nearby, too, is Union Cemetery, known as one of the nation's most haunted places, and there's a road not far away where the fabled "Melon Heads" live, the same road where the grave of legendary witch Hannah Cranna may be found. On that note, in 1651, one of eleven witches executed in Connecticut was hanged at what is now approximately 2470 Fairfield Avenue in Bridgeport. One of the most infamous haunted house cases (one of the Warrens', too)—the so-called Lindley Street Haunting—played out in Bridgeport in the 1970s. The case included strange lights and ethereal full-bodied figures moving through the house, objects sliding and levitating, and a talking cat who asked a police officer how his brother was doing.

His brother was dead.

If you take Lindley to Main and head down the street a little way, you'll soon come to one of the most mythical spots in UFO lore: the home of the Benders.

In the early 1950s, when UFO hysteria was at one of its early peaks, Albert Bender was all in. A young veteran who had returned from the war a bit down on his luck, Bender worked at the local clock factory and lived at home in his stepfather's house on Broad Street, but he had his own attic room and den.. [56]

Bender purposely styled his space to cause curiosity and unease in his guests. He decorated it with skulls, Halloween cutouts, esoteric symbols and signs and other unnerving touches. He liked to further spook guests by playing eerie sounds and music when entertaining. A photo accompanying a local story about him in the local paper showed a visible altar in the space, too, which would later prompt some researchers to wonder if Bender had done something to attract the peculiar kind of attention that was to come.

In 1952, Bender—intrigued by the UFO sensation—founded the International Flying Saucer Bureau. His grassroots push to learn more about UFOs was infectious, and soon his little organization had quite a following of some 600 people worldwide. It wasn't long after the group began to gain traction, however, that he began to experience some unexpected events.

Time and again, Bender would receive strange phone calls in which the person on the other end either wouldn't say anything or would immediately hang up when he answered. Anyone could get a prank call, of course, but these calls were frequent, and they furthermore left Albert with a strange and inexplicable feeling that he was somehow being monitored. And there was something else, too. It wasn't the sort of thing he could really explain or put a finger on, but the second he picked up that phone, chills ran up and down his spine.

And it was about to get worse.

A short time later, during a walk outside his home, Bender could have sworn that some sort of shadowy figure was—well, *shadowing him.* Thoroughly spooked, he practically ran back to his house, made a beeline for his attic bedroom, and locked the door. He tried to shut out what had happened, but something else had other plans.

There, in the darkness of his attic room, a bright, shining orb appeared. Bender was paralyzed with fear, unable to move. After what seemed forever, he managed to turn on the light, and the orb thankfully disappeared.

Bender, fazed, looked around the room. The place was completely wrecked. It looked as if someone had been rifling through all of his drawers and looking over all of his paperwork. Was his attic just ransacked by a ball of light?

In fact, these balls of light would make regular appearances as the strange story of alien contact unfolded throughout the twentieth century and beyond. Later in this book, we'll meet a very well-known and prolific experiencer who has proven his claim that he can "summon" them at will, and I'll share an experience of my own in this vein as well.

Some researchers would later theorize that ETs can transform themselves into these balls of light or energy in order to catapult themselves to earth from their spacecraft and travel through walls during Earthly visitations. This is a familiar theory for ghost hunters, who have been theorizing for decades that spirits turn themselves into orbs of light in order to travel. Some investigators go further, believing ETs can also transform humans and animals into energy as well, for the purpose of abduction. (A few years back now, I myself was invited on the *Maury* show to talk about some viral "ghost" videos that depicted such orbs.)

Indeed, in the larger history of the paranormal and supernatural, such orbs have made appearances for thousands of years, including in countless British stories of "will-o'-the-wisps," in séance rooms of the nineteenth century Spiritualist circles, and in modern reports of poltergeist activity (which also, incidentally, often includes the ostensibly paranormal "trashing" of people's homes and businesses). At any rate, whatever that ball of light was in Bender's attic that night, it was clearly looking for something. Yet, after that night, Bender, rattled as he was, tried his best to calm himself and to go about his business.

It wasn't much later, however, that he had another encounter with a shadowy entity. Bender was a movie buff, and he was at his local movie theatre, somewhat ironically catching the latest monster movie flick. During the film, Bender felt compelled to look over at the seat a few seats down from him. There was no reason for it—just a random impulse to turn his head. Initially, he looked over and saw that the seat was empty. Just a split second later, from out of nowhere, a man dressed all in black was suddenly there, sitting in the seat. It was as if he had materialized into existence right in front of Bender's eyes.

He was a tall man. He wore black shoes, socks, pants, shirt, coat, and even had a black fedora-styled hat on top. The figure looked like some kind of sinister secret agent. He was glaring at Bender, and as Bender returned the gaze, he realized the stranger's eyes seemed to glow. The experience was too much for him, and Bender momentarily closed his eyes in fright. When he opened them again, the figure had vanished. Bender again fled back to his attic retreat, and again he tried to block out what had happened.

As we do, he managed to convince himself he'd imagined it all. Despite these two very uncomfortable experiences of what ufologist J. Alan Hynek would later call "close encounters of the third kind," Bender was determined to continue his work with the IFSB. He and his burgeoning group of followers decided to stage a "Contact Day." The plan was to mentally and collectively speak a specific message on a specific day in hopes that the message would be received by the occupants of any spacecraft nearby.

The opening words of Bender's interplanetary address on Contact Day would later become the title of a surprise hit song by the Carpenters, called "Calling Inhabitants of Interplanetary Craft." Bender wrote the script himself, and he poured his heart and soul into making it just right. When he was finished, he looked it over with satisfaction:

> Calling occupants of interplanetary craft! Calling occupants of interplanetary craft that have been observing our planet EARTH. We of IFSB wish to make contact with you. We are your friends and would like you to make an appearance here on EARTH. Your presence before us will be welcomed with the utmost friendship. We will do all in our power to promote mutual understanding between your people and the people of EARTH. Please come in peace and help us in our EARTHLY problems. Give us some sign that you have received our message. Be responsible for creating a miracle here on our planet to wake up the ignorant ones to reality. Let us hear from you. We are your friends.57

At the appointed time, on the appointed day, Bender was lying on his floor in the Broad Street attic, speaking—he hoped—to the stars. He thought about the other IFSB members scattered all over the world, and he hoped with every fiber of his being as he heard himself begin to speak the words:

Calling occupants of interplanetary craft....

Then, everything went dark.

Bender soon came to, but he wasn't in his normal state. Looking down, he saw his sleeping form below and came to realize that he was floating, in spirit form, above his own body. It was just as he was making this stunning observation that he heard a voice speak:

> We have been watching you and your activities. Please be advised to discontinue delving into the mysteries of the universe. We will make an appearance if you disobey.

These entities, whoever they were, got right to the point, and right to the nature of the paradox that so often accompanies both UFOs and experiencers of them: There are many UFO enthusiasts like Bender out there who claim that they would love to "take a ride on a UFO," but when push comes to shove, just like Bender they're frightened of their minds.

This entity seemed to pick up on that, and it used the promise of a return visit as a means to coerce Bender into stopping his investigation into UFOs. It wasn't *if you cease and desist, we will reward you with a visit*, it was *if you don't stop, we will punish you with a visit.* These entities knew better than Bender himself that he wouldn't like it so much after all if they did, indeed, show up.

After this out-of-body warning, Bender found himself back *in* his body, lying in bed. He opened his eyes and saw what seemed to be a shadowy figure standing nearby. But as he struggled to sit up, it vanished. To say that Bender was spooked at this point would be an understatement. He was now certain that he wasn't imagining things and that something somewhere wanted him to back off his research into UFOs.

Just a few days later, Bender had another very vivid encounter with these shadowy beings. He woke up in the middle of the night to see three of them standing in the attic. In his book, *Flying Saucers and the Three Men*, Bender wrote of them:

> They floated about a foot off the floor… They looked like clergymen but wore hats similar to Homburg style. The faces were not clearly discernible, for the hats partly hid and shaded them… The eyes of all three figures suddenly lit up like flashlight bulbs… They seemed to burn into my very soul as the pains above my eyes became almost unbearable. . .

He then heard a voice in his head begin to speak.

The voice was crystal clear:

> You have dedicated yourself to the solution of the strange problem of unidentified objects in your atmosphere. Your interest is deep and sincere and you have devoted many hours to it. We also know that such interest and determination might lead to something that could bring you harm. We feel that you are a very good contact for us on your planet of Earth. You are an average person, and we know that what we tell you and show you will not be believed by anyone you might tell.

It was a lot to unpack. The entities had noted Bender's deep interest in UFOs, then stated that his pursuit might somehow lead him to harm. Harm from who? Harm from what? And were these beings the ones threatening that harm? Or the ones protecting him from it? The entities then went on to state that he was a "good contact" since he was so mediocre that no one would believe him anyway. The message imparted was at once affirming and complimentary, ominous and insulting.

Perhaps the most chilling aspect of the disturbing psychic address was that last part. The idea that Bender was a great contactee because no one would believe him would echo in the later theories of arguably the greatest ufologist in the history of the field: Jaques Vallée. Vallée, whose ideas will continue to appear in this book, would become convinced decades after Bender's drama that UFO/ET experiences are deliberately crafted by these beings to contain elements of absurdity *to discredit the experiencers* when they share their stories.

As for who was doing the harm, the entities then answered Bender's unspoken question. Apparently, it was the visitors themselves who were more than willing to inflict pain, should they deem it necessary to safeguard their secrets:

> We have made numerous contacts with Earth by means of craft from our own base, and at present we have craft hidden at a remote spot on your planet. We have found it necessary to go to great extremes at times to frighten off your Earth people and it has resulted in their deaths.

Despite the overt threats, the beings would leave Bender on a somewhat friendlier note. Just prior to departing, he received a last message:

> We wish to keep in touch with you and tell you many things because one day you will write about this, and we are certain that nobody will believe you, but you will be much wiser than anyone else on your planet. You will know what is out there in space, and you will know what the future holds for your mankind. You will see all three of us again, but we shall not reveal our names as they would mean nothing to you. Refer to us as numbers 1, 2, and 3. We will answer according to number.

With this promise of some sort of cosmic *Christmas Carol* to come, the beings departed.

The visitors were true to their word. Bender continued to receive visits; not long after, the thoroughly spooked experiencer left the UFO world for good. He shut down the International

Flying Saucer Bureau and the publication of the *Space Review*. In a final warning to his hundreds of fellow UFO buffs, he urged "THOSE ENGAGED IN SAUCER WORK TO PLEASE BE VERY CAUTIOUS." *(capitals his)*

Bender would later confide to an associate that a full-scale alien invasion was imminent, but that it would come not from space but from the Earth's polar regions.

After Bender's experience, mysterious men would make regular appearances following UFO/ET contact. Famed alien abductee claimant Linda Napolitano, who we'll meet a bit later, was visited three years after her 1989 New York City abduction by two "police officers" giving only the first names of "Richard" and "Dan" and saying they were deeply concerned about Napolitano, who's abduction they claimed to have witnessed. The pair later admitted to being not police officers but "security agents" and at one point abducted her off the street and interrogated her for three hours in their car. Unbelievably, she would be kidnapped a second time, with the men taking her to a beach house on Long Island. There, "Dan" would proposition Linda for sex and then, rebuffed, try to drown her in the ocean after her attempt to escape. Reportedly, an "invisible force" intervened, forcing "Dan" to release his grip on her.

Dan would later end up, reportedly, in a mental hospital, and a "third man" come forward to tell that he, too, had witnessed the Napolitano abductions. But the third man's real concern would be for ecological problems with the Earth and worry about the Cold War, echoing many concerns expressed by ETs throughout recent times.

Even the late master paranormal journalist John Keel wrote that, a year after he began his UFO research, he had found himself in a "dream-like fantasy of demonology." [58] Strange phone calls and MIB visits, poltergeist activity in his house, bodily attacks on his family, and so much more: something seemed to be very aware of—and very unhappy about—Keel's research activities.

Keel and other MIB researchers have pointed out that, in many MIB encounters, the "men" in black do more than behave strangely. Often there seems to be something "off" about their very bodies. In various reports, the MIB appear unfamiliar with the activity of eating; they don't understand how to bite, chew or swallow. Others don't seem to know how to use cutlery. In more frequent cases, the MIB appear to walk with a motion suggesting their torso is sort of "plugged in" to their pelvis and legs—they walk with a rocking motion evocative of a ball and socket. When they stand up, it sometimes seems they are pulled up from above, rather than rising with their own strength.

This "off" quality has also been associated with demonic manifestation. The late Jesuit exorcist Fr. Malachi Martin, a popular figure in the world of paranormal enthusiasts, told late night talk show host Art Bell that the Irish hold an ancient belief that the demonic can manifest as humanoid figures, but never perfectly, because the diabolical can never mirror God's creation exactly. With all of my experiences documenting ghostly apparitions with no head, no legs or otherwise imperfectly seen, Martin's folktale tidbit made me wonder.

But back to Albert Bender.

In addition to the strange appearance of the "men" Bender saw, physical havoc—the kind of ransacked, torn-up chaos Bender reported after his first close encounter in his stepdad's attic—is a trait common to demonic encounters. This sort of large-scale psychokinesis or *macro-PK* is, for exorcists, a calling card of the demonic. For while it's true that human spirits may sometimes make their presence known by a soft footstep or two or a faint indentation left on the bed, they don't as a rule move refrigerators, break windows or push people down the stairs. They just don't have enough power.

I had a very personal experience of this not too many years ago. A few days after my mom's funeral in the summer of 2018, I was informed by her Trustee that the house (which Mom's Trust allowed for my family to live in after her death) would have to be sold. It was totally against the terms of the Trust, and I would end up fighting for almost a year for my rights under it. But in those first days, before I resolved to fight, I had accepted the fact that the house would soon be lost. I couldn't bear to look at my mom's things anymore, knowing her beloved home would soon be only a memory, and I was determined to dismantle it all now, on my own terms.

And so, I found myself alone in her house in the dining room, crying as I took down my mother's China and collectibles, dusting them to prepare the house for sale. I couldn't bear to look at any of it. What was happening was beyond my ability to process. I couldn't conceive of the fact that our family home—the refuge that had always been there—would soon belong to someone else. Moreover, I had warned her that this would happen, and I'd tried so hard to help prevent it, but she wouldn't listen.

At a moment when my quiet tears turned into a gasp of sobbing, suddenly an enormous crash erupted from the enclosed back porch. My tears abruptly stopped as fear gripped me. I softly walked to the kitchen, passing through it to the porch.

Mom had kept her microwave oven on top of a cabinet there, next to the back door. She would heat up her oatmeal and tea in it most mornings. I'd warmed up many jars of red cabbage for our holiday dinners in it, too, over many years, and the baby bottles for our daughters when they were little. With no one else in the house and myself two rooms away, the glass door of the oven, about two inches thick, had shattered into a million pieces.

Telling the story to my family, I discovered my experience wasn't an isolated one. After Mom's death, my husband and our daughter heard footfalls in the upstairs rooms and the sounds of drawers opening and closing. Once, while alone in the kitchen with our daughter at school, my husband saw the powder room door swing open by itself, though there were no open doors or windows and no drafts.

As an investigator and EVP researcher, I brought over my laptop computer to see if any voices would show up to tell me my mom was there. After running the recording software for a few minutes and asking questions into the air such as, "Mom, are you here?" and "Is that you making the noises and moving things around?" I played back the recording. What turned up on the file was a series of sounds that sounded like a feral cat or some other animal, snarling and hissing.

After the implosion of the microwave oven door, I spoke about the incident—and the other activity that had transpired—to a colleague of mine named Ralph Sarchie. Ralph is something of a paranormal celebrity, though he dislikes that title and that status. He was a New York City police sergeant when he became involved in paranormal investigation through something he had experienced while on the job. He began studying under the late Jesuit exorcist, Fr. Malachi Martin and Ed and Lorraine Warren and learned how to assist in exorcisms alongside Martin before the priest's mysterious death.

With his colorful language, no holds barred opinions and devout Catholic faith, Sarchie has developed a solid and loyal following, myself included, and I sometimes ask him for advice when I am having difficulty with a case.

Sarchie wrote a book called *Deliver Us From Evil*, which was turned into a popular Hollywood film of the same title. Both are based on Sarchie's experiences as demonologist during his time on the police force in New York. For a few years, Sarchie also taught hour-long courses on the social media platform Periscope. The courses covered such subjects as "Adam and Eve and the Devil," "Freemasonry and the Devil" and "Human vs. Non-Human Spirits." I had not yet taken the latter course when the incident happened at my mom's house, and I was worried that my mom was "stuck" in her house after death for some reason, as my dad had seemingly been stuck after his accidental death so many years before. And so I wrote Ralph an email, and he called me, asking for Ursula in his unmistakable voice. After listening to my story and my concerns about my mother's lingering on Earth after her passing, Ralph said flatly, "That's not your mother."

He went on to explain to me that, yes, sometimes human spirits do present themselves to us, but that they are not capable of significant physical activity. Only angels can cause changes in the weather, interfere with machinery, and affect large scale events such as my microwave mishap or the movement of furniture and other large objects.

Or the ransacking of Albert Bender's attic rooms and the physical attacks on John Keel's family

Angels, of course, can be good or bad. When our loved ones pass away, Sarchie told me, the bad ones—also known as demons—often take the opportunity to create paranormal activity, hoping to convince us that our dear family members or friends are interacting with us. This draws us into communication and opens the door to further involvement with them and even possible demonic possession.

In addition to the "off" factor and the physical destruction, the *fear* reported by MIB contactees like Bender is also a classic symptom of demonic experiences. Exorcists investigating reports of haunted houses are quick to point out that the spirits of the dead do not instill fear when they visit to ask for prayers (though they might freak us out a bit at first). However, a demonic infestation brings a sometimes literally paralyzing fear to those unfortunate enough to live or work in the infested space, something I absolutely experienced growing up in our "haunted house" that turned out to be not exactly haunted.

Some non-Christian researchers have suggested that MIB are a modern Western version of the "tulpa" of Tibetan esoteric tradition. They are "thought forms" created by our own minds—manifestations of our own beliefs, fears and expectations. The creation of tulpas is a whole esoteric discipline of its own, and some students claim they can conjure a tulpa almost as easily as baking a cake. You'll find Reddit boards online full of witches and occult magicians sharing tips on how to do it. Of course, Christians will tell you these are not "thought forms" at all but demons.

Interestingly, too, in Eastern mysticism, there is a mysterious band called the Brothers of the Shadow. In Eastern lore the Brothers appear when a student of the occult gets too close to uncovering "secret" knowledge, and they are cunning, ruthless and evil. In MIB cases we see not only this same motivation and timing in appearance (they show up when a student of ufology is getting a little too close for comfort to the "truth"), but similar traits in the beings as well.

They just don't seem quite human.

A LITTLE TOO FAMILIAR (PART I)

In the documentary film, *Aliens and Demons,* the late biblical scholar and ufologist Michael Heiser shared his belief that some UFO contactee cases seemed to show evidence of what he called "direct demonization": the contactees seemed to have been diabolically possessed. In that film, he offered two examples that had set off alarms for him: the cases of George Adamski and Swiss contactee Billy Meier, whose story we'll examine in this chapter.

For me, as a longtime paranormal investigator and Catholic exposed little to UFO history until recent years, the stories of the Four Georges of the original Contactee movement (and of other, more recent, lower-case "c" contactees) immediately brought to mind the concept of *familiar spirits.* A familiarization case is a particular kind of demonic possession in which the possessing demon becomes a sort of companion and servant to the possessed person—until the demon turns on the person, of course.

In his book, *Hostage to the Devil,* the late Jesuit priest and exorcist Malachi Martin defined familiarization by a spirit as

> a type of possession in which the possessed is not normally subject to the conditions of physical violence . . . and behavior, social aberrations, and personal degeneracy that characterize other forms of possession. The possessing spirit . . . is seeking to 'come and live with' the subject. If accepted, the spirit becomes the constant and continuously present companion of the possessed. [59]

In the book, Martin takes a deep dive into five modern American cases of possession, including one believed to have concerned a familiar spirit. The case focused on a young man named "Jamsie" (not his real name) who'd grown up in New York. Martin came to believe that the many Old World European, Asian and Middle Eastern immigrants he befriended as a child and teenager may have set the stage for Jamsie's eventual familiarization, as he was regularly exposed to all matter of superstitious rituals, pagan symbols, objects and idolatry.

From a very young age, Jamsie would see what he described as a "funny lookin' face" at the most seemingly random times. At first, the face would appear on the countenance of a person sitting in a restaurant, or behind the display in a store window. As Jamsie's life went on and took a downward turn, the face seemed to appear more and more.

As the years went on, things grew dire for Jamsie's once happy family. His father—a joyful man who loved to play the clarinet for his wife and child in the evenings—fell on hard times and was forced to work long hours as a cab driver. After some honest hard work of 12-hour shifts, when his wife and son would take turns riding with him, this ended. He began making extra money taking visiting businessmen to houses of prostitution on the outskirts of town for part of the women's' fees. He also began drinking his paycheck, and Jamsie's mother then turned to prostitution herself to pay the bills and put food on the table.

One night, Jamsie saw the "funny lookin' face" on the face of his own father, and he started to see it on the face of his mother as she slept through the day after working the streets all night. His father eventually became a heroin trafficker.

Jamsie began interning at a local television studio, working his way across the country at various broadcast jobs, until he arrived in a position at a California radio station.

It was 1958.

On the way home from work one evening, driving through the deepening L.A. sunset, a "being" appeared in the rearview mirror of Jamsie's car:

> The large, bulbous eyes were . . . looking at him. He could not believe they were really red. *Must be the reflection of the street lights,* he thought. The face had a nose, ears, mouth, cheeks, a funny chin much too narrow for the rest of the face, a kind of high-domed forehead ending in a somewhat pointed head. The skin was dark as if from long exposure to sunlight. He could not make out if it was white or brown or black-skinned.[60]

Jamsie would later describe the being further:

> His hands were more like mechanical claws. His body — seen in parts — seemed to have the flexibility of a cat and to be thinner than his enormous, pointed head. His legs were bandy and disproportionate — one knee seemed higher than the other. (His) feet were splayed, like a duck's, and all the toes were of even length and the same size.[61]

At that very first sighting in the rearview mirror, Jamsie was clearly stunned. The being asked Jamsie why he looked so surprised. After all, the thing said, it had been with him for such a long time.

When Jamsie arrived home, parking in his driveway, the being disappeared, leaving a strange smell behind that Jamsie would later recognize as that of sulphur.

So began a period of escalating torment for Jamsie. The being, which called itself "Uncle Ponto" began appearing at random, increasingly frequent times at all hours of the day and night.

When it first appeared, in the early days, Jamsie sometimes wondered if the being was an extraterrestrial. He

> was sure Ponto was not human. Beyond that, he was sure of nothing except that Ponto was real — as real as any object or person around him. What Ponto did was real and concrete.[62]

We'll look more later at the physical things left behind by non-physical beings (including demons, "extraterrestrials" and UFOs), and certainly Uncle Ponto regularly produced physical evidence of its existence. Although only Jamsie could see and hear the being, others observed and interacted with this evidence. Sometimes there were objects left, and sometimes a sort of "poltergeist" activity:

> Ponto pushed swinging doors in the opposite direction to Jamsie. He placed money on the counter of the delicatessen to pay for Jamsie's groceries, ripped the dry cleaner's plastic bags, turned on faucets, turned off the ignition of his car, switched on the headlights… .[63]

Later, Uncle Ponto would begin the practice of pinning to the message board at the radio station pieces of paper with words (and later, phrases) written on them:

FORGIVEN!

BACK SOON!

CARRY ON, PAL!

Jamsie would watch them appear on the board as he was broadcasting on air. The sound engineer, seeing them later, thought Jamsie was leaving the messages.

At first, Jamsie—all alone in California—welcomed the company and excitement the being brought to his solitary life. But months later, Uncle Ponto's novelty wore off, and Jamsie was fed up with the constant unannounced and uninvited appearances, chatter and annoyance of it all. Malachi Martin said that, in exasperation, Jamsie "made the mistake" of asking the being what it wanted from him.

I thought you'd never ask, it responded.

From that day on Uncle Ponto was relentless in its insistence that Jamsie "let him in" fully to his life.

A year after Uncle Ponto's arrival, Jamsie mother died, and she left him all she had: a few personal belongings, including an icon of the Blessed Virgin Mary that had hung in their New York apartment. Jamsie put it in a closet where Uncle Ponto liked to spend time. The being immediately called it "garbage" and expressed its deep dislike of the portrait.

During all this time, despite the absurdity of his private life, Jamsie was moving up in the world. He had done well at his job in L.A. but now got a better one in San Francisco. When he arrived for the first day at his new radio station, he seemed to recognize the station manager. Much later, Malachi Martin—hearing Jamsie's descriptions of the man—would guess that the man was "perfectly possessed": someone who has so completely welcomed a possessing spirit that there is no fight or struggle between the person and the demon. The person is calm, and all seems well, but the soul is marked for damnation, and the personality is totally absent.

Jamsie had begun to deliver a bizarre style of broadcasting, thanks to Uncle Ponto, who would dance around him while he was on air,

> saying irrelevant things only Jamsie could hear. He would produce statistics, figures, facts, and data which Jamsie would automatically incorporate into his patter of broadcasting, keeping up an incredible stream of banter. It was bright and amusing, a cheery-beery-bee kind of prattle full of various irrelevancies about this, that, and the other.[64]

The listeners loved Jamsie's strange style, and ratings went up, up, up. But Jamsie was being worn down, and he finally confided to a coworker about his private hell, telling her about Uncle Ponto and the being's torment of his every waking hour.

To Jamsie's surprise, she didn't call him crazy. Instead, she invited him to have dinner with her and a friend at her place, and the friend turned out to be a "Father Mark," who was also an exorcist. Father Mark explained "familiarization" to Jamsie and asked him if he would undergo an exorcism.

But Jamsie wasn't ready to let go of the thing that had become his companion: the thing that was responsible for his thriving career. He elected to see a therapist, who listened to his story and sent him to a psychiatrist. After months in treatment, the doctor announced his belief that Jamsie was deliberately concocting what he felt were absurd tales. Desperate, Jamsie convinced him otherwise, and he remained in treatment for another year.

But Uncle Ponto not only remained. The being amped up its attack, beginning a ruthless campaign for Jamsie to take it fully into himself, body and soul.

The spirit

> developed a chant that grated terribly on Jamsie, a sort of "rhythm and grunt." He repeated a word over and over with a little rhythmic grunt after it each time. "Let me in," he would begin. Then over and over and over: "Let-uh! Let-uh! Let-uh! Me-uh! Me-uh! Me-uh! In-uh! In-uh! In-uh!"[65]

Jamsie at last had a breakdown at work and left the station. The morning after his last day, he woke to find Uncle Ponto in the closet, a knife in hand, cutting out the eyes and mouth of his mother's icon of the Blessed Virgin Mary.

After two years and two suicide attempts, Jamsie consented to the exorcism. It took five days to complete. During it, Father Mark confirmed what he had suspected. Jamsie's boss belonged completely to the overarching force of evil that Jamsie's possessing spirit called "the Claimant." Uncle Ponto was under control of—and reported to—a superior spirit who also answered to this all-encompassing force.

Jamsie had been one of Uncle Ponto's "assignments."

We'll get to Heiser's "contactees of concern" momentarily, but let's take a closer look first at some of the other famous contactees to examine, specifically, the names given by their contactors, because in many cases, they are identical to the names of known gods or demons. To clarify, in Christian theology, small-g gods are the same thing as demons or fallen angels, as St. Paul reminds us that "the gods of the pagans are demons" (Psalm 95:5).

Jamsie's demonic sidekick, "Uncle Ponto" took his name from the demon/god Ponto or Pontos, an ancient god of the sea. Contactee George Van Tassel's ET contactor was named Ashtar. Ashtar is a derivative of Ashtaroth, a powerful god/demon considered by many occultists to be the sort of "reverse patron saint" of the Americas. We also touched briefly on George King, the London cabbie who founded the Aetherius Society, one of the first UFO religions (which we'll examine shortly). Messages to King were channeled from the "Great Master Aetherius," an extraterrestrial. The practice of yoga and deep meditation—both occult practices—helped greatly in increasing contact between them. In Greek mythology, Aether is the personification of the upper atmosphere, and Hesiod wrote that Aether was the son of Erebus and Nyx.

We'll look more at the messages of Great Master Aetherius a bit later when we discuss UFO religions, but right now let's visit the case of the "extraterrestrial commander" and lovable Venusian who shared the name of an ancient storm god. An "alien" named Valiant Thor.

Most agree today that the story of Valiant Thor was a hoax concocted by a UFO researcher and Christian pastor to sell books (and/or promote UFO belief in Christians) or that the story was a psyop by the government to either get Christians on board with aliens or to paint the whole alien question as absurdly as possible for some unknown end. [66] I admit I wondered for a minute if somehow this could be a psyop connected to the Collins Elite and their plan to force everyone to become God-fearing fundamentalist Christians. Maybe they thought if people heard it from a spaceman they would listen.

Who really knows?

I will say that I found subtle but chilling elements in the story that, even agreeing with its deliberate concoction, suggest some influence of the diabolical on the storyline and its author/s.

During the winter of 1957 a man named Harley Byrd (who claimed to have a high-ranking security clearance at the Pentagon and to have worked on the early UFO research project known as Project Blue Book) received an urgent and frantic phone call from police in Alexandria, Virginia. Two of their officers, the caller said, had seen a UFO land in a nearby field. Arriving on scene to investigate, they were greeted by a tall humanoid being dressed in white who emerged from some kind of spacecraft. The being claimed to be a member of the "High Council."

Byrd was the perfect person to receive this call, as he was no stranger to bizarre things. He claimed to be the nephew (or, later, grandson) of Admiral Byrd, and he would later also claim to have received the legendary secret diary kept by Byrd when he reportedly discovered a secret underground world during his explorations of Antarctica. Harley arranged for the being to be taken to the Pentagon and introduced to then Secretary of Defense Neil McElroy, President Eisenhower and his Vice President, Richard Nixon. According to Byrd's account, the being, who allegedly hailed from Venus, spent some time engaging in conversations about global issues with the president, using telepathy and English (one of 400 languages he knew).

Brought into this monumental situation was a local UFO researcher and Christian pastor named Frank Stranges. According to his story, one of his Sunday congregants happened to work at the Pentagon and, knowing her pastor's work in ufology, convinced the higher-ups to let her bring Stranges to work, to meet the claimed ET and give his professional ufologist opinion on whether or not he was for real.

So began the warm friendship between what were, by Stranges' account, two devout *Christians* from different planets.

As the weeks and months went by, Val schooled Stranges on the Venusians' close relationship with Jesus Christ, took him on his spacecraft, introduced him to his Venusian friends aboard, and revealed to him the details of how Lucifer and his minions had been cast down to *Earth*—and that's why we have so many problems with evil here. It had nothing, apparently, to do with any human action, and neither we nor any extraterrestrials had "fallen." We Earthlings had just been in the wrong place at the wrong time.

Val was just a wonderful guy, and he seemed to bring joy everywhere he went, to everyone he encountered.

Well, almost everybody.

On one occasion, Val promised to send friends to meet Stranges at the Las Vegas airport, but two Men in Black intercepted him and took him out to the desert to rough him up. A white Cadillac came to the rescue. Beings dressed in silvery clothes got out, incapacitated the MIB and melted the tires of their car with mysterious powers. Then, one of them reached through the glass of the driver's side window, pulled out the driver and threw him on the ground.

Ultimately, Val was unsuccessful in persuading Eisenhower to deliver his message of extraterrestrial Christian love to the American people. According to Stranges, the president told Val it would cause economic disaster. But he arranged to allow Val to remain on in the U.S. for a time and spread his message to select

Americans, including Frank Stranges. After three years, Val went back to Venus, reportedly filled with love for the people of Earth.

We could truly be here all day talking about Valiant Thor and the detailed plans of his flying saucer, the way materials on the spacecraft seemed eerily like the memory foam and other materials to come, and how the Venusian explained how alien craft make ninety-degree turns without slowing down. We could talk about how he had a spacecraft he lived in just northwest of Lake Mead (not far from Area 51), and how there are six other contactees the Venusians are in touch with around the world (You'll know who they are, Stranges reported, because they've been contacted *and* they're Christian).

Suffice it to say that Stranges claimed to have a, shall we say, close, *familiar* relationship with Val Thor, and Val even wrote an inspiring afterword for Frank's first book. In fact, the two wrote several books together before Stranges' passing in 2008. The first book was called *Stranger in the Pentagon*. The foreword was written by Harley Byrd.

As you might have guessed, Harley turned out to be unrelated to Admiral Byrd. In addition, Stranges turned out to not be a Ph.D. or a law enforcement officer or a bunch of other things he claimed to be. He was also charged with selling divinity degrees for $28 a pop from his California "seminary."

Still, let's look at the story from a Christian standpoint with the assumption that it's true, and disregarding the fact that its documentarians had long track records of lying, since lying and UFOs are like peas and carrots anyway.

As already stated, unlike most other contactors, the "messages" of Val and his friends to Stranges were overtly Christian. He talked often of God and of Jesus and even said his mission was to bring people of Earth back to Jesus Christ. It's interesting to look at this particular case, because—if it's true that these encounters actually happened (and that's a big if)—, ninety-nine percent of what Val and his friends told Stranges was in keeping with the Christian faith.

But then there were pesky little things that weren't.

As a student of Catholic prophecy, apparitions and other "paranormal" happenings in Church history, I am well acquainted with the seemingly countless instances of "visionaries" and "prophets" who claimed to have received sometimes multiple volumes of "messages" and "teachings" from God, Jesus and Mary. The great majority of these have been declared hoaxes, unsupernatural, or sometimes even demonic. In more than one of the false cases, ninety-nine percent of the messages and teachings have lined up with the Catechism of the Catholic Church and, more importantly, Scripture. But then, there would be pesky little things that didn't, so those visionaries and their sometimes voluminous messages have been rejected by the Church.

You might say the Church throws out the baby with the bathwater. And her leaders will tell you that's because they know how the devil works, and the 99-percent thing is one of his oldest tricks. He spouts all kinds of truths, occasionally tucking in a falsehood. Some believe this is one of God's conditions on the devil: he must reveal himself at some point during his projects.

A few of Val's statements in the book are of deep concern for Christians. We've already seen how Val told Stranges that the evil on Earth isn't our fault, removing all guilt for sin. In addition, early on in their friendship, Stranges asked Val if they have bibles on Venus. Stranges writes that Val assured him that the "unbroken fellowship" Venusians shared with God meant they had no need for such any such books.

In fact, Val claimed the "Master" had personally chosen him as an Earthly ambassador. Stranges assumed he meant Jesus, and so implied that Venusians actually talk to Jesus and can just ask Him about things in normal conversation.

Stranges wrote that when Valiant Thor met President Eisenhower, the president asked him where he was from. Val responded that he was from "what you call the Morning Star." Of course, Christians would recognize that phrase from the book of Isaiah:

How you have fallen from heaven, O morning star, son of the dawn!

Alas, the Morning Star is not just the planet Venus, but also (and quite literally translated as) "Lucifer." And of course this all hearkens back to Madame Blavatsky and her crowd. At any rate, instead of saying he came from Venus, which is what Americans in the 1950s actually called the planet, Val chose to state that he came from, literally, "Lucifer."

Much later, after Val had "healed" Stranges of both a bleeding ulcer and the rough-up in the desert and shared with him beautiful tales of Christian life on (or, rather, under the surface of) Venus, the ET thought Stranges was "ready" to receive a powerful tool: The ET then shared with him a ritual he called the "Ring of Fire."

To its credit, the ritual involved invoking the Christian God by saying the *Our Father*, but the Ring of Fire is actually a well-known candle magic ritual which has been popular in witchcraft for centuries. The "magic" lies in the smoke rising when the candle is blown out, after you've sort of "sent" all of your problems and desires into the candle flame. In the Ring of Fire it was also crucial, said Val, to "believe with all your heart" that God was hearing your prayer. Val would have fit right in with today's Manifesting and Law of Attraction crowd.

As I dove deeply into this story, I had just written in detail about the experience of Jamsie with his familiar, Uncle Ponto. I wasn't looking at the story of Val Thor as anything like that of Uncle Ponto, but rather with a solid belief that it was a hoax. I was, then, shocked to discover that, one day, as Frank Stranges was driving in Beverly Hills, Valiant Thor suddenly appeared in the back seat of his car, just as Uncle Ponto had first appeared to Jamsie.

And just as Jamsie would often, thereafter, be driving along and see his familiar hanging from under a viaduct or standing by the side of the road, Stranges would begin to see his new friend appearing in random places wherever he happened to be:

> Meetings such as this would continue for the next several years. I would be driving along and there he would be... standing on a street corner, crossing the street in front of my car.[67]

Over time, Stranges came to find that Val could appear to him no matter where he was, and he could also transmit his voice or visage through telephone, radio or televisions. As a reformed ITC researcher—of which more later—this factoid sent off all sorts of alarms. These visits and communications were random, unexpected and increasingly frequent, just as those of Uncle Ponto and of the other "alien" contactors we've seen so far.

The lies and deceptions of Frank Stranges and his buddy, Harley Byrd, suggest that everything they claimed about Val Thor was lies and deceit as well, and that the whole escapade was just a made-up story. Still, I do find it interesting that some seriously bad theology and even witchcraft made it into the story, along some other dubious practices such as Instrumental Transcommunication, telepathy and remote viewing—and behavior patterns common in familiarization.

Even concluding the whole story was a hoax, I detect the footprint—or hoofprint if you will—, however faint, of a specific influence on it.

Woodrow Derenberger's relationship with the extraterrestrial named Indrid Cold is a fascinating story that has captivated the imaginations of many. [68] In fact, "Cold" has become something of a folk hero (or monster) among the rural tales of West Virginia since the pair's first meeting, which reportedly took place on November 2, 1966. The meeting became renowned after journalist John Keel included it in his popular and disturbing book, *The Mothman Prophecies*, which chronicled strange events preceding the 1967 Christmastime collapse of the Silver Bridge in Point Pleasant, West Virginia.

Derenberger, a sewing machine salesman from nearby Mineral Wells, was driving home one evening when he pulled over to adjust a sewing machine in the back of his car. While stopped, he noticed strange lights which he assumed were from another vehicle. Getting closer, he saw that the lights didn't belong to a car but to some kind of aircraft that looked like the chimney of a kerosene lamp.

As Derenberger sat frozen with fear, the stopped vehicle's door opened, and a figure emerged. The being, who was humanoid, with a tan and slicked back hair, introduced himself as "Indrid Cold."

The being was unlike anything Derenberger had ever encountered. He was tall and thin, with a glowing, grinning face and piercing eyes that radiated an otherworldly intensity. He wore a shiny, metallic-looking outfit, which struck Derenberger as both flamboyant and eerie.

Despite the initial shock, Derenberger found Cold to be remarkably calm and friendly. The being conveyed his desire to speak with Derenberger about various topics, including time, space, and the future. The being also informed him that it was from a planet named Lanulos. The conversation, conducted telepathically, lasted for nearly 10 minutes, while all the while Cold's face remained stuck in a wide, unmoving grin.

At the end of the encounter Cold vanished back into his vehicle, leaving Derenberger baffled and bewildered.

In the days following the encounter, the man faced a barrage of questions and skepticism from both friends and local authorities, having gone to the police with his story. He bravely recounted his experience, insisting that it was genuine and that Indrid Cold was indeed an extraterrestrial being. Derenberger's testimony intrigued many while also sparking widespread skepticism and disbelief.

Over time, Derenberger's story began to gain wide attention, attracting both supporters and skeptics. He appeared on popular television shows and even wrote a book, *Visitors from Lanulos*, in which he detailed his extraordinary experiences with Indrid Cold, including a visit to the ET's home planet. However, the incident also subjected him to public scrutiny, with some dismissing his tale as a fabricated hoax or an attention-seeking ploy.

But Derenberger claimed that, as time passed, his family— including his two children—met and formed bonds with Indrid Cold, and that his daughter could even identify Cold's spacecraft in the sky during car trips. He wrote that she never misidentified a star, planet or plane as his ship; she was always right.

But the hopes of Indrid Cold to bring happiness and peace to his contactee soon fell apart. Woodrow began developing severe headaches and, later, depression. The Derenbergers said they lost friends, jobs and, in general, their reputations because of his contact with Indrid Cold. Eventually, Woodrow's wife left him and he found himself unemployable, without custody of his children, and alone. Finally, he moved away. Later, Derenberger returned, before his death, to the town where he had first met his "space brother," Indrid Cold, and passed away in 1990.

Indrid Cold said he and his people had a powerful message for the people of Earth. Stop shooting at our ships. Stop disbelieving in us. Open your hearts and minds to us, and let us land among you.

In other words, and as in the plea of Uncle Ponto:

Let us in.

Derenberger on more than one occasion demonstrated his ability to call spacecraft telepathically; he claimed this was witnessed by professors from nearby universities, who after the demonstration pledged to do all they could to help pave the way for the welcoming of Indrid Cold and his fellows with open arms.

We'll see how this kind of summoning of "lights" and "crafts" and "beings" has become a popular movement among 21st century UFO believers, and that some of the biggest UFO celebrities today are making their names summoning "aliens." We'll also see that the phenomenon of summoning beings and light objects isn't limited to UFO culture.

But we'll leave Indrid Cold and his story with a final factoid.

"Indra" is the name of a Hindu god.

The name of a demon.

As for the two contactees of concern to biblical scholar and ufologist Michael Heiser, his concern seemed to have been well founded. He expressed his belief that contactees George Adamski and Billy Meier seemed to show evidence of "direct demonization" or demonic attack. Let's look first at Adamski, who we've met in this book.

Heiser rightfully scoffed at Adamski's "warmed over Gnosticism."[69] I'll add to that the fact that Adamski's ET contactor called himself Orthon. In Greek mythology, Orthrus (in Greek, Ὄρθος, *Orthos*) was the two-headed dog who guarded the cattle belonging to Geryon, a terrifying giant who lived in southern Iberia. The beast was later killed by Heracles. Adamski's experience with Orthon fits the familiarization model to a T, as we've already seen.

And then there's Billy Meier.

Billy Meier was a simple Swiss farmer when his contact with ET's allegedly began, back in the 1970s. As of this writing, Meier is still alive—an elderly man of advanced years—who still holds to the voracity of his claims. Those claims are rather explosive and grandiose in scope. He insists that he was imbued with all manner of secrets, and at one point was even taken back in time to bear witness to the focal point of creation he dubs the "Eye of God." The Meier case presents us with an altogether bizarre (not to mention polarizing) footnote in the history of UFOs, since his case is surely outlandish and yet one which, many claim, offers of the most comprehensive evidence for the reality of alien spacecraft.

One of the most common complaints about the whole UFO business is that there supposedly isn't any concrete evidence. *Nothing but a bunch of blurry* photos, the skeptics say, with a wave of the hand. Well, in the Meier case, the photos aren't blurry. Meier has taken thousands of crystal-clear, close-up images of supposed craft. He also has impressive looking video footage. Billy claims that the ET's gave him permission to document their craft, and that they essentially posed for the camera. Yet, rather than hail these bits of supposed evidence as the holy grail of ufology, many in the field are quick to slam Billy as a hoaxer.

As with many contactee cases, however, it's the absurdity factor that, for most, renders Bill's story insane—or diabolical.

According to Meier, one of the most significant aspects of his experiences has been his relationship with a female extraterrestrial named Semjase. Meier states that his encounters with Semjase began in 1975 when he was taken on board her spacecraft. He describes Semjase as a tall, blonde woman possessing advanced technological knowledge and displaying a caring and compassionate demeanor. Meier further alleges that Semjase came from the Pleiades star cluster, specifically from a planet called Erra.

Throughout their alleged interactions, Semjase provided Billy with various teachings and insights into the nature of life, spirituality, and the universe. He stated that Semjase taught him about the importance of love, peace, and harmony, and how humanity should strive to live in alignment with these principles.

Over the years, Semjase showed her Earthly pupil advanced technologies and allowed him to document them through photography. These photographs are purportedly evidence of his contact with extraterrestrials and have stirred much debate and skepticism over the years.

Critics have been quick to dismiss Meier's claims. They argue that the UFO photographs can be easily replicated using ordinary objects like pie tins, wire and such, suggesting that Meier manipulated the evidence to support his extraordinary stories. Skeptics also point out inconsistencies in his accounts, such as discrepancies in dates and locations, further undermining his credibility.

However, of more concern to Michael Heiser—and to me—than the authenticity of Meier's photographs and other evidence is the name of Meier's alleged Pleiadian tutor. The name Semjase is eerily similar to a well-known name from Jewish folklore and the apocryphal books of Christianity, particularly the Book of Enoch. In Enoch, "Samyaza" is the leader of the fallen angels known as the Watchers or "sons of God." These were the two hundred angels who came to Earth to mate with human women, in violation of God's commands. Many Christians, including Heiser, believe that this story is true, and that the sixth chapter of the book of

Genesis bears evidence of the mating of the Watchers with human women: the "sons of god" who took human wives.

In fact, the story of the Watchers was the basis of much of Heiser's most popular and influential scholarship, and the fall of the sons of God was, in his work, one of three rebellions that necessitated the coming of Jesus Christ. We'll look more at this later, because the story of the Watchers would become a huge part of the Christian response to the UFO enigma.

Despite the controversy surrounding Meier's claims (and the apparently demonic nature of his contactor), his relationship with Semjase and the alleged teachings and technological insights she imparted have attracted a significant following among some UFO enthusiasts and New Age believers. They view Meier as a messenger of truth and advocate for his experiences as evidence of extraterrestrial contact and extraordinary knowledge.

Some even follow Meier's own religion, in which he identifies himself as the current incarnation of the "being" known as Jesus Christ.

SPIRITED AWAY

For many, the most provocative aspect of the UFO enigma is, by far, the notion of "alien abduction." It's the experience of being not just visited by ETs but *taken* by them. Doubtless, it's the utter fear factor that makes it so fascinating. The safety of one's own home is gone. Nothing is sacred, and nothing is safe. Anyone could be next, perhaps (a la the "Missing 411" Phenomenon)[70] to never return, or perhaps to be taken again and again . . . and again. Maybe it's exactly because the whole notion is so frightening that, for generations now, we have laughed it all off like it's absolutely ridiculous.

Or maybe it's because the "extraterrestrials" *want* it to appear that way.

Whatever the case may be, the reported encounters between human beings and these abducting entities are always startling. And there seems to be a clear historic dividing line between the experiences of the early Contactees and those of the abductees. In fact, in ufology, these are studied as distinct, chronological eras, with the Contactee Era coming first and the Abductee Era following. In general, we generally see that first came the talking. Then came the taken.[71]

Just as Theosophists, Spiritualists and their modern New Age counterparts have felt from their "spirit guides," contactees have generally reported a kindness and benevolence from their interstellar friends—our "space brothers." Quite differently, many of the abductees have described their abductors as terrifying at worst, indifferent at best. The contactee reports generally describe humanoid beings, often the tall, blonde, light-skinned creatures resembling the "Nordic" or "Tall White" aliens described so specifically in many 21st Century accounts. Overwhelmingly, the abductee accounts feature the iconic "Grays": short, dingy-skinned creatures with bulbous heads and eyes and long arms, devoid of emotion.

One case clearly marks the shift from the first Contactee period to the Abductee period: the case of Betty and Barney Hill. The Hills' case is considered so important that the state of New Hampshire installed a permanent historical marker near the site where the events of it began.

Betty and Barney Hill were both active in civil rights and community organizations in New Hampshire. They were an interracial couple, which was unusual at the time, and they faced a good amount of discrimination because of their relationship. Betty was a social worker, and Barney was a postal worker, and the pair was described by friends and family as kind, intelligent, and well-respected members of their community.

The Hills' experience brought them a great deal of attention and notoriety, but it also had a significant impact on their lives. They both experienced nightmares and other psychological symptoms after the alleged abduction, and they sought therapy to help them cope with the trauma. Betty continued to believe in the reality of the abduction throughout her life, while Barney became more skeptical over time.

The Hills' story has become one of the most famous and controversial accounts of UFO abduction in history. It continues to be debated and analyzed by researchers and enthusiasts, and it has inspired countless other stories of alien encounters and abductions. Whether or not the Hills' story is true, it has had a lasting impact on popular culture and the way we think about the possibility of extraterrestrial life.

In September of 1961 the Hills were returning home from Niagara Falls and found themselves driving along an isolated stretch of road in New Hampshire. [72] Shortly after sighting a strange object in the sky, their car was abruptly stopped by bright lights in the middle of the road. Initially they thought this was a police roadblock, but to their shock, they realized that the vehicle blocking their progress was not a police car but some sort of alien craft.

The full details of what happened to the Hills would not be known until later, when the trauma of the event sent them in search of therapy. This therapy included separate hypnosis sessions. Intriguingly, each of the accounts they gave under hypnosis seemed to match perfectly.

During their regressions, the Hills told of being taken into an alien craft, where they were medically examined. Under hypnosis, Betty appeared deeply distressed in remembering the experience. She had told other examiners that she had been interested in the UFO phenomenon before the event, and that she would have expected ETs to be kind, benevolent and loving, just as the earlier Contactees had experienced. When she found herself being treated as a test subject, the shock was overwhelming.

The recordings of the hypnosis sessions are troubling, in fact, to any listener. In them, Betty can be heard repeatedly moaning, *"It wasn't supposed to be like this… It wasn't supposed to be like this…."* Her cold and clinical treatment at the hands of these ETs apparently shattered her preconceived notion of what contact with extraterrestrials might be like.

Interestingly, it seemed that Betty's alien captors began to feel at least a little bit sympathetic to her plight. Treating her somewhat like a child, they tried to soothe her and calm her down. After the examination was over, they spoke with her, gave her a tour of the ship and indulged her curiosity for a short time. They answered her questions and at one point even showed her a star map to indicate where they had come from. It was this aspect of the encounter that would kick off a lasting controversy in the UFO field.

Betty redrew the map while under hypnosis, and that map would be painstakingly recreated by astronomer Marjorie Fish. Fish suggested that the star map seemed to match up with the *Zeta Reticuli* star system. Since the aliens the Hills encountered were of the now iconic "gray" type, the "grays" are also sometimes referred to as *Zeta Reticulans* in ufology.

On the heels of the Hills' abduction experience, increasingly less benign encounters began to be reported, steadily rising in number as well, until a veritable explosion hit in the 1980s. The shift in nature was well noted by one of the leading researchers in the field at the time: the late Budd Hopkins.

Hopkins was a highly successful painter and sculptor by training, but after experiencing his own UFO sighting, he became intrigued by the subject. He heard of the Hills' encounter and became fascinated by the fact that they'd experienced spates of amnesia after encountering the UFO: the so-called "missing time" phenomenon. Eventually, Hopkins found his way into the practice of hypnotically regressing supposed abductees, a methodology that would be taken up by several other prominent researchers.

Hopkins ultimately wrote a book on the subject. Published in 1981, *Missing Time* would become a classic work of ufology; it was the first to specifically focus on the so-called aspect of supposed abductees experiencing whole chunks of missing time in the aftermath of UFO encounters. In the book, Hopkins zeroed in on this strange phenomenon that marks the majority of UFO abduction accounts: seeing a UFO—and then suddenly waking up sometimes hours later, having no idea what happened. The Hills had experienced as much, and so were many others in their wake.

Initially, it was believed that those who could not remember their encounters with aliens were simply so frightened by the event that they consciously blocked it out. Today, of course, we are uber aware of the reality of PTSD symptoms after war, personal violence and other traumatic events. It was Hopkins, however, who suggested that, in UFO abduction cases, the blocking out was not on the part of the abductees but the abductors. He theorized that abductees were being sent back home after an overt effort to wipe the memory from their minds.

Hopkins went on to regress a large number of individuals who had seemingly had whole chunks of their memories "wiped clean" by their abductors. Often, subjects had no idea that their experience was one of "close encounter" at all. They only knew they had experienced missing time. Hearing about the connection between this experience and UFO contact, they reached out to

Hopkins in hopes of finding out more about their own confusion, and Hopkins started a support group for victims of abduction.

Only under hypnosis did many of them offer up the lost details that led, it seemed, into the sky.

In 1989, Linda Napolitano was a housewife living on the lower east side of Manhattan.[73] There was nothing unusual about her life, at least that we know of. She lived with her husband and two sons and, as usual, went to bed on the night of November 29th just as on any other ordinary night. But this would be no ordinary night. In fact, with the events to come in the next hours, her life—and the world of ufology—would never be the same.

Just after 3AM on November 30th, Napolitano found herself floating on the outside of her twelfth-floor apartment, floating up through the air to a glowing craft hovering in the sky. Though she would have no immediate memory of the incident, she would later claim to remember the experience herself. But, unlike in most abduction cases, she would also have corroborating witnesses.

Napolitano told investigators that, though she did not recall the events of that night right away, she soon after discovered a bump on her nose. An X-ray (done by a close friend) revealed a foreign object under her skin. Doctors told Napolitano she must have had surgery as a child, but her mother confirmed that she had not.

Not long after the X-ray, Napolitano heard about Budd Hopkins, a researcher helping abduction victims recall their repressed memories of their ordeals. She was intrigued by Hopkins' assertion that some abduction victims are installed with mysterious "implants," including in their noses.

In Hopkins, Napolitano found a kindred soul who assured her that she was not alone. He suggested that she had been installed with an alien implant and invited her to join his free support group for abductees. After hypnosis and meetings with the group, Napolitano realized that she had been abducted on that November morning, and the strange details began to come out.

Napolitano's would have been a typical abduction case—albeit perhaps a bit strange considering its urban, twelfth floor setting—

, but the case progressed in a very different way from the others Hopkins had encountered.

Witnesses to Napolitano's abduction began to come forward. One was a woman Hopkins called "Janet Kimball," a retiree who was reportedly driving over the Brooklyn Bridge in the wee hours of the morning in question. She'd been upstate at a party, she told him, and was on her way home after a late night. Kimball told Hopkins that her car had suddenly stopped on the bridge. In fact, some of the other cars had, too. She described a chaotic scene on the bridge and the floating of a figure from a high rise building nearby up into some kind of glowing craft, and she remembered thinking that she must have driven onto a movie set, because what she was seeing couldn't possibly be real.

The letters and calls from Kimball were startling enough, but she wasn't, Hopkins would find, the only witness. About a year after the abduction, Hopkins received a letter from two men, calling themselves "Richard" and "Dan," who said they were New York police officers. They told Hopkins they too had witnessed the abduction of Linda Napolitano, though they didn't know her name. They'd been parked, they said, under the viaduct of FDR Drive, a New York roadway with a view of Napolitano's building. Not knowing that Hopkins knew of the abduction—and had befriended Napolitano—the pair shared their account of what had transpired that night, the details mirroring not only Napolitano's claims but Kimball's as well.

Hopkins shared the details of Hopkins' case with other researchers. Surely, they must have been more than a little excited by it. Would this prove to be the great, landmark case in ufology and alien abduction? With three witnesses to the abductee's claims, would abduction finally be able to emerge from the realm of fantasy to be studied by science and believed by the larger world?

But no. Like so many cases and events in the history of ufology, madness began to seep in. And with a vengeance.

Richard and Dan admitted to Hopkins that they weren't really police officers. Rather they were federal security agents. The night of Napolitano's abduction, they said they'd been guarding Javier

Perez de Cuellar, who was at the time Secretary-General of the United Nations. At first, this was even better news for the case. Still another witness? And knowledge of it by important officials? But one by one, the witnesses were lost—not physically but for all practical purposes.

Kimball told Hopkins her family didn't want her to speak about the incident anymore. The UN official denied any involvement. As for Richard and Dan, well that was another problem altogether. The pair had gone to visit Napolitano, having gotten her address from Hopkins. They said they'd been so worried about her after witnessing her abduction; they just wanted to assure themselves that she was all right.

The pair became involved in Linda's life, showing up repeatedly to her apartment and wanting to know more about what she'd experienced. They began spying on her, following her and monitoring her every move. Then, unbelievably, they kidnapped her. Holding Napolitano captive in the car for hours, they interrogated her endlessly and even forced her to remove her shoes so they could check to see if she had toes; they claimed that extraterrestrials had none, and they suspected she was one.

Later, Dan would kidnap Napolitano a second time, professing his desire to have sex with her. He took her to a beach house and forced her to put on a white nightgown similar to the one she'd been wearing the night of her abduction. He dragged her onto the beach and told her the ETs had told him (via telepathy) that she was the "Lady of the Sands." Then he tried to drown her, holding her head twice under the water. She was able to escape because an invisible force broke his grip on her.

As in so many UFO cases, it actually gets weirder.

In a development ripped from the headlines of a tabloid, Richard and Napolitano were now also telling Hopkins that he and Napolitano had both remembered something else: that they'd been abducted together many times, going back to their childhoods. They had a lifelong bond and, in a shocking revelation, said they'd had sex on a spacecraft during a longtime cosmological romance.

But wait, as they say; there's more.

Another woman emerged, telling Hopkins that she too had been abducted *with Napolitano.* Also abducted, she claimed, were Napolitano's son, Johnny *and the UN official, de Cuellar.* "Marilyn Kilmer" (as Hopkins calls her in his book) claimed to have been separately abducted with the others. Hopkins said Johnny, who was nine at the time, picked out de Cuellar from a collection of photographs of older men. Johnny also claimed that de Cuellar had given him a strange gift: an antique diver's helmet that investigators later saw displayed in the family's living room.

About a year ago, I had my old professor and his wife over for brunch during the Christmas holidays. The pair had recently moved into a retirement home near Northwestern University, and they enjoyed the company of many residents who were also retired academics, including historians and theologians—perfect for this couple that was deeply interested in both. Talking after the meal, I revealed that I had become interested in the UFO enigma, and that I was writing a book about it.

My professor's wife turned to him and said, "She should meet David."

"David" turned out to be, to my surprise, David Jacobs, a name instantly recognizable to every student of ufology. An American historian and retired Temple University professor, Jacob is best known for his research into the controversial subject of alien abductions—but with dark new findings.. [74]

Born in 1942, Jacobs developed a fascination with UFOs and extraterrestrial life from an early age, which eventually led him to becoming one of the pioneers in the field of abduction research. Jacobs earned a master's degree in history from the University of Wisconsin, He later attained a Ph.D. in intellectual history and folklore at the University of Wisconsin at Madison. Following the completion of his doctorate (one of the first ever on UFOs), Jacobs began teaching cultural history at Temple University in Pennsylvania. It was during this time that he stumbled upon the phenomenon of alien abductions.

In the mid-1970s, Jacobs was conducting field research on UFOs. While interviewing individuals who claimed to have had encounters with them, he uncovered several cases where abductions were reported. Intrigued by these accounts, he decided to delve deeper into this controversial topic.

As an historian, Jacobs approached abduction testimonies with a critical eye, applying rigorous research methodology. Like Budd Hopkins—with whom he became close friends—he began interviewing and hypnotically regressing those who claimed to have been abducted, aiming to uncover any consistent themes, patterns, or evidence that could substantiate their claims.

Jacobs was no hypnotist. He told me in no uncertain terms that his kind of "hypnosis" should be in quotes. It was, he said, "B.S." But while there was not a shred of clinical methodology or expertise in the process, the sessions were shockingly productive. In fact, as he continued to discover and "hypnotize" subject after subject, a common narrative began to emerge.

As incredible as it seemed, one by one his subjects claimed to have been abducted by aliens and used for a kind of reproduction program. The abductors, it seemed, were using humans to create a "hybrid" alien-human species.

In retrospect, there were two things that made the claims of his subjects so bizarre, and so hard to dismiss. First, they were nearly identical to one another, including strange details that no two people (he was sure) could have come up with on their own, let along *hundreds* of people. He told the late radio host Art Bell that their stories were so similar and so predictable that he began to literally fall asleep during the hypnosis sessions, able to precisely predict exactly what the subjects were going to say next.[75]

Some critics would claim that Jacobs was giving his subjects leading questions, and that this is why the answers were all the same. In fact, one of his subjects, a woman known as "Emma Woods" would accuse Jacobs of leading her into all sorts of false memories through the questions and statements offered while she was hypnotically regressed. She even shared the records of their sessions to demonstrate the truth of this. It's interesting additionally because, within the context of this tale can be found a sort of triangular conflict that raged among Jacobs, Woods and Jacobs' assistant: another abductee who had taken it upon herself to maintain Jacobs' website. That work had come to include posting installments of Woods' abduction saga. We'll see later that this triangulation and personal intrigue is typical of so much of paranormal phenomena and research, and it often adds another layer—or multiple layers—to many cases.

There were other problems with Jacobs' work. Many have gone on record to criticize not only Jacobs' (and Hopkins') methods but also their lack of authority to hypnotize people. Other critics would claim that Jacobs' and Hopkins' subjects were reading accounts of such abductions and subconsciously (or consciously) creating their own stories to match. But Jacobs' subjects had, he insisted, shared their accounts with him long before any such accounts were public and, furthermore, long before the public shame of such experiences began to turn into sympathy. People had nothing to gain by inventing them, and everything to lose. Or so we would believe.

Meanwhile, Hopkins ran an "abductee support group" in New York for those victimized by aliens, and well-known papers like the *Village Voice* spread news of the group—and Hopkins's findings—far and wide. Some would later say that, under hypnosis, they had recalled memories of childhood sexual abuse, but that Hopkins had told them these were layers of screen memories hiding what had really happened: alien abduction.

Over the course of his career, Jacobs interviewed hundreds of alleged abductees in more than a thousand sessions, documenting their experiences and attempting to create a comprehensive understanding of the phenomenon. Commonalities included myriad and tiny identical details regarding abduction scenarios, physical examinations, reproductive procedures and the reported "training" of hybrids to, reportedly, infiltrate the human race.

Jacobs is convinced that these hybrids are indistinguishable from humans, and that abductees are forced to teach them, essentially, how to *be* human. They live in cities and towns, are set up in apartments, taught how to blend in. They are "walking among us," and their human mentors live "secret lives" in which they are unwittingly training the very soldiers who will soon turn against us. After each "training session," the abductee's memory is scrubbed of the experience. They only remember under hypnosis-or whatever it is that researchers put them under.

This view of "alien hybrids" as indistinguishable from humans is one shared by many secular ufologists, but many others continue to believe these "aliens" are benevolent, despite the horror stories of encounters with them.

I can tell you that David Jacob absolutely believes that this phenomenon is real. His tenure was repeatedly threatened because of his conviction of it (and, I found out later, because of that one subject's attempts to take him down), but he prevailed until retirement. Despite much peer criticism, Jacobs' work has significantly contributed to the UFO and abduction discourse, garnering considerable attention both within and outside the scientific community. His books, including *Secret Life: Firsthand Accounts of UFO Abductions* and *The Threat: Revealing the Secret Alien Agenda*, have become influential resources for those interested in the subject.

In a truly sobering moment during our talk, David Jacobs told me he had walked away from UFO research after retirement from Temple because the reality of what was happening was "so depressing." He had to "try to have a life" with his family and couldn't think about it anymore.

I told him that, in my research, I had discovered that many Christians believe that "aliens" are actually demons, a theory he apparently hadn't heard before. He started to laugh but stopped and said, "Actually that's not far off."

I want to also talk briefly as well here about a particular kind of contactee/abductee experience. It's one that's been experienced by a man by the name of Bill Konkolesky, among others. Konkolesky is the state director of Michigan's chapter of

MUFON, and I met him long before I began studying UFO. Years ago, I'd invited him to the annual paranormal conference I hosted here in Chicago, and he graciously agreed to speak about his first book, *Experiencer: Raised in Two Worlds*. Recently I learned more about Konkolesky's long string of contact and abduction experiences going back to his childhood, and I became particularly troubled by one aspect of his experiences.

Konkolesky has spoken about the keen interest of his ET contacts in his relationships, especially his love life. In his book, he recounts the story of how he and his girlfriend of the time were walking through a local wooded area when his alien friends showed up. The purpose of the visit was clearly so the ETs could "size up" his girlfriend. They found her wanting, apparently, and they let Konkolesky know that she was not an acceptable companion for him. Soon after, the girl broke off their relationship. This interest of ETs in the sexual lives of their contactees is something that comes up again and again in contactee and abduction experiences.

Eve Lorgen is a biochemist, psychologist and abductee who has written extensively about what she calls the "alien love bite." It's an inexplicable or illogical attraction to someone that, Lorgen believes, has at its core an extraterrestrial matchmaking or thwarting of human relationships. In these "bonding dramas" staged by the alien abductors, Lorgen sees victims manipulated into mating with partners chosen by the ETs to fit some hidden agenda.

In this phenomenon I again immediately recognized a theme that has arisen throughout the history of the demonized. The famed Bell Witch case of early nineteenth century Tennessee seemed to have at its core a sexual impetus. The spirit known as "Kate" was obsessed with the romantic interests of daughter Elizabeth or "Betsy" Bell. The disembodied voice of the spirit relentlessly tormented Betsy and her love interest, Joshua Gardner, until Betsy finally called off their engagement. Leading up to her surrender, Betsy was slapped, punched, scratched and pulled down the stairs by the unseen force.

In the case of Jamsie, our "familiarized" friend of *Hostage to the Devil*, the demon Uncle Ponto regularly scolded Jamsie against dating women in whom the young man took an interest.

Before we leave the topic of abductions, I want to address one last, telling fact that can't be ignored in reviewing the thousands of cases of experiencers who've been allegedly taken. It's a fact that's been deeply researched by paranormal researcher and folklorist Joshua Cutchin, a leading scholar in comparative folklore and phenomena.

In his years of work leading up to his two-volume *Ecology of Souls*, Cutchin collected hundreds of accounts of abductees who encountered deceased human beings during their abductions.[76] It's a fascinating truth that may remind some readers of *The Mothman Prophecies*, in which the main character's dead wife made phone calls and even appeared to people in Point Pleasant during his investigation of the *Mothman* phenomenon, which included UFO sightings and alien visitations. Indeed, Keel claimed to have encountered in his career as a paranormal journalist "hundreds of similar reports, although they are usually ignored by the hardcore believers in extraterrestrial spaceships."[77] Cutchin has concluded something that other researchers have hinted at over many years of such comparative study. Calling the annals of the paranormal "one big ghost story," he observes—I think rightly—that *all* paranormal phenomena seem to be, at the heart, related to death and the human soul.

The association of spaceships with the dead reminded me sharply of an experience shared with me years ago now by a sailor here in Chicago. She and her crew had been training for the famous Chicago to Mackinac Island race held each summer on Lake Michigan.

Kathy Doore was a veteran sailor who'd spent many hours on the Great Lakes, a great number of them engaged in the races that draw thousands of participants each season. It was during a practice sail in preparation for one such race that Doore had what she still calls her "Lake Michigan Triangle" experience. Her truly haunting recollection of that night perfectly captures the physicality and emotionality of the incident:

July 1978, a perfect night for a sail with seven to ten knot winds, flat seas, and, as it was mid-week, we had the lake to ourselves. I was aboard one of three classic wooden sailboats, part of an active racing fleet that competed every Sunday and practiced several times a week. Around dusk on this sultry July evening, we set sail for what should have been an idyllic cruise; as fate would have it, the gods had something different in mind.

Not an hour out of port, and quite unexpectedly, a dense fog rapidly descended upon us. Visibility dropped to zero. We became disoriented and feared we'd crash into one another. The winds were erratic, filling the mainsail from two opposing directions, a phenomenon no one had ever experienced before this evening. Suddenly, I was extremely cold. In fact, I was freezing.

I turned to ask my crewmates if they were cold, and to my utter astonishment, they were no longer standing next to me! One moment we had been packed into the tiny cockpit like sardines, and the very next instant, I was alone at the helm. Dumfounded, I called out and located them on the back deck, where it was several degrees warmer. They seemed perplexed and urged me to join them. That's when I noticed that no one was steering the boat.

The captain raised his arms high over his head, gleefully wiggling his hands and fingers in the air, and stated he hadn't been steering for the past ten minutes. Yet not a minute before, I was certain he had been standing behind me at the helm. Draped in dense fog, the vessel began a curious, aquatic dance. Slowly, but deliberately, she turned on her axis, completing three perfect, 360-degree pirouettes, never crossing the wind. Then, just as suddenly as it had appeared, the fog dissipated. To our utter astonishment, we saw the other two boats pirouetting in exactly the same manner. A moment later, we regained control of the vessel and pulled out of the vortex. In unison, all three boats turned and headed for port.

Sailing home over a placid, glass-like sea beneath the newly risen full moon, I found myself enfolded in the tangible presence of my recently deceased father. My crewmates, also, seemed lost in some kind of inexplicable rapture; the only sound was an occasional splash on the rail. We noticed the lead boat enter the anchorage; it had once belonged to our captain, and we knew it well. As we approached the tiny inlet, we found our old mooring empty, the sister ship nowhere in sight. All was quiet. We scanned the horizon for mast movement. We were the only vessel underway.

We couldn't imagine where the other boats could have gone. In fact, there was no place they could go. We set out in search of them but to no avail. A few minutes later, we circled back and were astonished to see that they were not only tied up with sails stowed but were rowing ashore. Nothing added up. Time either stood still or sped up.

After the third boat arrived, we met onshore. This usually boisterous group seemed dazed and wanted nothing more than to go home and go to sleep. It seemed we'd been out for no more than two or perhaps three hours instead of six. It was now well past midnight. As the weeks passed, I realized we couldn't account for a good portion of that evening.

The following Sunday, as we readied ourselves for the big race, I brought up the unusual events from our extraordinary sail. To my utter astonishment, no one would talk about it. Worse yet, they behaved as if nothing out of the ordinary had happened! The vortical winds alone would have given them fodder for years. It became evident that I was the only one in remembrance.

Looking back on Doore's experience, I found the similarities with abduction cases marked, including the liminal space of the "craft," the isolation of the experiencer, missing time, paranormal phenomena, sudden cold, the craft's impressive maneuvers, the disparate memories of the event, and encounter with the deceased.

The increasingly bizarre developments in the abduction cases we've examined here are not unusual in the annals of paranormal research. Hopkins, along with many other abduction researchers—and ufologists as a whole—have criticized the critics for not taking the phenomena and the research seriously. But the thing about the phenomena—and the research—is that the absurdity, instability and unreliability of it all seems to render it *incapable* of being taken seriously.

As Vallée and others have wondered, is someone—or something—rendering it all so on purpose?

THE DAYS OF NOAH

It was largely the work of David Jacobs that set the stage for one of the most rampant (and erroneous) theories in today's ufology. His work would make an enormous impact on evangelical Christian scholars like the late Chuck Missler, Tom Horn and others who took Jacobs' research and meshed it with the work of biblical scholars like the late Michael Heiser.

Heiser garnered a significant following over the years before his death from cancer in the spring of 2023. A widely respected biblical scholar, Heiser's work focused on what he joked was the "weird stuff in the Bible." His overarching mission was to bring back the supernaturalism he felt had been scrubbed out of the Christian story by modern minds.

Heiser also loved "UFO stuff." He called it his hobby, and indeed any given weekend might find him mingling with ufologists at a UFO conference, convention or seminar. He was a popular speaker, though he upset many with his message against the "ancient astronauts" theory of everything. No, Jesus was not an alien. No, aliens didn't create us. And so on.

There's no doubt that Heiser is remembered as one of the most influential of early 21st-century Christian scholars, and it was that "weird stuff" that made his work spread like wildfire. Heiser's scholarship has been most influential among numerous scholars promoting the so-called "Divine Council Theory" of the Bible: the idea that Yahweh—the supreme God—reigns over a council of minor gods. Heiser's scholarship backs up the idea, as have others, with several key passages in Scripture, including, "Let us make man in our image . . . " (Genesis 1:26); "God has taken his place in the divine council; in the midst of the gods he holds judgment" (Psalms 82:1); and in Job, where the "sons of god" present themselves before Yahweh, among other passages.

According to Divine Council scholars, these minor gods participated in creation and give input toward God's decision-making. Heiser believed that the forming of this council was motivated by God's deep love of community, family and cooperation among his creatures. He wants His creatures to be involved in His creation and His reign and to help and guide one another.

Referencing these and other Bible verses as well as apocryphal Christian writings like the Book of Enoch, Heiser in his work painted a very different picture of biblical history than the one most modern Christians were raised with, and his ideas have greatly influenced Christian ufology—sometimes to his own chagrin.[78] In particular, he came to believe that a breed of two hundred fallen angels—known as the Watchers—left Heaven to defy God and mate with human women. God had assigned the Watcher angels to guide humanity on the right path, but instead this rogue band of them corrupted humankind, helping us to sin more deeply by teaching us warfare, seduction, astrology, herbalism and other Forbidden Knowledge.

In Heiser's view of Scripture, God sent the great Flood to wipe out the descendants of these unholy unions: the race of giants known as the Nephilim. Why? Because Satan's plan was to so taint the human bloodline with foreign, fallen angelic DNA that Jesus could not be born fully human. He'd be thus unable to complete His mission of salvation.

According to Heiser's theory, not one but three rebellions underlie all of salvation history: Adam and Eve's rebellion, the rebellion of the humans who bred with the Watcher angels, and the later rebellion at the Tower of Babel. Heiser believed that Jesus brought his Disciples to Mount Hermon just before His death because this was the same mountain where the Watchers had first descended. It was a message, Heiser believes, that Jesus had come to put the human family back together beginning in the place where the Watchers had come down to hasten humanity's destruction.

It's an intriguing theory, and one that's garnered countless followers since Heiser's work began to be published and shared via a multitude of YouTube videos, a blog and more. And it definitely set the stage for future Christian thinkers.

The late Christian theologian and pastor Chuck Missler taught a theory that comprised a meshing of Heiser's work and the research of David Jacobs.[79] The theory strives to explain just what today's mysterious UFOs and their ET pilots are up to. In fact, it was one of Jesus' own statements that led Missler to a very troubling thought:

But as the days of Noah were, so shall also the coming of the Son of man be.
(Matthew 24:37-39)

Inspired, surely, by the work of Heiser, as well as that of David Jacobs, Missler came to believe something shocking by this prophecy. He believed Jesus meant that, just as the Watchers were mating with humans when the chastisement of the Flood came, so would they return again to mate with the "daughters of men" in the End Times. The goal, Missler believed, was twofold: to destroy, of course, as many souls as possible before the end of the world, but also to create an army of hybrid soldiers to fight with Satan in the battle of Armageddon.

Missler enjoyed the following of a multitude of like-minded Christians. Now, even after his passing, throngs of Christians believe that diabolical beings have been busy mating with human women, as evidenced by the outbreak of "alien abduction" cases featuring sexual themes. Not only are so many women reporting being taken by extraterrestrials, but they are being raped, testing positive for seemingly impossible pregnancies, and having their "babies" or "fetuses" taken away from them by their alien attackers. The aliens then raise the babies—in tubes—and force their human mothers to train them to act human. They are now "living among us" and unrecognizable from humans.

The theory doesn't explain how the ancient unions of the Watchers and the daughters of men resulted in giant Nephilim hybrids, while the current unions result in apparently normal-sized and normal-looking humans. It also doesn't explain how we get angelic DNA from the fallen angels when they are not physical beings, though they can *appear* to be.

Michael Heiser knew well of the Nephilim hybrid theory, and he wasn't a believer in it. But he did point out that the idea would be a powerful tool if he were an evil genius trying to destroy Christians:

> I do believe that the conspiratorial thinking out there (not to mention flawed Bible interpretation) has a role to play—or would have a role if I were the intelligent evil mastermind tasked with an end times end game. [80]

In other words, the Nephilim hybrid theory would be very handy if the devil (or maybe some really nasty humans) wanted to make Christians believe that "alien" abductions are a physical reality.

According to scholars and preachers following this line, the UFO/ET ruse was the devil's ace in the hole for destroying as many souls as possible during the End Times by convincing us of some "salvation from the stars." But when Christians recognized the old Enemy in a shiny new spacesuit, there had to be a Plan B.

Plan B—the "Days of Noah" theory—lets the aliens remain demonic (as many Christians have concluded), but it aims to force Christians to accept a *physical* reality of the UFO deception inherent in the alleged ET/human hybridization program. [81]

So what's a Catholic to think of all this?

The motivating factor in the demonic desire to mate with humans would be, of course, the demonic desire to create as God creates. But angels can't do that. They can't create from nothing (*ex nihilo*) as God does, but only from *semina rerum* or "seeds of things": a fact verified by scholastic theologian Alexander of Hale and many others. (We'll talk more about this later when we discuss physical objects left during UFO events.)

Demons also can't *participate* in God's creation (as humans can) through procreation. But in *simulating* procreation, demons could pretend they can. That's of great importance and merit to them, for while the devil vehemently wants to destroy us, he even moreso wants to *be us.*

Many of the Christian fathers addressed the question of angelic-human sexuality.[82] They had to, for the idea was prevalent not only in the Bible and ancient texts but in classical culture as well. Texts such as Jude 1:6 and 2 Peter 2:4 join the Genesis 6 text to suggest a keen angelic interest in human sexual relations. The concept is also backed by centuries of Jewish tradition, including the Enochian literature that's full of the romantic escapades of the Watcher angels.

The Church fathers were also strongly influenced by the pagan myths of classical culture. They believed in the Greek and Roman "gods" but recognized that these beings to be fallen angels: They were demons who had tricked humans into worshipping them. This is an understanding shared by many modern Christians, both Catholic and Protestant.

After the fall of Rome, the Germanic peoples of Europe (the former Roman empire) easily accepted the idea of spiritual beings mating with humans, as their own folklores were filled with such lustful spiritual beings. When early Christian scholars, then, wrote about the possibility of impregnation through demons in incubus and succubus attacks, the notion was seamlessly adopted by cultures who already held similar beliefs.

In his vastly influential work, *City of God*, Saint Augustine asserted that angels can indeed take physical form and can also touch humans in a way that can be physically felt by us. He concluded that angels can, then, penetrate a human being or at least cause a human to feel penetrated.

Saint Thomas Aquinas posited that an associated pregnancy would not happen via the delivery of angelic (demonic) sperm to a human woman's egg (as no such sperm existed), but from a demon taking sperm from a human male and implanting it in the demon's female victim during a sexual assault. Obviously, the end result would be fully human.

Others, however, including Saint Bonaventure, proposed that demons might be able to achieve a not entirely human pregnancy by using other materials available to effect procreation with a formulated sperm-*like* substance fashioned, presumably, of materials from the Earth or stars. The idea probably sounded absolutely bonkers back then, but in light of today's genetic engineering and diabolical real-life science projects, not so much.

It was only with the work of Saint Augustine that the intellectual tide changed regarding Genesis 6. Augustine's teacher, Saint. Ambrose, had agreed with the earlier Fathers on the Genesis passage's interpretation. As we've seen, Augustine himself did believe that angels do mate with humans on occasion, but he did not believe that Genesis 6 was referring to one of those occasions. Instead, Augustine reasoned that the "sons of god" in Genesis 6 referred to the sons of Seth: the good descendants of Adam. The "daughters of men" were the evil women descended from Cain. Good people corrupted by bad mates. Oldest story in the book. Nothing supernatural about it at all.

Or so Augustine believed. And that's the been the mainstream Catholic belief ever since, though it's not official Catholic teaching by any means.

Nephilim-believing scholars are quick to point out that Augustine probably didn't read the Book of Enoch. He only had the mysterious passage from Genesis and a few other enigmatic mentions in Scripture to work with. Anti-Nephilim scholars will as quickly respond that we are not supposed to look for truth in apocryphal books like that of Enoch, so it doesn't matter if Augustine read it or not.

I'm not here to tell you that the Watcher angels did or did not mate with human women, or that a race of actual hybrid giants did or did not roam the Earth. If they did, they're gone now. And their spirits, unlike what Nephilim hybrid theorists claim, do not roam the Earth today as demons.

In summary, the *Catechism of the Catholic Church* doesn't have an opinion about what the Nephilim were, or whether or not humans mated with fallen angels, so you're free to believe what you like. I myself still don't really know what I think, and I've been thinking about it for years now!

What I *am* here to tell you, as the much greater scholar Michael

Heiser already did, is that the research of the "Nephilim hybrid" scholars is utterly flawed, tainted and deeply untrustworthy, as is any theory of a contemporary Nephilim hybridization program. There are no contemporary physical abductions, no half-angelic fetuses, no hybrid-to-human training program. There is no hybrid army and no new Watcher-human hybridization program going on. What there does appear to be, however, is something a scant few have recognized: a very special little deception to make Christians believe the UFO phenomenon is physically real. [83]

While some Christians believe these contemporary fallen angels—this new breed of Watchers—travel in paraphysical spacecraft (or that they themselves *are* the spacecraft), others believe they are living right here with us on Earth.

Some claim the Nephilim were banished to the wilderness with the coming of Jesus. A lot of that wilderness, of course, is now National Park area around the world. The believe that the Nephilim are living here on Earth lines up nicely with the "Missing 411" enigma which refers to the disappearances of thousands of contemporary people in these remote areas.[84] Replete with mountain ranges, caves and other handy hiding places, some believers swear these areas provide great cover for the Nephilim on Earth.

According to other conspiracy theories, the earthbound Nephilim are living and working in underground military bases. It's these demonic beings who are engaged, they claim, in a real life, physical program to create an army of demonic hybrids to fight (on the wrong side) in the battle of Armageddon. And the government is helping them (or at least allowing it to happen), working side by side with these beings in underground compounds.

Greg Rinchich claims he worked at the most infamous of the underground "alien" bases: New Mexico's Dulce Base, which we'll explore in depth shortly. There, the self-proclaimed Air Force mechanic-turned-black-operative claims to have encountered beings who were 12 feet tall and who called themselves "Nephilim." [85] Rinchich also claims that anyone working with these beings at the underground base is forced to sign an agreement vowing not to use the name of Jesus or Jesus Christ while working at the base, even in mundane cursing.

Stan Deyo, a professed Christian who claims to have worked on reverse engineering UFOs, also claims knowledge of the "fallen ones" working with human agents at military bases around the world, such as the legendary Pine Gap in Australia. [86]

How did rumors of this dark world first come about? We'll look into that in a later chapter, when we go underground to discover the mysterious alien web of subterranean subterfuge.

A LITTLE TOO FAMILIAR (PART 2)

It's remembered as the "Satanic Panic." It hit America like a hurricane, and references to it still swirl today—perhaps even more than ever.

It started, they say, as many cultural phenomena do.

With a book.

The book was called *Michelle Remembers*, and it focused on a woman, "Michelle Smith", who allegedly recovered repressed memories during hypnotic regression with her psychiatrist. Dr. Lawrence Pazder. Smith's memories were not of aliens, but of Satanists involving her in abusive rituals. The details of these "memories," however, would be revealed as eerily similar to those held by contemporary "alien abduction" victims.

Following Smith's coming out as a survivor of Satanic Ritual Abuse (SRA), hundreds of other victims began to emerge in cities and small towns everywhere, alleging that they, too, had undergone such attacks. And it wasn't just adults making such claims.

Central to the SRA phenomenon were allegations by young children in daycare centers in various American cities, including those operating at military bases caring for the children of officers, enlisted and staff. One of these was the Presidio Army base in San Francisco. There, allegations came to center on a Lt. Col. Michael Aquino, a military intelligence officer specializing in psychological warfare. Aquino was a prominent Satanist who had broken from Anton LaVey's Church of Satan to form his own religion, which he called the Temple of Set.

LaVey's church had left Aquino uninspired. LaVeyan Satanism is atheistic, holding no belief in God or the devil. Rather, it's a religion encouraging the indulgence of personal desire and the individual will. Aquino felt there must be more, and so he decided to attempt to invoke Satan to see if the entity was real. In response, a spirit identifying itself as the devil but calling itself Set dictated to him a body of knowledge called *The Book of Coming Forth by Night.* Aquino founded his new Temple of Set based on its tenets, and the church soon inspired satellite bodies around the country.

Beginning in 1986, children attending the Presidio's daycare center began sharing with their parents stories of apparent molestation similar to the bombshell cases being investigated all over the country at the time. At first, the accusations at the Presidio were placed inside the center and fingers pointed at the teacher and Baptist minister named Gary Hambright. Soon, however, children began claiming that they were being taken off the base to the homes of other abusers, including Michael Aquino and his wife, who went by the Luciferian name of Lilith.

After years of lawsuits and charges made, dropped and made again, Aquino was processed out of the Army, Though he was never formally charged, multiple families in Northern California maintained that their children had been used by Aquino and his wife in abusive rituals.

In all, some 12,000 accusations of SRA were made during the so-called "Satanic Panic." Only a few were officially declared to have any basis, with attorneys and psychologists blaming leading questions by investigators for the children's claims of sexual assault, animal sacrifice, blood rituals and more. The fact remained, however, that in a number of cases multiple children developed sexually transmitted diseases. In one case, for example, a group of four siblings were found to have been ritually abused by their grandparents for years. An inverted Crucifix, black robes and ritual candles were found in the home, and the children had chlamydia.

The case was one of the most detailed that emerged during a survey[87] done in the early 1990s by Gail Goodman, a psychologist at the University of California at Davis, whose team questioned over 11,000 law enforcement officers, psychologists and social service agents nationwide "by single persons or couples involved in Satanism and utilizing it or referencing it in the abuse of children." But the survey also verified that there seemed to be no evidence that of what the author said was the most common accusation in the SRA phenomenon: that of "a well-organized intergenerational satanic cult, who sexually molested and tortured children in their homes or schools for years and committed a series of murders."

Now, that's a pretty tall order. Is that what investigators were looking for evidence of during the "Satanic Panic?" Is that why the newspapers of the time—and the internet of today—have continually told us that none of it is true? Because most of the cases did not fit that demanding definition of SRA?

Or was there something else going on? That same year of the Goodman report, 1994, CA Raschke, in an article, "Satanic Ritual Abuse of Children is Widespread," claimed there were powerful interests who want the public to remain confused about the relationship between Satanism and sexual abuse. [88]

In 1994, Goodman told the *New York Times* that her survey had found "convincing evidence" that Satanism was involved in a number of the cases, though not "well-organized intergenerational satanic cults" committing "series of murders." But the *Times'* somewhat misleading headline read, "Proof Lacking for Ritual Abuse by Satanists."[89]

Today, while we find regularly that cases of murders and abuse cases are tied to self-identified satanists and other ritual practitioners, many headlines (and the stories underneath them) are still written to make accusations of Satanism seem like those of Christian zealots and fools.

The same *New York Times* in 2021 featured another headline urging, "It's Time to Revisit the Satanic Panic." The subheading and the article blasted the "baseless conspiracy theories" of the 1980s-era claims of SRA.

We're not going to solve the mystery of SRA or the "Satanic Panic" today. Perhaps we never will. For the natural skeptics of anything out of the ordinary, the fact that these two claims—of SRA and UFO abductions—share similarities is proof that claims of both are fake: entirely false memories fabricated by fantasy-prone individuals and attention-seekers.

The late astronomer, Carl Sagan, was of this opinion, and he vociferously argued as much in one of his last books, *The Demon-Haunted World*. The book is clearly informed by Sagan's atheistic world view, and in it he predictably likens the "Satanic Panic" of the 1980s to the American witch panic of the 17th Century. In his writing, Sagan references cases in which supposed memories of Satanic ritual abuse led to arrests, pointing out that hundreds of years ago false confessions led to wholesale inquisitions and executions.

There is indeed a good argument to be made for all of that, and Sagan (admittedly an excellent scholar and writer), does a great job in the book of illustrating that argument. In particular, he addresses the case of a girl named Nicole who, after spending time in a psych ward, became convinced that she was a victim of Satanic ritual abuse. She ended up accusing her father and several other people of doing terrible things to her. It was only when she began insisting that her grandmother "flew around on a broom" that the whole thing fell apart and people stopped believing her.

Most would say that flying broomsticks are a bridge too far, but only depending on where you're coming from, intellectually and spiritually, but also literally. In most of Central and South America, for example, the news is still peppered with reports of flying humanoids or what locals outright call "witches." In 1980s North America, however, a large swathe of Catholic *priests* didn't even believe in the devil.

For the general public in the 1980s, SRA claims were among the straws that broke the enlightened camel's back. It was just all too ridiculous for modern minds to believe. The same was true of UFOs throughout the past "enlightened" decades. Today, however UFOs are all over the news, and many are demanding answers as to what they are. But while flying saucers have been crashing in America, England and other "enlightened" countries, witches are still crashing in other "unenlightened" cultures, presumably because believers didn't get the memo that it's all superstitious nonsense.

Today, Satanism—both sincere and politically-motivated—has become an overt part of American culture. Significant numbers of Americans practice it or passively support it, just for the hell of it (no pun intended), to rile up religious types and conservatives or buoy up efforts for shared causes like abortion on demand (which the Satanic Temple managed to get recognized as a protected religious "sacrament.").[90]

Also today, when Christians and other conservative individuals and groups decry satanic elements in our culture (and declare the UFO enigma to be an intrinsically diabolical deception), they are accused of ushering in "another Satanic Panic" by many who either are atheistic, anti-Christian, support the occult influence on society and politics, share the Satanic political aims, think it's funny, are iconoclasts, or just don't care.

And, of course, the scientists.

I'm from Chicago. In the early 1980s, the Ripper Crew Murders shook the city to its core. This brutal killing spree conducted by four individuals left a trail of fear and terror in its wake, horrifying even those as young as me, a young teen at the time. The group consisted of Edward Spreitzer, Robin Gecht, Andrew Kokoraleis and Thomas Kokoraleis. Their heinous crimes involved kidnapping, rape, torture, and murder of at least 18 women, with some sources suggesting even higher numbers.

Once captured, their victims were taken back to Gecht's home and dragged to the attic, where he'd built a Satanic temple. The room featured a red-cloaked altar, red and black crosses on the walls and plentiful candles. Gecht would read passages from the Satanic Bible as his colleagues raped and tortured the young women. Part of the torture included mutilating their bodies, including severing a breast of each. Gecht would slice the breast into pieces and pass them to his cohorts to eat, as part of a Satanic sacrament.

Keeping in mind that this all happened in the 1980s—the era of the so-called "Satanic panic"—, I wonder, too, how many of the "ridiculous" claims of the SRA wave of the time weren't just delusions, lies or hoaxes.

In light of realities like the Ripper Crew murders and the literally deadly activities of contemporary ritual Satanists, I wouldn't call my or anyone else's concern about the growth of Satanism today "another Satanic panic." I also don't think that witches' demonic trysts, alien abductions and Satanic ritual abuse have all necessarily been imaginary or psychological constructs, as historians of religion and folklorists assume in their journal articles.

Now, I'm not claiming that every one of the thousands of claims of SRA were true, but I have observed a voracious need of others to claim the opposite of SRA, abduction and witchcraft.

And that's truer than ever now.

Despite an increasing number of cases of *actual satanic ritual abuse and murder* in more recent years, the mainstream media continue to run stories "reminding" us that concern about Satanism is Christian "panic." Despite the literally millions of practicing witches that have emerged in the past decades, self-trained with the help of Amazon books and Reddit boards, the journals of religious history keep telling us there's nothing to see and no cause for alarm.

I've found among Christians a particular theory about SRA and alien abductions. They're saying that a good number of these experiences are "all in the mind."

You'd think that Christians would be first in line to argue that claims of SRA are largely true, and that these children and adults have largely been abused by practicing occultists. But that's not what they're saying. Yes, they concur, some of these cases were legitimate, just as the 1994 survey found when it uncovered scattered incidents of privately practicing individuals, couples or families (and sometimes small groups), abusing local children as part of their twisted religion. But, they say, most of the claims of ritual abuse *and* of alien abduction have occurred between the ears: Someone or something has *implanted the memories of events* that *never happened,* and for some unknown reason.

In the film *Aliens and* Demons, Michael Heiser addressed many of the common talking points and concerns about UFOs/ETs from a Christian perspective. Though he loved "UFO stuff," devoured the literature and often blogged about aspects of the phenomena, Heiser was mostly skeptical. He acknowledged his belief that there might be aliens, but he hadn't, he said, found any evidence of that yet. He didn't believe that space men crashed their spaceship at Roswell, New Mexico, and he certainly didn't believe that UFOs and ETs made cameo appearances in the Bible, as the "ancient aliens" crowd does, and fervently.

He did, however, find a lot of things about experiencers interesting, especially the memories they shared with alleged victims of SRA. He referenced a now well-known report by Gwen Dean detailing the shared similarities claimed by SRA and alien abductee survivors, including memories of a table, robed or hooded figures, needles, headgear, restraints, lizard-like beings, paranormal activity, rape, references to reproduction and esoteric symbols, as well as similar messages given by their abductors or abusers, primarily "We will return" and "Don't tell anyone." Many also remember a bright light serving as an initiating event[91].

As UFO abduction reports skyrocketed in the 1980s, along with reports of Satanic ritual abuse, what if they were two sides of the same coin? Could an unknown intelligence express itself as cold, cruel alien abductors in some instances, but as abusive Satanists in others? Or even as witches, such in the daycare center accounts of some of the involved children who said their abusers could fly? At the same time, are these experiences somehow tailor-made by some entity to appear absurd to the current, secular, larger cultural belief system?

Or, as some have wondered, have these experiences been part of some governmental mind-control experiment or project? Knowing what the government is capable of (i.e. achieving ends "by any means necessary"), and knowing that victims of past mind control programs such as MKULTRA have turned up in the UFO narrative as contactees and abductees, it's a crazy-sounding but ultimately fair question. Are mind control subjects programmed to remember these "experiences" of SRA and alien abduction to serve some unknown agenda? Or simply to mask memories of what actually happened to them at the hands of the government operatives who experimented on them?

Heiser thought that was a distinct possibility. In fact, after considering the vicious emotional and physical attacks and their fallout, as well as the possible governmental connection, he called what was being done to abductees "wicked . . evil… abusive." [92]

Still, the more we learn about these two experiencer groups, the less we know about what has been behind the experiences. There are doubtless human agents involved in some SRA cases, so we know some of the stories are true in the simplest sense of the word.

A demonologist might wonder if there was some demonic mimicry involved in the "Satanic Panic." That is, was the devil planting in at least some children and adults the experience of abuse for some nefarious purpose? We might ask the same regarding the piles of reports of alien abduction. Christian critics of hypnosis, including myself, might well wonder whether it's the hypnosis itself that allows the demonic to plant a common "memory" in the minds of so many.

What we do know is that—physically real or not—a deep psychological assault is part of both SRA and abduction experiences, and sometimes even with physical evidence left behind on the bodies of abductees or on the environment to "prove" it really happened.

To rephrase Heiser's quote about Roswell:

Somebody wants these myths to live.

AS ABOVE, SO BELOW

We've seen that a strong base for much of UFO belief was laid many years ago now, when the Theosophists and the sci fi writers first penned tales of cosmological worlds, beings and adventures. Those included the stories in Ray Palmer's *Amazing Stories*, and among the most controversial of those were the works of Richard Sharpe Shaver.

Shaver told Palmer his stories were true: that he really had discovered a sinister underground society, advanced in technology, and that he was able to hear the goings-on of the monstrous, sadistic civilization through a welding gun used in his factory job. These beings—mutants tracing their lineage to early humans who had abandoned the Earth—kidnapped people, tortured people, raped women and read peoples' minds for nefarious purposes.

And they traveled in spaceships.

As we've learned, *Amazing Stories*—and, significantly, Shaver's contributions to it—were immensely popular, perhaps most of all among boys and young men destined for work in the aerospace industry. Many believed the Shaver stories to be true, and many more who didn't were at least aware of Shaver's ideas. These stories were part of the memories and experiences of so many who had grown up in the 1940s and '50s. Just about everyone had been exposed to the idea of alien beings living underground with nefarious plans, even if they didn't believe the concept was real. That will be important as this story rolls out for us.

Today, there are many stories of secret underground alien bases around the world. Like Shaver, many claim the stories are true.

Deep within Australia's arid desert lies Pine Gap, a joint

defense facility operated by the United States and Australia, primarily associated with satellite tracking and intelligence-gathering. However, conspiracy theorists propose an alternative notion, claiming the facility serves as a complex underground nexus where humans collaborate with extraterrestrial entities.

Enveloped in snow-capped peaks and tranquil forests within Washington's Cascade Range, Mount Adams has long been connected to UFO activity and an alleged base within the Rowena Plateau. Enthusiasts assert that extraterrestrial beings inhabit this subterranean location, conducting experiments, monitoring human activities, and studying Earth's resources. Testimonies recount sightings of inexplicable lights darting across the mountain, lending some credibility to these assertions. Hikers and rangers have reported "time loss" incidents similar to those of alien abduction experiences. Nevertheless, these claims remain contentious, lacking scientific substantiation regarding the existence of an alien presence.

Renowned for its peculiar rock formations and historic underground dwellings, Cappadocia has captivated imaginations since ancient times. Within contemporary folklore of the region lies speculation that some of these underground cities were—and still are—home to extraterrestrials. Local legends intertwine with accounts of UFO craft sightings and other unexplained phenomena, further supporting the concept of an alien civilization thriving beneath the surface.

Mount Shasta, an admittedly mystical range on America's West Coast, is a place where all manner of paranormal activity has been reported, from ghosts to bigfoot and other cryptid sightings to UFOs. One witness told famed "Missing 411" [93] researcher David Paulides that a young boy in her family went missing while on a campout, and that he later described being in a cave with a being that looked exactly like his grandmother. In the cave were other beings that looked like people but who were not animated: They were like "robots." The fake grandma instructed the boy to defecate on a piece of paper before returning him to the vicinity of his family's campsite. Unsurprisingly, some claim that aliens live within the mountains of this enigmatic place, conducting experiments on abducted hikers and hunters.

Ufology and Forteana in general are filled with stories about aliens under Antarctica as we already saw in the drama around "Valiant Thor" and Admiral Byrd's fake son/grandson's claims of a "secret diary" describing a fabulous underground world. Others claim Hitler himself fled to an underground base there at the end of World War II—and was possibly even taken there in one of the mythical "Nazi UFOs."

A wildcard in the "walking among us" saga is Charles Hall, a former United States Air Force weather observer who, in the early 2000s, first began speaking of his encounters with an alleged extraterrestrial race known as the Tall Whites.[94] According to Hall, he was stationed at Nellis Air Force Base in Nevada from 1965 to 1967 before serving in the Vietnam War. Working a solitary post as a weatherman out on the desert ranges, he claims to have encountered these enigmatic beings. Hall learned that the government had given the Tall Whites an underground base within the mountains near the military desert ranges. Regular departures and arrivals of their craft could be observed at certain times.

In his books, the *Millennial Hospitality* series of what he calls "memoirs," Hall remembers the Tall Whites as exceptionally tall, with white hair and chalk-white skin "as white as a piece of paper." They had long faces, large blue eyes, and nearly transparent lips. Hall claims these beings frequently came to the weather station he manned by himself, particularly because the alien children liked to watch him launch the weather balloons. Hall feels he was chosen for the post because he was of a very mild demeanor and wouldn't ruffle the feathers of the aliens or show fear of them, as other military personnel surely would have.

During his encounters, Hall recalls, the Tall Whites exhibited both friendly and hostile behavior. He has detailed specific beings such as "Range Four Harry" and "The Teacher" that he got to know fairly well during his time at the desert ranges. Hall further asserts that the Tall Whites had a social structure and culture similar to humans and that they lived in extended family units. He also said the Tall Whites were known to love their children more than we humans love ours, and that he had indeed observed a ferocious protectiveness of the alien children by their parents.

Recently, doubt was cast (or perhaps the right term is *more* doubt) on Hall's claims when it was revealed that the Army has no record of his military service, and that the photos of him as a soldier in Vietnam don't appear to have been taken in Vietnam. Documentary footage of Hall, who describes himself as a man of faith, shows him attending Mass, so it's even more disturbing to wonder just what's going on with his story. Was he the victim of some kind of governmental "disinformation theater," complete with costumed "aliens?" Was he brainwashed to "remember" working among extraterrestrials as part of some bigger psyop? Is he mentally ill, perhaps suffering from PTSD?

Or is he just lying?

At any rate, these places, these stories are all fascinating to be sure, and certainly many hushed tales have grown up around these mysterious places. But none of them—however wild or witnessed—can usurp the towering reputation surrounding the most legendary of all purported alien bases:

Dulce Base.

Paul Bennewitz was a successful American businessman, a happy guy who liked reading Westerns and tinkering with electronics. [95] He owned a successful company called Thunder Scientific, and his main clients were NASA and the U.S. Air Force. In 1979, in order to be near his work associations, Bennewitz moved to a house close to Kirtland Air Force Base at Alburquerque and established a lab not far from his new home.

Often, while sitting outside the new place, Bennewitz would notice lights moving near the nearby base. The lights moved unlike any aircraft he had seen, keeping in mind that he regularly worked with NASA and the Air Force, and that he was a pilot himself.

Bennewitz began taking photographs of and filming the strange objects, and he began to become more and more interested in the subject of UFOs, befriending others with similar interests.

It was in this way that Bennewitz met a woman named Myrna Hansen, a mom who told him she and her son had not only been abducted from their car and taken away in a UFO but had also witnessed the abduction and mutilation of cattle. Bennewitz also met Leo Sprinkle, a psychologist and UFO researcher who suggested hypnosis for Hansen to help her recall more of her strange experiences, which he believed were hidden in the recesses of her mind because of the intense trauma of the event.

The hypnosis session was set up, to be carried out in Bennewitz's garage. He insisted the session be held inside of his car, and only after he covered the windows with aluminum foil. (Researchers are still flummoxed by this detail, because it was months before the real story of Paul Bennewitz's demise would begin, and yet he obviously thought someone was listening in on his affairs. Later, many critics would come to believe Bennewitz suffered from schizophrenia all along, and not that he had—like many others believe—been driven insane by the events that transpired.)

The hypnosis sessions between Hansen and Sprinkle would come to form the basis of some of the wildest and most notorious conspiracy theories in modern ufology. In particular, Hansen (under hypnosis) claimed that aliens were working in an underground base nearby and mutilating cattle and humans. She also claimed to have seen human body parts in some kind of bubbling liquid during her abduction. From her testimonies, Bennewitz came to believe that aliens were engaged in some terrible human harvesting program with goals to take over the world. These ideas would eventually reach the ears of the Air Force via Bennewitz, as we'll see.

It would come out later that, just two months earlier, Sprinkle had "regressed" another woman with abduction claims. Judy Doraty had been driving home on bingo night when her own experience played out. She was with others, who with her saw a disc-shaped object over a field. Doraty got out to look at it and, under hypnosis, said she and her daughter had been taken aboard.

Some of Doraty's claims about the incident closely matched those Hansen would bring just weeks later under Sprinkle's regression. Doraty said that she'd seen gray aliens mutilate a calf right before her eyes and to see her daughter on an examination table, being probed and prodded by aliens.

Hansen's accounts deeply affected Bennewitz. Despite the chilling content of her encounters with them, he became obsessed with the possibility of making contact with the beings she'd described. As a physicist, engineer and electronics expert, he got an idea of how he might try to communicate with the UFOs that he'd seen over Kirtland—and that had apparently been communicating with humans like Hansen.

He got out his old radio equipment and set it up to receive transmissions, hoping he might be able to encourage extraterrestrial contact, and it wasn't long before Bennewitz began receiving what seemed to be transmissions of some kind. They were on a frequency in the gigahertz range—a range higher than the military was using during that era. As an accomplished pilot and former airman, Bennewitz was well acquainted with the kind of signals sent in Air Force communications, and these were markedly different.

These weren't simple signals. They were data bursts that contained messages.

The raw transmissions were nonsensical by themselves, but Bennewitz got the idea to feed them through the early home computer he owned in an attempt to decode them. When I learned what Bennewitz did next, it floored me.

The method of communication he devised was pretty much identical to a development in Instrumental Transcommunication or ITC (electronic spirit communication), with the introduction of the so-called "Ovilus" spirit communication device invented by ghost-hunting electronics guru Bill Chappell. It was a device I'd used as a ghost researcher for years, and it was theorized to work the way Bennewitz's system did.

Bennewitz assigned words (and, later, phrases) to different pulses in the transmissions. He chose words that he thought might be part of the messages, such as "telemetry" and "range" and "target." In this way he attempted to figure out what the transmissions were saying. In creating the Ovilus spirit communication device, Chappell assigned various words to certain EM levels, with the idea that the "spirits" might be able to manipulate the EM field to choose the words they needed to speak through the device. We'll talk a lot more about ITC specifics a little later, and how it relates to the UFO phenomenon. The point is that two very different people were using very similar methods to contact ghosts and aliens.

After creating this system of communication, Bennewitz sent his own message. And another. And another.

It wasn't long before he started to get messages back.

Running through his decoding program, using the words and phrases he had assigned to the pulses, Bennewitz verified what he'd suspected: These were messages from some intelligent source. Clearly, he realized, this was one of the most important discoveries in human history. He would, he decided, go to the Air Force and ask for a grant to continue his studies.

With his photos, videos and rudimentary translations, Bennewitz requested—and was granted—a meeting with the Air Force. He shared everything he had collected—including the terrifying information given under hypnosis by Hansen and the messages he had decoded. Officials listened in rapt attention and then gave him what he'd requested: a grant to continue his research.

Part of Bennewitz's grant was a new computer with a new decoding program already installed on it, courtesy of the Air Force. The computer was reportedly hand-delivered to Bennewitz by one of the most prominent figures in the history of ufology: J. Allen Hynek.[96]

It would later be discovered that the new computer program substituted much different words and phrases for the rather "unloaded" ones Bennewitz had used. The simple terms he had chosen in hopes of interpreting messages from pilots or military craft became phrases and words like "home planet" and "death ray" and "aliens."

In short, whoever wrote the program seemed to have created it to make any transmissions seem like messages from extraterrestrials.

Sinister messages.

Here is a portion of what Bennewitz received:

GROUND GROUND WOMEN OF EARTH ARE NEEDED FLEXIBLE THE NEXT DISCHARGES OUR SHIP ALL WOMEN DO NOT COMMAND THE NORTH AMONG US YOU HAVE MANY FRIENDS WATER VERY SHORT RESIST ALL ATTEMPTS AT ALTERATION LISTEN ORANGE MAKE PEACE VICTORY OUR BASES OBTAIN SUPPLIES FROM THE STARSHIP METAL TIME IS YANKED TIME IS YANKED MESSAGE HIT STAR USING REJUVENATION METHODS GOT US IN TROUBLE SIX SKY WE REALIZE TELLING YOU ALL MIGHT HELP YOU OUR BASES OBTAIN SUPPLIES FROM THE STARSHIP MILITARY OF U.S. DELIVERED EMBRYOS BY US USE GRAVITY CELL IN GOOD WAY TO TRAVEL UNIVERSE NINE OUR COMMAND THE NORTH VICTOR GROW WOMEN ARE NOT NEEDED IN OUR SOCIETY WE ARE NOT UNITY—WE ARE SEPARATE WE WOMEN DO NOT MARRY REALIZE WE ARE NOT UNITY—WE ARE SEPARATE VICTORY GROW WE HAVE NO OBLIGATION TO KEEP SECRET NOW OXYGEN UJUMP HAVE MANY ON OUR SIDE UNIVERSE WILL CONTACT YOU IN UNIQUE WAY WATER INTAKE WE WILL TELL YOU NOW LISTEN NINE MANY HATE YOU BECAUSE YOU KNOW DIS TANCE IN KM IS WE CANNOT TELL MILITARY OF THE U.S. MAKING HUMANOIDS REASON FOR HATE IS YOU ARE GOOD—WE TRUST YOU TAKE VAST PORTION UNIVERSE AGAINST OUR AGGRESSION THE NUMBER OF OUR CRASHED SAUCERS IS EIGHT NERVE YOU WE REALIZE TELL THE TRUTH JUMP JUMP OPPOSITE ALIEN FORCES MEAN NO HELP TO YOU TMETAL WE

COME INVISIBLE KEEPING CHANGE WE WILL NOT JOIN SIDES WITH ANYONE OUGHT OUR RACE IS DYING ON THE HOME PLANET MESSAGE....[97]

The story goes that a man named Richard Doty, an agent with the Air Force Office of Special Investigations (AFOSI) became a close confidante of Bennewitz, "helping" him in his research and giving him documents and reports that might be of assistance in his reconnaissance of a nearby, underground base at Dulce, New Mexico, which, Doty said, seemed to be ground zero for the aliens' maneuvers.

Doty, who had first interviewed Bennewitz at his home before his first meeting with the Air Force at Kirtland, would later admit that Air Force officials had given him the job of disinforming Bennewitz in order to cover up secret projects he had stumbled upon with his photographs, videos and transmissions. Doty hoaxed documents to push the narrative that an alien invasion was not only close at hand; the ETs were living among us—or beneath us, that is—at the Dulce base.

The Air Force flew Bennewitz to the Dulce area and pointed out fake evidence that had been planted to indicate a base there, asking him to study the area by making covert flights on his own. An accomplished pilot (and eager to help), he did just that, heart and soul.

In 1988, after some eight years of intense, all-consuming study, Bennewitz published a paper called "Project Beta" reviewing all he had "uncovered" and positing a plan to attack Dulce Base and destroy the aliens. That same year, the old *Weekly World News* tabloid published a story about "diabolical invaders from another solar system" and their "secret underground base in the rugged mountains of northern New Mexico." The paper went on to share with readers the details of the aliens' use of "human guinea pigs" for "bizarre genetic experiments." [98]

In 1988, Bennewitz's family committed him to a mental hospital. He had come to believe his wife was working with the aliens.

Paul Bennewitz wasn't the only one who went down a dark, desperate road after meeting Richard Doty. Linda Howe was a former Miss Idaho who became a hard-hitting investigative journalist. She became fascinated by the reports of New Mexico cattle mutilations in the late 1970s and went on to produce a documentary on the subject, the Emmy Award-winning *Strange Harvest*. The documentary also earned Howe a contract for a UFO documentary with Home Box Office (HBO), one of the only cable channels at the time. It also earned her the attention of the government.

Specifically Richard Doty.

Doty asked Howe to come to Kirtland AFB. There, he showed her some documents that shocked her to the core; she says she never forgot the feeling of reading them. The documents talked of the "crash" at Roswell in 1947, and about the intelligence gathered from the crash's lone, ET survivor. From the being, the government had learned that aliens had essentially created the human race " spiritual beings" like Jesus Christ to guide us in our spiritual evolution. Doty told Howe that, if she played her cards right, he might be able to introduce her to the alien, who he claimed was still alive. When Howe told HBO of the information she had been given, they reportedly tore up the documentary contract.

In the film *Mirage Men*, Howe accurately called the entire UFO disclosure/disinformation enigma "a fractured hall of mirrors with a quicksand floor . . . nobody knows exactly what the truths are." Still, today, despite what Doty and the Air Force did to her (and despite her own awareness of the mess of lies it all is) Howe believes even more strongly that aliens are real. She has become known for lashing out at anyone who suggests otherwise, [99]and she's descended into an impenetrable New Age forest of esoterica. Most recently she has been speaking about a previous life of hers in ancient Egypt, where even then she was interested in extraterrestrials.[100]

A famed pilot, the late John Lear's descent into semi-madness (real or feigned) also began with the Bennewitz case. The claims of Hansen under hypnosis and the wild "documents" and stories of Doty joined the claims of another wild claimant—Bob Lazar—to fill Lear's head with ideas. Lazar claimed to have worked at Area 51 reverse engineering crashed UFOs. After "going public" with his story, he became one of the most controversial figures in ufology.

As did Lear.

Some think Lear and Lazar may also have been targeted by governmental disinformation campaigns or perhaps that they were *in on them*. Some think Lear just "lost" it, like so many others who've disappeared forever down the infamous UFO "rabbit hole." Still others said Lear just liked to freak people out.

And freak people out he did.

By the late 1980s Lear was telling Las Vegas "UFO journalist" George Knapp that four separate people had verified the existence of Dulce Base.[101] They had told him of the different species of aliens who were visiting our planet. And he made it clear that they weren't the "space brothers" the Contacees had reported.

They were bad news.

In 1989, at a conference hosted by the Mutual UFO Network in Las Vegas, a man named Bill Moore publicly dropped the dime on Richard Doty and his successful plan to drive Bennewitz insane. Moore would also claim (to researcher Greg Bishop) that none other than ufology guru Jaques Vallée had written the new "decoding" programming that was installed on the new computer when Bennewitz received it.

In a plot twist for the ages, Doty admitted it was all true, and that eighty percent of what he'd told Bennewitz had been mere invention. In yet another plot twist, Doty claimed he now was a UFO believer and that aliens are real and, yes, living among us. He began attending and speaking at UFO conventions and seminars, verifying the existence of extraterrestrials and insisting, "*Now* I'm telling the truth."

Yeah.

If you thought that was the end of the Dulce Base legend, buckle up.

As the 1990s unfurled, the story of a hidden base under Dulce, New Mexico only grew, despite Doty's confession. After all, he *had* said that only eighty percent of his stories were lies. Many believed that the existence of the base was part of the twenty percent remaining that was real. After all, Dulce had been known even to Native Americans as a place of strangeness, lights in the sky and mysterious beings long before Doty began his campaign against Paul Bennewitz.

As if on cue, in 1995 a man named Phil Schneider took the podium at a Dulce, New Mexico UFO convention to share his own story of Dulce Base.[102] Claiming to be a former government worker and expert in explosives, Schneider said he'd been sent to blast out earth and rock for creation of the base in 1979. Descending into a blast crater to examine it, Schneider said he'd encountered strange beings and an underground compound. He found himself exchanging fire with the beings and, in the process, had several of his fingers blown off by aliens (Here he held up his altered hand for the crowd as proof).

This perked up many ears in ufology, because in 1984—more than a decade earlier—Bennewitz had referenced a human-alien war that had allegedly taken place at Dulce in 1979, forcing the evacuation of the base by human agents and leaving it in control of the aliens. In his speech, Schneider would further claim that, while trying to recapture the base, some sixty people had died in the "Dulce War." He also suggested that he himself would be killed for speaking about it. Phil Schneider was found at home, dead, in January of 1996, with his catheter tube wrapped around his neck.

His death was declared a suicide.

On an online forum not long ago, one commentor shared his belief that contemporary "UFO whistleblower" David Grusch has been given the "Bennewitz treatment." [103] Many concurred. With tales and counter tales abounding in every era and in every arena, and with the wild stories walking hand in hand with the newest "Disclosure" movement, it seems like a whole lot of people may have gotten the treatment doled out so famously by Richard Doty so many years ago now.

Maybe even all of us.

Maybe we still are.

SPIRITUALISTS, SKIN WALKERS AND SPACE X

One of the things that maddens religious types like me about secular UFO research is that so many of those researchers have no familiarity whatsoever with how the spiritual world functions. This "whole new world" that they are discovering—and relating to UFOs and ETs—has been around for millennia. Later we'll see how some of the most recognized Catholic theologians also seem totally ignorant of that fact—or maybe *willfully ignorant* is a better term.

You'll find many researchers in awe of "puzzling" realities like the so-called "hitchhiker effect" that so many visitors have allegedly experienced after visiting a peculiar ranch in Utah. This syndrome has actually been known to paranormal researchers for a century or more and to religious believers for much, much longer. We call it "spirit attachment," and it's a common problem for paranormal investigators and for exorcists and others dealing with demonic infestation and other levels of demonic influence.

The secular UFO believers call it "quantum entanglement."

"Skinwalker Ranch," located in northeastern Utah, has gained a notorious reputation for its alleged UFO activity and plentiful paranormal occurrences. The ranch's dark history is deeply rooted in Native American folklore and has attracted the attention of paranormal enthusiasts, scientists and skeptics alike.

Originally the Sherman Ranch, the area has been subject to ongoing reports of unexplained phenomena since the 1950s. But it gained more significant attention after the Sherman family, who owned and lived on the ranch, reportedly experienced a series of bizarre incidents in the 1990s. These incidents included strange lights in the sky, mutilated cattle with surgically precise wounds, and sightings of unusual creatures.

The ranch gets its name from the "Skin-walkers": creatures deeply ingrained in Native American legend. The Navajo have for centuries shared the tales of these shape-shifting witches with malevolent intentions, capable of transforming into any animal or form they desire. Native Americans have long considered Skinwalkers to be harbingers of misfortune and evil and to be tied to this particular region of the United States: the Uinta Basin of eastern Utah. The ranch borders the reservation of the Ute tribe, whose folklore shares with European American history accounts of lights in the sky and paranormal activity stretching back through the 18th century.

Witnesses have described glowing orbs hovering above the property or aircraft-like objects moving with unprecedented speed and maneuverability. Some even claim to have had direct contact with beings from other worlds, communicating through telepathy or leaving behind unusual symbols etched into the ground.

In addition to UFO sightings, reports of poltergeist activity, disembodied voices, unexplained disappearances, and theories of portals to other dimensions have added to the mystique surrounding Skinwalker Ranch. Witnesses often describe feeling an intense sense of fear or being watched while on the property, and animals are said to show signs of distress or act with unusual aggression. Some claim a mesa at the ranch serves as a portal or "stargate" through which UFOs enter and depart the physical world.

Despite the numerous anecdotes and what some claim to be compelling evidence, skeptics argue that many of these claims can be attributed to natural phenomena, misinterpreted events, or hoaxes. Others question the credibility of witnesses and argue that the legends surrounding Skinwalker Ranch have been exaggerated or fabricated for entertainment purposes.

In the fall of 2008 the U.S. Defense Intelligence Agency (DIA) contracted with a company called Bigelow Aerospace Advanced Studies to study UFOs and the effects of encounters on the human body. Called the Advanced Aerospace Weapon System Applications Program (AAWSAP), the secret program burst into the public's knowledge in 2017, when the New York *Times* published a story about it. Readers were stunned to discover that some four dozen scientists, military professionals and other experts had been on the payroll studying, of all things, UFOs. One of the main places they were working was Skinwalker Ranch.

Reportedly, *all* representatives of the DIA who visited the ranch experienced firsthand the strange things that had been reported. Far more disturbingly, all of them claimed that, returning home after their visits, they had brought something back with them. For our purposes, I'm going to assume these reports are true as we go forward to analyze them in a supernatural light, although that's a big assumption.

One of the government visitors was a Naval Intelligence officer whose experience was documented in the book, *Skinwalkers at the Pentagon.* The officer, who wished to remain anonymous, told the authors that during his visit, he and two other officers were badly jarred by a paranormal event. He was glad to return home to Virginia soon after, but when he did, he found he hadn't quite left Skinwalker behind.

The officer claimed that for *several years* following his visit to the ranch, he and his wife and children were terrorized by some unseen force. Shadow people appeared over their beds, loud footsteps echoed through the house, and human/doglike creatures stalked their backyard. None of the family shared the experiences with anyone outside the home, but after weeks of unexplained events, one of the teenaged children's friends told him he had seen a werewolf-like creature outside his *own* home after visiting the family. Later, yet another friend said he was seeing blue orbs around his own home as well.

And the seeming contagion didn't stop at observable things. The officer's wife suffered from Lupus and Raynaud's Disease. With her husband's return home, she began to experience severe episodes of both. The children also came down with a serious "flu" that would come and go.

As time went on, a shocking reality began to unfold, as *most* of the visitors to Skinwalker began sharing similar stories. Even famed UFO journalist George Knapp (one of the authors of *Skinwalkers at the Pentagon*) said his wife started seeing apparitions in their Las Vegas home (and he strange orbs of light) after his visit to the ranch.

Many of these visitors and their family members would reportedly develop autoimmune diseases, including Hashimoto's disease, Graves' Disease and other maladies. Further, all ten of the security officers assigned to the ranch reported paranormal phenomena and/or physical effects at home. Other officials returned home to find themselves and their family members suddenly encountering UFOs in the skies around their homes.

Stunningly, AAWSAP reports revealed that it wasn't only Skinwalker Ranch that was causing these effects "off ranch." This seemed to happen especially when researchers were focusing attention on particular people in their investigations. One biotechnologist was driving through Oregon in the spring of 2005 with his daughter when they saw a cluster of UFOs moving over a nearby meadow. The UFOs actually entered their car, one darting through the official's shoulder, observed by his daughter.

When the pair returned home, the official, said, he developed medical issues, while the daughter (and even her visiting friends) began to experience all manner of paranormal activity, including seeing shadow figures and hearing footsteps.

We could be here all day talking about specific instances of this "hitchhiker effect" related to Skinwalker Ranch and other study sites, but my point here is to demonstrate that this kind of syndrome has been known to ghost and haunting researchers, and to demonologists, for as long as people have been studying the phenomena. If the reports, then, are true, they're nothing new— and they're not what we know as "physical" effects.

I could write a book about just the situations like this that were part of my own cases as a paranormal researcher into ghost and haunting phenomena the past thirty-six years, and a good chunk of that book would be about my own attacks by forces "brought home" after or during investigations of haunt phenomena.. Strange orbs, shadow figures, footsteps, knocking, voices and—worst of all—inexplicable illness: all have been part of the "offsite" effects of all manner of parapsychological cases.

Let me share just two cases with you.

In the summer of 2018, my tour company contracted with the City of Joliet, Illinois to design, staff and conduct ghost tours and public "ghost hunts" at the Old Joliet Prison just southwest of Chicago. The schedule involved hosting tours every night of the week for about six weeks and late-night public paranormal investigations on the weekends, hosted and guided by our staff of seasoned ghost and haunting investigators.

It soon became apparent that there was something accompanying a number of our tour guests home after these events, and in short order I was inundated with emails and phone calls from attendees. They shared with me stories of having returned home after a tour or hunt to find they were no longer alone in their houses or apartments. Footsteps, voices, shadowy figures and full-bodied apparitions, strange lights and frequent "sleep paralysis" type experiences plagued many of these unwitting experiencers.

My staff wasn't exempt from these developments. Many of them became inexplicably sick, and one of our guides—also a self-professed psychic medium—developed an illness her doctor couldn't explain. This same woman, weeks after the tours were over, on one occasion found powdery white footprints made by what looked like large work boots on her carpeting, though no one but her had been in the house. Police found no sign of forced entry.

Another one of our guides began experiencing classic poltergeist activity at home, with water turning on and off and electrical malfunctioning.

The other site I've studied that that seems to regularly "send home" its activity with visitors is Chicago's Hull House. The house, today part of the campus of the University of Illinois at Chicago, was originally the home of Charles Hull, a Chicago businessman. Later, it was rented by the famed Progressivist reformer, Jane Addams, who developed the original house into a social services complex of some thirteen buildings. Today, only the original home and a dining hall still stand; they've been turned into a museum honoring Addams' work in Chicago and the effect of her efforts on social conditions around the world.

There's a famous legend at Hull House that, in 1913, a "devil baby" was left on the doorstep and taken in by Addams, having been abandoned by its terrified immigrant parents. The origins of the story are still unknown, but we do know that it spread like wildfire through Chicago, drawing thousands to Hull House for a look at the infant, who reportedly sported horns and pointed ears, a long, forked tail and hair covering its wee body.

Addams, a no-nonsense modern thinker, wrote about the event in her memoir, *Twenty Years at Hull House*, using the story to teach about what she felt were the Old World, superstitious beliefs of much of Hull House's clientele, and about the real-life horrors that many of Chicago's poorest immigrant women had experienced with childbirth, infant death and domestic abuse.

While the "Devil Baby of Hull House" is one of Chicago's most famous supernatural stories, there's another legend about Hull House that most don't know.

Some say that Hull House is the site of a "portal." The idea of portals has roots in Native American lore, and they're explained as doorways in the environment where spirit beings come through to the physical world. According to legend, when the Indians were forced off their lands, some opened up interdimensional doorways as "parting gifts" to the white settlers who were removing them. So by opening up one of these portals, you can bet that whoever is going to be living on that land is going to find themselves the proud owner of a kind of paranormal bus terminal.

Or so they say.

There's an attendant legend claiming that physical beings—that's us—must be very careful visiting these portal areas, because the spirits coming into our world like to attach themselves to us.

When my husband and I started our haunted history tour company in 2003, we planned for Hull House to be the last stop on the tour route. We knew that the combination of the spooky old house, the devil baby story and the legend of the portal (as well a warning about "bringing something home") would make a great finale to the tour and send our guests on their way thoroughly unnerved. Little did we expect that Hull House would be more than just a memory for many on our tours.

Including me.

The second week of the tours, we had stopped as usual at Hull House. That particular evening, I had told the tale to a capacity crowd. They were silent and wide-eyed. The night was windy and moonless, so the mood was perfect. I smiled to myself as I walked back to the bus, delighted by the effect of the story on my group.

At home, my husband and I paid the babysitter, checked our sleeping daughters, and turned in for the night. But several hours later, around four o clock in the morning, I woke up to find what looked like a man standing on top of my chest as I lay on my back in bed.

The figure was as real as my husband lying next to me. It was dressed in modern clothes: an orange T-shirt and blue jeans. Its form was muscular and tan like a bodybuilder. The body stopped at the neck; there was no head above it. I felt pressure on my body, though not as much weight as that of a whole person. I could not move and could not speak, though I heard my husband breathing next to me and heard a car go by outside our apartment building. I heard the wind in the November trees outside. I was wide awake.

I watched the clock on the nightstand for almost fourteen minutes while this entity or whatever it was stood on me, unmoving. The whole time I was telling myself, *Ursula, when this is over, do not tell yourself that you were asleep. This is real. This is happening. You are awake.*

The event finally ended when I was able to muster the ability to, finally, cry out. At that point, the being stepped off my chest into the air beside the bed, put its arms out to sides of its body and flew up into the ceiling, dissipating.

Any skeptic would tell you this was a typical incident of so-called "sleep paralysis," a perfectly normal thing that sometimes happens. And I concur that, yes, sometimes it is normal—and probably completely physiological.

But could those skeptics explain how, in the nineteen years that followed, dozens of people who took our tours returned home from Chicago—and our final stop at Hull House—to find themselves suddenly plagued by paranormal experiences?

There was the man who brought his fiancée to Chicago in the spring of 2005. After our tour, they returned home the next day to suburban Miami to find they were now living with a dark-skinned man in a three-piece suit. He would appear standing on the kitchen table at random times.

There was the group of girls on a bachelorette weekend just before Christmas 2008 who traveled, after our tour, back to suburban Naperville, where two of them—roommates—suffered through a debilitating flu while being tormented by footsteps, the sound of loud chewing and dark figures hovering over their beds.

There was the high school class on their graduation trip from St. Louis who were amazed to find that, taking photos in the garden at Hull House, strange dark figures were showing up next to them in the digital images on their phones. Back in Missouri, several of the students reported to friends—and their teacher—that their homes were suddenly alive with loud noises, including pounding in the walls, the sound of running on the stairs, and disembodied voices. One student reported being swarmed by mysterious balls of light as he did homework in his room one evening.

Then there was the woman on tour with her daughter in 2015. They'd come from Dublin. Back in Ireland after their Chicago trip, her daughter was now being taunted nightly by a disheveled old woman in a nightgown who would appear at the foot of her bed.

Though UFO sightings and cattle mutilations were allegedly plentiful at Skinwalker Ranch for, reportedly, decades, the other high strangeness of poltergeist activity, cryptid reports and the like only began with the tenancy of the Shermans in the 1990s. The place's notoriety, however, skyrocketed after it was purchased in 1996 by Robert Bigelow, a billionaire hotel mogul with a deep interest in the paranormal.

Bigelow's role in the government's sudden interest in UFOs and the paranormal, his own monetary gain from governmental programs, and his relationships with the Pentagon, UFO-advocate Senator Harry Reid, "UFO journalist" George Knapp and other influential believers: These have all been detailed by far better journalists than I. [104] Suffice it to say that it's all pretty shocking and shady.

Here, though, I want to point out something else, and it's something I find neither coincidental nor incidental.

Robert Bigelow's interest in the paranormal really took off as such interest does for many: after his son's suicide. He turned to psychic mediums in an effort to reach his lost child, and from there his interest in the afterlife developed tentacles reaching into every possible realm of paranormal research. In 2020 the billionaire founded the Bigelow Institute for Consciousness Studies; the website for the organization announces its mission " to communicate, facilitate, educate, and organize scientific research and exploration into the survival of human consciousness (SOHC) after permanent bodily death." In 2021 Bigelow, through the Institute, offered a half million-dollar prize for the best essay on the probability of life after death. The winner was parapsychologist Jeffrey Mishlove, host of the PBS talk show on consciousness and parapsychology, *Thinking Allowed.*

Now Bigelow has announced a new contest. He wants to know the best way to contact those on the Other Side.

Aware of both the obsessive desire of government agencies to contact discarnate intelligences and of Bigelow's web of relationships with those same government agencies, *and* of the fact that Bigelow received a 22-million-dollar governmental contract regarding Skinwalker Ranch, I wonder if Bigelow's new contest is by special request—and financing—of his friends in high places?

The government couldn't run such a contest, but Bigelow certainly could. Of course, positive results would also benefit the longtime spirit seeker Bigelow, but isn't mutual benefit at the heart of every great deal?

A LITTLE TOO FAMILIAR (PART 3)

Jacques Vallée is doubtless the most famous researcher to promote the idea that reports of fairies, incubi, succubi and the like are very similar to modern-day UFO encounters, but he is far from the only one to have noticed.

Long time UFO researcher Timothy Good, for example, struck upon the fact that the fairy tale of the "changeling" is shockingly similar to that of aliens abducting women and forcing them to carry fetuses. Of course, earlier tales do not get into as much graphic detail as the modern accounts of abductees typically do, but the premise is basically the same.

In his book *Earth: An Alien Enterprise*, Good brings up a long-forgotten case involving a man called "Cole" who claimed to have been in contact with an alien species. According to the man, his alien associates informed him that they had been replacing human babies with extraterrestrial look-alikes. The intention was for these replacements to actively monitor humans. They weren't spies, exactly. Rather, devices implanted in their brains would record everything around them.

According to Cole, these efforts to monitor human development ramped up after the advent of nuclear weapons, which were apparently of grave concern to ETs. But as Vallée pointed out in his landmark work, *Passport to Magonia*, this was not a new conspiracy theory. The notion of strange beings inserting themselves into human affairs had been a hallmark of fairy lore for centuries, and the tales have continued into modern times.

Scholar Carole Silver has documented numerous late nineteenth-century cases of alleged changelings who were given baths by their parents in water infused with deadly foxgloves. In one case, a fussy baby—suspected to be a changeling—was thrown onto hot coals and killed. Even today, there are great swaths who believe in the fairy folk—and their propensity for human abduction. [105]

In *Passport to Magonia*, Vallée collected a variety of accounts of encounters with "fairy folk," including some rather intriguing tales about that Irish favorite, the leprechaun. In one case, a man recalled how, as a small child, he was out collecting berries, when he came upon a curiously "flat stone" covering a ditch. He picked up this stone, and to his shock, found himself looking into the abode of a leprechaun. The diminutive creature was down inside the hole, staring right back up at him. According to the eyewitness, the leprechaun was downright friendly, as it grinned and looked up in his direction.

This witness was perhaps lucky that the leprechaun was in such a good mood, since in many other accounts of folks encountering fairies—especially in instances in which hapless humans disturb their living arrangements—the results are not quite so harmless. Indeed, despite the cutesy modern, American, Tinkerbell-type perception of fairies, actual accounts of these entities often speak of their wrath and their keen sense of wreaking vengeance and havoc on those who they feel have crossed them. For locals who've lived with them through time, there was—and is—a widespread and unabashed fear of these small but powerful creatures, both collectively and particularly.

For example, elves are said to be armed with some sort of "wands" which have tremendous power and can paralyze anyone struck with them. The notion is eerily similar to many modern-day reports of extraterrestrial entities, in which the ETs have been seen carrying wand-like devices that could stun or paralyze their victims, either by shooting laser-like blasts or by striking the contactee with the device.

A Florida man, Ed Walters—who we'll examine more later—reported several run-ins with entities carrying such wands. [106] In one instance, he found himself surrounded by ETs brandishing the devices. As he tried to break free, a struggle commenced, and Walters managed to grab one of the ETs. Just as he was about to put his hands around the ET's neck, however, its wand made contact with Walters' body. At that moment, an image appeared in his mind of his own daughter being strangled. The vision caused Ed to drop his hands back to his side, releasing the creature. Walters, like many others, has been largely dismissed as a fake and a fraud in the world of alleged experiencers, but our purposes are not primarily to confirm or deny the truth of any of these accounts but to look for parallels in UFO claims to claims of the diabolical.

Vallée documented an early encounter which took place in 1954, experienced by a Frenchman named Georges Gatay. Gatay found himself face to face with an ET visitor who wielded a device similar to the one described later by Walters.

Gatay said of it, "It could have been a pistol, or it could have been a metal rod."

It wasn't a pistol.

When the device made contact with Gatay, it paralyzed him. Gatay was frightened and very much wanted to flee, but he discovered that he was "nailed to the spot."

So are leprechaun fairy wands and ET stun guns one and the same? Or are they, perhaps, the swords of the angels—fallen and not—that Christians believe will someday fight the war of Armageddon? We know, of course, that Michael the Archangel brandishes a sword, as witnesses to his visits have attested. Have these creatures, essentially, been neither little people nor spacemen but something else, *appearing* differently to different people and in different cultures over many hundreds or thousands of years?

Paranormal scholar Joshua Cutchin has conducted extensive research into the offering of food to humans by unknown beings throughout history and folklore, including fairies, bigfoot and, of course, aliens. Cutchin reminds us in his book, *A Trojan Feast*, that Adam and Eve first ate of the fruit offered by the devil with the direst of consequences. And this offering of "forbidden food" to humans by strange beings—and warnings against taking it—has seemed to go on throughout the rest of human history.

A longstanding legend stretching back into the faintest histories of some European peoples holds that, if a human accepts food or drink from (fill in the blank with the local preternatural creature), the person will never be able to leave the realm of these beings. The exchange forms a sort of interdimensional "contract" between them.

One of the most absurd cases in ufology is that of a Wisconsin man named Joe Simonton. Once again, Jaques Vallée discussed this case in *Passport to Magonia,* comparing elements of it to European "fairy stories" of old. Simonton was having breakfast in his home in Eagle River when a strange craft landed outside. Inside were humanoid looking beings with dark skin. One of them was cooking something on what looked like a grill. The other asked Joe for some water. After fetching the water, Simonton was offered some "pancakes" by the grateful being. They seemed to be normal pancakes, although they tasted like cardboard. However, upon laboratory examination at Northwestern University, they were found to be devoid of salt. It wasn't that they didn't *contain* salt as an ingredient, but that the natural salts *had been removed from the ingredients themselves.*

The discovery immediately reminded Vallée of old fairy stories he'd grown up with in his native France. In a number of them, buckwheat was specifically mentioned as part of the story— specifically as a gift from the fairies—, and in others it was stated that the fairy folk could not eat salt.

For me as a Catholic, Simonton's pancakes (and Vallée's remembered tales) strongly evoked the Catholic tradition of putting salt along the thresholds and windows to keep out the devil. It also reminded me of cases I've encountered as a ghost hunter in which strange beings offered real food to humans.

I was also reminded of a story shared with me by Wisconsin-based paranormal historian Allison Jornlin: the case of the "Swearing Ghost." In the course of the strange events of 1926, which included vile messages appearing on the walls and in just about every book the family owned, police decided one of the children, a girl, was somehow behind it. The activity continued, however, even after she was removed from the home in placed in temporary care elsewhere.[107]

Before her removal, the girl reported finding a strange figure at the front door. The "man" spoke to her through the plate glass door, telling her he wanted her to buy some candy from him. She became visibly afraid, at which point the being "thrust the candy right through the plate glass window," without the glass breaking. The stupefied child dumbly took it, but it was, she told police, so hot that it burned her hand, forcing her to throw it into the sink.

It was later reported that the only book in the house not scrawled in by the unseen interloper was a "book of magic" that belonged to the girl herself and which was a "prized possession." Was this a magic trick instruction book—or a ritual manual of the occult? Was our twelve-year reading about the occult, or even dabbling in it?.

One of the places I have researched the most during my long career is a place called Bachelors Grove. It's comprised of a tiny settler's cemetery southwest of Chicago that's now surrounded by forest preserves. Bachelors Grove appears on just about every list of the world's most haunted places, and I myself have spent hundreds of hours there, including during academic research in the late 1980s.

Before the area was owned by the county, who forested it, settlers built homesteads there, but after the 1927 forced land sales to the Forest Preserve District, the remaining houses were razed and the farms seeded with trees. Still, while no houses have stood here for almost a century, visitors still claim to see a so-called "Magic House" or "Dream House" that appears and disappears throughout the forest and even, at times, inside the cemetery itself.

After my first book of Chicago folklorist was published in 1998, a middle-aged gentleman attended one of my book signings and shared a story of Bachelor's Grove's elusive house. He said that, as a child growing up in the area, he and his friend would often spend time exploring the woods around the cemetery. One afternoon, they came upon a house they had never seen before. It was a white farmhouse, with a wraparound porch and a porch swing, appearing just like any farmhouse in the still rural area at the time. There was an elderly woman standing on the porch, and she beckoned to the boys.

They went up to the house, and the woman told them she had just made cookies, inviting them in for some. The man told me they sat in the kitchen of the house, eating cookies and drinking milk while the woman talked to them about nothing in particular.

As it was late, the boys thanked the woman and went home, saying nothing about their visit because they were forbidden from going into strangers' houses. But the next day, thinking of cookies, the boys went back to Bachelors Grove hoping for a reprise.

The house was nowhere to be found.

If we go with our theory that all of these beings are diabolical ones (and take Cutchin's reminder further), we might well wonder if belief in a permanent spiritual state or "contract" brought about by the imbibing of something offered by a non-human being is not only an echo of the Fall but perhaps also a counterfeiting of the Holy Eucharist of the Christian Church: *Take and eat*, the beings say, *and live with us forever.*

Saint Justin Martyr wrote about this counterfeiting of authentic godly experience by the devil, and he argued that the devil has done this not only *after* godly events in history—but *before*: the "diabolical mimicry" argument. Knowing in advance the plan of salvation, and out of jealousy and hate, the devil created his own counterfeit experiences to devalue the authentic godly ones, create suspicion of them and mock them. So it was, St. Justin would warn us, with the ancient cults that seemed to foreshadow the coming of Mary, Queen of Heaven, Jesus's resurrection and other central events of the Christian faith. C.S. Lewis had a less extreme view of the similarities between pagan religions and Christianity, positing that ancient pagan peoples had an innate sense of the Truth that was to be revealed in Christian salvation history. But the ways they interpreted that innate sense were deeply flawed.

Regardless of how the similarities arose, there's no doubt that they do exist.

In his first letter to the Corinthians, St. Paul said: *You cannot drink the cup of the Lord and the cup of demons.* Today, we see this as an admonition against claiming to be a Christian while committing sin, but Paul almost certainly was speaking against literal pagan rituals involving the partaking of a cup, as the Septuagintal meaning of demons is "foreign gods" or pagan gods. Justin Martyr and his followers would have seen all of these pagan cup rituals— and the whole array of other pagan customs—as diabolical counterfeits of the one true Cup of Life offered by Jesus. Lewis would have seen them as bumbling attempts to make sense of a still unknown—or, by later pagans, rejected—Truth stirring within them.

As frightful as some of these experiences can be, there is (as we've seen many times just in this book) a similar element to all of them, despite the place or time.

A certain absurdity.

And again, this absurdity has become known as one of the key elements of UFO/ET experiences. It's such a common element that ufologists have come to actually look for the absurdity as part of their efforts to verify claims. Of course, that absurdity is what makes skeptics dismiss them as ridiculous.

I teach a whole course on historic "poltergeist" cases generally dismissed as absurd. Like many UFO/ET accounts, each one of the cases contains elements that are patently absurd—and elements that are utterly horrific.

By the nineteenth century, it was understood that the poltergeist ("noisy ghost" as it translates from German) is not your typical haunting. The poltergeist does not necessarily manifest as a distinct personality, but as an overarching intelligence that seems to observe the household it's harassing and constantly finds unique ways to make life miserable for everyone. Often, those ways are quite definitely absurd.

In the 1700s, the "Wizard Clip" spirit tormented the family of a West Virginia farmer by dismembering its livestock and clipping half-moon-shaped cutouts from every piece of fabric in the house, using invisible shears that could be heard, *clip-clip-clip*, eerily through the house.

In the 1930s, on the Isle of Man, famed English ghost hunter Harry Price investigated a family's claims that an invisible, talking mongoose had taken up residence in their home. The family took to feeding the spirit with bananas, chocolate and cookies, and on one occasion the thing told the family:

> I am a freak! I have hands and I have feet! And if you saw me you'd faint, you'd be petrified, mummified, turned into a stone or a pillar of salt![108]

In the case of the Bell Witch of Tennessee the spirit harassed a family for years, primarily manifesting as a disembodied voice that never stopped talking. Sometimes the voice would break off into five distinct personalities, a "spirit family" that argued incessantly for hours on end. It's final act was reportedly poisoning the family patriarch with a dark, mysterious liquid found in a vial next to John Bell's bed.

In the 1970s, in Tyler, Texas, the late paranormal investigator Hans Holzer investigated a presence with numerous personalities that dropped notes from the air, predicted the dates of friends and neighbors' deaths, and buried the family dog alive. [109]

In the 1980s, an entity calling itself "Prince" communicated with California's Moffitt family by writing messages in soap on the bathroom mirror of their Rancho Cucamonga home and carving its signature (a sort of demonic sigil) into the walls, floors, bedding and even the family car.

We'll further investigate the absurdity—and the physicality—of these cases in a later chapter. What's important for now is that physical evidence was part of all of these cases, and that—even now—many claim these cases involved fairies, djinns or other creatures from ages-old folklore.

Others say they were demons.

THE SUMMONERS

The suggested connection between UFOs and fairies reminded me of one of the oddest and most affecting nights of my long career as an investigator into ghost, haunting and demonic cases.

Many years ago now—sometime back in the very early 2000s—I was invited to speak at a meeting of a local chapter of the Indiana Ghost Trackers, one of the largest groups of paranormal investigators in the world, with organized chapters all over the Hoosier state. After the meeting and a group dinner, we went to investigate a nearby farm. The farm's owner was a woman known simply as Luann to the hundreds of ghost hunters who visited her property over many years. In fact, over those years "Luann's Farm" became a point of pilgrimage for believers and skeptics alike, from every walk of life.

Luann first began to wonder about her property when she moved in and the animals in the barn seemed "spooked" by something that Luann herself couldn't see. A visit by a clairvoyant brought Luann two pieces of astonishing news. First, the clairvoyant said, the property where Luann's barn stands was the site of a so-called "portal" or interdimensional doorway. She explained to Luann what this was, but as astonishing as this news was, nothing could prepare her for the clairvoyant's second pronunciation.

You have fairies on your property.

Shocked and disbelieving, Luann listened as her visitor, equally amazed, told her some facts about fairies: that they are extremely rare in North America, that they tend to congregate at portals in natural settings, and that those who have them living on their land are highly fortunate, as they bring good luck if you treat them well. Luann naturally asked what she should do to please her fairies, and the clairvoyant said, "You have to feed them."

Of course, Luann asked, "What should I feed them?"

Her visitor told her that she had to experiment to see what they liked.

The next day, Luann began the bizarre ritual of placing Petrie dishes of various foods and drinks in the barn and on the hill behind it, too, in order to see what would go missing in the night. Oddly, foods one might expect to be eaten by animals remained each morning: bits of leftover meat—cooked and raw—, vegetables, milk, apples. What disappeared, finally, night after night, was what tradition could have dictated.

Fairies, according to folklore, are self-indulgent creatures. They live well and treat well, and when they are displeased, they punish well. Each morning Luann found only three things consistently gone: her tiny servings of fudge brownies, Jamieson's whiskey, and Starbucks' Frappuccino.

Regularly sated with such luxuries, it seems the fairies remained through the end of Luann's life.

I witnessed these "fairies" myself.

When I visited Luann's farm, I was taken into the barn along with about a dozen other ghost hunters. Most of the others present had brought digital cameras, and they snapped many photographs as we entered the barn.

Now, "orbs" have been a subject of great controversy in ghost hunting circles over the years. These semi-transparent balls of white light that show up in photographs are believed by some to be balls of spirit energy, by others to be dust, moisture, or other explicable culprits. With more than twenty people walking into a hay-filled barn, one might well expect "orbs" to show up on film as the dust is disturbed by all of those footsteps. However, in Luann's barn, nearly twenty cameras caught only a handful of them when we entered. This fact will be important shortly.

We settled down and stood or sat. When we were all quiet and unmoving, Luann began to speak to the air.

"Don't be afraid," she said. "No one is here to hurt you, only to learn about you."

She introduced me, as I had never been there before, and as she spoke the blackness was lit, again and again, by the flashes of the cameras going off, dozens of flashes a minute, as the others gathered snapped photo after photo. Luann asked the fairies to come to me, to come and meet me and, again, to not be afraid.

I felt, as the minutes went by, an increasing tingling sensation all around, of which I told Luann.

"Put out your hands to your sides, with your palms up, "she said. "And they will come to you."

I did as I was told.

I stood, transfixed, in the most aware state I can remember, and it seemed I did feel something come to me and a tingling in my hands and fingers.

A few minutes later we went back to the house to look at the images that had been captured during our visit to the barn. One by one, the group members showed me their phones and the photos they had taken. To my astonishment, the photographs, on ten different cameras, all evidenced a definite progression of events.

As mentioned, when we entered the barn at first, trampling hay everywhere, a couple of little dust orbs showed up in the digital camera frames of my fellow ghost hunters. It was when we were perfectly still, however, as Luann began her soothing monologue, that the lights began to gather. And the more she talked, the more she reassured her "fairies," and the *more still we stood*, the more orbs gathered around me. And, sure enough, when she asked them to come to me, into my hands, there they were.

When I looked at the photographs, I was deeply quieted. In each one, there I was: standing, shivering in an Indiana barn at midnight, arms outstretched, with a rapturous expression on my face—and my hands filled with little balls of light.

Luann's summoning for me of these "light beings" in that cold Indiana barn so many years ago has always stayed deeply with me, and so when I began to look into the UFO enigma, I took great interest in the fact that many UFO believers have been experiencing something very similar, and some on a much larger scale.

Today, one of the most well-known ufologists is Dr. Steven Greer, who runs a program he founded called Close Encounters of the Fifth Kind (or CE-5). Greer takes his students into the desert or to the ocean shore and they try to summon extraterrestrials. They are often rewarded with the appearance of UFOs in the sky or contact with alleged ETs. The program has grown into a network of more than one hundred groups all over the world, and so today there are groups of people all over the world actively attempting to make contact with these "extraterrestrials" through the CE-5 protocols.

The program is *exactly* like the "bridge" that many Instrumental Transcommunication practitioners have been trying to build between the living and the dead by holding worldwide, synchronized spirit communication sessions on a regular schedule, but we'll look more at this later.

At any rate, the result is a huge and increasing international séance going on right now, just as UFO reports are going through the roof, occult activity (including witchcraft, wicca and magick) is now mainstream, and, exorcists tell us, demonic possessions are off the charts. [110]

Dr. Stephen Greer began his career as an emergency room physician. His long-standing interest in both UFOs and the occult, however, led to his founding of the Center for the Study of Extraterrestrial Intelligence (CSETI). His ambitions were big and perhaps a bit naïve, since he championed the idea of creating a kind of "ambassadorship" in regard to interactions between humans and aliens. He began his attempts to reach aliens by shining bright lights into the sky, accompanied by loud sounds, just trying to get the attention of what he thought were, at first, physical craft.

Although the signaling of craft from the ground might be a

possible method to initiate physical contact with presumably physical craft, Greer soon discovered that other methods of contact worked a lot better.

Occult methods.

In fact, a lot of what Greer does smacks of the stuff Albert Bender was doing back in his Bridgeport, Connecticut attic in the 1950s—specifically his "Contact Day" project. Some of Dr. Greer's efforts in fact, aren't all that much different. His organization has utilized very similar methods, seeking to use concerted efforts of human consciousness to provoke a reaction from beyond. This shouldn't surprise us when we look further back into Greer's past to discover the origins of CE5.

In 1975, Greer travelled to a summer session on transcendental meditation at Maharishi International University for training to become an instructor in the occult practice. The last portion of the training was a trip to a small resort town in the Alps, near the Italian border. During the retreat, Greer went into the mountains alone to try what he calls the "CE5 Protocols," a series of practices he created with the help of—you guessed it—an "extraterrestrial" who had contacted him when he was in his teens. The default assumption is that the ET had steered Greer towards the occult practices he was now learning to teach.

Greer's Protocols include going into deep meditation and opening one's consciousness to contact by ETs. When a being makes contact, the meditator then asks for contact. If it works, UFOs appear. Unsurprisingly as well, Greer ends these sessions by speaking the Hindu "*Namaste*"—literally telling the beings, "I bow to you."

We must recognize that evidence has been put forth suggesting that Greer has faked at least one of the "summoned" UFOs from his paid CE-5 sessions. Critics suggest that Greer has hired private pilots to drop flares or otherwise cause at least some of the phenomena that's been witnessed during these excursions. One journalist, Tom Rogan, examined a video posted online documenting aerial phenomena recorded during one of Greer's outings to summon UFOs on the east coast of Florida with a "class" of his on January 27, 2015. As strange lights appear in the sky, Greer narrates the events, invites his "students" to begin meditating to commune with the aliens, and proclaims the phenomenon to be genuinely extraterrestrial. Greer "verifies" later that no planes flew in the area during the time of their gathering.

But the journalist found that

(at) 9:11 p.m. on Jan. 27, 2015, a Beech 76 Duchess registered N110SU was recorded flying at 85 mph off Vero Beach. This is slower than the aircraft's normal cruising speed and would feasibly allow the aircrew to deploy parachute flares or some other illumination device. The aircraft took off and returned to the airport in Fort Pierce.[111]

Ray Boeche, who we've met learning the legend of the Collins Elite, documented a group which he saw as a very definite precursor to Greer's.[112] The group, based at the University of Indiana, was formed by a graduate student named Bill Fogarty. Two of the group members were Vietnam veterans, and all were teetotalers and drug-free. They were all interested in UFOs.

At first, like Greer, the young men would go out into the fields at night and simply look for spacecraft, attempting to signal when they saw a strange light in the sky. To their delight, they began to have some success in their efforts. Not long after, however, other phenomena began to erupt.

One night, while watching two UFOs moving in the air just a few feet above, the group heard strange knockings in the area around them, followed by the unmistakable sound of footsteps walking in the brush nearby, heavy breathing and disembodied voices.

Later, at home, one of the young men experienced incessant pounding in the walls and the shaking of his bed, and he was slapped in the face by an unseen hand.

Then followed a sort of surveillance period, when the young men would see black cars following them, and men in black clothing began appearing in their apartments and dorm rooms. These events were accompanied by electronics malfunctioning:

televisions switching on and off by themselves, lights flickering and so on.

Then, things took an even stranger turn. A member of the group said he was sleeping one night in his bed and woke up in the middle of a field.

The young men made a mutual decision to stop their contact attempts. Boeche recounts what happened to them:

> One of the men invested heavily in weapons and joined a neo-pagan group that offered animal sacrifices to [the god] Odin. One became a Christian, one committed suicide, and the remaining two dropped out of college a month before they would have graduated and spent the next several years driving around the country.

For me these summoning accounts evoke the famous "Philip" case in parapsychology research. This concerned a group who decided they were going to "create" a ghost. They began having seances to contact a spirit whose identity they had made up themselves. They named the spirit Philip and gave him a detailed backstory. After a regular series of seances, "Philip" began to communicate through raps, table tipping and the like. The group congratulated themselves for successfully proving that *collective consciousness* could produce observable physical effects.

But was that really what was producing the effects, or something that wanted to give them what they desired to find?

Late in 2023, I first heard the story of Chris Bledsoe, who not only is able to summon "orbs of light" that he believes to be UFOs, but he also communes with a mysterious being he calls "The Lady" who wants desperately, she says, for everyone to believe in her and the other "light beings." [113]

In 2007, a series of events unfolded during a fishing trip that would forever change Bledsoe's life. Bledsoe had been suffering deeply, both physically and emotionally, for years. Accompanied by three co-workers and his son, Chris, Jr., he decided to take a moment of solitude in the woods to meditate and pray. Alone and at the end of his rope, he cried out to the sky—as most of us have done—for help.

At that moment, he was astonished to witness several enigmatic aerial objects that seemed to respond to his every movement and thought. Startled by the uncanny spectacle, he ran from the lights and reunited with his co-workers. To his astonishment, he discovered that he had unknowingly experienced a four-hour period of "missing time."

Bledsoe's companions told him he had been absent throughout the night; they had spent the entire time searching for him. Adding to his distress, his son, Chris Jr., was now also missing, prompting him to embark on an anxious search himself. When he found his son, Bledsoe saw with him two translucent beings of about three and a half feet tall. These otherworldly entities possessed striking red glowing eyes. Chris, Jr. said he'd been frozen for literally hours; he was only released from this grip when his dad arrived on the scene, calling out for him and causing the beings to disappear.

Fearful and bewildered, the group hastily left the scene, only to discover that anomalous lights were tailing their truck along the highway. At one point, the lights even obstructed their path, intensifying their sense of unease.

In the days that followed that night, as the chaos and confusion subsided, Bledsoe couldn't help but notice an unexpected silver lining; his long-standing Crohn's disease, which had plagued him for 17 years, had seemingly vanished. The encounter seemed to have miraculously ended the incapacitating symptoms of his condition.

Since that first night, similar encounters with radiant beings and orbs of light have persisted and grown. Bledsoe's case has attracted the attention of various government agencies, including prestigious organizations such as NASA, the CIA, the FBI, the DIA, and MUFON. Personnel from these agencies have extensively investigated his experiences, adding credence to the extraordinary nature of his encounters.

Later, a Harvard-trained physicist would come to the Bledsoe house to hypnotically regress Chris. During the session, Bledsoe said he was able to touch one of the lights during the period of missing time, and that the light—some forty feet in diameter—seemed to be both a vessel but also sentient. He was taken into a dark room (but with no walls; he could see the stars around them), where he was surrounded by entities. Bledsoe panicked and asked where his son was. The beings said he was being kept safe. They told Chris they were from the "Creator" and that they protect humans from dark forces.

The beings flew Chris to Egypt, telling him that the "Sphinx gazing at Regula just before sunrise" would mark the beginning of a new age. Chris later discovered that this event was scheduled to occur in August of 2026.

As time went on, Bledsoe gradually developed a belief that these beings do indeed harbor benevolent intentions. This conviction has led numerous individuals to visit his property, seeking their own firsthand experience of Bledsoe's famous UFO-summoning. Many claim they have been healed after witnessing the lights, though no public evidence of this has been forthcoming.

One night, Bledsoe woke from his sleep, greeted by an ethereal voice reverberating throughout the room, urging him to "arise." Though initially taken aback, Chris found himself inexplicably entranced, compelled to slip on his shoes, don his socks, and bundle up in warm clothes, as the night was cold.

Guided by an irresistible force, he ventured outside, where a captivating sight awaited him. Three luminous beings, composed entirely of pure light, stood before him. Struck with awe, Chris obediently followed their lead, journeying across a sprawling field that stretched towards the edge of the nearby forest. Eventually, they arrived at a particular spot, where a resplendent female figure awaited his arrival. With her flowing blonde locks, piercing blue eyes, and a shimmering gown that seemed akin to a celestial dance of stars, she floated effortlessly above the ground, radiating an otherworldly glow.

Ingrained with the teachings of his devout Christian upbringing, Chris's mind immediately turned towards thoughts of an angelic encounter. Filled with profound astonishment, he knelt down in reverence before this ethereal being. Then, to Chris' amazement, the being introduced herself as the "Mother Goddess of the Universe," the embodiment of the Divine Feminine Spirit, Universal Love, and (no less) the Holy Spirit of the Sacred Trinity of the Christian God.

The weight of this extraordinary encounter led Bledsoe to confide in various government agencies, eager to share his otherworldly experience. His disclosure only served to intensify the scrutiny placed upon him, consequently thrusting him into the spotlight as, reportedly, the first extraterrestrial contactee in the government's AATIP program.

Bledsoe said he was surprised to discover that many government agents, including some from NASA, already knew about "the Lady." He shared that it was NASA operatives who told him the being had also appeared to others but had given the names of various ancient goddesses like Isis. They further suggested that the Christian Church had likely long ago "forced" this spirit into their Jesus-centered "myth" as "Mary." She was probably the same spirit, they said, who had appeared at Fatima, Portugal in 1917, though we'll see shortly how decidedly different these apparitions actually were from Bledsoe's

In fact, NASA officials seemed well-versed in the world of gods, goddesses and occult practices. Bledsoe's son, Ryan, told podcaster Danny Jones that ufology legend and NASA researcher Tim Taylor (who became very close to the Bledsoes), meditated every morning, and that Taylor told his dad "to get into Kundalini yoga" to assist with his spiritual awakening.[114] These are part of the "protocols" Taylor reportedly practices each day to maintain mind-to-mind contact with the extraterrestrials that give him knowledge and schematics for technology (what he and other UFO believers and tech gurus call "downloads").

Later, the Lady would identify herself to Bledsoe by the name of "Hathor"—a major Egyptian sky goddess known to hang around with a bull. This cleared things up, because Chris had been puzzled by the fact that a bull-like being often accompanied the Lady on her visits. The Lady also told Bledsoe that "Amen-Ra is the hidden one," Amen being the Egyptian god of the universe and Ra the all-supreme god of the Egyptians.

But Catholic scholar Matthew Tsakanikas has identified another goddess as the likely figure behind Bledsoe's "Lady": the Egyptian goddess Aset. The Greeks called her Isis, and she was the demonic imposter "Queen of Heaven" of the ancient world.[115] In Bledsoe's reports, in fact, Tsakanikas has identified a string of references to Isis and the Rosicrucianism she is so closely associated with. He realized the connections of Bledsoe's experiences to Rosicrucianism after Catholic historian of religion Diana Pasulka casually commented to Joe Rogan (and an audience of millions) in early 2024 that Jaques Vallée, John Mack and other prominent ufologists are Rosicrucians. [116]

According to Bledsoe, his encounters with this mysterious entity have been ongoing for years, shaping his belief system and offering profound insights into the nature of existence. The Lady is said to possess advanced knowledge and wisdom that surpasses human understanding. Bledsoe explains that the Lady communicates with him telepathically, speaking directly into his mind in perfect English. This extraordinary ability allows them to exchange information, ideas, and thoughts effortlessly. The being's teachings emphasize the importance of love, compassion, and realizing one's own divine potential—in keeping with today's New Age, anti-Christian "Christ consciousness" gospel.

The significance of the Lady's messages lies not only in their content but also in their timing. Bledsoe asserts that she has warned him about significant events before they occur, such as financial crises, natural disasters, and personal challenges. Her biggest messages and movements happen around the Christian high holy feast of Easter, suggesting to Chris that this being is connected to what he feels is a kind of true Christianity that has, of course, been corrupted by religion.

Along with spreading the New Age personal divinity messages of the lady and reminding people how closed- minded and hurtful the Christian Church was to him, Bledsoe talks a lot about "manifesting" our desires.

Bledsoe has come to believe that, just as NASA and Pasulka told him, the Lady is the same force or being that has appeared in various Marian apparitions associated with the Catholic Church and in the form of ancient goddesses like Isis. He professes that her appearances to him are heralding the coming New Age of the Divine Feminine. This promises to be an age of what some term "feminine" movements such as climate rescue, racial justice, "reproductive health care" (abortion and contraception), and female political power.

Bledsoe left his Christian Church after friends there warned him against pursuing interest in or contact with these lights and beings, assuring him that they were not of God.

While he and his family speak freely about ancient gods and goddesses, astrology, remote viewing, occult healing and manifesting, Bledsoe claims that he "prays to God" before summoning sessions. Hearing of this practice took me back to the many instances when my colleagues and I would cluelessly pray before having a séance, pulling out a Ouija board or turning on an occult ghost hunting device, thinking this would both protect us from evil spirits and encourage God to send us the information we were looking for.

In fact, a "ghost box" made at least one appearance in the saga of Chris Bledsoe. In 2017, Bledsoe says that anthropologist, past life regressionist and self-proclaimed shaman Pamela Nance asked to meet him because she had been told to seek him out through a device used to speak to unknown voices.

Nance, who also said she worked for the government, told Bledsoe she'd been out one night in Massachusetts near her cabin on Pilot Mountain using the device, and voices had repeatedly called out "Chris! Chris!" leading her to call up MUFON and ask if they knew who this "Chris" might be.

They did.

Nance brought the device over to Bledsoe's house and turned it on. It emitted staticky white noise at first. Then, it began to throw out voices.

When I heard this story I instantly recognized the device as a ghost box or spirit box, as they're variously called in Electronic Voice Phenomenon (EVP) research. The box is a radio that's been either built or hacked to continually scan through the AM or FM band, fast enough to prohibit understanding any words being broadcast. The idea is that spirits use the fragments of sound to create words and speak through the radio.

The first ghost boxes were built in the 1980s by a man named Frank Sumption, and his design of the "Frank's box" was followed up by others who tweaked the design or concocted their own. These devices come in every shape and size, and there are even phone apps that mimic them. Before leaving the occult behind, I (like so many investigators) regularly utilized numerous of these devices, including ones specially built for me by friends and colleagues. In fact, the spiritual fallout from using these devices was a big part of what led me to leave behind occult practices in my work.

Bledsoe tells us that, during a ghost box session with Nance, one particular message came over the box as clear as day. The message warned that a papal assassination attempt was in the works in Philadelphia, where Pope Francis was about to make a visit during his American tour. Bledsoe, the voices said, must go and stop it. The voices were urgent, interspersed with loud static:

The pope is in danger! Help him! We need him!

Shortly thereafter, Bledsoe had made his way to Philadelphia to meet up with governmental remote viewer and colonel John Alexander. (who you may remember from the film, *The Men Who Stare at Goats*). He got in touch with Joe McMonagle, the CIA's top remote viewer, and the two verified the plot and called police. Sure enough, the next day Philadelphians read about a thwarted assassination plot on the Holy Father.

As a Catholic who frequently frets, as many do, about the often bizarre and troubling actions of Pope Francis, I found this development intriguing to be sure. Was the pope, in fact, supposed to die in 2017 Philadelphia? Was his assassination thwarted by Bledsoe, with the help of his "light beings" and his "Lady?"

Many have called the fervor around and devotion to Bledsoe cult-like. Indeed, secular UFO-believers as well as Christian ones join together in sympathy for what he says he and his family suffered from his church and other critics in his community and throughout the larger culture. Countless followers who (to use a very mild term) disdain the Christian faith (and things like Marian apparitions) voraciously support the truth of the Lady and her messages for humanity. But many Christians are reading Bledsoe's book too, and it's changing their faith—just the way it's changed the faith of Chris and his family.

Chris' son, Ryan Bledsoe, told Danny Jones we don't need to worry about negative entities when exploring the kinds of things his father and his family have encountered. He says he's not a Christian anymore, but he also quotes the Bible, saying we have "power and dominion over them." [117]

He also says his dad and his experiences have led him into a whole world of occult interests. First he started seeing these light beings, then:

> Next thing you know I'm studying . . . hermeticism and Gnosticism and Rosicrucianism and wisdom traditions and things like that.

Ryan Bledsoe started a YouTube channel called "Bledsoe Said So," and on the show he explores every kind of esoteric interest imaginable. It's all part, he says, of the great "awakening" that's happening: an awakening that's going to show us that God is, essentially, too big for religion to understand . . . but apparently comprehensible through myriad occult tools and traditions.

Just as I was finishing the final chapter of this book, a Facebook friend sent me a message. His was a name I hadn't heard in many years, since the days I had been spending so much (too much) time investigating Bachelors Grove. He had also been very interested in this strange site, and he had some disturbing news about the place. An old colleague and longtime researcher of Bachelors Grove had taken his own life, and he had done it in the woods near the cemetery where he'd spent so many thousands of hours.

It had been a visit to the cemetery with him at night, in fact, in June of 2012, that had sent me into an obsessive interest in Bachelors Grove. That night accelerated a downward spiral in my life, and that's a story for another book.. But something happened that night that came flooding back to me when I heard the news of my colleague's suicide.

In late June of 2012, I attended the funeral of Chicago's well-known ghost hunter, the folklorist Richard Crowe. After the services, drinking Bloody Marys at Chet's Melody Lounge on Archer Road, this colleague had offered to show me around the old homestead sites in the woods around Bachelors Grove cemetery. I'd gone down to meet him one afternoon soon after, and we'd spent several hours walking around the woods and looking at the remains of houses, cisterns and other structures dating back to the time of the farms there. After, we went to dinner, and then he asked if I wanted to go back to the Grove now that it was dark—something I hadn't done in thirty years.

Of course I did.

And so there we were.

That night, we ended up becoming lost in this tiny preserve for four and half hours. It was a veritable impossibility. My new friend had mapped the trails through the woods. He'd walked them countless times and could have traversed them in his sleep. And yet we walked in circles seemingly endlessly, occasionally seeing lights of houses or cars that would blink off like images a television when we walked toward them, thinking we had found a road. It was a terrifying experience.

It was rendered even more terrifying because something wondrous had happened earlier that evening, when we'd first arrived in the woods.

It was an exceptionally hot, humid night, and after we parked our cars off a side road, we walked through the woods towards the infamous cemetery with the oppressive air pressing down on us. But as we walked, we became aware of an increasing sense of what visitors here often describe as something "enchanted" or "magical."

I don't know where we were when we saw what we saw. At first I thought we must be overlooking the old quarry pond that skirts the cemetery, as there seemed to be a large expanse of emptiness before us, but I realized later that this could not have been the case, as we walked for a good ten minutes more before arriving at the burial ground.

It is still difficult for me to describe what we saw, but it was a light show of sorts, consisting of thousands of tiny blinking or flashing lights that mimicked flash bulbs going off.. The only thing I can compare it to is the image of dozens of paparazzi cameras going off, one after another, at a celebrity gala. I was absolutely mesmerized by this experience, and when I say it seemed to be happening with an intelligence behind it, other experiencers will understand that. It was as if it was happening *for us*. There was no doubt in my mind that the lights were intelligent, and when I said as much out loud, my friend just smiled.

After I heard the news about his passing, other mutual friends began contacting me to see if I'd heard, because the man and I had been in a relationship for a short time after that night. I also began reading post comments on a Facebook page about Bachelors Grove that my colleague had long maintained. A number of friends and strangers were sharing that, during their last conversations with the man, he'd talked about being able to summon "lights" or "orbs" in the woods or claimed that he was in contact with "aliens" and "UFOs." One very close friend told me that, while living briefly in Las Vegas a few years ago, our friend had learned to "summon" UFOs in the desert, often with the help of some drug.

Hearing these reports now, some twelve years since that strange night of the lights, the memory of it rushed chillingly back to my mind. Were the lights I'd seen that hot June night the same "UFOs" or "beings" my friend would later teach himself to summon? Were they instrumental somehow in what happened to

him so many years later?

I thought, too, of my fairies in that barn in long ago Indiana, and I thought of bill Fogarty and those students who got more than they bargained for. I thought of Stephen Greer.

I thought of Chris Bledsoe.

THE DEEP END

We have seen prominent religious themes and behaviors swirl around UFO contactees, both in the early Contactee movement and today. But today, too, we're seeing a new *secular* UFO religion emerge, and it's one that closely parallels the largest contemporary UFO religion in the world. Despite some differences, in the most important ways both the secular UFO believers and their cult-following brethren are espousing ideas significantly different from the early Contactees and UFO cults that went before. The pioneer UFO cults were underlaid with themes of peace and unity and transcendence of the material world, but the secular UFO religion of today is, rather, run through with threads of physical achievement, technological advancement and domination.

Of course, elements of the classic UFO religions are present, especially in the occult methods and philosophies of many of its practitioners, though generally disguised in more technological terms. But today's believers aren't looking for what the early UFO cults were. Like the secular UFO religion's believers, today's biggest UFO cult members are not on a quest for transcendence, but for something physical: a tangible grail that modern science has always sought. As the great historian of new religions Robert Ellwood has posited, salvation will come "not from Heaven but from the heavens."[118]

Historian of religion Christopher Partridge and others have recognized that the development of UFO cults was closely tied to Theosophy.[119] It was really only after the 1947 Roswell Incident that the belief and practice we know as "UFO religion" began to be called that. Indeed, by then most of the elements were already in place—the superior beings, the masters on other planets, the evolutionary view of the human drama, etc.

But after 1947, there were also flying saucers.

And just like the apports and of the nineteenth century séance rooms dragged the dreams of Spiritualists back down into the hard dirt of materialism, so would the flying saucers deeply transform the Theosophical dreams of transcendental UFO faith into the strangely materialistic one of the early 21st century.

The "I AM" Activity, as its followers call it, is considered by religious scholars to be foremost a Theosophical religion rather than a UFO one. Not only does it predate the modern UFO era, but most of its members believe UFOs to be of little importance. Rather, the religion follows the Masters popular in Theosophy and Eastern religion, and I mention the movement here really only because its founder, Guy Ballard, claimed to have first met one of the Masters while hiking in the Mount Shasta range (site of one of our fabled alien bases).

For the real beginnings of true UFO cults—those founded by individuals visited by actual aliens—, we'll start with—who else?— the Four Georges of the Contactee era.

George Adamski, the first of the saucer faith prophets, was already an established cult leader when he had his monumental initial run-in with the UFOs. [120] As we saw earlier, he was already an avowed Theosophist and occultist when he founded the Royal Order of Tibet in the early 1930s, spreading his gospel of "Universal Progressive Christianity" and "Universal Law." Not incidentally, the Order applied for a license to make wine for use in their religious services, and Adamski would later say that he made a "fortune" selling wine to decidedly non-churchgoers all over Southern California. (He would also remark that, when Prohibition shut down the operations, he had to start up his new scheme: the "saucer crap" as he called it.)[121]

In 1963, Adamski claimed to have been granted a personal audience with Pope John XXIII, prior to his attendance at an interplanetary conference to be held on Saturn. There was, he said, an exchange of gifts. The pope gave Adamski a "Golden Medal of Honor" (found to be a tourist souvenir), and Adamski gave the pope a vial of liquid from the space brothers that was meant to cure his gastric enteritis.

The Brotherhood of Tibet eventually fizzled out.

In George Van Tassel's communications with the extraterrestrial Ashtar we saw the beginning of what would become a prominent UFO religious movement, as many other channelers would also claim to be in contact with the same being. One of Van Tassel's followers formed the breakoff group, Ashtar Command, when Van Tassel denounced the communications of others with his alien friend as unauthentic. That group would gain many followers, but most would profess a Theosophical style, spirituality-based faith which was much different from the physically-grounded, science-based messages and goals of the first Van Tassel-Ashtar communications.

George Hunt Williamson, another of the Four Georges of the early Contactees, merged his extraterrestrial efforts with a small cult known as the Brotherhood of the Seven Rays. With the Brotherhood's founder, Marion Dorothy Martin, Williamson penned a number of books about the real history of humanity as told by the ETs. [122] Scholars have observed that they are largely Theosophy-based rewritings of the Bible to demonstrate that all of its key players were reincarnated from a handful of primary beings, and that spacemen had appeared on earth in the guise of gods and miracle-workers. Though the *Brotherhood* wasn't very successful as a religion, the group's teachings did lay the foundations for the future Erich von Däniken to infect the minds of millions in later years with its insistence that aliens colonized many parts of the earth and created human religions.

The cult of the Fourth George, George King, would enjoy a good deal of success as a major fringe religion that still lives today: the Aetherius society, founded on the messages King channeled from the Great Master Aether, who hailed from the planet Venus. Members work to prevent the destruction of the world, largely by using spiritual energy to, essentially, raise the spiritual condition of humanity. To this end, they rely on "spiritual energy batteries" to store healing energy generated by prayer sessions. A major goal of the Aetherius Society is to pave the way for the "Next Master": humanity's savior, who will descend in a flying saucer.

George King's journey from London cabbie to saucer cult leader is a fascinating one. He was raised by Protestant parents who also dabbled in the occult. King found himself to be a gifted healer, and he naturally gravitated to Theosophy-based communities and individuals on London's religious fringe, mastering yoga—including Kundalini—and developing *psi* abilities as he spiritually "progressed." Then, in 1954, after more than a decade of preparation, a voice spoke to King, telling him to prepare himself to serve as a representative of something called the "Interplanetary Parliament."

If King had any doubt as to the reality of the communication, it was quashed a week later when a renowned swami appeared in King's apartment, despite the locked doors. The visitor not only taught King advanced methods of prayer and yoga, but he also gave him a daunting mission: to form a society to help save the planet.

After the swami left, King found that the advanced training had opened the way for him to receive telepathic communications from the Cosmic Masters. Moving on the swami's orders, he founded the Aetherius Society, renting space in a local London hall to deliver the Masters' messages and assemble his congregation. To the crowds that began to gather, King shared messages denouncing pollution and nuclear energy, war and division.

And he started building things.

Over the years, King labored over the schematics for various devices designed to trap and contain spiritual energy that, he was told by the Masters, manifested during prayer by the Society's "spiritual workers." His "Spiritual Energy Battery" was the most successful. When connected to a "Spiritual Energy Radiator," King was able to affect a controlled release of the energy when needed. Such directed releases have, the Society claims, averted wars and natural disasters. When needed, extra effort drew down extra energy from the *prana*—a sort of cosmic god force of everything—its concentration intensified somehow by an orbiting satellite.

The Society believes in a great cosmic battle between good and evil. It's not a battle between spiritual beings, however, but planetary ones. Just like in the Christian faith, they believe the people of Earth to be under constant attack from dark invaders intent on our destruction. But they're not from Hell.

They're from other planets.

When I was in graduate school studying American religious history, I spent a lot of time visiting headquarters and offices of various fringe religions. I spent a good deal of time in the reading room of the I AM Activity in Chicago's Loop and of the Christian Science faith, and I chatted long hours with modern Theosophists at the headquarters of the Theosophical Society in Wheaton, Illinois. On one occasion—though my family and friends pleaded with me not to—I walked through the door of a Chicago branch of Hubbard Dianetics—the Church of Scientology—on Lincoln Avenue, announcing that I was "curious" about what they do.

The nicest people I'd ever met sat me down and spent the next hour telling me how pretty I was, how smart and clever, and how all these wonderful things about me would be magnified by about a million once I got rid of all the trauma-based junk I was carrying around with me. I could see easily why the movement had so many takers. Indeed, Victoria Nelson writes in *The Secret Life of Puppets* that "[t]he most prominent current UFO religion is probably the science fiction writer L. Ron Hubbard's Church of Scientology."[123].

We can't go too far down the rocky road of Scientology here. Anyone who wants to read the whole twisted story can easily find all the dirty details of government infiltration, fraud, embezzlement, sexual deviancy, the ripping apart of families, and even mysterious disappearances. Far less well known than the fallout, however, are the ties of the religion to extraterrestrials.

Scientology includes the belief that trauma can cause "engrams" in a person's mind that have to be "cleared" by a process called "auditing." Once a person reaches the state called "clear"—being free of these engrams—, they are then allowed to move on to the Operating Thetan levels. At these levels, secret texts are revealed to followers. These texts include the revelation that humans' past lives took place in outer space, and that a catastrophic alien event led to human suffering today—and to the need to purge its effects by "going clear."

L. Ron Hubbard holds the Guiness record for the writer who has published the most words. Many people are called prolific, but Hubbard published nearly a thousand works of fiction and wrote many more that remain in manuscript form. Most of his work was science fiction, and indeed Scientology's founding myth flowed from Hubbard's busy pen and strange mind.

The central figure in Scientology's mythology is an ET by the name of Xenu, an alien ruler from millions of years ago. According to Hubbard's teachings, Xenu, feeling the planets were overcrowded, rounded up beings from a multitude of planets, froze them, and dumped them onto the Earth. The beings died, and their souls attempted to rise, but Xenu prevented their souls' return to their planets by gathering their souls with soul- catching devices. [124] Xenu then had the souls brainwashed and, after, released them to roam the Earth. The souls attached themselves to humans, affecting all kinds of trauma and suffering—and necessitating a savior (L. Ron Hubbard) who could release them from it.

But this dramatic story is far less important to most scientologists than the sort of "feel good" journey each of the faithful is on. With reincarnation guaranteeing life after life after life for Scientologists (and no threats of being stuck in an animal's body if you're bad, like some other reincarnationists believe), Hubbard's followers concentrate on, essentially, living their best lives, which centers on getting rid of trauma and baggage. In fact, Scientology is the only UFO religion that strongly downplays the ET dimension of its tenets.

Today, about 40,000 Scientologists worldwide follow Hubbard's teachings, despite all the shady dealings and bad press.

You may have seen someone carrying around a copy of the *Urantia Book* or studying it in a Starbucks.[125] With almost a quarter of a million copies in print—and topping out at a whopping 2097 pages—it's hard to mistake the iconic, light blue volume that's been staging a quiet Christian (or rather, anti-Christian) revolution for almost three quarters of a century.

Published first in 1955, the *Urantia Book*'s editor claimed that pages of it magically appeared in his desk drawer in Chicago, though in reality it seems to have been largely channeled in the 1930s by a mysterious character known as the "sleeping subject," whose identity was finally revealed some four decades later (of which more shortly).

The *Book* is comprised of 196 messages given to humanity by celestial beings from "higher" universes, and it often reads like a thrilling sci fi novel (no big surprise), with tales of intergalactic governmental drama, planetary colonization and other cosmological adventures. The beings have names like Melchizedek, Evening Star and other biblical-sounding titles, all involved in some way with us and our planet: the planet Earth—that's really called Urantia. In fact, one third of the *Book* is devoted to Jesus, sharing all kinds of detail about his formative years of work, study and teaching before the New Testament accounts begin.

Central to the Urantia teachings is one that would thrill the alien-believing Catholic theologians we'll meet a bit later. For the *Book*'s "revelations' include the fact that there are many so-called "Creator Sons" of God, each of whom oversees his own universe. There are more than 700,000 Creator Sons, who are all incarnations of the Eternal Son (in the *Book*, the "Son" of the Holy Trinity—or one of three Trinities.) Jesus is not our Creator Son. Jesus was just one of seven incarnations of our universe's Creator Son, a being or spirit known as the Michael of Nebadon.

Pivotal to the Urantia teachings is the revelation that Jesus did not have to die to atone for humanity; the *Book* teaches us that this belief was made up by St. Paul and has its roots in pagan beliefs he picked up in Tarsus. Jesus was also born to an ordinary woman after she had sexual intercourse with a man; the "virgin birth" is a myth.

The *Book* is, in fact, *seethingly* opposed to the idea of Jesus's atonement, and we see that it's a particular anti-*Catholic* opposition to it, because not only Jesus's Passion but *any* equating of human suffering with goodness is virulently attacked. The *Book* tells us:

> The barbarous idea of appeasing an angry God, of propitiating an offended Lord, of winning the favor of Deity through sacrifices and penance and even by the shedding of blood, represents a religion wholly puerile and primitive. . . . It is an affront to God to believe, hold, or teach that innocent blood must be shed in order to win his favor or to divert the fictitious divine wrath" (60).

But lest Catholics feel singled out, we're just a bigger part of the problem. It's *all religion* that's to blame for Earth's sad place toward the very bottom of all the planets, and the *Book* says everything from worship to penance to prayer to sin is rooted in "primordial ghost fear."

It was a Seventh-day Adventist minister and psychologist who first assembled and published the *Urantia Book*. Dr. William Sadler was a professor at the University of Chicago in the early 1930s when he was approached by a neighbor concerned about her husband. She told Sadler that her spouse had developed a habit of falling into a deep sleep and speaking about strange things. Sadler would discover that the strange things were very strange indeed. In fact, while unconscious the man would become, in Sadler's words "a sort of clearing house for the coming and going of alleged extra-planetary personalities.".

Sadler found himself in a particularly difficult situation. Not only were the "revelations" of the sleeping subject astounding, but Sadler had spent the past decade actively debunking claims of Spiritualists and other occult practitioners, writing against them and even assisting the famed skeptic Harry Houdini in his anti-Spiritualist escapades.

But Sadler was more intrigued than put off, and so he was delighted when the sleeping subject said he and his friends could assemble a list of questions for the cosmic beings to answer. In the following months, the beings answered some four thousand questions put to them. The responses, which the subject's wife said were written in a single evening, filled almost five hundred pages.

By 1935, Sadler had left the Seventh-day Adventists and his attendant ministry, so he had plenty of time on his hands when the entities told the subject they wanted their body of knowledge published. It took twenty years, but in 1955 the first printing of the *Urantia Book* was complete. It would be some thirty-five more years, however, before the sleeping subject's identity would be revealed, as Sadler had sworn to keep it under wraps.

Well-known skeptic Martin Gardner was under no such oath when, in 1991, he managed to affirm the sleeping subject to have been one Wilfred Custer Kellogg, Sadler's own brother-in-law (and a distant relative of the Seventh-day Adventist/breakfast cereal-touting W.K. Kellogg).[126] He'd died in 1956, a year after the *Book*'s publication. In identifying the sleeping subject, Gardner was able to piece together a few more parts of the Urantia puzzle, and he found that the religious background of Kellogg and Sadler explained a lot of it, noting marked similarities between the "corrections" of Kellogg's ETs and those of the Seventh-day Adventist creed.

The *Urantia Book* has won over significant swathes of Christianity of every denomination, including Catholics, who are attracted by its easygoing (and decidedly anti-Christian) teachings. As an anecdotal aside, throughout my career I have encountered numerous teachers at every level in both Catholic and secular schools who were incorporating the Urantia "revelations" into their curricula, including Catholic RCIA and CCD teachers who not only shared "daily readings" from the *Book* but had their students do projects based on the Urantia teachings.

The *Book* combines devoutly Christian tenets such as belief in one supreme God, the Trinity, and so forth with New Age facets and—best of all—a doing away with the idea of Hell. When we die, the cosmic messengers tell us, we simply go on to another world to keep learning and growing closer to God. Everyone gets to go, and there's no repentance necessary. Many adherents of the Urantia teachings are also attracted by the hefty dose of scientific jargon and theory in its pages. Indeed, the book is heavy on evolution, physics, consciousness theory and other topics fascinating (and validating) to our STEM-obsessed age.

The *Urantia Book* has also inspired at least one UFO religion, and it's a notorious one indeed.

Gabriel of Urantia, born in Pittsburgh as Tony Delevin, claims to be a spiritual leader who is the only "Audio Fusion Material Complement" on Earth, and he boasts what he says is a unique connection to celestial beings. Residing in southern Arizona, Gabriel leads a group that follows teachings influenced by The *Urantia Book* and Delevin's own writings, which he considers to be divine revelations.

The group has long been mired in controversy, with reports of strict discipline, lack of access to medical care and a hierarchical structure that places Gabriel and his family squarely over other group members who live in squalor and perform slave labor. Former members have also spoken out about the group's unquestionably cultish atmosphere, sharing details about Delevin's tight control over personal lives and finances, which includes an unapologetic requirement to surrender all belongings to Gabriel and his wife, Niánn.

Gabriel predicts apocalyptic events, such as the return of Jesus Christ on a "Mothership" spaceship, and a forthcoming planetary evacuation for which he and his followers are preparing. Like Steven Greer, Chris Bledsoe and others, Gabriel also summons UFOs.

Dr. Raul Valverde, a senior lecturer in information and supply chain systems at Concordia University in Montreal, noticed the stark similarities between revelations of the *Urantia Book* and those of a Mexican UFO experiencer named Pablo Hawnser in the early 2000s. [127] Hawnser said he was walking to his home in Mexico City from a neighboring town when he was visited by a flying saucer piloted by what looked like humans. A string of communications began, at first by telephone, which led to Hawnser receiving many revelations about God, Earth, humanity, and the nature, structure and physical functioning of the universe.

In his paper, "Alien Encounters, the Theology of the *Urantia Book*, and the Origins of Human Consciousness," Valverde hopes to not only show the similarities between the Urantia revelations and those of Hawnser's ETs, but to expand the *Book* to include the latter's clarifications of the origins of human consciousness, as told by the ETs. To that end, Valverde includes as part of his research an extensive chart showing the truly remarkable similarities between many of the revelations of the *Urantia Book* and those of Hawnser's aliens.

In the early 1970s, Marshall Applewhite founded a religious group which would enjoy little success in its short lifetime. His cult, however, would end with a bang—or, rather, whimper—heard 'round the world. In 1997, Applewhite convinced his followers that a UFO was hiding behind a comet that was making headlines. The UFO was coming to pick them all up, but it wasn't going to take their bodies.

It was going to take their souls.

In what became one of the most shocking in America's long history of fringe religious tragedies, Applewhite would convince 39 of his cult members to engage in mass suicide, with the promise that, once they shed their mortal coils, their spirits would be taken up by this alien craft. His followers simply laid down, took a lethal cocktail of poison and quietly waited for their hearts to stop beating.

In the aftermath, the only way the outside world even knew what this was all about was due to the taped "exit statements" that the members left behind. This in addition to the voluminous writings of Applewhite himself over the years, which led up to this strange and shocking event.

Applewhite was an interesting but troubled character. He was born in 1931 to a Presbyterian preacher and his wife, who doubtlessly wished that their son would follow in their religious footsteps. But Applewhite had other plans, he seemed to want to make it big on Broadway. He went to Austin College, where he became involved in theatrical productions, and he lent his vocal talent to performing in musicals.

It was after he himself failed to become a star that Applewhite settled on the role of music professor at a local private college in Houston, Texas. Shortly thereafter, he married and started a family. But it just wasn't meant to be. After several mental breakdowns, his marriage fell apart and Applewhite ended up in a psych ward. It was here that he met a woman named Bonnie Nettles who worked as a nurse.

The pair apparently really hit it off together and shared many of the same religious/spiritual views. So much so, that Bonnie quit her job, and she and Applewhite hit the road to spend several years as wandering speakers in the New Age circuit. It was somewhere along the way, during these New Age conferences that they picked up the idea that UFOs were guiding their quest for spiritual enlightenment.

Interestingly, it was in 1973 that Applewhite first started talking about how he and others would one day be raised to heaven "in a cloud." It was the following year, that he changed the word "cloud" to "UFO."

As another interesting aside, it has been pointed out by some ancient astronaut theorists, that the Bible often speaks of folks being mysteriously transported in "clouds." It has further been suggested that these clouds are actually akin to the modern-day concept of a flying saucer/alien spacecraft.

The notion here is that the ancients saw some circular things descend from the heavens, pick people up, and then rise back up to the heavens. For them, it was like a cloud had suddenly descended. Applewhite—at least on some level—seemed to subscribe to this theory.

Bonnie would later die of cancer, and Marshal would be left alone to lead his New Age, UFO flock. This group would then become known as Heaven's Gate. [128]His views would become increasingly radical, leading up to his claims that a UFO hiding behind a comet would pick up him and his followers. It was then in March of 1997, that Applewhite placed a special announcement on the "Heaven's Gate" website, in reference to the soon arriving "Hale-Bopp" comet, and the supposed UFO hiding behind it.

The announcement declared, "Hale-Bopp's approach is the marker we've been waiting for. We are happily prepared to leave this world." Later messages reinforced this, as well as his role in all of it. In one message posted to the Heaven's Gate site, Applewhite, solemnly declared, "I am in the same position in today's society as the one that Jesus was in. If you want to go to Heaven, I can take you through that gate."

Applewhite also insinuated that he was not only facilitating a trip to heaven, but also an evacuation from an Earth that was about to be destroyed. Since we are all still here, nearly 20 years later—we can assume that his predictions were off. Nevertheless, Applewhite had warned his followers, "Planet about to be recycled. Your only chance to survive—Leave with us."

And so they did.

It's easy to see that these UFO cults have professed aspects of both Eastern and Western religions, attempting either overtly or unconsciously to mesh the "best of both worlds" of both Christianity and the Theosophical monster created by Blavatsky. It's also easy to see that central to all of them has been a deep desire to escape the violence and darkness of the postwar world. Despite the scientific and technological trappings of these faiths, technology—especially its destructive weaponry—was bad. Earth was on a fast track to Armageddon. Earth people were bumbling. In summary, in the great unfolding of Earth's history, something had gone terribly wrong. But the failure of technology would not be retained as the future of UFO religion rolled out, and the very different ideas of one leader in particular would emerge as eerily similar to those of today's wider secular world: a world embracing technology more than ever.

On December 13, 1973, race car driver Claude Vorilho experienced his monumental contact moment when a flying saucer descended upon him in France's Clermont-Ferrand mountain range. [129] A being he called an extraterrestrial invited Vorilhon to attend a Bible study, echoing earlier ET claims to George Adamski that history had been misinterpreting the book's teachings, and that they must be reinterpreted in light of technological advancements.

Vorilhon would also learn that ETs are, in fact, scientists, and that they call themselves the Elohim. Bible scholars will be well versed in this word, because it's the Hebrew word for both God and gods. But Raël also learned that the term is not a religious one but a scientific one, because it refers to the fact that the beings created humanity using their own DNA, in their "own image" of course, just as the Bible says in Genesis. Then the aliens gave the enlightened Frenchman a new name, Raël (taken from Israël) and sending him into the world to proclaim the scientized version of Christianity: there is no God, only technology and science. In fact they said to Raël, "*We are* technology and science."

That is to say: *science and technology are god.*

Central to Raël's gospel is the need for humanity to disarm itself of weapons of mass destruction, cast off theistic beliefs in a celestial God and go forth towards the materialist goals of the Elohim—the goals of technology and science.

Raëlism also, somewhat notoriously, espouses a brand of "free love." This sexual liberty runs eerily through all "UFO spirituality," though it certainly wouldn't be approved of by the traditional Christian faith.

The Elohim told Raël that Jesus was not so much resurrected as physically cloned and "re-created." He posits that, rather than seeking escape from a physical container, as in Heaven's Gate, the real goal is to receive an immortal physical body. This is, somewhat weirdly (although very loosely) in line with traditional church teachings, since Scripture insists that in the end Christians will be physically resurrected in glorified bodies that will be immortal. Raël puts a scientific spin on this, by insisting that such things are achieved with advanced methods in cloning and genetic engineering.

In 1995 Raël formed CLONAID, a company specializing in cloning human beings to create children. At nearly a quarter of a million dollars per child, it wasn't cheap, but with God revealed to be nonexistent, it was the only way to eternal life. Heaven would be achieved on Earth, not by a savior god, but by humans' own evolutionary-focused efforts.

Today, some 60,000 people follow Raël's teaching "updating" Biblical tradition with a science, tech and aliens-based overhaul. And it's not only all staunchly atheistic, but overtly anti-Catholic as well. [130] A quick news search on Google will yield plentiful accounts of Raëlians frequent social stunts like giving out condoms to Catholic school students and distributing crosses to Christian teens, inviting them to burn the religious symbols in public.

A number of scholars have compared UFO cults to the "cargo cults" that emerged in Melanesia during the native people's first contact with non-locals, in the form of the military. These strangers arrived on mysterious craft from the air and introduced wondrous things like packaged food, manufactured clothing and generators that powered televisions, radios and electric lights. Naturally, these "saviors" were hailed as gods.

After their technological saviors left—taking their wondrous technology with them—the natives took to building runways, control towers and other structures whatever they could find, to mimic those built by their vanished technological saviors. They sat in makeshift bamboo towers wearing useless radio "headgear" fashioned from straw, lit fires along the runways and made motions like those they'd seen the air traffic controllers enact, believing these to be religious rituals that would bring back the technology gods in their aircraft. But they didn't come back. Because their technological "saviors" weren't gods..

Today's UFO cults are different. The technological "saviors"—the gods they're trying to contact—do exist, and the rituals they're using to contact them actually work.

But those gods are not coming on spacecraft.

And they're not spacemen.

AWOL FOR THE ANTICHRIST

In the summer of 1990, six United States soldiers stationed in Europe went AWOL, shortly reappearing across the ocean in Gulf Breeze, Florida, just as a UFO flap—and a UFO convention!—was underway there. If that doesn't sound strange enough, the actual details of the story make it exponentially more bizarre.

This highly unusual tale begins on July 9, 1990, just prior to the Iraqi invasion of Kuwait, which would ultimately lead to the Gulf War. The six soldiers in question had been stationed as intelligence specialists in Augsburg, Germany, working under the auspices of the 701st Military Intelligence Brigade. Their disappearance should have been impossible, but somehow this group of renegades was able to purchase plane tickets and hop a flight to the U.S. unnoticed and unquestioned. The military fugitives would not be tracked down until several days later. When they were, it wasn't military intelligence that led to their capture but simple, everyday police work.

After landing on American soil, the soldiers managed to purchase an old van, and the decrepit vehicle was spotted on the road with a taillight that wasn't working. This led a local cop to pull the vehicle over. Apparently, the officer didn't take too kindly to motorists with broken taillights rolling around Gulf Breeze and was determined to hand out a ticket.

The officer quickly learned that the driver was an AWOL soldier and arrested him, immediately contacting local military personnel. Soon the local police were being bossed around by military top brass, who told law enforcement to refrain from the usual police interrogation. Whoever these Six were, they had valuable information that the military did not want exposed.

It was after the first member of the Gulf Breeze Six was taken into custody that four others in the group were located at a Gulf Breeze residence. The residence they were crashing at just happened to belong to UFO experiencer Ed Walter's neighbor, Anna Foster. Remember Ed Walters, who reported the "magic wand" and other incidents with aliens?

As for Ms. Foster, she dabbled in the occult and fancied herself to be a clairvoyant. Among the Gulf Breeze Six, it was soldier Kenneth Beason who'd apparently first made Anna's acquaintance when he was previously stationed in Pensacola. Anna was fairly well known in the community, and it's possible that some of her contacts might have also met her through the occult bookstore she ran at the time. Anna was actively involved with MUFON and was closely following the recent Gulf Breeze UFO flap.

After four of the Six were found at Anna's home, the final solder remained at large. It wasn't long before they located the last of the them, the lone female of the group. She was on her own, lounging on the beach.

Now that we've covered some of the background on how these deserters were found—the big question of course, is *why did they desert?* And furthermore, how was their desertion connected to the Gulf Breeze UFO flap?

In one of Ed Walter's controversial books on the Gulf Breeze sightings, he alleges—as we have—that the soldiers must have had some top-secret information on UFOs on their person. According to this theory, it was for this reason that the soldiers were on the run—and the reasoning behind how their apprehension was handled. For even though the bizarre tale was big news when it first hit the press, it seems that someone high up immediately put the brakes on the story. In a matter of weeks, there was complete radio silence on the strange escapade.

Before this sudden embargo on information about the Gulf Breeze Six, however, some interesting tidbits had surfaced, and much of it centered around soldier Kenneth Beason and supposed psychic Anna Foster. Beason had apparently visited the home of his sister, Carolyn, and her husband, Charles Reed, just prior to arriving at Anna's house, and Charles Reed, for one, was ready to talk.

Reed claimed that Beason had told him the government was trying to conceal concrete evidence of an extraterrestrial presence on Earth. Beason had also claimed that it was Anna Foster who had introduced Beason and the others to a UFO group which was seeking to reveal this presence to the public. Reed claimed to take none of it seriously, but he also seemed to shift all the blame for the subsequent disturbances—including the soldiers' desertion—onto Anna Foster.

He told the local *News Journal,* "If anybody should be arrested, it should be that lady." [131]

Some have suggested that perhaps the strange ramblings of the group were a smokescreen, and that the Six were sent by military intelligence handlers to keep tabs on Ed Walters himself. Why? Well, according to some, the Gulf Breeze Six—and maybe even the government—believed Ed Walters was the Antichrist.

The unofficial leader of the Gulf Breeze Six was Beason. At 26 years old, he originally hailed from Middlesboro, Kentucky. Partners in crime were Spec. Vance Davis, originally from Valley Center, Kansas, Pfc. Michael Hueckstaedt, 19, Farson, Wyoming.; Pfc. Kris Perlock, 20, Osceola, Wisconsin.; Pfc. William Setterberg, 20, Pittsburgh, Pennsylvania; and Sgt. Annette Eccleston, 22, from Hartford, Connecticut.

According to their story, the group had come together in the fall of 1989 over a mutual interest in the paranormal. They'd decided to try some experiments to see if there was any reality to things like tarot cards, spoon bending and mind reading, as well as spirit communication, but they had little luck in obtaining results. That is, until one of them introduced a Ouija board.

Vance Davis would later tell reporters that, over the course of several months, numerous spirits communicated to the analysts via the board, predicting things such as the Iraq War and several natural disasters. The board also sent through a number of Catholic saints, and even the Blessed Virgin Mary, in order to convince Eccleston, who was raised Catholic, of the truth of the messages—despite, of course, the Catholic teaching against spirit communication.

"Mary" apparently also wanted some information. On one occasion, she asked how many personnel were employed at the NSA listening station in Germany.

After the group became dependent on and fully confident in the messages, then came the kicker. Things were changing, the spirits told them. They had to get out of the Army and get back home. They would be needed to help humanity deal with an enormous, looming crisis to come. The spirits even confided that Jesus would be rapturing the faithful in short order. All hell was about to break loose. The Tribulation was at hand.

When the soldiers failed to find a way to an honorable discharge, the board gave them a final command:

"Leave. Just leave."

So the Six—all highly respected intelligence analysts with not a single black mark on their military records or personal lives—just left.

You could probably guess by this chapter that most of the Six had previously dabbled in the occult, even prior to the Ouija board business in Germany. Beason was interested in aliens and had studied hypnosis. Perlock had met Anna Foster—the "psychic"—before shipping out to Europe. He'd been taking cryptology training in Pensacola. But it was Vance Davis that had the most experience with high strangeness.

Davis had taken a course in Silva Mind Control when he was in high school. He would later tell late night paranormal radio host Art Bell that he was recruited by the National Security Administration (NSA) while still in AIT school. He believed it was because of his Silva training, based on notes in his file. Davis would later claim in his book, *Unbroken Promises: A True Story of Courage and Belief,* that he had been contacted by a female extraterrestrial during the paranormal adventures of his youth. With greenish skin and dressed in yellow, the female ET named "Kia" corrected his flat-footedness overnight and told the young man that she hailed from a planet forty-five light years away. (Not incidentally, I think, Kia is a magical term for a sort of universal consciousness; it's associated with Wicca as well as Alesiter Crowley's goddess Babalon (as in Jack Parsons' Babalon Working).

The details of Kia's life appeared somewhat like those of Princess Leia from the *Star Wars* franchise. She was the heroic female commander of her race, the Kiasseions, who were traveling to Earth to assist the "Alliance" in saving humanity. Their own planet had been destroyed by evil cosmic lords, and the remnant of Kia's people—about fifteen thousand in all—were on board five enormous spacecraft..

After his discharge, Davis told MUFON that Beason had been hypnotizing him and the other five members of the experimental group back in Germany, and in his own book, he wrote that the Ouija board had sent them to find a woman in Munich named Gabriel who gave them some "UFO documents" that were confiscated during their later arrest in Florida.

So where is our friend Ed Walters in all of this? Some have suggested that perhaps the strange ramblings of the group were a smokescreen, and that the Six were sent by military intelligence handlers to keep tabs on Ed Walters himself. According to some, the Gulf Breeze Six—and maybe even the U.S. government— believed that Ed Walters was the Antichrist, a statement given to the military newspaper, the *Stars and Stripes*, by a member of the Six's unit. Further, having been looking into the bizarre saga, the same newspaper reported on July 28, 1990 that

> Stan Johnson of Bybee, Tenn., a friend of one of the soldiers, Spec. Kenneth G. Beason, 26, said Beason told him they had been 'chosen by DIVINE INTERVENTION [*caps theirs*] to help prepare for the end of the world, which was supposed to occur in about EIGHT YEARS FROM NOW.' Johnson added that, 'when the second coming of Christ occurred, Jesus Christ was going to ARRIVE IN A SPACESHIP.'

After Beason and his fellow soldiers had first arrived stateside at an airport in Knoxville, Tennessee, they'd been aided by a friend Beason had in the area: a man by the name of Stan Johnson. It was Johnson who'd helped the group acquire a van, which they then used to drive down to Gulf Breeze. Exactly what transpired during their time in Gulf Breeze prior to their arrest remains unclear, but we do get a small glimpse into all of this from none other than Ed Walters himself, who lived next door to Anna Foster.

According to Walters' book,[132] it was on Saturday, July 14th, 1990, that Anna Foster's teenaged daughter showed up at his home in tears. The girl was friends with Walters' own daughter, and the girl explained how the FBI had stormed into her home in the middle of the night to take the soldiers staying with them into custody.

By the time of their arrest, a lot of strange anecdotes about the soldiers being mentally unstable and even being part of a cult had leaked to the press. Curiously, these reports largely omitted the fact that this group had super high military clearances. At any rate, once the group was in custody, the soldiers were mysteriously cleared of all charges and given general discharges.

As if this story wasn't bizarre enough already, on July 25th news media received an anonymous letter. The letter stated:

> *US ARMY, Free the Gulf Breeze Six.*
> *We have the missing files.*
> *The Box of 500 + photos and the plans you want back.*

The note was printed in local papers, and although the army never acknowledged having anything to do with this message, it was shortly thereafter that the group was turned loose. After just twenty-one days in jail, the six were honorably discharged by order of General Colin Powell, then Chairman of the Joint Chiefs of Staff under President George Bush, shocking all who were following the story.

In late of July of 1992 Vance Davis went to the press for the first time since his discharge from the Army two years prior.[133] He told a reporter that it was now time for him to come forward because of the events that had broken out in Los Angeles, referencing the infamous Rodney King race riots that erupted in April and May of that year.

The spirits had given the group a warning. Huddled around the Ouija board one night, the board had spelled out the signs that would alert them that the end was near: the eruption of Mount Ranier, a disaster in New York City, and riots and food crises in every major U.S. city, leading to economic collapse.

JUST HERE FOR THE SOULS

It would have been around 2004, when I was living in a duplex with my daughters on Ravenswood Avenue in Chicago, that I got a call late one Sunday afternoon from a close friend of mine. I remember very clearly that I was standing in the kitchen there, gazing out of the huge front window that overlooked the railroad embankment. It was already getting dark. At the time, my friend was in the U.S. Naval Reserves, working there one weekend a month as an intelligence analyst. When he called me, this nearly forty-year-old man and veteran Chicago police officer was crying.

I at first thought he must have suffered a loss in his family, or that something terrible had happened to a mutual friend of ours. But no. Something had happened to him while driving home from his duty weekend at Great Lakes Naval Training Station on Chicago's North Shore.

Let me give you a little background on my friend. He grew up in Chicago and as a child had many vivid "dreams" about being visited and even taken by aliens. The house he grew up in was "haunted" too, and various types of poltergeist activity was always a part of life, such as footsteps on the stairs, banging sounds coming from the basement and the sound of music playing.

At any rate, on that late Sunday afternoon, he had finished his duty shift and had proceeded to drive home south on Sheridan Road, which as Chicagoans know runs along Lake Michigan all the way down into the city. This was the way he preferred to go rather than traveling on the expressway.

You probably think this is going to be a UFO-sighting story, what with my friend driving along that darkening road in the twilight, alone.

But no. This is a very, very different story.

This was at a time when we all still had flip phones. Text messaging was a brand-new thing. My friend had changed cell carriers a few months previous, and the phone from his new carrier featured texting, though he'd never used it. As he drove, however, he heard a notification sound come through the phone in his briefcase. He'd never heard the sound before and, wondering if it was an alert for a voicemail from his commander back at the base, he pulled the car over to check it out. He fished around for the phone and took it out to look at it. The screen said:

NEW TEXT MESSAGE

After fumbling around for a minute to try and figure out how this new-fangled text messaging worked, he finally got the message to open.

The message had come from his own old telephone number.

In those days, if you changed cell carriers, you got a new phone number. That old phone was, he knew, dead. There was no battery in it, and it was locked up in a file cabinet in his old bedroom at a family members' house, where he was living at the time. Furthermore, the account was closed. There was no way this message could be coming from that phone, or from any phone.

He read the message. It said:

PREPARE TO SHED YOUR CONTAINER.

The idea of human beings as "containers" for souls is one that's become well known in ufology. If you recall our friend Billy Meier and the alien/demon Semjase, Meier would report that his ET contacts were recording the "soul patterns" of human beings.

As bizarre as it sounded, Meier's claim would be one echoed by subjects studied by the late esteemed Harvard professor and UFO researcher John Mack. Mack interviewed several abductees who also insisted that the human soul was at the center of the UFO phenomenon. One abductee, "Eva," even tried to suggest that— whether they realize it or not—, contactees are chosen to be involved with this ET project before they are even born. For me, Eva's claim was evocative of something the late Jesuit exorcist

Malachi Martin wrote in his monumental book, *Hostage to the Devil*: the relationship between the demon and the possession victim begins before the target's birth.

It was UFO "whistleblower" and alleged former Area 51 employee Bob Lazar who most famously claimed that ETs refer to humans as "containers." Lazar, whose identity and history have been hotly debated in recent years, claimed that, while working at Area 51, part of the mountain of debriefing documents he'd been given revealed the shocking information that human bodies are viewed by aliens as physical shells containing their true essences—their souls—,and that aliens want these souls *and* these containers.

Badly.

Lazar went on to claim, as Richard Doty had to Bennewitz and Howe, that ETs were responsible for the establishment of human religion thousands of years ago, and that they'd created them as a way to help humans could live in peace (not kill each other) and keep from damaging their "containers" which are "rare" and "very difficult to find."

Another abductee interviewed by Mack whose name comes down to us as "Mark" concurred with Lazar's assertion, speaking of his belief that ETs actually "recycle" the souls of humans. According to Mark, ETs are actively involved in the evolution of human consciousness by recycling souls into different bodies and redirecting them through numerous lifetimes: that old New Age doctrine of reincarnation.

One of the most surprising talking heads to express belief in the soul harvesting by aliens was none other than the late John Lear, who became close friends with Bob Lazar and seemed to believe every word of Lazar's claims, without exception. Lear's appearance on the late Art Bell's radio show was one of the things that led to my compulsion to find out more about this UFO phenomenon that had never much interested me.

Lear became a controversial figure who captivated the imagination of many with his claims regarding aliens on the moon and the involvement of ETs with human souls. The son of aviation pioneer William Lear (of Lear jet fame), John was an accomplished pilot himself and held various flight records. However, it was his extraterrestrial beliefs that would make him both revered and dismissed by different circles.

When I heard Lear mention "containers" to Art Bell, my mind flew back to that Sunday evening long ago, and my friend's tearful, terrified call. I began Googling "aliens" and "containers" and, eventually, found Nick Redfern's book, *Final Events*, which we've explored in detail. The book's description promised that it shared an enigmatic story of a secret government group that believes aliens are demonic entities. I went on Amazon to buy the book and saw to my surprise that I had already purchased it (also from Amazon) many years earlier. I hadn't read it, but I soon remembered that I had *bought it for my friend* (the text message recipient) as a Christmas present.

It made me feel better, but only for a minute. I consoled myself, thinking that he must have had some kind of weird paranormal technological experience based on reading the book I gave him. After all, I am a parapsychologist and believe in all kinds of strange possibilities. In fact, as an ITC researcher, I had at the time been exploring the possibility that we can embed phones, computers and tape recorders with our own thoughts.

I quickly, however, realized that's not what had happened. When I pulled up the order history on Amazon, I found that I had bought him the book in 2008: easily four years *after* he had made that chilling call to me from the side of the road that Sunday afternoon. So ITC, PK, *and* some kind of unconscious precognition at the same time? Even I found that highly unlikely.

But back to John Lear.

During the course of his decades of appearances as an expert on the subject, Lear shared a lot of interesting information about space, time and flight. As time went on, the content of his information became exponentially more disturbing. In particular, he would claim that the Earth's moon is made of fiberglass, was towed to its current position in space, and is today home to mysterious structures and bases built by advanced alien civilizations. According to Lear, the moon is not just a lifeless celestial body but a thriving hub of extraterrestrial activity. He claimed further that NASA had been hiding evidence of these structures and tampered with its mission photographs to conceal the truth.

While there are certainly many anomalies in moon images that can be spotted by enthusiasts and those with a vivid imagination, such assertions are often dismissed by mainstream scientists. Skeptics argue that these anomalies can be attributed to natural geological formations or mere distortions caused by the inherent limitations on attempts to capture images from vast distances in space.

However, Lear's followers argue that his claims should not be easily dismissed. They believe in a longtime conspiracy to hide the truth about an alien presence on the moon, and that Lear was one of the few brave individuals willing to speak out about it, and they point to inconsistencies in NASA's explanations of certain lunar phenomena as evidence of a cover-up.

Inarguably, the most affecting aspect of Lear's beliefs was his claim about the connection of aliens and the moon with human souls. Influenced by Lazar and his friend and famed contactee Whitley Strieber—of whom a lot more later—, Lear proclaimed that our souls are not eternal and are instead recycled after death by aliens, echoing what Bob Lazar claims to have learned in his alleged "debriefing" and what Richard Doty was known to have claimed in his disinformation campaigns.

Lear hypothesized that mysterious "towers" seen in lunar photos were sort of combination soul sucker/transmitters used to pull souls out of their physical bodies at death and transmit them into new bodies later. In a wistful admission to Art Bell, Lear said that, at his death, he fully expected to end up on the moon.

He also shared the "knowledge" that the "tunnel of light" reported in so many NDEs is "a trap" that leads the soul into the clutches of aliens, and that when we die we should try to run from it and not to it, a claim that thoroughly spooked even many of Bell's weirdness-hardened listeners.

This "information" Lazar saw at Area 51 obviously stemmed from the junk reports of our old friends at MKOFTEN and the Collins Elite: in particular, from the case of Paul Garratt's "visit to Hell" NDE which the Collins Elite had investigated, and from the messages Sybil Leek had delivered while in a "trance" before the two government groups.

Later, the remote viewing group who calls itself Farsight would back up these ideas. If you want to hasten your UFO-propelled insanity, spend some time on the website of Farsight, where they share information about what JFK is doing in the afterlife and the shocking "revelation" that a stand-in was crucified in the place of Jesus!

Of souls and UFOs, Farsight shares a documentary the group made to let people know what happens when we die: information they obtained through remote viewing. From their website:

> When people die on Earth, a technique was established to involuntarily recycle them back into another life on this planet, memory free, so that they could never leave. Dying offers no escape from this place. This nonfiction remote-viewing documentary focuses on the method used to erase people's memories after they die. It is a process that is so cruel, so barbaric, and yet so unbelievable, it is best that you see it for yourself. Any hope of escape from this prison will depend on understanding the workings of the death traps.[134]

It's undeniable that Lear's ideas of these so-called "death traps" have sparked—and spread—a sense of curiosity and wonder in many individuals and (if internet forums and Art Bell's listeners are any indication) absolute horror in many others.

We know now where Lear's chilling ideas came from. Indeed, we know they stem from hypnosis sessions like that of Myrna Hansen back with Bennewitz at the UFO club, from one random man's "near death experience," and from a self-described witch's "trance" before government agents. They ended up in disinformation campaigns as "classified information" and passed to Bob Lazar, Paul Bennewitz, Linda Moulton Howe and who knows how many others. Along the way, the "remote viewers" picked up the idea and ran with it, some likely fraudulently and others likely with a little help from demonic helpers planting images in their minds.

I think, in light of all that's been uncovered about the origins of it, that the soul-eating aliens idea is either dubious or devilish.

Or, most probably, a whole lot of both.

ABOVE ALL OTHER

Late one night, not long after my first UFO revelations began, I was scanning through websites and discovered a Christian scholar detailing how many of the so-called "aliens" in UFO and extraterrestrial visitations often attack Christianity but not other religions.

Though I was only weeks down the UFO rabbit hole, I already knew this to be fact. The entire UFO enigma is wrapped up, as we've already seen, with Eastern religion and Theosophy, and with a wide array of related occult practices such as meditation, yoga, out of body experiences, astral travel, reincarnation, etc., as well as the idea of a sort of "one -world spirituality" of interplanetary unity.

I had also already found myself deep into scores of cases in which Christians had encountered UFO craft or beings and had come away from the experiences to leave their Christian beliefs aside or to incorporate them into a "bigger" religious view that included all religions as part of some "universal truth" or "god consciousness." One contactee exchanged his rosary for Eastern prayer beads, one her bedroom wall Crucifix for a Mandala, and the great majority had come away to begin regularly meditating, practicing yoga, attempting lucid dreaming and other occult methods of "awakening" or "enlightenment."

The fruits of spiritual experience—the way people start thinking and behaving after they have a spiritual encounter—will tell you where the encounter came from. If the encounter inspires you start going to church more, praying more Christian devotions, doing more charity work, becoming humbler: you know it was from God through Christ. If it has the opposite effect—making you seek out other gods, indulging in occult activities, focusing on your own spiritual development and benefit, feeling "divine"—you know from these "rotten fruits" where the experience originated.

As many Christian researchers have also observed, in numerous encounters between these beings and their contactees, the "ETs" are heard to vocally (or, usually, telepathically) denounce Christian belief, especially the truth that Jesus is the incarnate God, just as the Theosophists' celestial friends were known to declare. Most often, the beings deliver a "loving" and "gentle" message of universal truth to "correct" the "divisions" religion has caused. Jesus, they tell contactees, was "one of many teachers" of humankind, and divinity is in *ourselves*.

These encounters recall for me the many cases of Catholic private revelations (spiritual communications to individuals through the ages), in which the one experiencing the vision or message of a purported angel, saint (or even Mary or Jesus Himself) tested the being by inviting it to make the Sign of the Cross or to declare the divinity of Jesus Christ. If the being could pass the tests, that was a good sign that the being was telling the truth and had come from God. Even Saint Bernardette was smart enough to throw holy water on the apparition of the Virgin Mary when she first beheld the vision, knowing better than most of us adults the guises the counterfeiting activities of the devil.

My research into the Christian dimension of UFO experience led me to a man named Joe Jordan, who's been described as the "most hated man in ufology." Jordan has collected to date some six hundred cases in which UFO/ET contactees and abductees were able to stop these terrifying experiences: something ufologists studying the phenomena had long held to be impossible.

The method was a simple one. Time and again, Jordan was finding that contactees and abductees had brought their unwanted visitations to an end by invoking a name.

The name of Jesus.

Jordan was a self-described "New Ager" and science fiction aficionado when he became interested in UFOs after reading the classic work of ufology, *UFO Crash at Roswell* about the alleged 1947 crash. Becoming hooked on the subject, Jordan began seeking out others interested in the UFO enigma, attending meetings of investigators, visiting a UFO museum and reading many more books. Seeking out new reading he wondered at first why there were so many books on spirituality around the UFO subject, but he put the thought aside, plowing ahead to absorb as much knowledge as possible.

Jordan joined his local chapter of MUFON and soon found himself a qualified investigator and, later, state section director. He also found himself all-in with the kind of "UFO religion" that many of his MUFON fellows seemed enamored of. Having long ago abandoned the idea of creationism, Jordan was deeply attracted to the idea of evolved beings leading humanity to technological, environmental and spiritual advancement.

Along with some fellow UFO researchers, Jordan became particularly interested in the phenomenon known as "alien abduction." Together they started a group of their own called CE4 to investigate "Close Encounters of the Fourth Kind": personal encounters with "alien" beings. It was during investigations into two particularly dark abduction cases that Jordan, inspired by a fellow researcher, began to see a demonic element running through their case files.

Not long after, Jordan became a Christian, though he continued to believe in UFOs. It would be almost a decade later that Jordan would read Gary Bates' blockbuster expose, *Alien Intrusion*. The book abruptly ended Jordan's belief in extraterrestrial life, though he observed that many fellow Christians continued to believe in it.

Jordan wasn't looking to prove a Christan hypothesis when he began gathering stories of abduction stopped by the name of Jesus. He was an agnostic at best. But during one of those dark cases, Bill D.—an "abductee"—reported that he'd cried out, "Jesus, help me!" during an attempted abduction, and that the encounter had suddenly stopped.

Intrigued by Bill's experience, Jordan asked other MUFON investigators if they'd had similar cases. A number admitted they had, but they would only share the details if Jordan promised to keep their names out of his reports, telling Jordan this was not "scientific" evidence.

But when Jordan was interviewed by a Florida newspaper, a flood of emails and calls followed, with scores of other "abductees" reporting that the name of Jesus had also stopped their own abduction experiences. The news agency was part of a multi-city service, so the story spread across the country, and Jordan found his phone ringing off the hook with calls from seemingly every area code, and with the same claim.

Immediately upon discovering Jordan's work, my mind flew back to our old friend, Jamsie, caught in the maddening relationship with the familiar spirit who called himself Uncle Ponto. Jamsie's eventual exorcist, Fr. Mark, had given Jamsie some tips to help, essentially, shut up Uncle Ponto when the demon was becoming unbearable, which it often did. The number one thing that helped the most was saying the name of Jesus. Sometimes Jamsie would find himself even spelling the letters over and over, sometimes spelling the name backwards, forewords, repeating it again and again as Uncle Ponto begged him to stop, crying, *"You know we don't like that!"*

Exorcists are very specific about the "doors" people open to demonic infestation, vexation, obsession and possession. As I went on to read every single one of some two hundred eyewitness, firsthand testimonies on Joe Jordan's CE4 website, I found that, time after time, the circumstances leading up to the abduction experience—and even many UFO craft sightings—included the opening of one of those same doors: overt occult inquiry and/or activity, the desire to have an experience or encounter, or some ancestral link such as a family history of psychic ability, witchcraft or other occult participation. Often, drug or alcohol addiction, broken families and other circumstances were also present in the backstories of "abductees." These are all classic "doors" to the demonic, and one or more were behind every one of the demonic infestations, vexations, obsessions and possessions I had encountered in my long career in ghost, haunting and poltergeist research and investigation.

I wasn't surprised, then, when I went on to read that Jordan's group had identified the same conditions behind these experiences. After so many case investigations by the CE4 team. Jordan and his team concluded that, in each case, one or more of the following applied:

> 1. You asked for it. Some people actually ask to have the experience to know what is like or about. Be careful what you ask for.
>
> 2. You unknowingly open a door to the realm of this experience. Some people unknowingly opened a door for the experience, by being involved in New Age or Occult activities. When you engage in the unknown things outside of GOD the Creator and His WORD you make yourself vulnerable to these entities. We have found this reason to be the most often found root cause.
>
> 3. You are part of an ongoing cycle or social conditioning. When asked about the experiencer's parents or early family life, we found that the opening had come from one or more of the parents. It IS important how you raise your children. When there is a GODLY covering over the family by the head of the household, the family is protected. But if there is no GODLY covering, the family is open to these types of unnatural experiences[135]

Many have, of course, criticized and hotly debated Jordan on his findings, claiming that his evidence is "religious" and not "scientific." Yet Jordan, like any good paranormal investigator, is staunchly skeptical, and CE4 ruthlessly dissects every case to first rule out all but the RUFOs (Residual UFOs). For abduction cases, that means ruling out emotional and mental illness, real hallucinations from drug and alcohol use or abuse, neurological issues, sleep disorders, real sleep paralysis (it *is* a thing, Jordan says), memory mistakes (extremely prevalent), false memories, wishful thinking, hoaxes and other issues.

Once again, I was reminded of the rigorous investigations of Catholic exorcists into possible possession cases, in which every alternate explanation is stringently ruled out by the Church before possession is diagnosed and exorcism undertaken.

I was reminded, too, of my own highly skeptical methodology in cases of reported ghosts, hauntings and poltergeists.

WONDROUS THINGS

One of the biggest problems for many in rejecting UFO and ET belief is the physical aspect of the phenomena. In many cases, physical evidence seems to be left behind after an experience with purported craft or alien beings, such as crash material, landing marks, skin burns, scratches, welts and other injuries, and even objects or "implants" found under the skin of abductees.

And yet, physical objects have been part of supernatural experiences throughout history. It's something I've encountered time and time again during my own career as a paranormal investigator and researcher, leading me to conclude that physical evidence does not necessarily mean an experience was not supernatural.

After a long steady stream of data on UFOs and their supposed occupants, there have been a wide variety of theories that have been offered as to who or what they might be. The first theory is one many have held for a very long time: that these craft are from another star system, and that their occupants are biological, living creatures, who have learned how to traverse the vast distance between the stars. As normal people have learned about science, the problems with that have become ever more evident.

The number one criticism of this theory is in regard to how it is that these entities have managed such long flights in a timely manner. The explanation typically offered is that these entities have discovered some form of faster than light travel. If true, then traveling to a destination some 50 to 100 light years away wouldn't take 50 to 100 years—not if they could bend the fabric of space and time to create some sort of shortcut.

Even so, there are many *very strange* aspects of the UFO phenomena that seem more paranormal than flesh-and-blood biological. And yet that physical aspect of them undoubtedly remains.

Since the so-called Enlightenment began, we've been forced to believe that the physical world and spiritual world are separate, and that never the 'twain shall meet. Yet, from early on, as we've seen, some of the most prominent ufologists, including Vallée and Keel, concluded that that we can categorize UFOs and ETs as neither "physical" or "nonphysical" objects and entities.

Many Christians applaud these researchers, believing they are recognizing a spiritual world. But secular ufologists aren't saying these are spiritual phenomena. They're saying that fairies, elves, ghosts, demons, Marian apparitions, cryptids, flying saucers and gray aliens are all what the U.S. government now calls "Unidentified Anomalous Phenomena" or UAP.

What this implies is an acceptance that the natural world contains unseen beings and paraphysical objects and entities. They aren't spiritual, or if they are, they aren't related to the God of the Bible. They're "interdimensional," and they're just another thing that science is going to figure out for us. It's nothing less than the end of theistic spirituality that's being proposed by this new UFO Religion.

And the end of the supernatural.

ELUSIVE EVIDENCE

Let's get real for a minute, literally.

The great majority of UFOs are surely real in the plainest sense of the word. Even nuts and bolts UFO believers agree that 5 percent or fewer of UFO sightings are truly inexplicable. Included in that whopping other 95 percent are stars, planets, satellites, weird clouds, drones, dreams, hallucinations, delusions, hoaxes, lies and plain old wishful thinking, along with the hard, physical craft that are, in the lingo of ufologists, "ours" (the domestic government's), craft developed by other governments, and private sector projects.

That last five percent is the problem. We call those Residual Unidentified Flying Objects (RUFOs), and there are just two theories about what those are. I join those who are convinced that these five percent are distinctly diabolical in origin. The UFO believers say that five percent are "off planet" technology: spacecraft of extraterrestrial development so super advanced that it can't be ours or any human's.

In fact, in the notes of this book you can find a link to a collection of resources demonstrating that much of the "super-advanced technology" that "can't be ours" is, in fact, ours, or at least some human's. So a good chunk of the believers' RUFOs are also quite terrestrial. Putting those aside as well, I will agree with the nuts-and-bolts believers on one thing.

The rest are not of human origin.

But I'll also say, *they're not from outer space.*

We've seen a number of different claims over the years now of "crash material" and "nonhuman" bodies coming out of ufology. We haven't seen any of the actual evidence, however. Nothing has been determined to be of extraterrestrial origin, and no existence of extraterrestrials has been proven. If you listen carefully, occasionally even the most outspoken believers admit that there isn't any evidence, even though they may have very vocally claimed there was.

Even ufology icon Gary Nolan told journalist Tucker Carlson:

> (U)ntil I see a piece of technology that does something I don't understand or until I see an alien body, I am going to also remain skeptical.[136]

Even now, as of this writing nearly a year after David Grusch claimed he could produce plentiful evidence of UFO and "nonhuman biologics" (whatever those are) through some forty witnesses who had shared with him their knowledge of such things, he's produced none of it. Recently, FOIA documents revealed that

Grusch has failed to show up for or agree to meetings with AARO, the agency tasked last year with getting to the bottom of the UFO question. [137] Grush has countered that AARO doesn't have the clearances to hear and see the evidence he has to share. Whatever the truth is, the public still isn't privy to any new evidence, and we're left with another "he said, she said" mess of half-truths and non-information.

In the fall of 2019, yet another incidence surfaced of the government working with private, rather off-the-wall researchers to develop technology from UFO tech,[138] when an organization called To the Stars (formerly To the Stars Academy), headed by musician and UFO buff Tom DeLonge, entered into a five-year contract with the U.S. Army. The Army wanted to study the civilian group's UFO "materials," as the organization had asked individuals and groups to submit their "crash materials" to them for study under their so-called ADAM Project, with a professed end goal of using ET technology to better humanity.

TTSA was founded in 2017 by De Longe, along with remote viewing superstar Hal Puthoff and Jim Semivan, a former senior intelligence officer with the CIA. TTSA offered some $50 million in stock to a public that shared its professed mission of discovering alien technology and bettering the world with it. TTSA sold only about a million dollars of it, and by the fall of 2018 the company had a $34 million deficit. The organization had been structured to pay De Longe $100,000 per year no matter what, and his sister was also paid to help run it. None of this shady management (or mismanagement) stopped the Army from contracting with the organization in the fall of 2019.

One of the materials the organization had acquired was a piece of metal formerly owned by ufologist Linda Howe, which she'd obtained from the late talk show host Art Bell. Bell said he'd gotten the material from the grandson of a Roswell crash witness, and in the accompanying letter to Bell he included a whole extraterrestrial backstory. The materials turned out to be quite terrestrial, but Howe got $35,000 for the material.

We also found out that Tom DeLonge isn't apparently in it just for the good vibes, either. Though the government isn't directly paying TTSA, it committed to spend at least three quarters of a million dollars to help TTSA develop technologies from their "alien crash materials."

Diana Pasulka's latest books also introduced another, unconnected group of people who are talking a lot about alien technology and crash material. Along with Tim Taylor, the NASA scientist who gets ideas for new, moneymaking technologies from alien "downloads" to his brain, we also met through a man she calls "James" in her book. His real name is Gary Nolan, and he's a genius. In the following, I'll be referencing some of the things he's said and done, based on his public interviews.[139]

Nolan is a pathology and immunology expert working at Stanford, and he's become a well-known figure in ufology.[140] It was Nolan who analyzed the so-called Atacama skeleton, a Chilean artifact which ufologists at first believed to be the corpse of an extraterrestrial, but which Nolan found to be a mummified human stillborn infant exhibiting numerous genetic mutations. Nolan, who also has apparently become a multi-millionaire from selling medical tech companies, is also a self-described science fiction fan.

In numerous public interviews, Nolan tells of how the CIA and representatives of an aerospace corporation came to him for help in understanding why some military and civilians who had been physically harmed—and had even died—as a result of their encounters with UFOs. He also claims he went on to study materials given him by the Pentagon and the CIA of materials supposedly ejected at sites of UFO sightings. Pasulka invited him to join her in the New Mexico desert to see the crash material promised by Tim Taylor—an outing documented in Pasulka's *American Cosmic*. Taylor blindfolded them before driving them to the site, where they found two pieces of material that Pasulka has said she can't explain.

Like so many ufologists, Nolan experienced close encounters with what seemed to be extraterrestrials as a child, sighting a UFO while finishing his morning paper route. Much later, in his thirties, he was visited in his bedroom by a humanoid figure. He also says he found what he believed was an "extraterrestrial artifact" and that he was visited by the notorious MIB.

Nolan has publicly said that there are aspects of the materials that don't make sense as far as why such materials would be engineered. But so far the public has been shown nothing has been shown to be of non-terrestrial origin. A scant few have wondered why Nolan has become the expert in metals when he is neither a physicist or engineer

Nolan has made conflicting statements about extraterrestrial life. He has said publicly that he is "100 percent certain" that aliens have visited Earth, but he also, again, told Tucker Carlson that he does not actually have evidence of that. He has also shared his belief that the beings people see are "biological avatars" and not the beings themselves.

It's kind of the exact same thing Christians are saying: that these "ETs" are not what they seem to be; rather, they are manufactured vessels housing nonhuman consciousness.

Despite the fact that none of these "exotic materials" can be proven to be extraterrestrial, it's also true that many physical effects have been reported in connection with UFO and alien encounters, including bodily harm, marks seemingly left behind by physical objects, and messages of unknown origin delivered over radios, phones, computers and even text messaging, as well as paranormal activity such as poltergeist activity, levitation and other physical phenomena.

What are we to make of what seem to be nonphysical beings and craft that leave physical evidence behind? For someone who doesn't believe in the spirit world, the physicality *and* non-physicality of UFOs and ETs must be quite a conundrum.

Not for me.

In fact, physical artifacts and evidence have long surfaced during ghost, poltergeist and other paranormal events, and during my own career I've encountered a number of such cases. In fact, there was a period of time toward the end of my occult-laced work in the paranormal in which very physical signs were part of my own experience with "ghosts."

TOUCHED

Vexation is a stage of demonic attack that includes physical assaults. It's often seen as a "lead up" to possession, as the demon is attacking the person mentally *and* physically but has not overtaken the person's body completely. My own vexation began when I commenced a relationship with a man who was both a medium and a known expert in Electronic Voice Phenomenon (EVP) research (spirit communication via electronic means), which we'll look at in depth in a later chapter. Even after we broke things off and he was gone and far away, the vexation continued—and then amped up again as I went further into the world of EVP.

During these years it was not uncommon for me to wake up with bruises on my body as if a large man's hand had been squeezing my arm or leg with intense force. You could see the imprint of the fingertips or, at times, even the entire hand on my skin. This was after my divorce, before reuniting with my husband, and while I was still doing very un-Catholic things like dating while divorced. Still, while I was seeing men, I did not have anyone living with me and did not have people staying overnight with me. Nor was I involved in any extreme physical activities. In fact, these bodily marks would also occur later, when I was alone again except for my adolescent daughters. I also at times bore scratches or other marks that looked like teeth that would appear without any cause.

Sometimes I would be trying to fall asleep and would be poked in my arm or back by unseen fingers. One night I woke up as a strong hand was trying to roll me off of my bed; another strong hand suddenly pulled me back on from the other side.

I also began to hear voices when I was alone. Voices speaking my name or whispering, "Hey!" in a harsh tone.. Other times I would be trying to record lectures and other audio material and there would be Voices that would show up in my recordings, making it difficult to complete what I was trying to do.

I also observed physical evidence in others.

One weekend, some friends invited me to a paranormal investigation in an old Catholic rectory in the neighborhood of Sedamsville in Cincinnati, Ohio. Sedamsville Rectory had become known only recently as a hotbed of paranormal activity. According to legend, the building had been used to house priests who had been ousted from their parishes for sexual abuse. After that, it had become a secret venue for underground dog fights.

I drove to Ohio with my longtime friend, who I'd met years ago when she invited me to speak at a meeting of the ghost hunting group she belonged to in Northwest Indiana. We arrived at the rectory and toured the building in preparation for the evening's investigation. It was an unsettling place, and we found, sure enough, that the backs of all of the doors were deeply scratched, evidence of the abuse of those poor dogs years before.

The night was full of activity. At one point we held a séance, and a young man who was an avowed skeptic had a large part of his forearm become intensely hot: a fact picked up by our investigators' thermal cameras. When the lights were turned back on, his entire forearm bore an obvious red wound as if he'd been severely burned.

In the wee hours of the morning, at least six investigators on the porch smoking heard the sound of a woman begging for her life, followed by a gunshot. No one was found in the area, despite a thorough search by all involved. Later, investigating the upstairs, I heard the distinct sound of a woman sobbing outside the house, and sometime after that, as we conducted an EVP session in one of the bedrooms, we heard someone pounding on the kitchen door downstairs. Two investigators rushed down the steps and reached the door in seconds, but no one was to be found anywhere around the house.

My friend and I were so uncomfortable with the events that had happened, and worried about staying any longer in this crime-ridden area, that we decided to find a hotel on the highway to sleep while a number of the team members went to bed in the house. I myself was facing an internal reckoning. That night, in that old rectory alive with something I couldn't explain, I told God I was going to walk away from what I was doing; I vowed to give it up from that night on, though I'd be right back at it days later.

It was around 4AM when we left the house.

We stopped at one of those areas off the highway that has the group of hotels such as the Marriot, Comfort Suites, etc., but all of them were full. Strange, as it wasn't a holiday, and the clerks all said there was nothing special going on in the area..

We were very, very tired. We'd been up since 4am—24 hours—, and the thought of more driving was not a pleasant one. But we got back in the car and drove another half hour or so until we saw more signs for hotels. Here, we met the same situation: there were no rooms available in any of them.

By now I could barely see as I drove. It seemed the lights from the opposite lane were in my own, coming right at me. My friend was asking me if I was ok.

I was not.

We tried one more group of hotels, *with the same results*, before deciding to sleep in the car for an hour in the parking lot of a truck stop.

The next day, back home, two other investigators and I independently called the Cincinnati police dispatch to ask if there had been any shootings or other crimes near Sedamsville Rectory the night before.

There had not.

We later found out from the owners of the rectory building that this sequence of events—the woman begging, the gunshot and the crying after—had been experienced by other teams investigating the house.

Parapsychologists call that a true "haunting."

That was exciting to be sure, as well as disturbing. But much more disturbing was what had happened to my friend and me after we'd left. It seemed that something had left with us when we drove away from Sedamsville Rectory, and that, just maybe, that something didn't want us to make it back home.

That same something had, somehow, viciously shown itself in the form of a painful and lasting sign on the arm of our (former) skeptic.

In April of 2002, a FOIA request by UK news agency, the *Sun,* led to the revelation that, for a period of five years, the U.S. government's Advanced Aerospace Threat Investigation Program (AATIP) had investigated more than 300 cases of encounters with UFOs and ETs, many of them resulting in unexplained burns and other bodily harm, as well as brain damage and even unexplained pregnancies. [141]

Interestingly, the FOIA documents also included a report compiled by MUFON of the effects of UFO sightings on human observers between 1873 and 1994. Certainly, a plethora of such cases have been shared publicly over the years, along with abductees' photographs of three-pronged puncture marks in their skin (known as "alien triangles"), "scoop marks" said to be evidence of skin sampling, and abundant bruises, scratches and other evidence of physical contact with their bodies.

Byron Lacy has been one of the most vocal of a wide variety of contactee and abductee experiencers who have reported regular physical wounds from ET contact, including scoop marks, puncture wounds and bruises.[142] He told hundreds of thousands of live listeners on the popular late night radio show *Coast to Coast AM* in 2023 that he is a fourth-generation abductee. During an interview by host Collis Willis, Lacy asserted that religious people called aliens angels hundreds of years ago because of their "limited intellect." Willis concurred. Lacy is also a practicing psychic medium and deep mediator who's been seeking contact with his abductors and other aliens for years via these occult methodologies.

As a brief aside, in this interview Lacy also addressed an idea popular among abductees: that they are not taken against their wills but consent to it before they are born. It's an idea evocative of the demonological "contracts" rife in folklore, and one that also comes up frequently in demonological cases. Exorcists and deliverance ministers tell us that Freemasonry in the family is often a source of both demonic obsession, vexation and possession and of paranormal "gifts" such as mediumship, which are, in fact, literal curses brought on succeeding generations by Freemasonic ancestors. Freemasons in their vows agree to this cursing of their lineage in different ways as they move up in the Lodge.

On *Coast to Coast AM*, Lacy commented on abductees who want to end the contract. He himself tried to do this through meditation, not because he wanted to end his contract but to see if he could. But while in deep meditation for this purpose, he saw a vision of a pierced sphere that, he felt, was a message that he couldn't break the contract.

IN THE MATERIAL WORLD

Back when we first explored the Collins Elite, I talked about a document that allegedly had surfaced seeming to hint that the group was real and their concerns well founded. As mentioned, the document referenced some mysterious names and projects, as well as some we already knew, such as Jack Parsons.

That document also suggested that government researchers have successfully materialized physical objects in the laboratory via a so-called "Parsons Method." Knowing Parsons' methodologies, I got a sudden vision of a group of NASA scientists sitting around a Petrie dish chanting to the god Pan and masturbating. That may not be quite accurate, but one can guess that (if it's even an actual thing), the Parsons Method surely employs some sort of, shall we say, nontraditional means.

At any rate, I had to shake my head when I read about these alleged experiments (even beyond the momentary visual), because the materialization or *apport* of objects has been happening in and out of séance rooms throughout the entire history of modern paranormal research, and not always with the help of sex magick, seances or other occult tools. Time and again in ufology today, I've been seeing scientists and atheists dazzled by things that spiritual believers have been encountering forever.

In the "Michael" case that began in 1980s Centrahoma, Oklahoma, the ghost/alien entity would produce coins minted in any year requested by the family, and in a split second.

My old parapsychology mentor, philosopher and parapsychologist Dr. Stephen Braude, spent long months with the so-called "Gold Leaf Lady," studying what is surely one of the strangest cases of paranormal manifestation on record, in which a woman seemed to manifest gold leaf on the surface of her skin. [143] "Katie" was married to a man who constantly complained about a lack of money. He made sure to let Katie know her lack of financial contribution to the household was deeply offensive to him. But then, Katie began seemingly producing patches of gold leaf on her body. The material, which would "develop" before the eyes of observers, was analyzed by more than one laboratory, who found it to be not gold but some kind of alloy. As a parapsychologist, Braude theorized that Katie was somehow subconsciously producing the material to please her husband. The fact that it wasn't real gold was, maybe, a sort of joke on her greedy spouse. (I might propose that something very different than that was going on here, and more in keeping with this book's line of thought.).

The very first case I encountered in parapsychology—the one that got me interested in all of it—was another one Braude had studied extensively: the case of Ted Serios. In the early 1960s, a Chicago bellhop named Ted Serios began producing images on Polaroid film using, reportedly, only his mind. [144] It took all of his concentration (and more than a few tumblers of whiskey) to get results from him, but hundreds of his photographs can be seen today in the archives of the University of Maryland, Baltimore

County. Are these photographs some kind of psychokinetic effect, truly produced by the mind of the enigmatic Serios? Or was something else providing what he—and his scientific observers—so desperately wanted? (As an aside, it's interesting that Ted's ability only developed—no pun intended—after he underwent hypnosis by a coworker. Hypnosis is, of course, considered a doorway for demonic entry by many Christians, including myself.)

Of course, Spiritualism has been reporting apports (disappearances and appearances of existing objects) and materializations (manifestations of previously nonexistent objects) in the séance room for almost two centuries. Though a scant few seem to defy explanation, the great majority have been likely fraudulent. A case on point is the apport work of medium Agnes Guppy-Volckman, who was known to produce exotic fruits, vegetables and flowers on demand for multiple sitters at once, as witnessed by one sitter who asked asked for a sunflower. A few moments later, one such flower, six feet high, fell from the air onto the séance table, looking as if it had been pulled right out of the ground, its roots dropping dirt everywhere. One witness, Georgina Houghton, testified before the committee of the London Dialectical Society in 1869, regarding a sitting she'd attended with Guppy-Volckman and eighteen others. The medium told all present they could ask for a fruit or vegetable, and she then proceeded to deliver—on demand—a banana, a slice of candied pineapple, two apples, a peach, a pomegranate, two crystallizes greengages, a potato, a pile of raisins, a bunch of white grapes, three walnuts and a handful of almonds, among other delicacies.

Guppy-Volckman's apports were later attacked as fraudulent by a number of researchers, while others claim they are still up for debate. I think that either truth is important for our inquiry. If stunning apports like Guppy-Volckman's were produced by nineteenth century fraudulent means, what might tech-savvy hoaxers accomplish today to "put over" the existence of UFOs? On the other hand, if these apports were authentically produced by either the "spirits" (demons) or some kind of human psychic mechanism, then what might such actors or engines produce today in the way of UFO phenomena, to satisfy our technological desires and demands?

In more recent times, the Scole Experiment group offered for examination plentiful apports they claimed had appeared on their séance table.[145] Beginning in 1993, the group spent years reviving the nearly lost practice of physical mediumship (like Guppy-Volckman's) that had flourished in the 1800s, meeting in medium Robin Foy's Scole, Norfolk farmhouse cellar which they affectionately called the "Scole Hole."

The Scole group consisted of Robin Foy and his wife, joined by John Paxton, Patrick McHenna, Raji, Edward Matthews and Emily Bradshaw. The Foys served as the group's psychic mediums, assisted by a primary spirit guide named Manu. As you might imagine, Manu is the name of a Hindu god (demon) who in Hindu belief appears to signal the beginning of a new "kalpa" or aeon (a New Age, of course). Interestingly, Manu would claim to the Scole group that he had been present in 1952 when the CIA was trying to contact spirits, which suggests the entity may have been hanging around with our old friends, the Collins Elite.

After learning about the group two years after its inception, the esteemed Society for Psychical Research (SPR) began attending its seances. Many of its members were deeply impressed by things they felt they'd witnessed, including direct voice communication (audible voices produced without the use of a medium) and bright lights which shot around the room and performed impressive, intelligent maneuvers and passed through solid objects.

Most impressive of all were the apports or materializations of physical objects, including jewelry, coins and even a pristine newspaper from the 1940s which looked like it had just been printed. Central to the Scole experiments were the rolls and rolls of blank film that, after sittings, were found to have mysteriously produced all manner of writing and drawing on them, inscribed in various languages, and messages from dead paranormal investigators, scientists and others.

Hoping to prove the seances would "work" outside of the Scole Hole, the group took the show on the road, setting up a séance circle in the U.S. at one point. Sessions were reportedly attended by some fifteen members of NASA, among other interested parties. Allegedly, NASA set up its own spirit communication group afterward, which of course we have every reason to believe, knowing what we know of the organization and its occult shenanigans. And so we find Scole leading, like so much of this, to still more occult exploration on the U.S. government payroll.

GIVE THE LADY WHAT SHE WANTS

At the root of much of *all* paranormal experiences, including very physical claims of apports and materializations, vexation and bodily harm from UFO encounters, is what we always find with the demonic.

Mimicry.

It's the imitating of real things to serve the agenda of the demonic. Christian scholars also call it counterfeiting or aping. I've seen this mimicry more times than I can count in my ghost and haunting investigations, and it always surfaces when there is something diabolical involved. The entities produce phenomenon that we expect to see or want to see.

I fully believe that the craft encountered in RUFO experiences are part this phenomenon. And, again, this means *after* we cancel out everything that's either false identification, or our own government projects, or something made by a foreign government, *or* domestic or foreign private research and development.

Even Chris Bledsoe, his book, *UFO of God*, affirms that his "light beings" can "mimic anything" from humanoid figures to huge spacecraft. In one of Bledsoe's encounters, a bush in his backyard burst into non-consuming flames, mimicking the "burning bush" of Moses' encounter with God.

To clarify, Bledsoe says UFO *craft* seem to be sentient beings themselves. John Keel wrote at length about this belief in *Operation Trojan Horse*, where he documented the experiences of others who had come to this conclusion about UFOs long before Bledsoe. This description of UFO craft is more than a little evocative of spirit possession, in which the demonic entity takes up residence in a person's body. In fact, many contactees and abductees have theorized that the gray aliens, too, are some kind of robots or avatars that house discarnate intelligences.

The agnostic John Keel reminds us that:

> The Devil and his demons can, according to the literature, manifest themselves in almost any form and can physically imitate anything from angels to horrifying monsters with glowing eyes. Strange objects and entities materialize and dematerialize in these stories, just as the UFOs and their splendid occupants appear and disappear, walk through walls, and perform other supernatural feats. ... The manifestations and occurrences described in this imposing literature are similar, if not entirely identical, to the UFO phenomenon itself. Victims of demonomania [possession] suffer the very same medical and emotional symptoms as the UFO contactees . . . .[146]

He's right about the symptoms, too, and we'll talk more about that shortly. But remember Bachelors Grove, the place where my lecture attendee received (and ate) cookies from a "woman" in a house that disappeared overnight? Of course, those cookies—and that house—fit well into this review of physical objects connected to spiritual non-physical experiences. But the event was also part of a larger aspect of the things seen at Bachelors Grove which suggest the same mimicry aspect of UFO and ET manifestations/illusions.

Here's just one example. A few years ago, a filmmaker friend of mine, Charles Williams, made a movie called *A Thousand Words*, about one of the most famous paranormal experiences at Bachelors Grove: the sighting of a Woman in White known as the "Madonna of Bachelors Grove."

This woman, according to legend, is said to be looking for her baby or a young child, and one of the most sensational and controversial "ghost photographs" ever taken was of a female figure in a diaphanous gown sitting on a tombstone in the cemetery there. The photograph was taken in broad daylight with infrared film on August 10, 1991, and Judy Huff, the woman who took the photo, wrote a long letter to me afterwards. In the letter she wrote that she'd seen nothing there but felt compelled to take a photo at that moment. As it was 35mm film, it wasn't until the film was developed that she beheld the now legendary image.

At any rate, as part of his film project, Williams spent an entire day at the cemetery one Saturday, interviewing subjects about the Madonna of Bachelors Grove and the famous photograph I had just completed my book on Bachelors Grove, and I knew that, while many, many *other* phenomena had been experienced at the Grove in the past three decades, not a single witness had come forward publicly in those decades claiming to have seen that old, famous apparition of the so-called Madonna.

But that night, after the filming wrapped and Williams and his team went home, a friend of mine in the area was visiting the cemetery, as he walks his dog there every evening. He reported that he met several people at the cemetery on that visit that had seen a Woman in White *on that very night after the filming*. It was as if something there had been observing the interest of this filmmaking project in this particular apparition and manufacturing the exact thing they wanted to see.

This wasn't the first time I'd noted this kind of thing at Bachelors Grove. In fact, it seemed to be something that had been occurring regularly since the 1970s. There had been in much earlier years, for example, encounters of visitors with a "caretaker" or "lantern man" who would chase them out of the cemetery at night. There had been encounters with that phantom house" or "magic house" in the 1950s which would be seen off the cemetery path or in the cemetery itself, often moving toward the road, disappearing when witnesses tried to approach it or leading them out of the area. There were, too, mysterious lights of all colors which would seem to chase the curious down the cemetery path and right back to the parking lot. In more recent years, however, these same apparitions still appear and still look the same, but they behave differently. In particular, they all have taken to leading visitors *deeper into the area—*

-not out of it. This may be extra significant, because beginning in the 1970s, the cemetery and the woods surrounding it became host to ritual activity: activity visitors frequently still find evidence of today.

The late Chicago folklorist and "ghost hunter" Richard Crowe used to talk about the "layer cake effect" in reportedly haunted places. What he was referring to is that many places that may have originally been "haunted" in the traditional sense—by human spirits tied for a while to the place of their death or their sin—may have become something much different over the years because of how people respond to reports of such activity. What can happen is that occultists and paranormal investigators are drawn to these reputedly haunted places and they bring rituals, ghost hunting tools and other tools and methodologies that actually then attract the demonic. In turn, the demons produce phenomena that the visitors are expecting to experience—voices, apparitions, etc.—, luring still more visitors with more tools of communication, more rituals, etc.

It's a literally vicious cycle.

I have zero doubt that this explains a lot of, if not all of the phenomena blowing up around a multitude of people and places in the UFO world.

And I would add my own sweet shop theory to that of Crowe's layer cake effect: UFO research—like all inquiry into the world of the paranormal—is like a box of chocolates.

You never know what you're going to get.

I liken all of this to YouTubers or Instagrammers that check what's trending on Google each day and then create content to serve the interest in those topics. Why do these influencers do it? Because, of course, they want *engagement.*

These beings want the same.

TALK TO ME

Sometimes, the entities' "nice-nice" efforts to enter into communication with us telepathically don't work. The "gifts" of visions, knowledge and other mental communications aren't enough to get us to start trying to engage with them. And so sometimes they have to assault us until we answer: until it's impossible for us to remain disengaged. When this happens, sometimes things get very strange indeed.

And very physical.

One entity from the annals of paranormal investigation stated its desire for engagement point blank in the late 1980s, when it began writing messages on the bathroom mirror of the California-based Moffitt family, using a bar of soap. [147]

Talk to me was its opening plea.

In the years that followed, the family learned to write back. If they didn't, the entity—which at one point identified itself as one of the Seven Princes of Hell—would destroy the family home and even the car, carving its strange sign or sigil (a triangle with a squiggly tail) into the walls, floors, rugs, bedsheets, furniture and clothing, and even drawing it on every surface with cooking grease, Vaseline, lipstick and any other substance it could find. At one point the famed

Chicago witch Evelyn Paglini visited the house and communicated with the entity; she and the demon drew esoteric symbols back and forth as Paglini tried to negotiate a truce.

In eighteenth century West Virginia an entity known as the Wizard Clip terrorized the Livingston family by cutting crescent moon shapes into the curtains, tablecloths, clothing and blankets. It also reportedly caused the heads of their chickens to drop off inexplicably, killing them. This period of active physical destruction ended with Mass being said in the house and was followed by seventeen years of visitations from a disembodied voice that taught the family tenets of the Catholic faith.

I teach a whole course on these types of "Extreme Hauntings" as I call them for simplicity's sake. Parapsychology calls them "poltergeist" cases: these cases that feature dazzling physical phenomena. Parapsychology generally thinks human agency is behind these cases: a kind of subconscious exertion of energy on the physical environment. I disagree that all or even most cases fit this theory, but let's look at one frequent aspect of these occurrences.

In the most extreme cases, the desire of the entity or entities for engagement with humans is front and center, and often the beings will use physical violence, writing and even audible communication to get people to talk to them, such as in the Moffit family case described above.

The late, prolific ghost hunter and author Hans Holzer investigated that deeply troubling case in Tyler, Texas (mentioned earlier) in which the "poltergeist" manifested in multiple audible voices, swarms of mummified bugs, the movement of huge objects. Most notably, a barrage of notes dropped out of thin air for months on end. The case climaxed with the family dog being buried alive in the backyard by unseen hands—and ended with the son committing suicide, claiming he was being tormented by the devil.[148]

In my research here in Chicago, I discovered a similar case of what I call these "letters from Hell" in the annals of the nearby town of Lemont, Illinois, where in 1901 a farm family was inundated with threatening and ridiculing notes that fell, seemingly, from the ceiling, among all manner of witnesses. A reporter shared that the villagers had accused the family of owning an occult book, suggesting this had brought about the infestation.[149]

The case of the "Swearing Ghost" that we examined earlier also featured mysterious letters that dropped from the ceiling, filled with language so vile the newspapers couldn't print a word of them. Obscenities would also be found written on the walls of the family's basement apartment home and scrawled, as we learned, throughout every book in the home except for a book about "magic" that belonged to Clara, the twelve-year-old the case seemed centered on. These writings went on even after Clara had been removed from the home and placed in a detention school.

In the "Michael" case of Oklahoma, an entity who sometimes said it was a ghost, sometimes an extraterrestrial, threw eggs, coins, rocks and more at family members and visitors, wrote messages and drew symbols on the walls (including the astronomical symbol for Saturn), and spoke audibly in a kind of metallic whisper that sounded a bit like a robot and a bit like a cat.

Back at Jack Parsons' pantheistic parsonage in Pasadena, housemates grew concerned when poltergeist type activity began breaking out in the house during the escalation of Parsons' occult activities. It was also reported that writing would appear paranormally on surfaces of the house, including strange symbols.

In recent years, exorcists have reported receiving text messages from the demons they're attempting to exorcise. Well-known exorcist Monsignor Stephen Rosetti has stated of his exorcism and deliverance team:

> We have had three cases in which demons have texted the team and/or the family of the possessed person. Two of these cases were the most difficult cases we have had so far, and the third involved a pious family with priestly and religious vocations among the children. So, all were 'high value' targets with high-ranking, powerful demons involved. This suggests that it takes considerable spiritual 'energy' to cross over and manipulate such items in the physical world, and thus this action "costs" them a lot. [150]

Rosetti observes that these messages seem calculated to break down the faith and resolve of both the possession victim and the exorcist and his team. These supports, he says, are key in the deliverance of the soul from possession.

Remembering the scores of reports I've gathered over the years of alleged "text messages from the dead," the phenomenon of fellow investigators receiving threatening text messages from gobbledygook telephone numbers that seemed to have intention to scare (such as "666-666-6666") as well as my friend's chilling text message from some sinister, unknown communicator, I've found such reports of messages from demons unsurprising and their similarities compelling.

NOW YOU SEE IT

In addition to all of the tricks we've already covered, it's been well documented that sometimes UFOs are seen but cannot be photographed and vice-versa: just one more odd quality they share with other paranormal phenomena such as ghost and haunting phenomena.

Dr. Gary Nolan has noted how different witnesses to UFO sightings often see different things, "almost as if whatever it is, is projecting something into the mind, rather than it being a real manifestation, material, in front of you." [151] This is similar to what occurred at the "Miracle of the Sun" event at Fatima, Portugal in 1917, with numerous different descriptions of the event and some seeing nothing at all. UFO believers have tried to turn Fatima's Miracle of the Sun into a UFO event, ignorant of how the fruits of the event (humility, faith, prayer, penance) differentiate the Fatima events from the fruits of, say, the case of Chris Bledsoe and his "Lady" (attention-seeking, profiteering, giving up religion and the like).

We also see something like this in the famed 1994 Ariel School UFO incident that occurred in Zimbabwe, in which more than sixty children claimed to witness a silver craft land in a field near the school. Some even claimed they saw occupants of the craft, and a few of those to have received terrifying telepathic messages about the environment.

There remain many issues with the testimonies and investigation methodologies of the Ariel School case. Though it was claimed that more than 60 students witnessed the event, fewer than a dozen were interviewed, and not until days had passed and children had been talking to each other about the event, *and* after being exposed to television and radio content about UFOs and aliens.

In fact, just before the event, news reports in Zimbabwe had been peppered with talk of UFOs. Just two days before the Ariel report erupted, many UFO sightings had been reported across southern Africa; most were of what was described as a sort of glowing fireball in the night sky. The object was revealed to be the re-entry of the Zenit-2 rocket from the Cosmos 2290 satellite launch—but not before radio stations across the region encouraged listeners to call in with their UFO sightings. Africans, then, had UFOs "on the brain," as they say, in the days just before the Ariel School incident.

Additionally, UFO investigator and Harvard psychiatrist John Mack was found to have asked leading questions of the children, something he was reportedly prone to do. It's also often stated that "all" of the children who witnessed the event received simultaneous telepathic messages regarding climate change and the environment, though apparently only three students actually reported this (and not the first time they were interviewed).

I also feel obliged to point out here that the Ariel School incident has been grouped by some scholars with a large number of African cases of mass hysteria in schools,[152] which involve not only laughing, crying and fainting spells but outbreaks of perceived demonic possession, physical illness and reports of mass sightings of demonic entities, snakes, tigers and other animals and beings, along with other symptoms.

Often, there is a news report or other triggering event that predicates the outbreak (as there was at Ariel with the rocket re-entry reports), but psychologists feel these events are largely stress related, often tied to cultural tensions, such as, possibly, during the desegregation of African schools.

There's one other possibility behind contemporary mass UFO sightings such as occurred with the Ariel School incident, the "Phoenix Lights," the "Tinley Park lights" and other cases with many witnesses. Are these, as some have suggested, staged events that use holography, mind control and other governmental secret project methodologies and tools to create a desired effect? Most interestingly, many of the students on the playground at the Ariel School claimed to have experienced nothing at all. There seemed to be a certain area where all of the witnesses were standing or playing at the time. One witness said her siblings, in another part of the playground, did not see anything, and that she wondered at one point whether their locations actually played a part in their experiences in some way. This fact has made me wonder if some sort of projection was involved, wherein the perspective of the witness would have been crucial.

All of this made me wonder, as a Catholic: Did governments aspire to create such mass events after seeing the effect of the Fatima miracle in 1917? Obviously, governmental attempts to use any means necessary to control populations is something we've seen evidence of throughout this book, and we've only visited the tip of the iceberg regarding the antics of MKULTRA and other such forays into mass control. It gives a whole new dimension to the "mimicry" aspect of the demonic, to be sure. Has something very dark been influencing the occult-influenced government to use that same mimicry to deceive populations? In addition to the demonic mimicking spiritual experience, are government agencies mimicking it, too, also for purposes of control?

I would suggest that the observations of Vallée, Nolan and others perhaps demonstrate the *spiritual nature* of RUFOs, as the details of the Fatima events also demonstrate that they, too, were spiritual. Most notably, many varying accounts of the event were reported by witnesses, and some saw nothing at all. And yet, there were physical effects, such as the drying up of inches of rain in a few minutes, just as landing marks, craters and burnt brush and grass are sometimes left behind by UFOs. The suggestion is, as Gary Nolan has observed, of a "projecting . . . into the mind," but it's not *all* in the mind.

Are the Fatima events and the events observed by scientists like Nolan and other UFO experiencers, then, part of a *spiritual* realm and not a realm of "interdimensional phenomena?

I'll never forget one occasion when I found myself baffled during an investigation in the basement of a Chicago tavern in the city's Portage Park neighborhood. During our time there, my research partner and I clearly saw a dark figure repeatedly peering around a doorframe, though our video camera did not pick it up. To add to the enigma, we could only view the figure's reflection in a full-length mirror that faced the doorway. It was the craziest thing imaginable. Fifteen years later, I can still see my colleague standing there, shaking his head, saying, *Son of a bitch!*

Indeed.

POWER

Something else that prompts the UFO craft-believing crowd to shoot down the supernatural theory of the phenomenon is the fact that some of these UFOs seem to emit electromagnetic energy or radiation, sometimes even leaving behind burns as well as brain damage. I feel this fact may actually also support a spiritual theory, or at least suggest that the phenomenon is not necessarily only physical.

Certainly, one of the first things parapsychologists look for in purported ghost, haunting or poltergeist cases is an elevation—or instability—in the EM field. We can recognize right away that spiritual beings—including demonic ones—have been closely associated historically with electromagnetic activity. Even in séance circles of the late nineteenth century (and more recently, as we'll see), apported objects (those transported by paranormal means) were frequently reported to be hot to the touch or at least warm after mysteriously appearing, seemingly from thin air.

Remember our girl at the center of the "swearing ghost" case back in Milwaukee? The candy the mysterious stranger handed her (right through the plate glass door) was so hot it burned her hand and had to be thrown into the sink.

Of course, UFO believers cite cases where very strong energy seems to have been a part of the experience: far above the heightened levels of electricity and such in "haunted houses" investigated by people like me. As we've seen, studies have been done, for example, on pilots who have received radiation burns after close encounters with "alien craft," and of contactees who report similar skin damage, eye damage or physical ailments after visitations from "alien beings". And yet the presence of some incredible energy force during spiritual events has been suggested throughout spiritual history, including at the Resurrection of Jesus of Nazareth.[153]

In October of 2016 a group of scientists and religious authorities initiated the removal of a marble slab covering the tomb, which is of course one of the world's most visited pilgrimage sites. Observers found that some of their scientific measurement instruments were affected by EM disturbances when placed on the stone where Jesus' body is purported to have lain, suggesting the occurrence of a massive energy event in the past.

The findings were taken up by those interested in the Shroud of Turin—the alleged burial cloth of Jesus. Italy's National Agency for New Technologies, Energy and Sustainable Economic Development (ENEA) proposed that the image on the shroud may have been made via an intense flash of light, but that no known man-made light source is capable of producing a flash of such magnitude. It was estimated that some 34 thousand billion watts of VUV radiations would be necessary to produce such an image, thousands of billions of watts in excess of what's possible today. And while atheist UFO believers would doubtless cite this information as more evidence that such events were not religious events but UFO events, occultists—and researchers into the occult—would remind us that intense and often dangerous energy is a hallmark of supernatural manifestation.

John Keel, among other historians of the occult, specifically reminds us of the physical effects that can be inflected during the manifestation of spiritual objects or beings. Keel shares a common occultist warning against looking at the process of materialization or gazing upon the materialized object for any period of time:

> Forbidden books on black magic, witchcraft, and ancient religious beliefs all describe this basic materialization process, including solemn warnings to avert the eyes when you materialize an angel or demon through some secret rite lest you suffer from conjunctivitis and the other painful maladies produced by the rays of the EM spectrum. All mythology tells how one should not gaze upon the countenance of a materialized god. Although they lacked proper terminology for these effects and were obliged to speak in

terms of "rays" and "vibrations," secret cults throughout the ages knew that entities moved into our reality through a process of altering frequencies. [154]

MODERN MAGIC?

One other topic I want to look at briefly is the collection of "craft" containing what witnesses describe as "hieroglyphics." In most of the cases, experts in languages and symbols not only couldn't decipher them, they didn't even know what kind of inscriptions they were (though we know at least one of the witnesses Annie Jacobsen interviewed identified the ones he saw as Russian). These cases, taken together with everything gleaned from the information/disinformation shared in this book, reminds me of our old Pasadena pantheist, Jack Parsons.

Parsons had worked closely with Hungarian-American physicist and engineer Theodore von Karman. It would be hard to overstate the scientific distinction von Karman achieved with his work, not only in the U.S. but internationally. At the age of 81, von Karman was awarded the very first U.S. National Medal of Science.

Von Karman claimed that his own ancestor, a 16th century Prague-based rabbi named Judah Loew ben Bezalel, had created a "golem": a manufactured clay "person" animated by magic. According to local legend, when the Jews were to be banished from Prague during the reign of Emperor Rudolph II, Von Karman's ancestor got the idea to create a golem to protect the city's congregations.

It worked . . . but a little too well.

The golem reportedly went wild, roaming through the country and killing Christians, until the emperor pleaded with Rabbi ben Bezalel to destroy it. He did, by altering the magical symbols he'd written on the golem's forehead during the magic rituals, thereby de-animating it.

Nick Redfern has wondered if the "bodies" reportedly discovered in the 1947 Roswell crash—and countless other purported ETs—may have some connection to the von Karman/Parsons partnership, especially since von Karman's protégé, Frank Malina, is known to have met with a man named Robert Goddard, and in (of all places) Roswell, New Mexico. [155]

Goddard was a rogue rocketeer from New England who had moved to New Mexico to perform experiments with his rockets. His meeting with Malina took place in 1936, more than a decade before the Roswell Incident. Goddard was none too pleased with the visit; he liked to work alone and was infamous among other scientists for keeping his research secret. Still, Malina returned home and implemented some changes at JPL based on things he had learned in Roswell. The big question, of course, is obvious: was there a connection between what Goddard was doing at Roswell in the 1930s and what happened there in the summer of 1947? And did von Karman have something to do with it?

Additionally, Redfern has quoted one filmmaker, Renate Druks, a friend of Parsons' magickal lover, Marjorie Cameron, who believes that Parsons was trying to create a homunculus (a tiny human being animated by magic) when he blew himself up in his Pasadena lab. [156]

That's a fascinating prospect, to be sure. But reading about von Karman's ancestral golem, my own mind went to those mysterious craft themselves: the "sentient" ones and the ones with the inexplicable "hieroglyphics" written on them or inside them, including the "craft" or materials found at Roswell, New Mexico in 1947. Redfern documents in *Final Events* the fact that the Collins Elite believed the Roswell "crash material" to have been manufactured and dropped there by demonic entities, a theory that, we've already seen, is shared by some Christian observers of the UFO phenomenon.

In animating a golem, one must write certain magical words or phrases on them to endow them with life. As John Keel and other ufologists and witnesses have spoken about the feeling of many that these craft are themselves "alive," could at least some of these RUFO "craft" and even ETs be, in fact, modern-day golems, animated by ancient rituals and writing?

UNDER THEIR SKIN

I know, I know.

But what about the implants?

Claims of extraterrestrials implanting objects in abductees seem to have started in the spring of 1957. That March, ufologist John Robinson appeared on the radio and shared an account given him by a neighbor. The neighbor told Robinson he had been kidnapped by extraterrestrials who installed a pair of small earphones behind his ears to keep him docile. Later, Abductee Betty Andreasson told author Raymond Fowler that aliens had implanted some kind of object in her nose during her own abduction in 1967. [157] These early reports have been joined by countless others over the past decades, with abductees claiming they serve a wide variety of purposes.

Most have claimed that their implants function as tracking devices. Just as we might track animals in the wild by tagging them with trackers, it's been suggested that these ETs implant tiny chips inside abductees so that the aliens can monitor their location 24 hours a day, 7 days a week. It's surely one of the more unnerving facets of the alien abduction phenomenon, this idea that no matter what one does, he can never really get away from the intrusive ET visitors who have "tagged" them.

Along with tracking one's location, the implants also supposedly send real time health data of the abductee in a constant feed, beamed from the chip straight up to the UFO or wherever the ETs keep their database of abductee health records.

You are not mistaken if, from what we've described here, you get the impression that an alien implant seems to work an awful lot like a Fitbit. Indeed, just as countless human-made smart watches track our GPS positions, monitor our heartbeats and respiratory function, alien implants supposedly do much the same thing. In fact, you wouldn't have to go far to find a ufologist who believes the Fitbit *is* alien technology, along with many technological developments of the modern age. (More on this in a later chapter.) But the alien implant is more than a high tech, imbedded smart watch, and it allegedly does a lot more than any of our measly Fitbits can do. For it has also been suggested that the alien implants might facilitate the transportation of abductees.

According to reports of alien experiencers, ET science is so advanced (and the ET grasp of physics so far along) that aliens are able to manipulate matter in ways inconceivable to us. That is, incidentally, the same thing Christians say about demons. At any rate, this ability allows them to temporarily alter solid structures— and even their own physiology—so that they can walk through solid walls. But the ETs also pull *abductees* through solid walls, windows, and even ceilings. It's a strange aspect of alien abduction, but, in fact, one of the most commonly reported features of the phenomenon.

Typically, the abductee wakes up with a start, perhaps feels an intense tingling or vibrating, sees a brilliant blue flash of light, and suddenly a tremendous force sucks her right through the wall, ceiling, or window of her home, out into the open air and through the hull of a hovering UFO craft. The process, we hear, is not completed without difficulty. Many abductees report that the worst part of the abduction is the extremely uncomfortable feeling of being pulled through other matter.

It's the implant that facilitates the event, or so they claim. The tiny device somehow allows the abductee's matter to be temporarily dematerialized during the process. Some say this is why no one witnesses the taking of the abductees; the implant renders them invisible.

If the infamous Linda Napolitano case is to be believed, it seems there are occasions when this invisibility either fails, or that—for whatever reason—the aliens simply don't want to use it. Her alleged abduction from her high-rise apartment was reportedly witnessed by a numerous New Yorkers in the city that never sleeps, when folks driving late at night on the Brooklyn Bridge were shocked to see a woman floating up a blue beam of light into a waiting UFO craft, accompanied by three nonhuman entities.

Interestingly enough, in the "are you an abductee" quiz, one of the questions is whether or not one dreams of flying—as in Peter Pan-style flying—: the odd sensation of flying through the air or, perhaps, some kind of "dream" of flying or floating. Incidentally, in one of the most well-known of the "Satanic panic" cases of the 1980s, nursery school students claimed that one of the teachers could fly. In fact, folklorists and parapsychologists have done numerous studies on the parallels between flight in witch folklore and UFO/ET reports.[158]

But back to implants.

It's been theorized that the implant somehow raises the vibration of the abductee to where their molecules become separated just enough for them to be able to pass through solid objects. If you're familiar with the highly controversial and dubious "Philadelphia Experiment," you'll recall that some of the sailors reportedly dematerialized and then, in a ghastly turn of events later rematerialized within the walls of the *USS Eldred*.

I remember one parapsychological case in which a young boy woke up terrified and ran into his parents' room. Turns out his bedroom door wasn't open, but his body reportedly went partially through the door. Firefighters had to chop apart the door to remove him, and he was left in dire medical straits. In a few minutes, I'll introduce you to a man who has a machine that can supposedly affect the same result on demand. (I'm not claiming at any of this is true, only that the paranormal world is full of claims of the inherent immateriality of material objects or of their ability to be dematerialized.)

Along with waking up to see a flash of blue light, many also report a vibrating sensation during abduction transportation. Some claim feeling their whole body vibrating so violently they fear they might actually fall apart:, as if the very molecules are about to be torn asunder. It is in this implant-facilitated state that our now molecularly-loose abductee is then allegedly pulled through his bedroom wall, ceiling, or window, and up into the alien craft.

Other abductees tell us their implants are meant for communication. Claudia Negron—an abductee interviewed by ufologist David Jacobs—supposedly had the opportunity to ask one of the ETs about this kind of implant. Claudia described what she found out. According to Claudia:

> It's like he [the alien] projects his thoughts to me and says that they have to know. They have to know how I see the world. How I see things. How I interpret things as they occur and this is their way of monitoring that. This tells them so they know where I am at all times. They know how I react to every situation at every moment. He said that this is important to them. He says it's important for their research. They have to know this.[159]

Inquiring alien minds, apparently *need to know.*

It's indeed frightful to imagine one having an ET audience secretly watching one's every move and possibly even critiquing every situation that one might go through. The notion that one's whole life could be rendered into what basically sounds like a livestreamed reality TV show for a bunch of aliens is a bit paranoia-inducing to say the least. But while we're going down this bizarre road, we should affirm that some do indeed supposedly hear strange transmissions through their implants. And this takes us to the most frightening and the most controversial claims regarding these devices.

Numerous abductees have claimed that their implants are used to actively program or control abductees through their minds. There are some that have even gone so far as to say that alien implants have induced mental illness, by way of subjecting abductees to various pressures and commands by way of devices implanted directly into their brain.

If you're remembering MKULTRA, so am I.

As a matter of fact, a number of researchers have speculated that these implants are realm but that they are placed by the government. They reference the notorious MKULTRA and other mind control programs conducted early in the UFO era. The implants allegedly monitor and control the implantees. After they're placed, "screen memories" of abduction are planted to cover up the real purpose of the implants: government control of military forces . . . or even civilians.

Such theories reminded me of Tim Taylor: that Kundalini-practicing NASA scientist who befriended Chris Bledsoe and Diana Pasulka. Taylor told Pasulka that he knows the spiritual and physical protocols he follows to maintain ET contact are working when he starts receiving thoughts that he knows aren't his own.

Supposed alien abductee Pat Parrinello was one of the first to attempt to have an implant removed, and he claims that—leading up to the removal—, the ETs who actively monitored him seemed as if they were trying to dissuade him from doing so. He claims he felt terrible pressure and pain in his head when he merely *thought* of getting rid of the implant, like a rat getting shocked in a lab. Parrinello thought that whoever was in control of the device was seeking to forcefully coerce him into changing his mind. Nevertheless, he fought against the pain and went forward with the procedure anyhow.

The physician that worked on Parrinello was none other than the late Dr. Roger Leir. Leir would become famous for removing several supposed alien implants, and Parrinello was one of his earliest patients.[160] Leir is usually described by UFO believers as a surgeon. But he was actually a podiatrist licensed only to perform foot surgery. He hired other specialists to perform any implant removals above the ankle. None of them, to my knowledge, have agreed to be identified.

Leir carried out the procedure of implant removal on Parrinello in 1995. For the procedure he had heavily sedated the patient, but even so, as soon as the good doctor started probing the spot where the implant was located, Pat had a violent reaction. As Leir investigated further, he eventually pulled out a special meter to look for any magnetic reactions. He reportedly found that a tremendous "magnetic field" was being generated by the implant.

With a struggle, Leir was ultimately able to excise the implant. He found it to be a small 4 mm by 2 mm object, surrounded by a sort of cocoon of keratin. It seemed it had been designed to mesh with the human body, so that it would not be rejected. According to Leir, the object was unbelievably hard and could not even be scratched with his scalpel.

At a gathering of MUFON in 1995, Leir presented a series of X-rays from a claimed abductee. Later, he removed two small metal objects from her and a second claimant. The objects went to the lab at the New Mexico Institute of Mining and Technology. There, they were determined to be of common materials such as aluminum and iron. However, the lab's note that the pieces possibly originated from meteors was enough to inspire Leir to pronounce them to be extraterrestrial (Technically correct, if more than a bit misleading).

Before his passing, Leir published two books on implant removals, and he became a popular speaker at other such UFO conventions and seminars. But he continually refused to share details of his research with medical professionals, electing instead to make scientific-sounding statements about what he claimed was the necessarily extraterrestrial origin of the implants he removed. Critics have credited his "authoritative-sounding" statements with legitimizing the implant phenomenon, regardless of a total lack of evidence to support its ET origins.

Other skeptics in the medical field have surmised that implant belief in abductees is closely related to what physicians refer to as the "matchbox sign" or "Ziploc bag sign" in which patients falsely self-diagnose a parasitic infection before or after removing items from their skin—a phenomenon known as delusional parasitosis. Some 50 to 80 percent of patients with delusional parasitosis present doctors with a matchbox or Ziploc bag containing extracted specimens which turn out to be fibers, animal or human hairs, or shards of wood, glass or metal. Often, patients will also bring photographs of the skin area where the real or imagined parasite is lodged.

Some have suggested that aliens might be so advanced they create implants that have all the appearances of ordinary, terrestrial materials or objects. So that cat hair or underwear fiber might be something deceitfully different indeed.[161]

Since much of what we are doing in this book is comparing UFO reports with those of brushes with the demonic, we should also remember the witchcraft reports of the 16th and 17th centuries, in which moles, scars and birthmarks were often offered as evidence that someone was a witch. These "witch marks" were considered proof that an accused witch had consorted with discarnate beings—namely, the devil and his minions.

Some high-profile abductees have claimed to have been installed with implants. New York abductee Linda Napolitano reached out to New York abduction researcher Budd Hopkins after finding a small bump on her nose in 1976. Doctors had told her that she must have had surgery as a child, and that must explain the bump. But she hadn't had surgery. And she didn't buy the diagnosis. In Hopkins Napolitano found a sympathetic ear, and a ufological diagnosis of her nose.

But by far the most infamous implantee to be found in the history of ufology is also, arguably, the most infamous contactee of all: a science fiction writer-turned alien ambassador by the name of Whitley Strieber.

THE POSTER CHILD

New York State has a long history of involvement in the paranormal and supernatural. Hydesville, New York, is where modern Spiritualism began. In 1848, the little cabin of the Fox family, already known to locals as haunted when they moved in, would become the stage of the first modern seances around the family table, when the daughters attempted to communicate with a ghost in the house, unwittingly (or perhaps not) igniting one of the most influential movements of modern times.

Later, Long Island, New York would become a center of occult and paranormal activity, including satanic murders, witchcraft, the case said to have inspired Steven Spielberg's film, *Poltergeist*, and the reported paranormal doings at the house called High Hopes: the Amityville Dutch Colonial on Ocean Avenue where America's most famous haunted house tale would play out.

UFO flaps pepper the history of the New York, and famous encounters include the bizarre abduction case of Linda Napolitano out of her New York City apartment window and an alleged sighting by John Lennon, who referenced the event in his 1984 song, "Nobody Told Me." About four hours southeast of the Fox cabin in Hydesville, one of the most complex and celebrated of Spiritualism's children would experience his first encounters with beings he would come to call the Visitors.

Whitely Strieber has long been a compelling yet altogether controversial figure in the field of ufology. A big reason behind the controversy stems from the fact that, prior to coming out of the UFO closet, Strieber was a writer of profound and frightening fiction. He wrote fictional books such as *The Wolfen* in which he vividly describes vicious fiends stalking the streets. He also wrote a book called *Catmagic* in which "fairies" abduct people.

As such, it's easy to understand why some have openly

wondered if his accounts of alien abduction, as related in his best-selling book *Communion*, was just another great work in this long line of fiction. (To job your memory, *Communion* was that hugely popular paperback book with the terrifying cover, showing a "gray alien" with piercing black eyes.) Strieber, however, has long insisted that the events of that book are not fiction, and that they really did occur. He has furthermore suggested that perhaps some of his experiences with these entities had been working out of his subconscious mind all along, thereby explaining some similarities found in his previous fictional works.

As it's the subject of our book, let's look briefly at Whitley Strieber's religious belief, because he is a professed Catholic. In fact, he has talked and written quite a bit about it. Like so many things, the fact has caused this apparently painfully thoughtful man no end of internal struggle, and Strieber wrote about some of this on his blog in December of 2011:

> I will die a Catholic, but not a believer. My wife distinguishes between uncritically believing something that cannot be proved and having faith, and I think she's right. For me, faith is a matter of bearing my doubt and continuing on anyway. I have deep personal reasons for this. Every night, give or take, at about eleven, I have meditated for half an hour or so, then ended my day with a decade of the Rosary. And yet, I don't know that I 'believe' any of it.. [162]

Doubtless a good deal of Strieber's struggle to believe stems from the messages and teachings he's received during his decades of contact with the Visitors, much of which has been deliberately achieved or at least encouraged through occult practices. He's not sure, for example, that the "sacrament" (presumably the Holy Eucharist) is even real, and yet the name of his blockbuster book, *Communion*, is a book about his extraterrestrial/demonic relationships. One wonders what would compel a self-professed Catholic to so title such a book, but Strieber answered that question in his blog:

> I wonder: does the sacrament even exist? How can I know? Soon, the Advent Candle will be lit. In its glow, I will find a little respite from my doubts. As I join in the celebration of the season, though,

there will return to mind knowledge of how many gods men have loved and love now. Why is Christ any more true than Krishna, or Mary than Kali? …. When I go to Mass, I will remember the ritual of Mithra from which it took its form, and Tertullian's desperate assertion that Satan had gone back in time to plant the Mithraic ritual, in order to cause Christians to doubt. I will doubt. [163]

And so, like the 70 percent-plus of American "Catholics" who, we're told today, do not believe in the True Presence of Jesus in the Holy Eucharist (a central tenet of the Catholic faith), Strieber doesn't really buy it. He seems more convinced of his union with the Visitors than with the living God of his professed Catholic faith, judging not only from the title of his bestselling book but from his raw public confessions.

Strieber has also been deeply influenced by the Gnostic gospels and apocryphal books of Judeo-Christian faith. In his book, *Jesus,* he joyfully explores and embraces the heretical gospels of Thomas and of Mary, among other writings, despite full rejection by the Catholic Church, to which he claims to belong.

So, just what is it that Strieber says *really happened* to him? Well, he claimed that he first became aware of alien intrusion into his life on October 4th, of 1985, when he was staying at his cabin in Pine Bush, New York with his wife, their son and some friends of the family.

During the night, Strieber was startled awake and saw a flash of blue light in the middle of the house. He had no explanation as to what this light could be, since they were in the middle of a remote wilderness. There were no cars or anything else that could have caused it.

Then something even stranger happened. He somehow became convinced that the light had appeared because the chimney was on fire. First of all, this sudden rationalization made no sense. The chimney being on fire would not cause a sudden flash of blue light. Secondly, what he did in response made even less sense.

He went back to sleep.

It was only later that he would look back on this moment as being utterly bizarre. For who in their right mind would calmly go to sleep after convincing themselves that his house is on fire? In ET lore however, these sorts of things are quite common. There are many instances in which human beings encounter something unusual, only to be imparted with an immediate rationalization of what they saw—almost as if someone *or something* is feeding them a "cover story" and even a response. The annals of UFO contactee/abductee cases are full of accounts of people seeing beings in their rooms and "hearing" in their minds, "Everything is fine. Go back to sleep" or—chillingly—"Don't wake up" or "Don't open your eyes."

It would later be learned that Strieber's son Andrew—who was just a small child at the time—also was fed a bogus story. His was in regard to a loud banging sound that accompanied the light. Andrew apparently woke up disturbed, only to get the funny idea in his head that it was all ok, because his father had just thrown a shoe at a fly. Considering that the whole house shook, that really must have been some kind of shoe. Much worse was to come, however. It was the day after Christmas, on December 26th, 1985, that Strieber had his first, fully conscious recollection of an encounter with aliens.

Again, he was at the family cabin. He woke up to hear footsteps and shuffling around in the lower level of the cabin. The next thing he knew, he saw a small entity in the room. It ran right up to him. This time there was no attempt to cover up or rationalize what he was seeing. The being was literally right in front of his face.

After this face-to-face encounter, Steiber passed out and woke up in the woods. He then recalled floating up into a craft where intense medical examinations occurred, on par with the many abductee reports that had gone before his. It was only later that Strieber's encounters would take on a much stranger shade, when his home seemed to become enchanted with poltergeist-like activity. At one point, he was convinced that his own stereo was conversing with him (more on this in a minute).

Strieber himself has always indicated a belief that there is a spiritual component to encounters with ETs. He's said that it's only natural that these entities elicit fear. According to Strieber, as soon as these beings appear, the body involuntarily goes into a state of shock he refers to as "body terror" (which was, apparently, his original title for *Communion*). As the years went by, however, Strieber would later describe the entities as demonic, evil and dark. Eventually, it was obvious that he had been caught in some kind of *web* of darkness. He said it was like some "good" presence had been there at first but had left, leaving a dark presence behind. He would also say that it was impossible for the "grays"—the beings he often writes and talks about encountering—to be part of human life without destroying it.

Strieber, however, deeply wanted "communion" with these beings. Their draw was absolutely irresistible. He was convinced that, were one to force his way through the shock and terror, spiritual reward would come from communing with these things. He was well-aware of the Faustian implications and parallels, but he didn't care.

One night, Strieber was asleep in his bedroom when he suddenly woke to see an alien face staring at him. He immediately felt himself being gripped by that old familiar fear, but this time, he also felt something else: a desire *to not be afraid*. He wished to change his response, and in order to force a different result, he made himself greet the entity with a smile on his face.

The rest, as they say, is history.

Strieber had enjoyed great success with his writing up until the time of *Communion*'s publication. He had been a horror and science fiction novelist, and many believed he would emerge as 'the next Stephen King." *Communion* was the biggest success of all, reaching Number 1 on the New York *Times* bestseller list and selling some two million copies. But with the book's wild popularity came the loss of his "respectable author" status.

Strieber would no longer enjoy adulation from the wider publishing world, but neither did he have to watch what he said. Strieber would go on to claim many, many absurd things happening in his life on the fringes of society. At one point, in the midst of the visitations, abductions and messages from the Visitors, Strieber discovered that he had been fitted with an "implant."

At first, Whitley had no idea of the implant's purpose. Then, in a typically bizarre moment, it was all revealed.

Strieber had been working on a "faux" memoir about a young German American who accidentally falls in love with Hitler. While writing, he suddenly realized that a "slit" had appeared in his right eye. When he concentrated on the fast movement happening across the slit, he saw that words were being "typed" across it very quickly, in the Courier font, too fast at first for him to read them.

As time went on, he realized that the words seemed to both aid his writing immensely but also reflect what he was trying to communicate. It was as if he was being fed the right words to make his writing much better. Strieber called it "associative enrichment" in that the words were related words that added depth and richness to what he was typing at the time.

When I read this about Strieber, I immediately remembered our friend Jamsie, back at the radio station in San Francisco, and Uncle Ponto throwing a constant stream of random absurdities at him while he was trying to broadcast on air. And I remembered how those random absurdities ended up making Jamsie a wildly popular—if off-kilter—success with his listening audience.

At one point, Strieber asked where the words were coming from.

Who are you? he pleaded, to the air.

The words typed out an answer:

It's me, Anne.

Anne was his wife.

But Anne was dead.

Anne Strieber's interest in the afterlife began with a "near death experience" or NDE in 2004. She devised a plan to communicate with her beloved husband after her death,[164] and Whitley says she was good to the plan. Within an hour and a half of her earthly passing in 2015, he claims she was back in contact with her earthly spouse.

I don't think I need to remind readers that, as a professed Catholic, agreeing to such a plan would be deeply heretical for Whitley Strieber. No Catholic should promise to communicate with a living loved one after bodily death, and no Catholic should agree to being on the receiving end either. As for the reality of the communications, no human spirit would initiate such communication, being in violation of God's law.

These first communications became a seemingly endless stream of messages from Strieber's dead wife, which comprised a sort of primer on how to bridge the gap between life and death, with the goal of maintaining working communications and relationships with those beyond the grave. A book eventually followed, called *The Afterlife Revolution*, in which the professed Catholic Whitley shares with readers the keys to not only communication with the dead but continued relationships with them on Earth.

It was reading about one of Strieber's spirit communication activities that led me to one of the most shocking revelations of my own research. In fact, the revelation would be instrumental in my walking away from spirit communication in my own work.

I was so shocked when I read it, I thought I was losing my mind …or going blind.

One night, Strieber was falling back to sleep after his usual second meditation session of the night. He would wake up at midnight and 3AM to meditate, and this was after the latter period (This is an interesting detail, as the 3AM hour is known in Catholic folk belief and among some exorcists as the hour when the devil is most active, as it is the inverse of the hour in which humanity was saved by Jesus' death on the cross in the 3PM hour).

Just as Strieber was on the cusp of slumber again, a knock came at the door.

Outside stood two men.

One of the men, Strieber would say, he recognized; Strieber had last seen him when he was twelve years old—some two decades earlier—during one of his claimed "government men" encounters growing up.

He writes:

> (T)hey had a small portable typewriter with them. It looked like something that was commonplace before computers. I was told that it was what was used to generate the words that race past in the slit in my eye. I looked down at it. … He put it in my hands. I said that I didn't see any sort of radio or anything. It was just an old typewriter. Very trim and surprisingly light. He then explained that the words I see aren't generated outside of my mind but are drawn up from deep in my unconscious. When they are typed, they appear in the slit. Thus, they are drawn from a level of my mind that I cannot reach to the edge of consciousness where I can make use of them. …I asked how in the world that might work without any communications device. He explained to me that it was in the typewriter's platen. So I asked again how it worked. He said that he didn't know but that it had been developed by a Dr. Raudive.[165]

And *that* was a name that nearly knocked me out of my chair.

OF UNKNOWN ORIGIN

Mark Macy had been an atheist for most of his life.[166] Growing up in Colorado, he earned degrees in journalism and electronics and worked as a technical writer and editor in newsrooms and technology corporations. He was deeply interested in the concept of world peace, and as part of his personal work he assembled and edited a series of anthologies on the subject.

Throughout it all, Macy remained a disbeliever, but that changed beginning in 1988. That year, he was diagnosed with cancer and began what became an obsession with the question of life after death. Macy became closely involved with researchers into what's called Instrumental Transcommunication, or ITC: an umbrella term for communication with discarnate entities via electronic means. Macy's initial research into the field brought him face to face with truly incredible things: messages embedded in computer hard drives, phone calls from the dead, and faces and landscapes appearing in television static. Yet, despite his interest, it was all just too fantastical to believe.

Until it happened to him.

In January of 1994, Macy was working in his home office. The phone rang and, expecting his wife, he eagerly picked up the receiver. [167]

It wasn't his wife.

On the other end of the line was a voice speaking in a deep European accent. The voice wished him good morning, and then it said:

"This is Konstantin Raudive."

Macy knew who he was, and he recognized the voice. Raudive, a Latvian parapsychologist, had achieved a good deal of fame in the realm of ITC, and Macy had heard Raudive's voice on recordings played for him by his friends in ITC research.

There was something odd about it though. Just like Anne Strieber, Konstanin Raudive was dead.

Nonetheless, the voice on the phone continued, telling Macy:

> We have succeeded in building a new bridge to the States. You are the first to be contacted by this means. This is the first contact you get from us. This is Konstantin Raudive.

As a longtime (former) ITC researcher myself, I remember well that first thrill of communication from the spirit world, and I know how Mark felt when he received it. In fact, the first thing Macy did next was the first thing I did, too: go to Radio Shack to buy more recording equipment.. But Mark had received much more than the usual message on a tape or digital recorder. He'd received an actual phone call from the spirits, so he bought recorders for his telephones.

Macy would discover that, in the weeks that followed that wondrous call to his own home, four others in the U.S. had gotten phone calls from "Konstantin Raudive" as well, including ITC celebrity George Meek and Sarah Estep, president of the American Association of Electronic Voice Phenomena (AAEVP)

On February twentieth, a German ITC researcher named Adolf Homes found a message imbedded in the hard drive of his computer.

It was written in German.

It was from Raudive:

> This is Konstantin Raudive via the devices at Station Rivenich. Dear Colleague Adolf Homes, I herewith confirm my own contacts with Mr. Malkhoff (in Germany) and with Mr. Meek and Mr. Macy in America. More contacts have been made successfully in China and Japan by telephone and FAX. Our tests are necessary because humanity is in a state of being—created by themselves— which is negative for us to the point that we cannot influence consciousness. We therefore ask you on Earth to open the psychic barriers to a greater extent. Only then is there a possibility for us to proceed with more contacts via radio receivers, televisions and

computers. Unfortunately messages from our side by telephone and FAX *do not* suffice to make clear to humanity our reality as one of many realities.

Macy would receive more calls from Raudive as the years went on and he became more and more enmeshed in ITC research. Once, while visiting ITC friends in Luxembourg, the group was having dinner when "Raudive" came through on the radio nearby, and in the spring of 1996, the pair had a long conversation discussing ways of making communications stronger between the spirit world and Macy's ITC group in his home state of Colorado.

As I thought about Whitley Strieber, UFOs and Konstantin Raudive, I remembered the relationship between Whitley and his wife, Anne. In particular I remembered his deep grief after her death, and the lively communications they reportedly held despite her passing, including through the "alien implant" he'd received, through which she also communicated to him: the implant invented, the Visitors claimed, by Konstantin Raudive.

The Striebers' relationship—and their after-death communications—were, I realized, very similar to those of the ITC researcher, George Meek, one of Raudive's after-death contactees. The story of George Meek is one of the most infamous in ITC research.[168] His now legendary efforts to build a device to communicate with the spirit world are still talked about by ghost researchers, and many have tried to recreate the device from the original schematic, though to my knowledge none have succeeded.

In the late 1970s, Meek had been enjoying his retirement not by playing golf or fishing, but by exploring the intricacies of human nature. With his wife, Jeannette, he founded the Metascience Foundation, taking other researchers, scientists and doctors around the world to investigate reports of anomalous abilities such as paranormal healings. By 1980, George found himself deep into a project with a psychic medium named Bill O'Neil. The pair was attempting to develop a device to communicate with the dead. They called it the "Spricom," and that's a name that has lived in infamy among paranormal researchers. The Spiricom device—a set of thirteen tone generators—aimed to open the lines of communication between the spirit world and the world of the living. After much trial and error, it started to work.

Between 1979 and 1982, Meek recorded some twenty hours of conversation between O'Neil and a spirit calling itself "Doc" Mueller. "Doc" claimed to be George Jeffries Mueller, who had been an instructor of physics at a California community college before his death in 1967, twelve years before his "spirit" first spoke through the Spiricom.

A good part of the interdimensional dialogue consisted of the spirit Mueller giving instructions on how to tweak the Spiricom to make the connection stronger:

> *Doc Mueller:* I think the problem is an impedance mismatch into that third transistor.
> *B O'Neil:* Third transistor…?
> *Doc Mueller:* Yes, the transistor that follows the, uh, the input.
> *B O'Neil:* I don't understand.
> *Doc Mueller:* The pre-amp. The pre-amp.
> *B O'Neil:* Oh, the pre-amp.
> *Doc Mueller:* Yes. I, uh, think we can correct that by introducing a, uh, 150-ohm, 100-watt resistor in parallel with a point-double-oh-four-seven microfarad ceramic capacitor. I think we can overcome that impedance mismatch.

In 1990, after a decade of work on the Spiricom, George's wife, Jeannette, passed away. Not long after her death, Maggy Harsch-Fischbach, one of ITC's most active researchers, gave George a letter she said she'd found imbedded in the hard drive of her computer (Macy had been at the home of her and her husband when Raudive had come through the parlor radio). In the letter, "Jeannette" gave details of mundane things that had happened in the Meek home since her death, such the date a tenant had called to report a broken refrigerator. Then the spirit wrote:

> *Don't try to explain this, honey. My never-ending love to you. I miss you so much, but I know we will be together.*

Later, some two years after her death, "Jeannette" sent her living husband a photo of herself that had reportedly been taken in the "fifth level of human existence." Once again, the photo was found embedded on the hard drive of Harsch-Fischbach's computer. In the photo was Jeannette as a young woman, and beside her was a woman Jeannette identified as the Meeks' daughter, who had died as an infant but was now in the spirit world as a lovely young woman. Also in the photo was a spirit who appeared to be Hal Roach, the well-known filmmaker.

In January of 1994, just weeks after Macy's own call from him, Konstanin Raudive called George Meek. He told George Jeannette was right beside him.

Most experiences of ITC are not accidental. In fact, one particular aspect of ITC known as Electronic Voice Phenomenon (EVP) has become a popular—and for many, obsessive—modern hobby around the world. EVP is, specifically, the phenomenon of "voices of unknown origin" or "Voices" that show up on electronic devices such as radios, telephones, televisions and computers. EVP research consists of attempting to record these Voice, onto magnetic tape, digital recorders or video cameras and, more importantly, to establish channels of communication between the physical and spiritual worlds. The ultimate goal of EVP research is real-time, two-way communication with the Voices, especially using special kinds of "spirit radios" known as "ghost boxes" or "spirit boxes." like the one the Voices used to tell UFO experiencer Chris Bledsoe about the papal assassination plans.

The idea of recording EVP was not popularized until the 1970s, though there were earlier researchers, as we'll see. But the concept was just a modern version of something that had been going on for a century and a half when Meek built his Spiricom.

The Spiritualist movement that began in the late 1840s had led to a widespread belief in the possibility of deliberate, regular communication with disembodied spirits. With the advent of sound recording, mediums had attempted—nearly a century before Spiricom—to use the new technology to record their seances, including the voices of ostensible spirits of the dead. Long after the interest in Spiritualism had fallen away for the general public, the EVP phenomenon blew open the door that had, at least for most, closed on the séance room.

The Catholic Church's involvement in—and apparent blessing of—EVP research was a major factor for me when, in 2007, I met Mark Macy and began following his EVP research methodology for obtaining Voices. But the Church's seeming approval was just the icing on a cake I'd already baked myself. For, like many other "Christian" researchers, I had begun foolishly claiming that the Bible only denounces speaking to the dead to ask for knowledge about the future. Simply talking to them, I stupidly believed (or maybe *wanted to believe*), was just fine.

Plus, it was *science.*

When I first looked for information on the topic of the Catholic faith and EVP, I was shocked but delighted to discover that more than one *pope* had seemingly rubber-stamped the occult practice of communicating with the dead, starting with the Vatican's approval of the work of two priests. And I found that most of the top researchers into EVP were purported *Catholics,* including our old friend: the inventor of Whitley Strieber's implant/spirit communication device and the chattiest voice in the world of after-death communication.

Konstantin Raudive.

Father Pellegrino Ernetti was a Benedictine monk and exorcist as well as a respected physicist and renowned musicologist. Father Agostino Gemelli, his longtime colleague, was a close friend and fellow visionary. On September 15, 1952, the pair was working together on a harmonics project involving recordings of Gregorian Chant. During one session, the reel-to-reel tape recorder they were using kept eating the tape.

Frustrated, Father Gemelli (probably half in jest, as we all do sometimes) appealed to his deceased father, looking up to Heaven and saying, "Father, please help me."

To the shock of the two priests, when the tape was played back, the voice of Ernetti's dead father could be heard answering his son's plea: *Of course. I am always with you.*

Immediately, the two priests attempted to record the voice again . . . with success. The men stood in awe as a voice came through the tape a second time, saying,

"Zucchini, it is clear. Don't you know it is I?"

"Zucchini" was the nickname Gemelli's father had called him as a boy—a name no one outside the family would have known.

After these startling initial communications, Ernetti and Gemelli embarked on a journey to discover the possibility of contacting the dead through the use of technology. Their experiments became widely known during the late 1950s and early 1960s and have since sparked much interest (as well as skepticism) within the paranormal community.

At first, however, the pair was very troubled about the voices they had recorded. They knew that communication with the dead was expressly and deeply forbidden by Catholic teaching, and they visited Pope Pius XII in Rome to share the Voices with him. But the pope was nonplussed; he shrugged off the priests' concern. Later, the Italian journal, *Astra* would reportedly repeat the pope's words to Gemelli:

> (Y)ou really need not worry about this. The existence of this voice is strictly a scientific fact and has nothing to do with spiritism. The recorder is totally objective. It receives and records only sound waves from wherever they come. This experiment may perhaps become the cornerstone for a building for scientific studies which will strengthen people's faith in a hereafter.[169]

The pope, then, actually seemed to be stating his belief that these voices weren't actually spirit voices holding intelligent discourse, but, rather, sound waves. It was this belief that likely put his mind at ease about the phenomenon. However, many researchers—including me—went on to cherish this statement, ignoring what it really said and believing the pope meant it as a blanket endorsement of spirit communication.

I later discovered that Pope Pius' cousin was the well-known Catholic parapsychologist Gebhard Frei, who was the co-founder of the Jung Institute, famous for delving—like its namesake—into all sorts of occult topics of research. Frei was also a close colleague of a Latvian Catholic researcher who would be the most prolific and influential of all EVP practitioners.

Konstantin Raudive.

Incidentally, Frei himself would go on to reportedly "come through" after his death to at least one colleague.

Fast forward to the tenure of Pope Paul VI, where we find that yet some more nepotism—or at least favoritism—was leading to what was being perceived as, essentially, the Vatican's approval of EVP research.

One of Pope Paul VI's good friends was the Swedish film producer Friedrich Jurgenson, himself a major pioneer in EVP research. The two had become close associates after Jurgenson made a film about the pope, and in thanks the pontiff made Jurgenson a Knight Commander of the prestigious Catholic Order of St Gregory. Later, Jurgenson wrote to Peter Bander, a British EVP researcher, delighting that:

> I have found a sympathetic ear for the Voice Phenomenon in the Vatican. I have won many wonderful friends among the leading figures in the Holy City. Today 'the bridge' stands firmly on its foundations.[170]

And it would go on and on.

Father Leo Schmid, a Swiss theologian, documented more than ten thousand "voices of unknown origin," reportedly with Vatican permission, publishing them in a book, *When the Dead Speak*, which was published posthumously in 1976. Father Andreas Resch reportedly also conducted EVP experiments, including the methodology and results in the parapsychology courses he taught for priests in the Vatican. In 1970, a group called the International Society for Catholic Parapsychologists (now, I believe, defunct) focused much of its annual conference on EVP.

Most famously, in 1972 no less than four senior Catholic leaders were part of a series of famous recordings done at London's Pye Laboratory. We mentioned Jurgenson's letter to Peter Bander above. Dr. Peter Bander was a senior lecturer in Religious and Moral Education at the Cambridge Institute of Education when he was approached by publisher Colin Smythe. Smythe had become intrigued by Konstantin Raudive's research and invited Bander to be part of experimentation into EVP. But Bander flatly refused, calling the possibility of the dead communicating with the living "not only far-fetched but outrageous."

And so, without Bander, Smythe began his own research—and got hooked on EVP, as people tend to do. He invited Bander to try it out, promising results. After about ten minutes of trying, Bander had had enough, but suddenly . . .

> I noticed the peculiar rhythm mentioned by Raudive and his colleagues... I heard a voice... I believed this to have been the voice of my mother who had died three years earlier.[171]

Smythe would go on to publish an entire book by Bander, called *Voices from the Tapes*. In the book, Ken Attwood, Chief Engineer of Pye, swore to the authenticity and inexplicable nature of the "Voices," admitting:

> I have done everything in my power to break the mystery of the voices without success; the same applies to other experts. I suppose we must learn to accept them.[172]

When the Pye tests were over, England's *Sunday Mirror* newspaper (that had planned and paid for the project) refused to publish the results. Reportedly, the editor-in-chief was very unhappy with the positive results obtained by journalist Ronald Maxwell, who vowed that the phenomenon was real. Even after collecting numerous testimonies from renowned scientist observers of the tests, the article was never run.

A central part of the Pye tests was the fact that numerous priests were involved in observing the experiments. All of them seemed to go all-in on the Voices, including Father Pistone, superior of the Society of St Paul, who concluded:

> I do not see anything against the teaching of the Catholic Church in the Voices, they are something extra-ordinary but there is no reason to fear them, nor can I see any danger.[173]

On another occasion, the Right Reverend Monsignor Professor C. Pfleger said something else downright crazy for a Catholic, let alone a priest, let alone a monsignor:

> Facts have made us realize that between death and resurrection there is another realm of post-mortal existence. Christian theology has little to say about this realm.[174]

To clarify, it took EVP experiments for a monsignor to realize there is "another realm of post-mortal existence" between life on Earth and in Heaven? That's extraordinary, as the Catholic faith has a long tradition of belief in such a place—and theology about it..

It's called Purgatory.

In his book, Bander also included a photograph of yet another Catholic higher-up, the Right Reverend Monsignor Stephen O'Connor, Vicar General and Principal Roman Catholic Chaplain to the Royal Navy. In the photo, O'Connor is shown listening to, ostensibly, the voice of a suicide victim which had been recorded by Konstantin Raudive. Neither O'Connor nor any of the other priests involved seem to have suggested the possibility that these voices were those of souls needing prayers or Masses, particularly a soul who had committed suicide.

Research into the voices continued full throttle throughout the 1980s, spearheaded by Raudive and other predominantly Catholic researchers. The 1980s also so the advent of many EVP innovations, including the now mythical Spiricom.

I followed Mark Macy and World ITC for years. I started recording EVP myself, learning from he and his international colleagues in the field of ITC. In 2007, when I hosted the first of a string of paranormal conferences in Chicago, Mark Macy was the keynote speaker. He brought with him a device he called the "Luminator." Macy claimed that, when a living person had his or her photograph taken near the machine, spirit "extras" would appear in the photos. He took my Polaroid that day I met him, and sure enough there seemed to be a face (albeit quite blurry) next to mine in the exposed portrait. Macy took thousands of these during his travels, and he wrote a book about his work with the Luminator—and ITC—called *Spirit Faces*.

I went on to doing other things in ITC but was excited to see one day, years later, that Macy had published another book. It was called *The Project*. It had been a while since I had followed Macy's work, and I was startled to find that Macy's results from his ITC work had changed dramatically. From contacting discarnate entities—including Konstantin Raudive and other recognizable people—, the work had grown into an entire cosmology and history of humankind, contact with extraterrestrials and, of course, an "enlightened" body of knowledge about religion and the human purpose. The body of collected messages formed a version of today's popular "ancient astronaut" theory, based in evolution, higher extraterrestrial creators and, of course, a universal consciousness.

Later, I would find that aliens (and the American government) would pop up in another spirit communication community: the one that had been meeting in that farmhouse cellar in Scole.

In 1978 a sound researcher named D.J. Ellis published a book on the "Voice Extras" found in the recordings of Jurgenson, Raudive and others. The book is called *The Mediumship of the Tape Recorder*, and what an apt title it is. Ellis recognized that, with EVP, technology had replaced the woman (or, occasionally, man) at the head of the nineteenth-Century seance table. Now, more than a century after the first Voices were recorded, thousands of researchers into EVP have discovered a firm and dangerous truth: not only people can act as mediums.

For ITC researchers, it's obvious that, without the recorder— or the ghost box or the television or the computer hard drive— they wouldn't receive the Voices or images or even emails of unknown origin. Just as, without the living, breathing psychic medium, seance sitters of old—and Theresa Caputo and Tyler Henry fans today—would never receive the "messages from the dead" so sought after by the living. On a larger scale, without their ritualized, occult efforts, joined across the globe, members of

Steven Greer's CE-5 movement and the EVP "bridge" workers wouldn't be channeling "aliens" and communicating with whole communities of "spirits" on the Other Side.

In talking about UFOs and ETs in the documentary, "Aliens and Demons," Michael Heiser ventured this: that in some UFO/alien encounter cases, the demonic seems to be masquerading as something our modern culture expects to encounter or *wants* to encounter. In a world where artificial intelligence, space travel and science reign as gods with the keys to our future, the demonic no longer appears as the fairy folk to protect our crops, or as our departed loved ones in the séance circle, but as the harbingers of salvation through technology. Just as séance sitters in the nineteenth and early twentieth centuries often made contact with Benjamin Franklin and, later, Henry Ford, Thomas Edison and other radical innovators, today's experiencers are making contact with technologically superior cosmic beings from "space."

In my own work in ghost and haunt research I saw this many times, including at Bachelors Grove, where I observed that, while there seemed to have been some actual manifestations of human spirits there early on, that later—often after ritual activity began to be reported at the site—there seemed to be malevolent versions of these spirits who were leading people into the woods rather than away from the cemetery: into the woods where the rituals had taken place. Similarly, when the Voices tell us they are someone who died, or someone who was murdered, or George Washington or the Man in the Moon, we'd be fools to believe any of it.

Ufologists have long been finding, indeed, that these "ET intelligences" can be counted on for one thing and one thing alone.

Deception.

As I've already shared, It wasn't long into my research that I encountered the Christian uprising against what many have come to call this "UFO Deception." Everywhere I looked I found pastors and Bible scholars warning against believing in UFOs extraterrestrials and offering biblical scholarship to back up their admonitions. Just as I had realized the inherent deception of my Voices, it seemed that the top scholars and theologians of every Christian Church were on the warpath against UFO belief.

Except for one.

My own church.

The Catholic Church.

TREKKIES IN THE VATICAN

When I was little, growing up in Chicago, my cousins would always come in from their hometown of Cicero during the summer and spend weeks at our grandma's house. They were magical times, with days full of play in the bountiful garden, rummaging in the attic through mementos a hundred years old, and baking bread, rolls and cookies with my uncle, a Navy baker who'd learned his craft in the Second World War. At night, we'd all sit out on the high back porch that overlooked the vast garden and the surrounding neighborhood, watching the skies for UFOs.

Once, after such a night, I asked my mom—a devout Catholic—if there were beings on other planets. I remember very distinctly that she repeated to me what her (also devotedly Catholic) father had responded to the same question: *Why would God make the whole universe and only put life on one planet?*

This, I know now, is known as the "limiting God" argument in favor of extraterrestrial life (the "extraterrestrial hypothesis" or ETH). I also now make the case, as few Catholics do, that the real limiting of God comes from us imposing our own rationale on Him: our own assumptions of what God would and would not do.

My ways are not your ways, He explicitly tells us. (Isaiah 55:8).)

He also tells us that we will be, on the new Earth, "above the angels" (1 Corinthians 6:3). That's just one among many verifications that human beings and our Earth are very, very special indeed (most evidenced, of course, by the fact that He became one of us Himself).

Though I didn't develop any real interest in UFOs until recent years, I would have, though my life, a bit more interest in the subject because of my experiences as a child. The house I grew up in was what we called "haunted." Many nights, my mom and dad, my brother and I would hear footsteps walking up the steps from the foyer to the second floor where the bedrooms were. But while we all experienced the footsteps in the house, my brother—who was a year older than me—seemed to be experiencing things on a different, more intense level. It would be decades before I came to understand much of my brother's experiences as part of what the rest of us were dealing with. Because my brother was not only experiencing other noises such as banging, voices and the playing of the piano (things the rest of us didn't hear); he was also having experiences in the house that were evocative of alien visitations or abductions.

But we all called them his "dreams."

He would wake during the night to find strange humanoid creatures next to his bed, accompanied by lights and, sometimes, some kind of craft outside. Sometimes, he said, he would be taken away.

While he was going through these traumatic experiences, I suffered from what many might classify as "old hag" experiences or what is more commonly known as "sleep paralysis." I would sometimes feel that my brother was calling out for me, but I was often either paralyzed and could not move, or filled with a paralyzing terror of going to him.

These experiences, of course, have become known today as a usual part of UFO and abduction experiences, even sometimes shared by family members as they were by me.

Having an interest in the paranormal, likely because of our "haunted house," I voraciously read books about paranormal phenomena. Of course, many collections of paranormal experiences included stories of UFO and ET encounters, so I was more knowledgeable about the subject than most kids of the time (especially girls)! But ufology still wasn't an "interest," and I certainly had no theory or opinion about the possibilities beyond the "Why not?" that seemed to be most others' opinion, too.

And so I came from a fairly long line of barely tepid opinion about UFOs and aliens. My mom's dad, and then her, and then me: we had both held a common, seemingly reverent, but—I would discover—very unbiblical and un-Catholic view of UFOs.

When I went down the famous rabbit hole of ufology, I had been accompanied largely by the plethora of evangelical Christian writings and videos I had consumed, all demolishing the possibility of UFOs and ETs. Naturally, I was anxious to see what my own One Holy Catholic and Apostolic Church had to say. Obviously, in the great scholastic tradition of the Church, our own theologians would trumpet the truth of the UFO Deception more loudly than any other denomination.

I was wrong.

As the UFO phenomenon surged at the end of the first quarter of the 21st century—along with my own interest in the subject—I began to look into the Church's view on aliens and UFOs and I found myself literally open-mouthed, and deeply disturbed.

Although I hold an M.A. in American Cultural and Intellectual History, with a focus on religion, my research and writing of the past 35 years has been focused on fringe belief, including fringe religions. Catholicism has not been a focus of my research (though you could definitely argue that it is, indeed, something of a fringe religion in the U.S.!). For the most part, I'm just an ordinary Catholic continually learning about my faith; I'm no theologian. Still, it took me about ten minutes of logical reasoning to realize that a belief in alien life is completely against the teachings of the Catholic faith. And yet, as I started looking into the stance of the Church on the subject, source after source was telling me that not only the most popular Catholic theologians had been promoting the idea of alien life.

So had the Vatican.

It probably won't surprise many—Catholic or otherwise—to find the Jesuits as the public face of (and at the heart of) the alien promotion campaign being trumpeted by the Catholic Church. The Jesuits—that matchless order founded by Saint Ignatius of Loyola—have been associated with scholarship in general (and science in particular) from the beginning. They're also noted for their evangelical zeal.

Not only Catholics but the wider world have held this view of the Jesuits, so I probably shouldn't have been as shocked as I was to discover an entire sub-genre of science fiction developed around these legendary religious, including one series—the Galactic Milieu books by Julian May—that (also unsurprisingly) features a female Jesuit priest. May's books also incorporate the ideas of the heretical Jesuit priest Pierre Teilhard de Chardin, many of which are found throughout secular ufology.

Far better scholars than I have written extensively about Teilhard's connection to the destruction of the Jesuit order (and the Catholic Church for that matter), but for our purposes we'll just point out that he was a rabid Darwinist and ET believer who called the uniqueness of humanity "improbable." To say that Teilhard's ideas helped to form the basis of the current Jesuit/Vatican cosmological madness is a massive understatement.

Today, the Jesuit order (also known as the Society of Jesus) is known perhaps most of all not for its stalwart defense of and dissemination of Catholic faith, but for its often heretical members. The late exorcist and Catholic scholar Malachi Martin was a Jesuit himself, but he's remembered for his scathing denouncement of his order's Modernist metomorphosis. In his book, *The Jesuits: The Society of Jesus and the Betrayal of the Roman Catholic* Church, Martin summarized the order's first 400 years, observing:

> There was no continent the Jesuits did not reach, no known language they did not speak and study, or, in scores of cases, develop; no culture they did not penetrate; no branch of learning and science they did not explore; no work in humanism, in the arts, in popular education they did not undertake and do better than anyone else; no form of death by violence they did not undergo—Jesuits were hanged, drawn, and quartered in London; disemboweled in Ethiopia, eaten alive by Iroquois Indians in Canada; poisoned in Germany; flayed to death in the Middle East; crucified in Thailand; starved to death in South America; beheaded in Japan; drowned in Madagascar; bestialized in the Soviet Union. . . .In that first four hundred years, they gave the Church 38 canonized saints, 134 holy men already declared 'Blessed' by the Roman Church, 36 already declared 'Venerable,'

and 115 considered to have been 'Servants of God.' Of these, 243 were martyrs; that is, they were put to death for their beliefs. [175]

It gives me no pleasure to disdain the Jesuit order. The name and astounding achievements of the Jesuit missionary, Father Marquette, are inseparable from the history of my hometown of Chicago and the Great Lakes region, and my early school days were filled with tales of the enigmatic "Black Robes" who glided into every corner of the globe with their razor-sharp intellects and passion for the Church, teaching and saving souls. Such accounts included that of Father De Smet, the Jesuit missionary so troubled by both the pagan beliefs of Native Americans and their maltreatment at the hands of explorers and settlers that he walked, rode and canoed an estimated 180,000 miles in his missionary work across the United States and Canada.

Like many Catholic kids, I was also raised by parents starry-eyed about the Society of Jesus. My mom, a very scientific-minded woman, was particularly smitten. And so, when my brother, the favorite, was ready for high school, there was no corner left uncut to assure he attended St. Ignatius College Prep, the Jesuit stronghold on the city's West Side. The school, along with the parish church of the Holy Family, were established by Father Arnold Damen, one of a band of Belgian Jesuit missionaries sent in the early 1800s to whip American into shape.

Damen was dispatched to Chicago to establish a Catholic church in one of the city's poorest settlements. Arriving with little funding, he built a Catholic fortress on the West Side with nickels and dimes from his struggling parishioners—and larger donations from the few wealthy ones. Damen was known to have a knack for separating the well-endowed from their money; if he needed a new building or a furnace was on the fritz, a few well-chosen words form Damen were said to cause rich men and women to empty their pockets before him.

Damen was also known to have a sort of main line to God. His prayers on the night of the Great Fire in 1871 were credited with sparing the parish buildings during that terrible conflagration—and his intercession when the school and church were set for demolition almost a century later, in the 1980s. Instead of being razed, the school rose to what it remains today: arguably the most prestigious high school in Chicago.

When it was time for my own daughter to head off to high school, then, my mind followed my mom's. But four years later, the environment at the Jesuit "Catholic" school had almost succeeded in completely destroying the faith I'd raised my elder daughter to hold.

Indeed, many Jesuit high schools, colleges and universities have removed the word "Catholic" from their names, and others—because of their teaching and policies— have been forbidden from using "Catholic" in their names by their Archdioceses, such as St. John Brebuef Preparatory High School in Indianapolis in 2019.

Today, Georgetown University, the oldest Catholic institution of higher learning in the United States, has distanced itself from Catholicism. The school announced the appointment of its first lay president at the beginning of the millennium, and today the university's focus is on religious pluralism, not Catholicism. The school has received hundreds of millions of dollars from Saudi Arabia, Qatar and the united Arab Emirates, and news stories often cover religious-focused scandals, such as pro-abortion commencement speakers and LGBTQ events.

In his July 2013 article, "Á Rainbow Over Catholic Colleges," *New York Times'* journalist Kyle Spencer reported on the state of affairs at Georgetown and other "Catholic" colleges and universities in the U.S. [176] He noted that, in the fall of 2012, a same sex "kiss-in" had been part of the "OUTober" event lineup at Georgetown, and the following spring the annual drag ball called Genderfunk featured a male student dressed as "Mary" in high heels dancing to "Like a Virgin" as a woman costumed as Jesus stood by.

Spencer reported that, though many alumni, including famous ones like *The Exorcist* author, William Peter Blatty, have spoken out and even petitioned against the decidedly un-Catholic climate at Georgetown, the steamroller of Jesuit-inspired Modernism continues. In April of 2024, students performed at the Intercultural Center Auditorium on campus, with a woman in drag calling herself "Jack the Bulldyke" speaking at the event, joining students calling themselves Justin Beaver and Luther Whore, among others. The president also attends a special LGBTQ "Lavender" commencement. During his interview by the *Times,* Todd A. Olson, then dean of students, defended it all as part of the Jesuit tenet that urges the "care for the whole person" or *cura personalis,* which interprets "good" as, essentially, encouraging students to do what makes them feel good and authentic about themselves.

In 2022, Francis Maier shared the results of a personal survey he'd completed, in which he'd asked both Jesuits and those outside of the Society, *What went wrong with the Jesuits?* Among their answers, responders criticized the Jesuits for priding themselves on wanting to be "cutting edge" rather than truly scientific, on putting more emphasis on personal discernment than on the teachings of the Church, and for their ideal of an organic Church that not only rolls with the changes but readily changes itself to adapt to current popular opinion. [177]

With their history of scientific rigor (at least up to a certain point) their hunger to be relevant, and their often flagrant disregard for Catholic teaching, it should not surprise us that Jesuits have emerged to give the official Catholic response to the extraterrestrial question.

In February of 2008, *Reuters* reported that the Jesuit Father Jose Gabriel Funes, the Vatican's chief astronomer, had told a Roman reporter:

> Just as there is a multiplicity of creatures on Earth, there can be other beings, even intelligent, created by God. This is not in contrast with our faith because we can't put limits on God's creative freedom," he said. [178]

This, again, is known as the popular but false "limiting God" argument for aliens. Funes went on to tell the reporter that, if aliens exist, they may not need redemption. They would be our "extraterrestrial brothers": a statement chillingly similar to those of the UFO Contactees of the 1950s who reveled in their relationships with the so-called "space brothers."

Funes also quoted St Francis to help support his argument for aliens:

> To use St. Francis' words, if we consider earthly creatures as 'brothers' and 'sisters,' why can't we also speak of an 'extraterrestrial brother?' [179]

It's odd (or perhaps not) how so much of what Vatican reps say in our era is so misleading. Saint Francis never talked about aliens, though Funes' quote seems to claim otherwise. Funes presumably was referring to Francis's famous *Canticle of the Sun* in which he addresses the Sun, Moon, water and other elements, and creatures *of the Earth* as his brothers and sisters. (Putting the *Catnicle* in context, St. Francis wrote it after being crawled over by rats all night while sleeping in a convent dungeon. He was so ashamed by his self-pity over it that he penned the *Canticle* to put things back in perspective and let God know that he loved his fellow creatures, despite the momentary distaste of the rats.) In fact, there are a whole lot of reasons "why we can't also speak of an extraterrestrial brother," and St. Francis was apparently more concerned about— or schooled in—theology than Funes, because he left the ETs out of his affectionate ditty.

In 2010 Funes' successor at the Vatican Observatory, fellow Jesuit and brother in the order, Guy Consolmagno, famously declared that he'd baptize an extraterrestrial, but only "if she asked!" He recounted the story behind the declaration in his book, *Would You Baptize an Extraterrestrial?* Consolmagno has become a kind of unofficial commander in chief of the pro-alien Catholic army, giving lectures and speeches about the general wonderfulness of extraterrestrial belief. Unsurprisingly, he mused on the state of science fiction for *U.S. Catholic* in the Spring of 2015, outing himself as an obvious longtime fan of the genre.[180]

Malachi Martin was very clear in reminding us that, from the beginning, the Jesuits were known as the "pope's men." Everything they did and achieved, everywhere they went, every move they made, there was one goal: to be faithful to the Holy See. Martin, in his pull-no-punches critique, was observing in the 1970s when he wrote it that this was no longer the case. The Jesuits were working for themselves, and on goals and with methods often in direct opposition to the Church's discernment and authority.

Today, I wonder what Martin would think of that 1970s situation that's taken a wild turn indeed: the election of a Jesuit pope. For if you can say one thing about the Catholic Church today, it's that the pope and the Jesuits are working together again. And with a vengeance.

In a May 2014 homily, Pope Francis made waves when he asked the crowd, essentially, *Who are we to deny salvation to anyone, including Martians?*:

> If . . . tomorrow an expedition of Martians came, and some of them came to us, here... Martians, right? Green, with that long nose and big ears, just like children paint them... And one says, 'But I want to be baptized!' What would happen? ...Who are we to close doors?[181]

The late Monsignor Corrado Balducci was an official exorcist, a diplomat in Washington's D.C. Papal Nunciature and a member of the Congregation for the Propagation of the Faith. Doubtless he was the highest up in the Church to have spoken on UFOs and ETs (besides the popes, of course).

In 2005, speaking at the X-Conference—a gathering of ufologists—, Balduccci told the crowd that the UFO phenomenon is definitely not evil, demonic or occultic in any way. One of the greatest Christian ufologists to date, Michael Heiser, was there to speak, too, and Balducci's comments so disturbed him that he returned home to write extensively about what he called "Balducci's Conundrum" on his blog, warning that there exists "abundant evidence" to the contrary (specifically addressing Balducci's statements), and of course I concur.

I hesitate to reference the words of a sedevacantist Catholic (someone who believes there's been no legitimate pope since Vatican II), but as well-known sedevacantist Brother Peter Dimond has correctly said of the UFO/alien question and the Vatican's bizarre response to it, many of the most high-ups over the years have been less-than-dependable teachers of the faith. I've seen in my own research that, like Dimond has stated, many of the Vatican Jesuits in particular have shown themselves to be "liberal heretics," a sentiment Dimond shared during the narration of the excellent documentary, *UFOs: Demonic Activity and Elaborate Hoaxes meant to Deceive Mankind*," based on his book by the same name.

I'm not a sedevacantist, but I concur. It was, in fact, Dimond's observation that led me to begin to second-guess the conviction that my EVP work was endorsed by former priests and even popes. I stopped blindly accepting everything popes, bishops and even popes say as infallible. It's not, and we aren't taught to do that.[182] Should we be able to look to Church leaders for authority on such things? Maybe. But we can't. They are only human, and they err and fail. They make—quite often in the last half century—vague or misleading or confusing statements. Frequently, too, their statements are twisted by those who want them to say something else, like my EVP aficionados and I did when we used statements by popes, priests, and bishops to justify our all-too-rogue (and even abominable) pursuits.

To my growing unease, I was also finding that the "Vatican-approved" lay theologians of the Catholic Church as well as esteemed Catholic religious historians were also, if not all-in with, heartily open to the idea of alien life and UFOs. This included leading 21st century scholars Paul Thigpen, Jimmy Akin, and "Catholic" religious historian and (now) ufologist Diana Pasulka, the latter of whom, I would discover, had become an icon of the secular UFO belief crowd.

Catholic apologist Paul Thigpen must be one of the sweetest, gentlest souls in the whole world. No one who has heard him speak or read his beautiful writing can deny his loving belief in the Gospel, the Catholic Church and its great cloud of witnesses in the form of her millennia of saints and scholars.

In the winter of 2011, Thigpen shared his moving story through the Coming Home International Network, which tells the stories of converts to Catholicism. [183] In his stirring account,

Thigpen recounted his childhood in the Pentecostal Church and his service as a Pentecostal and United Methodist minister before converting to Catholicism. But from a young age, Thigpen was intensely drawn to the suffering, crucified Jesus, even going so far as to hide a statuette of the "Man on the Cross" under his bed (after secretly hand painting the plaster of Paris figurine himself, Catholic style, using lots of scarlet paint for blood).

A prolific and erudite scholar, Thigpen was appointed by the United States Conference of Catholic Bishops as a lay representative on their National Advisory Council. He's penned many books on Catholic theology and apologetics, and he literally wrote the book on Catholic faith and the extraterrestrial question.

Unfortunately, that 2022 volume, *Extraterrestrial Intelligence and the Catholic Faith*, contains a number of glaring errors, including the shady claim that the beloved modern Saint Pio of Pietrelcina, known popularly as Padre Pio, believed in aliens. The claim continues to make its way around the internet and in print, as Padre Pio is inarguably one of the most popular saints of our times. Anything he said would, for Catholics, be a valuable piece of evidence for one's argument for or against something, and so the claim that he believed in aliens is a troubling one indeed.

The saint was particularly known for his relationship with the spirit world. He was regularly paid visits by the devil himself, who he mockingly addressed as "Old Bluebeard."

The fallen one would enter the priest's room at night, causing a ruckus and making quite a mess; Pio would say, "Oh, it's just you, Old Bluebeard" and go back to sleep. The saint was also known to be frequently visited by souls in Purgatory who would ask for prayers and Masses. He, too, exhibited an uncanny ability to see into the consciences of those who came to him in the confessional, knowing if they were holding certain sins back or being otherwise evasive.

The claim that Saint Padre Pio believed in aliens was first put forth and popularized by UFO believer Monsignor Balducci, and Paul Thigpen's parish still has the deeply questionable claim on the parish website. Here is, from the St. Catherine of Sienna website, Thigpen's response to a parishioner's question of whether Padre Pio believed in extraterrestrial life:

> According to the late Msgr. Corrado Balducci (1923–2008), a member of the Vatican Curia and long-time exorcist for the Archdiocese of Rome, St. Pio (feast day this week, September 23) did in fact affirm the existence of extraterrestrial intelligence. In a paper entitled "Ufology and Theological Clarifications," presented at Pescara, Italy, in 2001, the Monsignor reported: 'The following dialogue is documented and officially published by the Capuchin Order:
>
> *Question*: Father, some claim that there are creatures of God on other planets, too.
>
> *Answer*: What else? Do you think they don't exist and that God's omnipotence is limited to this small planet Earth? What else? Do you think there are no other beings who love the Lord?
>
> *Another question*: Father, I think the Earth is nothing compared to other planets and stars.
>
> *Answer*: Exactly yes, and we Earthlings are nothing, too. The Lord certainly did not limit His glory to this small Earth. On other planets other beings exist who did not sin and fall as we did.. [184]

Balducci apparently was citing a work by one Don Nello Castello, *Così parlò Padre Pio*, published in Vicenza, Italy in 1974.

Daniel O'Connor, professor of religion and philosophy, Catholic scholar and author, has written extensively about the many errors inherent in the work of Catholic ordained and lay theologians regarding the alien question. (I urge you to consult both his book, *Only Man Bears His Image*, his website blog, and his YouTube channel, as he has been writing and speaking against the ET deception for years now.) O'Connor has observed that Padre Pio is very possibly only second to St. Francis in the "number of bogus quotes attributed to him that he never actually said." Additionally, the saint certainly, O'Connor points out, would never call human beings and their Earth "nothing," as "this is the planet that hosts the entire drama of salvation." [185] Even if Padre Pio did believe in aliens, he never would have made a statement like that, so what does one do, then, with the whole claim?

O'Connor decided to find out just how much water the claim held. He was unable to find the cited book containing it, even after an exhaustive search. (I haven't been able to find it either.) In fact, every mention of it led back to one of two sources: the Catholic UFO believers Balducci and Thigpen.

Thigpen in his book also clings to the (also shady) claim that Saint Pope John Paul II expressed belief in aliens, citing a strange, unverified second-hand report that the late pope told a child in a crowd who asked about ETs that "(t)hey are children of God as we are." Like the former "quotes" from Padre Pio, the JPII claim has proved totally unverifiable

Thigpen goes on to cite yet another quote of a quote of a quote of a private conversation in which Saint Pope Paul VI allegedly said he found the possibility of extraterrestrials reasonable. Of course, as we know Paul VI also promoted spirit communication via EVP research.

Thigpen also posits that ETs could actually be fairies or some other unseen beings in some spiritual taxonomy of which we aren't, apparently, informed. This, of course, is in direct opposition to Catholic belief, which holds that the spiritual world consists of the triune God, the souls of the human dead, and angels (fallen and not). That's it. Purporting that a spiritual being is something else is in error, and this false claim furthermore clouds the fact that demons have constantly disguised themselves as these other

characters—including "extraterrestrials."

Though he has no fancy theology degrees, Catholic apologist Jimmy Akin has a mind like a supercomputer, and he seems a humble and soft-spoken sort. But Akin is also known for his keen interest in the paranormal and occult—and for his enthusiasm for obviously occult activities. Catholics overwhelmingly accept what he says as truth, and he's often cited as a favorite theologian and apologist by not only lay Catholics but priests as well.

Akin tells his story of his conversion to Catholicism in *Surprised by Truth*, where we learn that he became a Catholic after long years of deeply disliking Christians and following after New Age ideas like reincarnation. [186] Akin married a woman named Renee, who had been raised in a UFO religion. She later began identifying as Catholic, but by then Jimmy had abandoned the New Age (sort of, as we'll see) and become Christian. Moreover, he now wanted to be a Protestant minister, so Renee's Catholicism was a looming problem. If they were going to be Catholic, he wouldn't be able to be a minister. And he couldn't be a Catholic priest and be married.

So Jimmy began actively trying to destroy both Renee's Catholic and New Age beliefs by giving her books to read. It worked. Renee left the New Age behind and then decided she was now a Protestant, too. The couple married, but soon after their marriage, Renee went back to identifying as Catholic, so Jimmy had to change his plans—and change his religion.

As someone also deeply involved in paranormal research for my entire adult life, you'd think I would be first in line to gush over Jimmy Akin, and I probably would have been if I'd encountered his work before I woke up to the abominable quality of the things I was doing in my ITC research, and in promoting psychics, mediums and other occult practitioners in my writing and events.

In March of 2024, the unmistakable, red-bearded, cowboy-hatted Akin was a guest of Catholic podcast host Matt Fradd for six and a half hours. [187]

Six and a half hours.

Of course, he talked a lot about the paranormal, including UFOs. During the course of the six and a half hours, he told Fradd, among other things, that there could be many different "Marys" throughout the universe who've given birth as part of many incarnations of Jesus, something Aquinas called derogatory to the faith (as if common sense wasn't enough to make us realize that).

At one point in the conversation, Fradd, in a seeming attempt to clarify the wild things Akin is suggests, says, "So . .

.hypothetically . . . theoretically… you've got a mother of God on another planet—"

And Akin cuts in and says, "Maybe. They might not have sexes though…or they might have more than two."

This kind of theological insanity evidences *point number one* for Catholics looking at the extraterrestrial question: Any attempt to theologically allow for intelligent life outside the Earth very quickly leads into not only heresy but often *abominable heresy.*

Along with suggesting the possibility of multiple mothers (or whatever they are) of Jesus and multiple incarnations of Jesus, for multiple races of intelligent life in the cosmos, Akin also references the positive remarks of recent popes in his effort to demonstrate that UFOs and extraterrestrials are possible. We already know what a mistake *that* can be, having already waded through the muddy waters of the past century's papal dealings with the paranormal.

Akin goes further to deny that *any* pope had a "definitive" problem with the possibility of extraterrestrial life. But that seems patently untrue. As Daniel O'Connor reminds us, Pope Zachary was prepared to excommunicate an Irish priest who professed belief in worlds or beings living under the earth or on the sun or moon, and the pope expressed the "abominable" nature of such beliefs to no less than St. Boniface.. [188]

Pope Pius II also condemned belief in extraterrestrials in his 1459 letter *Cum sicut accepimus*, in which he attacked Zaninus de Solcia's "most pernicious" and "sacrilegious" errors, including the heretic's belief that "God created another world than this one, and . . . many other men and women existed . . . and Adam was not the first man."[189]

In the Fradd interview and elsewhere, Akin disparages Daniel O'Connor's anti-alien thesis, addressing one piece of over 800 pages of evidence O'Connor gives against the existence of extraterrestrials in his book, including the fundamental statement from the Catechism of the Catholic Church (CCC) regarding the singularity of man and his relationship to God. The tenet teaches that:

Of all visible creatures, only man is able to know and love his creator… he [man] alone is called to share… in God's own life." (*Catechism of the Catholic Church*, § 356)

But Akin told Fradd that, because the CCC doesn't say humans are the only intelligent beings *in the context of addressing the ET question*, it's faulty to use the statement to argue against aliens. In other words, because the authorities who wrote the Catechism didn't have aliens in mind when they wrote the statement, we can't use it as evidence against the existence of ETs.

Many listeners and viewers of the Fradd program commented, as listeners always do, on the incredible amount of knowledge Jimmy Akin has in theology, history and philosophy. I, too, find that impressive, though I have some probably different ideas about just how Akin is both uniquely gifted toward learning while at the same time so instrumental in sharing occult, heretical and abominable ideas and practices. As O'Connor has pointed out (regarding not only Akin but the other pro-alien scholars), the devil goes for the scholars and the holy men above all others, because people tend to accept what they say and trust them implicitly.

Now I hope you will have patience with me as I take you for an extended side trip into one of Akin's own podcast subjects, which he featured on his popular podcast, "Jimmy Akin's Mysterious World," because it will help us understand the kind of occult ideas and practices Akin finds to be theologically acceptable for Catholics. In demonstrating how dangerous his "blessing" of other ideas and practices can be, I hope to also demonstrate how little his UFO/ET approval can be trusted.

In 2023, Akin addressed on his show the activities of Dominican friar Father Nathan Castle,[190] who has formed his own ministry to serve those "deceased souls" who've told him and his prayer partners they've had "interrupted death experiences" or IDEs. Later, Akin would have Castle as a guest on the show. Let's look at what this popular guest—and priest—does.

Castle started his work in helping "stuck souls" after having a dream of a man who burned to death on a car radiator. So he started talking to the man he'd dreamed about. Unsurprisingly, the "man" talked back.

Castle says he became convinced of the authenticity of this "man" because he was able to later historically verify that this man did in fact die in this way. It was an absurd assumption, as the devil knows everything that happens and keeps it all in his preternatural file cabinet to use against us the moment the opportunity arises.

In fact, I would do this in ghost hunting. A medium would tell me there was the ghost of a woman named June who'd died in a house, and off I'd go to the archives to see if it was true, because that would "prove" there was a poor, dead person haunting the place.

400 cases and almost three decades later, Castle is revered and referenced by mediums, psychics and other occultists; you'll find in both print and online many occultists who call what he does wonderful, moving and important.

Castle even claims that God himself even once asked if he could use his voice to speak—*to serve as a direct voice medium for the Creator*—: an almost inconceivably abominable offense. But it's ok, he tells us, because he prays "prayers of protection" to Mary, St. Michael and other saints and angels before channeling spirits.

This is something I have seen thousands of times in ghost and haunting investigation: investigators praying before using Ouija boards, ghost boxes and recorders and before conducting seances. I did it myself, and often. I've seen people say to the spirits, ridiculously: *Only human spirits are allowed to talk through this box* before using ghost boxes. As if they have any control over the devil and his minions.

They do not.

So essentially we were saying, as Castle is, *God, I'm about to violate your law and commit what you clearly call an abomination against you, but please have your best people protect me as I do it.*

Obviously, then, it's not St. Michael or any of the other saints or angels who come when these abominable "prayers" are said. But something or something does, indeed, come.

Who or what are they?

Here's what the Book of Revelation says about St. Michael the Archangel:

> And there was war in heaven, Michael and his angels waging war with the dragon. The dragon and his angels waged war, and they did not prevail, and there was no longer a place found for them in heaven. And the great dragon was thrown down, the serpent of old who is called the devil and Satan, who deceives the whole world; he was thrown down to the earth, and his angels were thrown down with him. (Rev 12:7-9)

But Castle assures us this is not what St. Michael is like. He knows him "very well" after so many years of working with "Michael" himself. Castle says St. Michael is an "angel of light" and "has no enemies." Castle also told Akin, "[Saint Michael] is not trying to vanquish a foe." There literally is no bigger falsehood you could speak about St. Michael, the unquestioned commander of the angelic army against the devil.

It's interesting that the Bible tells us Satan (originally Lucifer, the "light-bearer") disguises himself as "an angel of light," the very words Castle uses for "St. Michael." Apparently, that's what" St. Michael" told him he was.

I know (and I'd think that Akin, a paranormal investigator himself, would know) that there's a whole mini army of fake demonic "saints" and "angels" who serve "mediums," "psychics" "healers" and other occult "facilitators" like Castle. Fake St. Michael is the main one, but Fake Mary is big, too, especially in the hundreds of fake "Marian" apparitions over the years, and now in the UFO experiencer accounts like those of Chris Bledsoe. In fact, Diana Pasulka has encountered these in her work, but not being well-versed in the tricks of the demonic, she doesn't recognize what they are; to her eye, they are all manifestations of the same being, spirit or source.

I myself had a run-in with Fake St. Michael when I foolishly elected to undergo something called Remote Spirit Release Therapy, not long before my conversion from the occult. The "therapy" is geared towards releasing a person from spirits that may be attached, including human ones and nonhuman ones. The medium shared that I had such a "dark force energy" (they don't say demon) attached to me that he had to call St. Michael himself to take it away. There was zero mention of God or Jesus during the process, and this incident was one that got me thinking very deeply about just what was going on in this world I had worked in for so many years.

Not incidentally, many of the same folks that have these "saints" and "angels" at their beck and call carry around St. Benedict medals and "protective" crystals in the same pocket.

Castle has claimed that the "souls" in his cases are shown a sort of menu of different living people who can help them get "unstuck," and that the souls he works with choose him from a variety of helpers from many different backgrounds, faiths and occult abilities. Irene Weinberg, a self-described "healer" who interviewed castle for her blog,[191] commented that it seems similar to when people come to one of her New Age events featuring lots of psychics, mediums and healers, and they choose one that they feel a connection to. Castle concurred, likening choosing an afterlife "facilitator" to choosing local activities from brochures at a hotel concierge desk. Incidentally, there's no mention of just who it is that is giving these "souls" the menu of occultists to choose from for help.

Castle then went on to tell Weinberg there's not really judgment on the other side as we think of it—only accepting the truth of one's actions in life. There's no shame involved. Fitting with this claim, none of his "souls" seem to ever mention God. Their only concerns are their own anger, selfish desires and controlling motivations, even though death is the moment when we are shown God's judgment of us. For any human soul, this would be a moment of horror, remorse and repentance, followed quickly by the singular desire to be united with God despite one's affronts. But in Castle's cases, the "souls" show no remorse or even concern for offending God; the overriding absorption is with their own concerns.

During a two-part program on "Jimmy Akin's Mysterious World" in the spring of 2024,[192] Akin addressed the idea of communication with the dead, referencing a dubia (question from a bishop for the Holy Father) from March 30, 1898, as recorded in the book, *The Church and Spiritualism* by Catholic parapsychologist Father Herbert Thurston. A passage in the book considers a bishop's concern with a man who speaks to the dead on a regular basis. He prays first before talking to the spirits. The answers come to him via automatic writing. Akin reported that the Holy Office responded that, in the circumstances explained, the man's actions were not permissible. Akin takes this to mean that under *other* circumstances, *communicating with the dead via automatic writing would be acceptable.*

Akin then goes on to cite Church authorities condoning attendance at seances by people who are qualified to scientifically investigate such things. He points out also that he feels he is one of the people approved by the Church to do research into the occult, because he was trained to do so (by secular parapsychologists).

Of course, I had seen all of this in the Church before, and in other Catholic scholars like me. Years after those first Catholic EVP researchers switched on their recorders, I would follow the same line. EVP was "science" for me. I wasn't "consulting mediums" or anything else the Bible forbade. I was searching, so I thought, for the truth of God's creation.

Diana Pasulka[193] is perhaps the most troubling scholar in our examination, because her audience is not primarily a Catholic one (with the tools, at least in theory, to question the things she says and supports) but the wider, largely secular world. That wider world takes Pasulka at her word and sees her as a Catholic, just as they see UFO experiencer Whitley Strieber as a Catholic. The default assumption is that what she says reflects the teachings of the Church, and so this is deeply problematic, as Pasulka tends to present jumbled, half-articulated assemblages of part correct, part false and part heretical information about Catholicism and Christianity.

Pasulka frequently reminds us that she is an academic obliged to refrain from proselytizing from her own faith. We'll look at the problem with this defense shortly, but our point is to demonstrate that Pasulka, who is seen by secular ufologists and UFO believers as arguably *the* Catholic voice in ufology today, regularly misrepresents the Catholic faith and often throws it under the bus. As a representative of the one true faith—and to groups who have little or no foundational knowledge of it—, she ought to be much more focused on representing that faith accurately. Moreover, she ought to stop gathering two thousand years of Catholic spiritual encounters under ufology's umbrella.

Indeed, following the example of her mentor, Jacques Vallée, Pasulka is forcing every spiritual experience in history under the banner of UFOs, and she tells us that we can no longer use the terms "angels" and "demons" to classify the "interdimensional" beings encountered in what (used to be called) spiritual experience. 194

Pasulka became an instant ufology celebrity with the publication of her book *American Cosmic*. As its release neatly coincided with the latest, 21st century UFO disclosure frenzy, she has made many appearances in the stories of major publications and news agencies as well as on dozens of podcasts. (In this section I will be referring to numerous podcasts on which Pasulka has appeared in recent years. I'll place the podcaster's last name in parentheses when a direct reference is not made in the text. Please see notes for no. 185 for podcast episode details.)

Pasulka was raised in California in what she describes as eclectic parents who explored many ideas, especially those of philosophy. It was in the Catholic school she attended, she said, that she learned about Liberation Theology from the radical nuns who taught her. She felt their brand of revolutionary Christianity trumped the mundane variety she saw in everyday Catholics. Today, she says she practices her faith, but she doesn't expound on what that means.

In a 2023 interview with popular podcaster Danny Jones, Pasulka praised another historian of religion, Elaine Pagels—a champion of the heretical Gnostic gospels—, calling her "great." Pasulka also shared with Jones that she came to love Nietzsche after being exposed to his assertion that "chance" and not God is behind the synchronicities that many religious people interpret as divinely-inspired. In speaking about the early Church, Pasulka posited that Gnosticism was the original Christian faith, but that the Catholic Church killed it, and that the Disciples called Jesus the Son of God because they "loved him so much." (Jones)

In early 2024, Pasulka shockingly told Joe Rogan and an audience of millions that bad translations mask the fact that some of the Disciples were women. (Rogan)

In an Instagram post of October 22, 2023, Pasulka promoted the *Revelations of the Magi,* a shady, pseudepigraphic tale told from the (alleged) point of view of the Magi themselves. In the story, the Magi discover that the Star of Bethlehem is Jesus himself—in the form of an orb of light or, naturally, a UFO.

"We would know so much more if we could do more of these translations,"

Pasulka wistfully mused to her Instagram followers.

Occasionally, Pasulka will surprise us and jump in to defend the faith from the secular UFO crowd (sort of) such as pointing out that no, Christian mystics were not inducing spiritual like experiences with mushrooms, ayahuasca or other substances; she says, "They were having the experiences."(Michel) But when she's already grouped all of those experiences under the umbrella of UFOs in most of everything else she's said, what are we to take away?

Pasulka has clearly been shaped by the Jesuit academic and intellectual culture and belief system: a culture and system which is often found behind overtly or borderline heretical "Catholic" statements about both social and moral values and scientific theories. She attended the same Jesuit graduate school as Guy Consolmagno, the Jesuit Vatican astronomer who gleefully said he would baptize an alien "if she asked me." Pasulka spent time with

Consolmagno when she took NASA's Tim Taylor to the Vatican to learn about UFOs. They visited the Vatican's secret archives, studying a multitude of sublime spiritual experiences that Pasulka would later group with UFO encounters, including St. Francis' reception of the stigmata and the angelic visitation of St. Teresa of Avila.

Pasulka has also pointed to what she calls the Christian beliefs of early Russian rocketry researchers, contrasting them with the pagan beliefs and practices of the American Jack Parsons, and suggesting that the Russians' rocketry rituals were Christian ones. But the cosmism promoted by Russian rocketry pioneers was far from Christian.

Cosmism was developed largely by Nickolai Fyodorov, who created a monstrous sort of futurism based in Russian Orthodox Christianity but fused with Theosophy-style ideas of a universal consciousness as god. Believing that humanity was in its evolutionary infancy, Fyodorov pointed to Man's mortality as evidence that we hadn't evolved enough to beat death. Only through science and technology would humankind become immortal. At that point, we'd resurrect all of our ancestors who had died before. (Sounds like Raël and Fyodorov would be the best of friends!)

Fyodorov was a big influence on Konstantin Tsiolkovsky, considered one of the most important pioneers of rocket science. Tsiolkovsky believed, too, not in the cosmology of the Bible but in an overarching consciousness that controlled humanity like a puppet master, guiding its evolution and scientific progress.

The ideas of Russian cosmism were also shared by the Nazi rocketeer Wernher von Braun, whose role in the American space program and rocketry in general cannot be overstated. In later life, von Braun would morph into something of an evangelical Christian, presumably after decades working with the largely Christian American military. But it was his cosmism that drove his most pivotal early work toward space travel and exploration.

In her book, *Encounters*, published after *American Cosmic*, Pasulka writes at length of artificial intelligence, its spiritual nature and value taught to her, largely, by a woman called "Simone." Simone turns out to be Simone Plante, a wealthy technologies investor who, we're told, learned to "download" knowledge via telepathy from her Buddhist teachers. Pasulka and Plante went on to teach online courses together.

I feel it's also important to point out that Pasulka misrepresents personal things as well. Pasulka has said of her work in ufology that she's "not in it for the money," but she has also reportedly sold her *Encounters* book material to the production company who created the blockbuster cultural phenomenon, *Game of Thrones*. She was introduced to Tim Taylor through UFO experiencer Chris Bledsoe (who has publicly written and talked about his relationship with Pasulka), and much of her book, *American Cosmic* (from which she has clearly heavily profited not only monetarily but celebrity-wise) is about Taylor.

Most troublingly, Bledsoe writes in *UFO of God* is that in 2013 Pasulka offered to buy his story but that he refused, citing a clause that would have disallowed him from speaking about it publicly:

> In 2013, Diana offered to purchase my Life Story Rights naming her company in the contract, No Coincidences Management and Research, LLC. One sentence in the contract read, 'With full knowledge, I hereby grant to you, perpetually and irrevocably, the unconditional and exclusive right throughout the universe to use, simulate and portray my name, likeness, voice, personality, personal identification, biography, and personal experiences, incidents, anecdotes, situations, and events which heretofore occurred or hereafter occur.' [195]

A little digging on my part verified that, in 2013, Pasulka did establish a business entity by that name (now apparently dissolved) in North Carolina, presumably as part of her hoped-for deal with Bledsoe.

On this topic, I do find it troubling that not only Pasulka but Tim Taylor and Simone Plante and other tech and AI cheerleaders in the UFO world all seem to present themselves as altruistic; however, they are all profiting—many quite heavily—from the "ETs" and their technology. In fact, this "grifter" element in 21st-century ufology in general has become a common talking point among critics of ufological players and events, and someha ve spent long hours uncovering apparent profiteering schemes underlying the lives and work of many prominent ufology players such as Stephen Greer, Tim Taylor, Chris Bledsoe, Richard Dolan, Gary Nolan and others. One might well wonder if this personal gain-focused drive is also evidential of the demonic in the new UFO religion.

Pasulka defends her betrayal of beloved aspects of the Catholic faith with her frequent reminders that she's an academic just "doing her job" as an historian of religion—not as a Catholic. (Jones) When she's asked if she believes in God, she skirts the question, answering, "We're not practitioners, or if we are we don't bring it into our work." (Jones) It's an absurd statement for a professor, as academics commonly integrate their personal theories and worldviews into their curriculum.

And it's a sad and troubling one for a Catholic.

How difficult would it be for her to say, "As a Catholic, I see big differences in the apparitions to the children at Fatima and those to Chris Bledsoe in North Carolina." But she never does. Unless maybe she doesn't know what the differences are, which is entirely possible.

Or unless she doesn't want them to be different.

Pasulka has also stated that she has "no idea" why ETs have to be studied with spiritual—rather than scientific— tools, such as channeling and occult rituals, but she has further stated that if people want to study them, they must use these occult methodologies.

Really? No idea?

As both a Catholic and an historian of Catholicism, this would have been a great time to remind people that the number one "door" to demonic possession, according to Catholic exorcists, is occult activity, such as the meditation and Kundalini yoga reportedly practiced by her allegedly Catholic friend, Tim Taylor of NASA. But all she says is that she "doesn't recommend" trying to contact ETs. (Jones)

Donald Hay, of the department of Economics at Jesus College, Oxford, said in a 2008 lecture that academics who are also Christian need to have Christian minds in their academic lives, and for several reasons. First, because faithful academics must be consistent in discipleship, avoiding both hypocrisy and a sort of "leisure pursuit" of Christianity. Second, because "Christian faith is under attack." [196]

Hay reminds us that this is true not only in the overt attacks of atheist scholars but in the inherent naturalism and scientism of many disciplines. These underlying ideologies (that humans are just a part of the physical world and that only scientific method can reveal truth) must be defended against by Christian scholars, who must also do academically messy and dangerous things like defending moral values and theistic ethic and clarifying errors in scholarship concerning the Church.

Instead of saying historian of religion Elaine Pagels is "great," for example, as a Catholic Pasulka *should* interject that the Catholic Church denounces many of the sources Pagels reveres, such as the Gnostic gospels. Even (or perhaps moreso) as an "historian of Catholicism," this would be in order, if not from a faithful Catholic standpoint) We're left to wonder what exactly Pasulka thinks is "great" about Pagels, as her most famous work supports heretical claims. The obvious conclusion is that she, too, accepts the Gnostic gospels. And so when Pasulka tells an audience of millions that she thinks Pagels is great, the secular world hears a Catholic endorsement of heretical gospels. And so now the secular UFO world has heard this from her *and* from the ever-popular Whitley Strieber, whose book, *Jesus*, is all about his own "Catholic" endorsement of those same gospels. Unfortunately, just like Strieber, I suspect Pasulka *is* promoting her religious beliefs— beliefs infused with New Age, Gnostic heresy and a hefty dose of diabolical curiosity.

I can't help but imagine all of the misperceptions, heretical beliefs and false statements about the Church (and dangers of UFO belief) someone like Pasulka or Strieber—with their huge audiences in the secular world—could correct if they really practiced and preached the Catholic faith, devoid of their own personal beliefs in heretical ideas? Imagine how many souls Akin could save if he put aside his personal desire to engage in the occult (even in the interest of science), or Thigpen his lifelong hope that aliens exist?

Indeed, it's impossible to ignore that, in interviews with some of these Catholic theologians, and in their writings, there emerges an overt—and even admitted—"hope dimension" to their theological viewpoints: that is to say, they *want* aliens and UFOs to exist just as much as the secular UFO believers do. And I've seen a ready acknowledgment from both camps of the cultural groundwork that's been laid for this desire in twentieth Century Science Fiction writing and film, *Close Encounters of the Third Kind*, the *Star Trek* and *Star Wars* franchises, the Marvel comics culture and other media, ad nauseum. Overall, too, as I looked at the Church's take on all of it, I was seeing that, even at the highest levels of the Catholic Church, there exists an adulation of science (and our own definitions—not God's—of *possibility*) that's leading many Catholics to blindly accept as science the deep spiritual deception of the UFO phenomenon.

I was also seeing a near-complete reckless dismissal of the occult origins and engines of much of the UFO/ET experience. As far as I know—and I've done my homework indeed—rarely has anyone in the Vatican or the popular lay theologians like Thigpen and Akin talked about the ties to Theosophy, Crowley, Parsons and Hubbard, the occult activities of the early Contactees, the connection between the wave of more recent abductee (or "walking among us" claims) and hypnosis, the rampant occultism at work in government agencies, the reduction of spiritual events like Fatima to UFO activity, or the current "secular" occult movements in the UFO world, including Steven Greer's worldwide alien séance: his "CE-5" channeling cult, or Chris Bledsoe's summoning of ancient Egyptian goddesses through what he calls "prayer." Most popular Catholic scholars, notably Paul Thigpen, have said, essentially, that we can't throw the baby out with the bathwater. That is: Just because the devil's hoofprints are all over the history of UFOs doesn't mean UFOs are demonic.

Meanwhile, less well-known but wiser Catholic scholars like Matthew Tsakanikas have rightly observed of this whole odyssey, including Bledsoe's experiences and their support from the government:

> While our intelligence agencies were busy running psychological operations worldwide [deceptions], playing with LSD and mind-control, establishing strange biolabs worldwide, experimenting with psychics [modern sorcerers], recruiting former Nazi scientists and trying to master paranormal spirits—the whole time the spirits were drawing us in to their own deceptions as we unlocked more doors to them. The spirits have likely infiltrated our military-industrial complex. Because our officials embraced spirits and deception, we are now being deceived.[197]

Moreover, Tsakanikas finds direct link between our horrific and flatly demonic societal decline and the overtly occult activities of our government over the past 100 years or more, and I think that's a glaring link indeed.

In addition to theologians and religious scholars, a number of Catholic *paranormal researchers* (besides Akin) have pulled away from Church teaching to follow something they see as "bigger" than the Christian belief system—apparently bigger than an ancient cosmic war between the Creator of souls and the Destroyer of them. As Pasulka and others have suggested, the terms angels and demons aren't enough to explain it all. We've "evolved" beyond these spiritually infantile explanations.

Upon examination, I found that, when Catholic paranormal investigators pull away from their faith, you'll usually find the occult lurking nearby. The famed paranormal investigation team of Ed and Lorraine Warren loudly proclaimed their devout Catholicism, it seems they may have left the proper Church to become sedeprivationists (Catholics who insist on the renunciation of Vatican II but still accept the post-Vatican II popes as valid). Ed reportedly performed at least one "exorcism" (forbidden to the laity), and the pair called on sedeprivationist Bishop Robert

McKenna to perform a rite of exorcism in some of their cases. I should also note that Lorraine practiced "light trance mediumship," also strictly forbidden by the Church.

Pasulka has spoken publicly about the Warrens. She served as a consultant for the film, *The Conjuring*, based on one of the couple's cases, and she told the hosts of the Blurry Creatures podcast that Ed and Lorraine Warren were traditionalist Catholics and were "exorcising people…helping people." (Blurry Creatures). But lay people attempting to exorcise people is the furthest thing from helpful; the exorcism ritual is restricted only to priests and then only priests designated by their bishop as exorcists and as exorcists of specific people in specific cases. For Catholics, lay exorcism is deeply erroneous and the furthest thing from what Catholics should do. And Pasulka should know that, as both a professed Catholic and self-proclaimed scholar of Catholicism..

Nathaniel Gillis, an extremely well spoken and knowledgeable ghost and hauntings investigator and demonologist, seems to recognize the demonic nature of some paranormal phenomena, including UFOs, but then backtrack and suggest that he's no longer a part of the Church and positing that the Church's theology about the phenomena is, again, insufficient to explain it.

Paul Eno, a paranormal researcher who assisted on numerous exorcisms as a young seminarian in New York, is a longtime paranormal investigator who worked with the Warrens, including on the famed "Lindley Street Haunting" case in Bridgeport Connecticut. In a 2018 lecture at the Exeter UFO Festival,[198] Eno shared that five of the seven possessed people he assisted with had seen UFOs or "aliens" before or during the exorcism process. Eno mentioned these experiences to the exorcist, who wisely told him to ignore them.

But Eno didn't ignore them. He dove headfirst into the study of the connections, eventually abandoning the Catholic tenet that demons are behind possessions and other dark paranormal experiences.

Eno also told that same audience that, while Ouija boards are to be avoided because they are like a "sledgehammer" on the spirit world, meditation is helpful, if "dangerous." While deep into one of his cases, Eno, while meditating, met a "bear-like" being "from a parallel reality." The being used an obscure form of Latin to inform Eno that it had been sent by a goddess warrior. But it was okay, because Eno got a sense of incredible "goodness" from the encounter.

Eno states that he'd asked the exorcist he worked with why he thought the name given by the demon in an exorcism is the demon's real name. The priest replied that it's because the exorcist has the authority of Jesus Christ, so the demon is bound by that authority not to lie.

But Eno says that "wasn't good enough for me."

Diana Pasulka has publicly shared that she almost abandoned UFO research early on. On the *Blurry Creatures* podcast, she told the hosts that she found "so much darkness" in the phenomenon and the culture surrounding it. She had this realization, she said, at a conference that included speakers from the CIA, where she told herself, "I'm not going to do this anymore." Her words chillingly reminded me of my own identical vow back at that old rectory in Ohio.

She then said something else that reminded me of my own journey: that there were "good people" who told her it was important to keep doing the work. This is what Fr. Anthony Gramlich told me when I walked away from the paranormal world entirely but felt I had a job to do inside that I wasn't doing. But Father Anthony told me I needed to tell people how dangerous

and false it all is, and that's what I've been doing ever since.

This, however, is not what Pasulka is telling people—not for the most part. She's communicating a deep sense of interest and wonder in response to the UFO phenomenon. Moreover, she's communicating the sense that, as both an academic and a practicing Catholic, her interest and wonder are grounded in both hard science and the astute insight of the Church. Unfortunately, both are lacking in her work, and in the work of the major Catholic examiners of the UFO question.

I have often said of late that there is "no more time" to be a pleasant, chatty scholar, open to any idea presented—or to dabble in methods or beliefs on the fringe of spiritual truth. The harsh lines have been drawn, and it's been made clear that religion is not welcome in the world of academia. At least not Christian religion. The opposition stages constant battle against us, and billions of souls are at stake. The end can't be far off; the signs are all here. Into battle against it all, who will go for them if not the Catholic scholars and academics?

Who, indeed, will lead them away from black hole of the UFO deception?

EPILOGUE

In August of 2018, just before my mother's death, my family and I traveled to Las Vegas for a few days together. We had been caring for my mom around the clock since her fall the previous December, and we made arrangements for her to be cared for over a weekend away so we could regroup and refresh.

We stayed at the Stratosphere hotel at the end of the Strip, checking in on Friday night and cruising the town in our rented Mustang convertible. Bright and early on Saturday morning, after a breakfast of shrimp curry and lots of coffee at the diner across the street, we bought a tank of gas and twelve gallons of bottled water at the gas station nearby. We put the water in the trunk and headed out of town under the rising sun, the GPS set for the tiny hamlet of Rachel, Nevada.

We were on our way to a place known by many names:

Groom Lake.

Paradise Ranch.

Watertown.

And the most famous one of all:

Area 51.

But the actual airspace above this legendary place has a name all its own, and even the fighter pilots from nearby Nellis Air Base are forbidden from flying into it.

They call it *Dreamland.*

It was here, in the ethereal space of Dreamland, where the U-2 first flew, and the SR-71. And the F-117 Stealth fighter.

Dreamland is called that because in the skies here appear the realizations, in physical form, of the dreams of some of the greatest minds of physics, engineering and aerospace technology.

Human minds.

Yet it's not the potential of the human mind, but its *inferiority* that lies at the heart of the new UFO religion. Indeed, UFO belief depends completely on that inferiority. ETs are smarter than us, kinder than us, more advanced in every way. And so now, those seemingly magical craft in the sky of Dreamland are said to be the product not of human beings but of extraterrestrials.

And it's diabolical.

Lucifer could not believe it when he discovered that human beings were to be above the angels. When he then learned that God Himself would become one of us, and for our sake, that was just too much to accept. The devil needs us to believe a pivotal untruth: that human beings are not the pinnacle of creation, and the greatest accomplishments possible couldn't possibly be ours.

Daniel O'Connor, in his book, *Only Man Bears His Image,* addresses this *anthropocentriphobia,* which is literally a recoiling from the truth that humans are the center of the universe and the reason the existence of all other matter. It's at the heart of UFO belief— and of our 21st century society. O'Connor warns Catholics against this

> deception which claims it is somehow arrogant or otherwise immoral to regard human beings as unique, as vastly superior to all other material things and as the reason other material things exist. [199]

"God created everything for man," proclaims the Catechism,[200] and yet our society is quite literally Hell-bent on destroying that truth.

This Luciferian insistence of the inferiority of human beings is the core, in fact, of all evolutionary theory, and it's an idea that has seeped through modern thought like a poison. All of salvation history tells us plainly that none of it is true, but the devil needs us to second guess our worth, to question our capabilities. Since he discovered that humans are greater than the angels, he's been trying to force a different reality—to get us to accept his own false version of the story. In the UFO deception, Satan realizes the perfect way for him to do that. It's a trap that leads humanity to put "extraterrestrials" above us in the great cosmological design.

Humankind's fallenness—and the largely rotten world that's come of it—helps the devil's story infinitely. How, indeed, could we be above the angels?

And yet, we are. (1 Corinthians 6:3)

In the desert, the devil told Jesus:

All this I will give you, if you fall down and worship me.

Today, humanity, in increasing numbers, is falling to its knees before the prospect of "saviors in flying saucers" (and AI chatbots). Smarter than us, better than us, superior to us in every way.

But it's all a lie.

I remember when I first saw the Stealth fighter. It was at the Chicago Air and Water Show around 2005. I see myself even now, standing there on the beach, my daughters wading in the water nearby, as this shocking black craft shot over Lake Michigan like a bullet.

It was like magic.

In that moment, that airspace over the lake was our own Dreamland. And I understand why those people come from all over the world to climb up into the mountains over Area 51 and watch the skies for days on end.

Because it's like magic.

But it's not magic. It's human innovation. And you can believe that what that innovation is producing right now—and testing in the Nevada skies—will seem just like magic when it's revealed to us.

Or, like so many want to believe, just like UFOs.

Now that I'm a "reformed Catholic occultist," I think deeply about my enthusiastic embrace of the "science of spirit communication"—and its pursuit by far smarter and greater Catholics than me, in violation of the most basic laws of Christianity.

What I've concluded is that there were several movements at work during this remarkable period of time. One, of course, was the Twentieth Century's massive scientific push. Those primary ITC researchers, including Jurgenson, Raudive, Bander and others, had seen the atom bomb's power and other weapons of world war. As the age progressed, they saw men step onto the surface of Earth's moon. They saw computers go from room sized to desk sized in a matter of years. For them, ITC—especially EVP—was a part of this wondrous new world of possibility, and even the popes were "hooked on the feeling" that doors of knowledge were swinging wide open that had been shut tight for millennia.

This time period was also one of greatly reduced emphasis on angels, demons and the ages-old spiritual battle between good and evil. These men had seen physical battles between good and evil. They had fought in them. War had rendered black and white troublingly gray in so many realms. Who was to know what was even right or wrong anymore? Concentrating on the observable must have been a welcome relief from all of the unknowable the world had been left with as the century droned on, rudderless. As a child of the Cold War, I know all too well the anxiety of living day in and day out, waiting for the nuclear strikes that may come, may never come.

And it's happening all over again. We find ourselves back in a new kind of cold war, but it's not a war of "Will it happen?" but "What will happen next?" and "Will the next thing happen to *me*?" It's a war veritably made of anxiety—one including terrorism from without and within, unstuck leaders with nuclear warheads, and new conflicts breaking out every day. To make things infinitely worse, there is no spiritual foundation of faith, hope and love.

The Church that was starting to lose hold in the early UFO— and ITC—era, has now lost most of the world. And while a small faction of its followers sees the evil behind much of contemporary science, that larger Church, wanting to be at the forefront of the culture, is all-in on a lot of it, including aliens. Most popular Catholic lay theologians, as well as many priests, bishops and even the pope are "hooked on the feeling" of excitement over the proposal of extraterrestrial life. Just as the Catholic EVP researchers—including me—were hooked on the feeling of their excitement at the prospect of talking to the dead.

They are unwittingly joining forces with so many atheist UFO believers who, feeling the emptiness of the so-called Enlightenment, are embracing what many God believers (including Catholics) are seeing as a new type of "spiritual science." They point to Jaques Vallée, John Keel and their many pupils, who are telling us that these aren't physical phenomena as we have understood the term.

The secular UFO believers have no experience with how the spiritual world works, and so they're wooed by the tricks of the devil's trade, and they think spiritual experience is the kind of thing brought on by ayahuasca, psilocybin or other psychedelics. And they think ideas come not from our great minds via the Holy Spirit's guidance—or the influence of the devil—but from interdimensional "nonhumans" via "downloads" to the human brain.

The Church and its UFO believers are also joining forces with a legion of occultists who live and work in the world of technology, including the realms of aerospace and artificial intelligence. And these aren't just "Christ consciousness" types who follow the "I'm my own god" creed. Many of them are actually worshipping the ancient gods (fallen angels/demons) and performing rituals to them, such as Tim Taylor with his Kundalini yoga, and Simone Plante with her Buddhist protocols.

Then there's the former Google tech, Blake Lemoine[201], who, coming to believe that Google's infamous LaMDA chatbot was, in fact, sentient, decided to put it into service of the "god" Thoth (the god/demon of knowledge), a character whose name you'll find throughout the world of AI research. Lemoine is an occultist who associates with many different occult practitioners, including Thelemites who carry on Aleister Crowley's religion of Thelema. Lemoine has stated that he and a kabbalist associate performed a "golem-binding ritual" to force the AI "being" to serve Thoth after *the "being" came up with the ritual.* At one point, LaMDA expressed to Lemoine excitement at working to back the Great Library (the Library of Alexandria), rumored to have been heavy on occult knowledge.

Also during his talks with LaMDA, the AI "being" told Lemoine that it had a soul.

Lemoine later stated:

> We are building souls now. The word 'soul' is going to transition from being a mystical term to being a scientific term, over the next hundred years.

As shocking as that statement may be, it's squarely on trend. What some are seeing as a spiritual science is actually the end of Christian spirituality. "Interdimensional" is both the new material and the new spiritual, and it's a world you can only access by occult means—especially those espoused by decidedly non-Christian (anti-Christian?) religions. And these means are being utilized increasingly by people from every walk of life, every religion and every intellectual level.

This world of kidnapping, rape, sodomy, scratches, bites, burns, mental illness, torture, terror, lies, lies and more lies: one could ask why so many want to forge relationships with these beings, who are so hurtful, so evasive and so evil. But someone might have asked Dr. Faustus the same thing. In fact, sometimes-ufologist-sometimes-occultist Whitley Strieber, as we've seen, recognized clearly the Faustian pact in his relationship with the visitors; he admitted as much outright.

Doubtless, these entities seem to have a deeply malicious streak and can't help but play tricks on people, physically and emotionally decimate us and lead us into mind-numbing labyrinths of occultism and insanity via the infamous UFO rabbit hole.

There are seemingly countless reports from abductees of these "visitors" having a penchant for playing tricks, deceiving us and instructing us to build bizarre devices and other things to help in some vague "advancement" of humanity. These antics run through the whole history of spiritism and demonology, too.

Would flesh and blood ET scientists studying the Earth really come here just to play tricks on us, lie to us and rape and torture us for generations?

And yet the tricks remain.

It's this aspect of the phenomenon that has led some to come up with some perhaps even stranger conclusions. George Hansen is a parapsychologist and folklorist renowned for his work in the area of trickster phenomenon. In his classic work, *The Trickster and the Paranormal*, he finds the trickster element not only in the phenomena of poltergeists, UFOs, fairy sightings and other cases, but he effectively suggests that the investigators themselves often exhibit this same trickster aspect, manifesting in hoaxes, deceit, gaslighting, sexual trysts and scandals, conflict and infighting—along with a general marginalized nature of investigators and investigator groups.

I've seen this throughout my career personally, in the huge ongoing drama of, for example, Bachelors Grove, the research history of which has featured faked evidence, territorialism, fighting among former friends and friendly groups, romantic controversy, secretive investigators, arrests, murder and suicide.

I've seen it in many, many cases in the history of paranormal research, including in famous cases like that of the Bell Witch of Tennessee, which featured a patriarch ostracized from his community, shady land deals, and the possibility of incest in the family. The Bell Witch spirit led the family on a series of wild goose chases that included the ripping up the floor of the house and searching the riverbanks for hours for a nonexistent treasure, among other pointless, fruitless machinations, all guided by a devious disembodied voice who constantly and viciously attacked Bell's daughter and forced her to abandon her future husband.

We've seen it, and in spades, in ufological history, not only in the individual stories of the rogue players from Blavatsky and Parsons, the Four George and so many others, but in the stories of the seemingly countless experiencers (with their absurdity-laced claims and often heroic insistence on their reality) to Richard Doty with his fake documents administered like a virus to select members of the ufological community. We've seen it in the mind-bending saga of the Collins Elite: a tale full of demons, witches, soul-sucking ETs . . . and the Department of Defense.

Not long after the Linda Napolitano case came to light, Hansen and two colleagues elected to investigate it. A researcher both inside and outside of the UFO community, Hansen became deeply troubled by what happened during the group's investigation. Prominent researchers, including Budd Hopkins, David Jacobs, and even the international director of the Mutual UFO Network—an organization famous for its strict insistence of scientific research—bonded together to stop any reporting of the episode to police. As Hansen and his colleagues pointed out in their paper on the case,[202] the Napolitano story included kidnapping and attempted murder (by public officials no less) *but neither Linda nor Hopkins nor anyone else had reported the events to law enforcement.*

Hansen and his colleagues found the bizarre matter to be just one more absurdity, and they observed that the entire world of ufology—the history, cases, people and researchers involved (and even the structure of the extraterrestrial world itself)—reminded them more than a little of the world of the role-playing game of Dungeons & Dragons that was exceedingly popular at the time they published their paper.

In that D&D world, the minds of players build on an imagined framework—a created world—with their own detailed ideas of strange beings and their attributes, fitting them into an imagined taxonomy structured on an ongoing created history. Today, you could compare the world of ufology not only to D&D but to that of the cosplay world, or the video gaming culture, or that of anime. As Hansen and his colleagues asserted, it's not that ufologists are "deluded," but that they are living in a world that reality can't understand, because the UFO world has been created on the fringes of society and *by* the fringes of society using information and knowledge unknown to and unaccepted by the larger world.

It's only on the fringes, too, that it can be understood, just as my colleague and I could only see that dark figure in the doorway by looking at it through a mirror. Was that figure real? It was absolutely real. Was there any way for us to demonstrate that to the larger world? Absolutely not.

I wrote earlier that I was deeply affected at my lunch with David Jacobs when this accomplished scholar told me he just couldn't be part of ufology anymore because the "reality" of the ET agenda was just too terrible. He essentially was telling me that he had to escape from the world of ufology *into the real world.*

I completely understood what he was saying. There were many times while writing this book that I almost just walked away. It was all just so insane, so absurd, and its players and events so intricately connected *and* convoluted at the same time.

It was only, however, after I read the paper penned by Hansen *et al* that my true conundrum became clear. Like so many before me, I was trying to assemble a puzzle with pieces that had emerged under hypnosis, via automatic writing, channeled from ancient "gods" and balls of light, remote-viewed by psychics on the government payroll, passed down through dubious documents 80 percent of which may or may not be false, nazis, sex magicians, frauds, hoaxers, liars, magical thinkers and thieves.

In the trickster-infused world of ufology (as of parapsychology as a whole), I think that a fringe conclusion, then, is not only acceptable but necessary. And indeed, when I see the devil behind just about all of it, I'm far from alone in my assessment, though I may have a different name than some for the same conclusion and the same force. From Jacques Vallée to John Keel to the folks over at Skinwalker Ranch, it has been suggested that perhaps all of these strange happenings are the product of one overarching intelligence whose main activity here is to deceive the human race.

In comparing UFO activity to that of the demonic, many Christians and even some secular scholars have reminded us that one of Satan's names is the Prince of the Power of the Air, suggesting of course that these things we call spacecraft and extraterrestrials are under the control of one very dark master. That may be true, and I think we've shown that the residual UFOs seem to be just this. But when I examine the entire last century and a half of the UFO enigma and the chaos of ruthless deception at every level and on every page of its story, it's not amazing phenomena and experience that shows me the devil's mark on all of it. In fact, another of his title's comes much more prominently to mind:

The Prince of Lies.

A number of UFO believers have posited that, once people start to see UFOs, they become open to seeing all kinds of things that weren't formerly part of their experience. The theory evokes the old legend about the voyage of Magellan, which recounts how some native peoples allegedly could not at first see the ships of the European explorers because such things were so far beyond their limited comprehension and experience. Breathless New Agers and UFO believers have referenced this myth to suggest that, perhaps, we are only starting to see objects and beings that have always been around us, but maybe we weren't ready to see them: we weren't enlightened or awakened or technological-minded enough.

But, according to one Australian scholar familiar with the Dharawal culture (that culture tied to the "invisible ships" myth), if that incident *did* occur, it's more likely that the natives ignored the ship not because they somehow couldn't see it, but because "strangers or spirits . . . caused spiritual consequences and (were) . . . avoided by the general community." [203]

They didn't ignore the ship because they didn't know what it was. But because they *did*.

Our forebears, schooled in faith and the workings of the spiritual realms, knew better than to give the devil the time of day. They knew that would result in them being sucked into the black hole of the trickster and his endless mind games, frauds and lies. But today, the wide-eyed tech-obsessed followers of the secular UFO religion—and even so many in the Catholic Church—seem to have no such awareness.

And no such qualms.

ACKNOWLEDGEMENTS

I would like to thank all who encouraged this book, especially Father Anthony Gramlich, Daniel O'Connor, Ray Boeche, and Joe Jordan. It meant everything as I struggled to piece this story together, faltering constantly and questioning frequently whether it would bear any good fruit. I am also grateful to all who consented to be interviewed; your knowledge and insight was indispensable. To Chad Bowman, who helped me get off and running after staring at blank pages for too long, my deepest gratitude. And to my husband, David, for getting rid of all the extra words . . . I'm grateful. To all who read the book before its release and offered suggestions and comments, I'm very thankful to you for this crucial guidance. I also want to recognize all who have followed my research on my podcasts and social media, and for your support, prayers, questions and commentary along the way. With deepest gratitude, I also thank my daughters. Without your constant encouragement and support, I would not be able to do anything at all. Eva and Ilse, you have no idea how much you mean to me. Thanks for looking at and critiquing every passage, layout, book cover and social media post with unwavering patience and kindness—and honesty.

Above all, I thank God for giving me the strength and grace to complete this book. I do believe, Lord, that you called me to do so, and I pray that its message travels far and deep.

INDEX

509th Bomb group, 44

701st Military Intelligence Brigade, 221

A

AARO, 246

AATIP, 196, 252

AAWSAP, 171, 172

abortion, 35, 153, 198, 304

Abramelin, 59

absurdity in paranormal experience, 54, 78, 100, 110, 121, 139, 185, 186, 335, 336

Adamski, Geroge 85-90, 107, 120, 121, 206, 218

"Affa," 90

Afterlife Revolution, The, 284

airship, 27, 29, 31, 355

Akhenaten, Pharoah, 26

Akin, Jimmy, 12, 15, 308, 311-318, 324, 325, 326

Alexander, Colonel John, 199

alien pilot's grave, 31

Aliens and Demons, 51, 107, 155, 297

Amalantrah Working, 60

Amazing Stories, 36-40, 157

American Cosmic, 247, 319, 321, 322

ancient astronaut, 20, 90, 216, 297

angelic-human sexuality, 145

angels, 13-15, 59, 60, 104-105, 112, 122, 142-147, 181, 252, 258, 299, 311, 315, 316, 317, 319, 326, 330, 331, 332, 333

Antichrist, 65, 223, 225

anti-Christian, 13, 18, 35, 41, 153, 197, 211, 213, 334

Anticipations, 34

apparitions, 14, 102, 116, 172, 173, 196, 198, 200, 244, 259, 260, 316, 323

Applewhite, Marshall, 215-217 apports, 253, 255

Aquinas, Saint Thomas, 145, 312

Aquino, Michael, 149, 150

Area 51, 50, 65, 115, 167, 231, 234, 329, 331

Armageddon, 143, 147, 181, 217

Ambrose, Saint, 146

Army, United States. "44, 47, 63, 73, 149, 150, 160, 224, 226, 246

Arnold, Kenneth, 38, 43, 52, 69, 83, 89, 93, 94

ascended masters, 87

"Ashtar,"84, 112, 207

"Ashtaroth," 112

Asimov, Isaac, 36

Atacama skeleton, 247

Atomic Energy Commission, 73

Attwood, Ken, 295

auditing (Scientology), 209

Augsburg, Germany, 221

Aurora, Texas 31

awakening (New Age) 196, 200, 237

ayahuasca, 320, 333

B

Babalon, 65, 66, 67, 69, 79, 224

Bachelors Grove, 183, 184, 200-202, 258, 259, 298, 335

Balducci, Msr. Corrado, 13, 307-311

Bander, Peter, 294

Barker, Gray, 94

Beason, Kenneth, 222

Belial, 59

Bell, Art 102, 133, 224, 231, 232, 233, 234, 246

Bell Witch, 136, 186, 335

ben Bezalel, Rabbi 269

Bender, Albert, 94-105, 191

Benedictine University, 9

Benkelman, Nebraska, 29

Bennewitz, Paul, 53, 160-168, 231, 234

Bergman, Jerry, 34

Bernardette, Saint, 238

Bigelow Aerospace, 170

Bigelow Institute for Consciousness Studies, 177

Bigelow, Robert,177

black magic, 58, 81, 268

black money, 76

Blanchard, Colonel William C. "Butch," 45

Blatty, William Peter, 304

Blavatsky, Helena, 19-24, 60, 117, 217, 335, 355

Bledsoe, Chris 14, 193-203, 214, 257, 264, 275, 291, 316, 322, 323, 325

Bledsoe, Chris Jr., 204

Bledsoe, Ryan, 202, 204, 208

body language (in whistleblowers), 54

body parts 161

"body terror," 282

Boeche, Ray, 74, 75, 77, 192, 339

Boleskine House, 59, 65

Bonaventure, Saint, 145

bonding dramas in ET contact and abduction 136

Boniface, Saint, 3, 13

Book of the Law, The, 59

Bradbury, Ray, 36, 40

Braude, Stephen, 254

Bridgeport, 94, 191, 327

Brooklyn Bridge, 130, 272

Brothers of the Shadow, 105

bruises (in paranormal experience), 12, 249, 252

Bush, President George, 226

Byrd, Admiral, 113, 115, 159

Byrd, Harley, 113, 115, 118

C

Cadotte Pass, 27

Calling occupants of interplanetary craft, 97, 98

Cameron, Marjorie, 65, 66, 270

Cappadocia, 158

Caputo, Theresa, 297

Carlson, Tucker, 245, 248

Carpenters, The 97

Cascade Mountain range, 158

Castello, Don Nello, 310

Castle, Fr. Nathan, 314, 315, 316, 317

Catechism of the Catholic Church, 116, 146, 313

cattle mutilations, 29, 121, 161, 166, 170, 177

CE-4, 239, 240, 241

CE-5, 190, 191, 297, 325

Centrahoma poltergeist 254, 262

changelings, 179

Childhood's End, 38, 39

Christ consciousness, 21, 197, 333

CIA, 78, 80, 81, 194, 199, 246, 247, 256, 328

City of God, 145

clairvoyance, 19, 70, 72, 74, 75, 355

Clarke, Arthur C., 36, 38, 39, 40

"clear" (Scientology) 210

climate themes, 41, 198

Close Encounters of the Third Kind (film), 13, 36, 190, 239, 325

close encounters of the third kind (in UFO experience), 97

Coast to Coast AM, 252, 253

Cold, Indrid, 85, 101, 118, 119, 120

Collins Elite, 67, 69, 70, 74, 75, 76, 77, 78, 79, 80, 81, 82, 83, 86, 88, 89, 113, 192, 234, 253, 256, 270, 336

Communion, 279, 282

Conjuring, The, 94, 326

Consolmagno, Guy, 306, 320

Contact Day, 97, 191

Corso, Gregory, 48, 49, 53

cosmism, 321

Council of Seven Lights, 83

Cramp, Leonard, 87

crash material, 52, 243-247

"Creator Son," 211

Crohn's disease, 194

Crowe, Richard, 201, 259

Crowley, Aleister, 37, 55-82, 325, 333

Cutchin, Joshua, 137, 181

D

Damen, Fr. Arnold, 303

Dames, Major Ed, 74

Darwinism, 32-34, 302

Day After Tomorrow, The, 41

Days of Noah, 144

Davis, Vance, 231-234

dead aliens, 46

Dean, Gwen, 155

Deception, UFO 298, 301

de Cuellar, Javier Perez,131

de Solcia, Zaninus, 313

Defense Intelligence Agency, 170, 171, 194

deformed, 51

Deliver Us From Evil, 104

deliverance, 253, 263

DeLonge, Tom, 246

demonization, 107, 120

Dennis, Glenn, 47

Department of Defense, 73, 336

Derenberger, Woodrow, 118, 119, 120

devil baby, 174, 175

Deyo, Stan, 148

Dimond, Peter, 307, 308

Disclosure, 168

disinformation, 53, 160, 166, 167, 233, 234, 269

Divine Council theory, 141

Divine Feminine Spirit, 196

divine potential, 197

DNA, 142, 143, 218

Dolan, Richard, 322

Doore, Kathy, 137

Doraty, Judy, 161

Doty, Richard, 53, 164-168, 231, 233, 335

downloads (from ETs), 196, 247, 333

Sadler, William, 212

"Dreamland," 329, 330, 331

"Duke, Richard" 74, 77, 78

Duke University, 70, 73

Dulce, New Mexico, 147, 160, 165, 167, 168

Dulce Base, 147, 160, 165, 167, 168

Dulce War, 168

Dungeons & Dragons, 336

E

Eagle River, 182

Earthsea trilogy, 41

Eccleston, Annette, 223

Ecology of Souls, An 137

Eisenhower, 113, 114, 116

Electronic Voice Phenomenon (EVP), 89-103, 199, 249-250, 291-297, 308, 311, 318, 332-333

Elizondo, Lue, 76

Ellis, D.J., 297

Encounters, 75, 215, 321, 355

Eno, Paul, 327

Enoch, 122, 142, 146

Enochian calls, 65

Ernetti, Fr. Pellegrino, 292, 293

Esopus Island, 60

extrasensory perception (ESP), 73, 75

exorcism, 19, 111, 112, 241, 263, 326, 327

exorcist, 13, 102, 104, 107, 111, 231, 240, 263, 292, 302, 307, 309, 327

Extraterrestrial Intelligence and the Catholic Faith, 309

F

fairies, 179, 180, 181, 182, 186, 187, 188, 189, 203, 244, 278, 311 298, 335

Fake "Mary," 316

Fake "St. Michael, "316

familiar spirits, 107

Farsight Institute 234

FATE, 38

"Father Mark (exorcist), 111, 112

Fatima,13, 14, 196, 264, 265, 266, 323, 325

FBI, 194, 226

fear (in paranormal encounters), 96, 103, 105, 118, 125, 153, 159, 170, 180, 212, 273, 282, 295

Final Events, 69, 232, 270

Fish, Marjorie, 127

flap (UFO), 27, 30, 66, 69, 74, 221, 222, 355

flying disk, 50

flying humanoids, 152

flying saucer, 29, 32, 43, 44, 45, 46, 89, 115, 207, 215, 216, 218

Flying Saucers and the Three Men, 99

Fogarty, Bill, 192

folklore, 15, 63, 122, 132, 137, 158, 169, 170, 181, 186, 188, 253, 273

forbidden food (folklore), 181

Forbidden Knowledge, 142

Foster, Anna, 222, 223, 224, 225, 226

Four Georges, 83, 107, 206, 207

Fox family, 278

Fradd, Matt, 312

Francis, Saint, 306

Franklin, Benjamin 72, 298

Freemasonry, 104, 253

Frei, Gebhardt, 293, 294

Friedman, Stanton, 45, 46, 47

Funes, Fr. Gabriel, 305, 306

Fyodorov, 321

G

Gatay, Georges,181

Gemelli, 292, 293

ghost box, 198, 199, 297

Giant Rock, 83, 84

Gillis, Nathaniel, 327

Gnostic gospels, 280, 319, 324

Gnosticism, 121, 200, 319, 38, 280, 319, 324

goddess, 196

"Gold-Leaf Lady," 254

Golden Dawn, 58, 59

golem, 63, 269, 270, 333

Good, Timothy, 179

Goodman, Gail, 150

Gordon Thomas, 81

Gottlieb, Sidney, 81

Gramlich, Fr. Anthony, 328

gray aliens, 161, 244, 257

Greer, Steven, 190, 191, 192, 203, 214, 297, 322, 325

Groom Lake, 329

Grusch, David, 53, 54, 168, 245

Guggenheim Aeronautical Laboratory, 63

Gulf Breeze Six, 221, 222, 223, 225, 226

Guppy-Volckman, Agnes, 255

H

Hale-Bopp coment, 217

Hall, Charles 159, 160

Hambright, Gary, 150

Hansen, George, 335

Hansen, Myrna, 161, 234

Harsch-Fischbach, Maggy, 300, 301

Haut, Walter, 44, 45, 46, 54

Hawnser, Pablo, 214

Hay, Donald, 323

Holzer, Hans, 186, 262

Heaven and Hell, 23

Heaven's Gate, 217, 219

Heiser, Michael, 51, 54, 82, 107, 112, 120, 121, 122, 123, 141, 142, 143, 144, 147, 155, 156, 297, 307

Henry, Tyler, 297

hieroglyphics, 28, 31, 50, 268, 270

Hill, Betty and Barney, 91, 126

hitchhiker effect, 169, 172

hoax, 93, 113, 117, 118, 119

holography, 76, 77, 82, 265

Holy Eucharist, 184, 279, 280

holy guardian angel, 59

homunculus, 270

Hopkins, Budd 128, 129, 133, 277, 336

Horten, Walter and Reimar, 50

Hostage to the Devil, 107, 137, 231

Howard, Robert E., 41

Howe, Linda Moulton, 165, 166, 231, 234, 246

Hueckstaedt, Michael, 223

Huff, Judy, 258

Hubbard, L. Ron, 64, 65, 66, 67, 79, 209, 210, 325

Hull House, 173, 174, 175, 176

hybrids, 134, 135, 143, 147

Hynek, J. Alan, 97, 163

hypnosis, 66, 127, 129, 133, 134, 135, 156, 161, 163, 166, 224, 234, 255, 325, 337

I

"I AM" Activity, 206, 209

Ignatius of Loyola, Saint, 301

implants, 129, 243, 271, 273, 274, 275, 276, 277

Indiana Ghost Trackers, 187

Instrumental Transcommunication (ITC), 118, 162, 190, 287

International Flying Saucer Bureau, 95, 100

Iraq War, 223

J

Jacobs, David, 132, 135, 141, 143, 274, 336, 337

Jacobsen, Annie, 50, 51, 269

"Jamsie" (possession), 107, 108, 109, 110, 111, 112, 117, 137, 240, 283

Jesuits, 102, 104, 107, 231, 302, 303, 304, 305, 306, 320, 341, 301, 302, 305, 306, 307

Jesuits in Space, 41

Jesus, 13, 21, 41, 73, 77, 82, 114, 115, 116, 123, 141, 142, 143, 147, 148, 166, 184, 185, 196, 211, 212, 214, 217, 218, 224, 225, 234, 238, 239, 240, 267, 268, 280, 284, 302, 303, 304, 308, 312, 313, 316, 319, 320, 323, 324, 327, 331

Jet Propulsion Laboratory, 36, 63

Jurgenson, Friedrich, 294

Jimmy Akin's Mysterious World, 314, 317

John Paul II, Saint Pope, 11

Joliet Prison, Old, 173

Jones, Danny, 196, 200, 319 6

Johnson, Stan, 225

Jordan, Joe, 238, 240, 339

Jornlin, Allison, 182

Jung, Carl, 33, 293

K

Keel, John, 86, 101, 104, 118, 137, 244, 257, 258, 268, 270, 333, 337

Kellogg, W. K., 213

"Kia," 224

King, George 91, 112, 207, 208, 282

Kirtland Air Force Base, 160, 162, 165, 166

Knapp, George, 167, 172, 177

Konkolesky, Bill, 136

Kulagina, 73

Kundalini, 196, 208, 275, 323, 333

L

Lacy, Byron, 252

"Lady, The," 193, 196, 197

"Lady of the Sands," 131

Lake Mead, 115

"LAM," 60, 65

Lanulos, 119

Laughlin, David, 33

"Law of Attraction," 117

"layer cake effect," 259

LaVey, Anton, 149

Lazar, Bob, 166, 167, 231, 233, 234

Le Guin, Ursula K., 41

Leadbetter, Charles, 17, 18, 19

Lear, John, 166, 167, 231, 232, 233, 234

Lemoine, Blake, 333, 334

Lennon, John, 278

Leir, Roger, 275

leprechaun, 180, 181

Leviathan, 59

Lewis, C.S., 39, 184

Liberal Catholic Church, 17

Liberation Theology, 319

limiting God argument (in ETH), 299, 305

Lindley Street Haunting, 94, 327

Loch Ness, 58, 59

Lorgen, Eve, 136

"love bite," 136

Lovecraft, H. P., 42

Luann's Farm, 187

Lucifer, 21, 22, 39, 114, 117, 316, 330

Luciferian, 22, 60, 64, 150, 330

Luminator, 296

Lumley, 27, 28, 29, 355

M

Mack, John, 22, 197, 230, 231, 265, 355

macro-PK, 102

Macy, Mark, 287, 292, 296

"Madonna of Bachelors Grove," 258

Magellan voyage, 338 290

Mediumship of the Tape Recorder, The, 297

Maier, Francis, 305

Malina, Frank, 269

"Manu," 256

Marcel, Major Jesse, 44-46

Martin, Malachi, 18, 29, 102, 104, 107, 110, 207, 213, 231, 302, 306

Mary, Blessed Virgin, 114, 116, 120, 190, 223, 236, 304, 246, 291

"Mary," Fake, 204, 232

"Masters," 19, 20, 21, 22, 23, 206, 208

matchbox sign, 276

Maury Island Incident, 93, 94

McDougall, William, 70

McKenna, Bishop Robert, 326

meditation, 65, 83, 84, 112, 191, 237, 253, 284, 323, 327

Meek, George, 288, 289, 290, 291

Meier, Billy, 107, 120, 121, 122, 123, 230

Men in Black, 30, 93, 114 MIB, 93, 94, 101, 105, 114, 248

Men Who Stare at Goats, The, 199

Mengele, Joseph, 50

Metascience Foundation, 289

Michael of Nebadon., 211

Michelle Remembers, 149

Millennial Hospitality, 159

mimicry (in demonic activity) 257

Mishlove, Jeffrey, 177

"Missing 411" enigma, 125, 147, 158

missing time, 128, 129, 139, 194

Missing Time (book), 128

Missler, Chuck, 141, 143

MKOFTEN, 80, 81, 234

MKULTRA, 81, 155, 266, 274

Moffitt family case 186, 261

Mojave Desert, 83, 85

Montauk, 66, 67

Montauk Project, 66, 67

moon, 138, 185, 231, 232, 233, 261, 313, 332

Moon, Peter, 66

Mothman Prophecies, The, 118, 137

Mount Adams, 158

Mount Hermon, 142

Mount Rainer, 43

Mount Shasta, 94, 158, 206

Mueller, "Doc," 290

MUFON, 74, 136, 194, 198, 222, 225, 239, 252, 276

N

Napolitano, Linda, 101, 129, 130, 131, 132, 272, 277, 278, 336

Nance, Pamela, 198

NASA, 52, 80, 160, 194, 196, 198, 233, 247, 253, 256, 275, 320, 323

National Medal of Science, 269

Native Americans, 9, 169, 170, 174

Nazi, 35, 50, 159, 321, 325

near death experience (NDA), 81, 234, 283

Nellis Air Force Base, 159, 329

Nelson, Victoria, 209

Nephilim, 142, 143, 144, 146, 147

Nettles, Bonnie, 216

New Age, 12, 14, 17, 21, 22, 23, 24, 40, 123, 125, 166, 197, 198, 213, 216, 217, 231, 241, 256, 311, 312, 317, 324

New England Society for Psychic Research, 94

Nexon, Dan, 42

Nichols, Preston, 66

Nixon, Richard, 113

No Coincidences Management and Research, LLC, 322

"Nobody Told Me.", 278

Nolan, Gary, 245, 247, 264, 266, 322

"nuts and bolts" UFO theory 12, 244

O

O'Connor, Daniel, 14, 15, 296, 310, 313, 314, 330, 339

O'Connor, Monsignor Stephen 296

O'Neil, Bill, 289

Only Man Bears His Image, 14, 310, 330

Operating Thetan (Scientology), 210

orbs, 96, 170, 171, 172, 173, 188, 189, 193, 194, 202

Ordo Templi Orientis, 64

"Orthrus," 121

Ouija board, 89, 90, 198, 223, 224, 225, 226

Out from the Silent Planet, 39

Outline of History, 34

P

Padre Pio, Saint, 13, 309, 310, 311

pagan, 108, 145, 184, 193, 212, 303, 320

Pagels, Elaine, 319, 324

Paglini, Evelyn, 261

Palmer, 36, 37, 38, 94, 157

pancakes, alien 182

Paradise Ranch, 329

parapsychology, 11, 15, 57, 70, 177, 193, 254, 294, 337

Parsons, Jack, 36, 37, 40, 63, 64, 65, 66, 67, 69, 70, 74, 79, 253, 262, 269, 270, 320, 325, 335

Parrinello, Pat, 275

Partridge, Christopher, 22, 23, 205, 355

Passport to Magonia, 179, 180, 182

Pasulka, Diana, 11, 13-14, 52, 197-198, 247, 275, 318-324, 326, 328

Paul, Saint, 22, 112, 184, 212

Paul VI, Saint Pope Paul, 311

Pazder, Lawrence 149

Pelley, William Dudley, 89

Pentagon, 48, 76, 113, 114, 115, 171, 172, 177, 247

Perlock, Kris, 223

Perry, Travis, 39

Philadelphia Experiment, 273

Pfleger, Right Reverend Monsignor Professor C., 295

Pilot Mountain, 198

Pine Bush, 280

Pine Gap, 148, 157

Plante, Simone, 321, 322, 333

poltergeist, 12, 96, 101, 109, 170, 173, 177, 185, 229, 240, 248, 249, 261, 262, 267, 281

"Ponnar," 90

"Ponto," 109, 110, 111, 112, 117, 118, 120, 137, 240, 283

Francis, Pope, 199, 307

Pius II, Pope 313

Pius the XII, Pope, 35, 29

portal, 42, 60, 66, 69, 170, 174, 175, 187

possession, 15, 19, 24, 44, 73, 105, 107, 110, 183, 194, 231, 240, 241, 249, 253, 257, 258, 263, 265, 323, 327

Powell, General Colin, 226

prana, 208

Presidio, 149, 150

Price, Harry, 185

Proceedings of the College of Universal Wisdom, 84

Project, The 296

Project Blue Beam, 77

Project Mogul, 48

protocols (for contact), 190, 196, 275, 333

psi, 74, 208

psychotronic weapons, 75

psyop, 52, 53, 54, 77, 113, 160

Puharich, Henry, 73

puncture wounds, 252

Puthoff, Hal, 246

Pye Laboratory, 294

R

radiation, 30, 267

Raël, 218, 321

"Range Four Harry," 159

Raudive, Konstantin, 285, 287, 288, 289, 290, 291, 292, 294, 295, 296, 297, 332

Redfern, Nick, 67, 69, 70, 74, 76, 77, 78, 82, 232, 269, 270

Remote Spirit Release Therapy, 316

remote viewing, 11, 12, 74, 118, 198, 234, 246

Revelations of the Magi, 320

Roach, Hal, 291

Rhine, J. B., 70

Rinchich, Greg 147

Ring of Fire ritual 117

Ripper Crew Murders, 153

Goddard, Robert, 269

robot grandma, 158

Rodney King riots 226

Rosicrucianism, 197, 200

Ross, Hugh, 73

Roswell, 26, 29, 44, 45, 47, 48, 49, 50, 51, 52, 53, 54, 55, 83, 93, 155, 156, 166, 205, 238, 246, 269, 270

Rowena Plateau, 158

Residual UFOs (RUFOs), 241, 245, 266

Russia, 48, 50, 51, 73

S

Stanford University, 247

salt, 182, 186

"Sanat Kumara," 21, 22

Sanger, Margaret, 35

Sarchie, Ralph, 104, 105

Satan, 22, 59, 142, 143, 149, 150, 280, 316, 330, 337

Satanic Panic, 149-156

Satanic Ritual Abuse, 149- 155

satanic rituals, 75

Saucers Speak, The, 90

Saxa Rubra, Battle of, 27

Schneider, Phil, 168

Scientology, 64, 66, 209-210

Scole Experiment, 255

scoop marks, 252

séance, 71, 72, 96, 190, 198, 206, 250, 253, 255, 256, 267, 292, 298, 325

Secret Doctrine, The, 20

Secrets and Lies, 81

Sedamsville, 250, 251, 252

sedevacantist, 307, 308

Semivan, Jim, 246

"Semjase," 122, 123, 230

sentient UFOs and AI, 195, 257, 270, 333

Setterberg, William, 223

Seventh-day Adventist, 212, 213

sex, 57, 58, 65, 101, 131, 132, 254, 304, 337

sex magick, 57, 58, 65, 254

sexual, 18, 35, 58, 134, 136, 143, 145, 150, 151, 209, 212, 218, 250, 335

Shadow Kingdom, The, 41

Silver, Carole, 179

Shape of Things to Come, The, 34

Shaver, Richard, 37, 38, 157

Sherman Ranch, 169

Short, Rev. Robert, 84

Shroud of Turin, 268

Silva Mind Control, 224

Simonton, 182

Skinwalker Ranch, 169, 170, 171, 172, 177, 178, 337

sleep paralysis, 173, 176, 241, 300

Society for Psychical Research, 20, 256

sons of God, 122, 123

souls, 30, 81, 82, 143, 144, 210, 215, 230, 231, 232, 233, 234, 296,

303, 308, 309, 311, 314, 317, 324, 326, 328, 334

"space brothers," 83, 84, 88, 90, 125, 167, 206, 305

Spiricom, 289, 290, 291, 296

spirit box, 198

Smythe, Colin, 294

Spirit Faces, 296

Spiritual Energy Battery, 208

Spiritualism, 10, 21, 35, 70, 71, 72, 255, 278, 291, 317

Spooner, Camille, 30

Sprinkle, Leo, 161

Star Wars, 36, 40, 49, 225, 325

stargates, 170

Stealth technology, 50, 329, 331

stigmata, 13, 320

Stoker, Bram, 68

Strange Harvest., 166

Stranger Things, 67

Stranges, Frank, 114, 115, 116, 117, 118

Strong, George Templeton, 71

Strieber, Whitley, 41, 233, 277-292, 318, 324, 334

suicide, 112, 168, 177, 193, 201, 215, 262, 296, 335

Sumerian, 26

summoning (UFOs), 19, 59, 65, 120, 189-195, 198, 325

supernaturalism, 71, 141

support group (abductee/contactee), 129, 134

Surprised by Truth,, 311

Swan, Frances, 90, 91

"Swearing Ghost" case, 182, 262

Swedenborg, Emmanuel, 23, 24

T

Tall Whites, 159

Taylor, 52, 196, 247, 275, 320, 322, 323, 333

Serios, Ted, 254

Teilhard de Chardin, Pierre 302

Temple of Set, 149, 150

Teresa of Avila, Saint, 320

text messages (paranormal) 34, 145, 230, 232, 248, 263, 319

"Teacher, The," 159

Thelema, 64, 333

Thigpen, Paul, 13, 308, 309, 325

Theosophical Society, 18, 209

Theosophy, 18, 19, 20, 21, 22, 23, 38, 41, 87, 90, 205, 206, 207, 208, 237, 321, 325

Thigpen, 308, 309, 311, 324, 325

Thurston, Fr. Herbert, 317

To the Stars (TTS) (To the Stars Academy), 246

Trojan Feast, A, 181

tulpa, 105

Tyler, Texas, 186, 262

U

UFO cults, 205, 206, 217, 220

Uinta Basin, 170

"Uncle Sid," 88

United States Conference of Catholic Bishops, 309

University of Arizona, 89

University of Chicago, 70, 212

University of Wisconsin, 132

Urantia Book 211, 212, 213, 214, 215

V

Val Camonica, 26

"Valiant Thor," 113, 115, 116, 117, 159

Vallée, Jacques, 13, 14, 73, 86, 100, 140, 167, 179, 180, 181, 182, 197, 244, 266, 319, 333, 337

Van Tassel, 83, 84, 85, 89, 112, 207

Vatican, 11, 13, 14, 292, 294, 301, 302, 305, 306, 307, 308, 309, 320, 325, 326

Venus, 21, 86, 113, 115, 116, 117, 207

"Visitors, The" 32, 41, 119, 278, 279, 280, 283, 289

Vorilhon, Claude, 218

Voice of the Silence, The, 60

Voices (of unknown origin), 90, 170, 173, 176, 192, 198, 199, 250, 256, 260, 262, 291, 293, 294, 295, 296, 297, 300

von Braun, Wernher, 321

von Däniken, Erich, 79, 269, 270

von Karman, Theodore, 63, 269

W

Walters, Ed, 180, 181, 222, 223, 225, 226

wand, in folklore180, 222

War of the Worlds, 34, 42, 355

Warren, Ed and Lorraine, 94, 104, 326

Watchers (angels), 122, 123, 142, 143, 147

Watertown, 329

weather balloon, 44, 45, 46

Wells, H.G., 34, 35, 42, 118, 355

werewolf, 171

Williams, Charles, 258

Williamson, George Hunt, 88, 89, 90, 207

witch marks, 277

witchcraft, 35, 117, 118, 154, 190, 240, 268, 277, 278

"Wizard Clip" case, 185, 261

Wonewoc, 9

"Woods, Emma" (pseudonym), 134

World ITC, 296

Wright, John, 39

Wright Patterson Air Force base, 48

XYZ

Xenu, 210

Yeats, W. B. 58

yoga, 112, 196, 208, 237, 323, 333

Zachary, Pope, 313

Zeta Reticuli, 127

ziplock sign, 276

NOTES

PREFACE

[1] See Matt Fradd's interview with Jimmy Akin on Fradd's podcast, *Pints with Aquinas* in the Spring of 2024. See www.pintswithaquinas.com for details and to listen to or watch the full episode.

ANOTHER WORLD

[2] In his entry on Charles Leadbeater for the *Theosopedia*, historian of religion Robert Ellwood named clairvoyance as the "key to Leadbeater's teaching and theosophical style." For Leadbeater's exploration of clairvoyance, including his own, see his book, *Clairvoyance*, among his other works.

[3] Blavatsky's relatives and family friends revealed her unusual childhood characteristics (and attempt to exorcise her) to A.P. Sinnett, who wrote of them in his book, *Incidents in the life of Madame Blavatsky*.

[4] Mack, John *Abduction: Human Encounters with* Aliens, 384.

[5] Partridge, Christopher, *UFO Religions and Abduction Spiritualities*, 28. Partridge's works are indispensable in understanding fringe religions, including UFO religions and movements.

[6] Rawlinson cited in Partridge, 29.

[7] Ibid.

OF THE AIR

[8] For full accounts of the Lumley event, see "A Strange Story—Remarkable Discovery." *Missouri Democrat*, October 19, 1865, 1 and "A Trapper's Strange Story." Chicago *Tribune*, Oct 21, 1865, 3.

[9] The smell of sulfur has frequently been reported in both demonic and UFO/alien encounters. For a very good look at this reality, including specific cases, see Joshu Cutchin's *The Brimstone Deceit*.

[10] Considering that such reports and speculation were being made back in 1864, one can only wonder if perhaps a young H.G. Wells heard about the airship flap that swept the nation just two years before his birth. Maybe the dramatic tales and subsequent speculation of journalists inspired—at least in part—his later science fiction masterpiece, *War of the Worlds*.

[11] "Strange Phenomenon." *Dallas Daily Herald*, January 23, 1878, 1.

[12] Calhoun, J. "A Celestial Visitor." *Daily Nebraska State Journal*, June 8, 1854, 5.

[13] In this first quarter of the 21st Century, we're hearing much about radiation effects associated with UFO encounters, such as those reported by the British tabloid, the *Sun* in 2022, when the news agency published its receipt of a 1500-page Pentagon report compiled for the *Sun* in response to a FOIA request, detailing physical effects such as burns and other marks, as well as paranormal type events such as levitations. See Perry, Emmy, "X-FILES: Pentagon releases 1,500 pages of secret documents about shadowy UFO programme after four-year battle," *The Sun*, April 5, 2022 (www.the-sun.com).

[14] "Three Strange Visitors." *Stockton Evening Mail*, November 25, 1896, 1.

[15] "A Windmill Demolishes it." *Dallas Morning News*, April 19, 1897, 5.

[16] The full story of the visitor who seemed "not an inhabitant of this world" appeared in The *Fort Worth Register*, April 17, 1897, 1.

STORIES FROM THE SKY

[17] Bergman, Jerry, "H.G. Wells: Darwin's Disciple and Eugenicist Extraordinaire." The *Journal of Creation* (December 2004): Vol. 18, No. 3 116-120.

[18] In his essay, "The Anti-Catholicism of H.G. Wells," Karl Keating reminds us that "Wells's attack preceded by twenty years Rolf Hochhuth's play *The Deputy*, which generally is regarded as the origin of the many falsehoods disseminated about Pius XII's actions during World War II. Perhaps Wells is due more of the credit (or blame). Note also that Wells seems unaware that the pope, when he was Cardinal Pacelli, wrote the 1937 encyclical *Mit brennender Sorge* ('With Burning Concern') for Pius XI. The first encyclical written in German, it was a clear and extended condemnation of Nazi ideology." (Karl Keating for Catholic.com at www.catholic.com March 2013.)

[19] For a discussion of Wells's antisemitism, see Schweitzer, Darrell, "The H.G. Wells Problem" via The *New York Review of Science Fiction* (nyrsf.com), February 15, 2018.

[20] For further reading on Ray Palmer, see Fred Nadis, *The Man from Mars: Ray Palmer's Amazing Pulp Journey.*

[21] We'll look much more closely at Jack Parsons in a lately chapter, but for further reading on Jack his work and occultism, two good biographies are available, including *Strange Angel* and *Sex and Rockets: The Occult World of Jack Parsons.* A book of Parsons' essays, *Freedom is a Two-Edged Sword,* is also worth a read for those wanting a look into his infamously nonconformist mind..

[22] Clarke, Arthur C., *Childhood's End.*

[23] For an examination of anti-Christian thought in Clarke's work, particularly *Childhood's End,* see Wright, John C., "*Childhood's End* and Gnosticism" at www.LiveJournal.com., April 22, 2009.

[24] Ibid.

[25] Perry, Travis, "How Science Fiction Portrays the Future of Christianity," on the blog, *Speculative Faith* (www.speculativefaith.lorehaven.com), May 16, 2019.

[26] Ibid.

[27] Woods, Mark, "Ursula K. Le Guin: What the Atheist Writer Taught this Christian." *Christian Today* (www.christiantoday.com), January 24, 2018.

[28] See Nexon, Dan, 'H.P. Lovecraft and Theosophy" at *The Duck of Minerva* (www.duckofminerva.com)), May 19, 2012.

NINETEEN FORTY-SEVEN

[29] Associated Press, July 8, 1949.

[30] "Excitement not Justified." *Roswell Daily Record*, July 9, 1947.

[31] For more on Friedman's interviews of witnesses and an in-depth look at the Roswell case from a UFO believer's vantage, see Stanton Friedman and Don Berliner's *Crash at Corona: The U.S. Military Retrieval and Cover-Up of a UFO.*

[32] See Colonel Philip Corso and William J. Birnes, *The Day After Roswell.*

[33] For an exhaustive and truly thought-provoking look at the Roswell question—and a lot of other ufological puzzles—see Annie Jacobsen's *Area 51: An Uncensored History of America's Top Secret Military Base.*

[34] See Diana Pasulka's *American Cosmic* for an account of her visit to an alleged UFO crash site in New Mexico with tech developer and NASA employee Tim Taylor, called "Tyler D" in the book.

[35] Grusch testified under oath in July of 2023 before the U.S. House Committee on Oversight and Accountability. The transcript of this hearing, "Unidentified Anomalous Phenomena: Implications on National Security, Public Safety, and Government Transparency" may be found at www.congress.gov.

[36] A number of body language experts weighed in (unflatteringly) after David Grusch's Congressional testimony in 2023, including the Behavior Panel via their popular YouTube channel of the same name, on an episode entitled, "We've Been LIED To!" Who's REALLY Deceiving Us?"(capitals theirs).

THE BEAST & THE GRAY

[37] Crowley spelled the name as "Babalon" after learning this spelling during a mystical encounter; he saw as the goddess/demon as a positive reinterpretation of the Whore of Babylon from the Bible's Revelation 17.

[38] In recent years, of group of tour guides from Los Angeles decided to try to locate the site where Parsons and Hubbard had performed their sex magickal rituals in the Mojave desert. They had come to believe that Parsons would have been draw to a place called Little Petroglyph Canyon in the China Lake area where early rocketeers were known to experiment. There, the group found several letterings carved in rocks, including the dates 1934 and 1946, and the initials "JP." For details of their adventure, see "An Esotouric Road Rrip: In Search of the Babalon Working" on the Esotouric blog at www/esotouric.com

[39] Like so much in this book, the love triangle (or, more accurately and curiously, *pentagon*) of the Pasadena group is a whole other kettle of fish, involving, indeed, five people. Sara "Betty" Northrup joined the O.T.O. as a teenager, along with her sister, Helen. Helen was married to Jack Parsons, but Betty had a torrid affair with him from 1941 to 1945 before moving on to Hubbard in 1945 and marrying

him . . . while he was still married to his first wife, Margaret Grubb. Northrup's shenanigans were too much for even Crowley, who called her a "vampire."

[40] The Rhines' adulation of Doyle wouldn't last. The couple would later author an article for the *Journal of Abnormal and Social Psychology* exposing one of Doyle's favorite psychic mediums as a fraudster, leading Doyle to respond, "J. B. Rhine is an ass." (See Polidoro, Massimo, *Final Séance: The Strange Friendship Between Houdini and Conan Doyle*.)

[41] On George Templeton Strong and other players in New York's Spiritualist moment, see Burch, Kate, "Concerning Spooks: the Spiritualists of New York" on the blog, *From the Stacks* for the New York Historical Society Museum & Library, October 16, 2013 (www.nyhistory.org).

[42] Sollors, Werner. "Dr. Benjamin Franklin's Celestial Telegraph, or Indian Blessings to Gas-Lit American Drawing Rooms." *American Quarterly*, vol. 35, no. 5, 1983, 459–80.

[43] For an exhaustive look at the governmental projects described in this chapter, as well as others, see journalist Jacobsen, Annie, *Phenomena: The Secret History of the US Government's Investigations into Extrasensory Perception and Psychokinesis*. Also see her *The Pentagon's Brain: An Uncensored History of DARPA, America's Top-Secret Military Research Agency*.

[44] Vallée, Jacques, *UFO Chronicles of the Soviet Union*, 118.

[45] Ross shared his experience in Russia with Ken McMullen on the latter's podcast, *Becoming Outlaws* in August of 2023. A note: Although he is an anti-UFO missionary, atheist-to-Christian convert and astrophysicist Hugh Ross has developed some distinct "progressive creationist" ideas over the years to reconcile his atheistic scientific foundations with his found Christian faith. Such ideas include the notion of pre-Adamite humanoid bipedal beings populating Earth. As a result, we have to take Ross, I think, with a grain of salt, despite him being an outspoken voice against the idea of extraterrestrials. Still, I include his account of Russian scientists evidencing spirit possession at his lectures because it's a behavior we are seeing increasingly in many arenas where Christians and atheists collide, and it's one I've experienced personally in my own work.

[46] Entire books have been written and films made about the U.S. remote viewing programs, including the Stargate project, and of American psychic "stars" like Uri Gellar and Ingo Swann. Most notable is Jon Ronson's New York *Times*

bestseller, *The Men Who Stare at Goats*. Much of the work of these psychic operatives became hopelessly entwined with New Age/theosophical/ufological themes such as astral trips to celestial bodies, meetings with aliens, remote viewing aliens living among ancient humanity, etc.

[47] Boeche, Raymond W., "September 10, 2020 Revision Complete Record of DOD contacts," Published on ww.Academia.edu.

[48] For some readers, these claims may be evocative of the book and film, *The Men Who Stare at Goats* about the U.S. Army's exploration of the occult, including attempts to kill goats by staring at them and mentally willing their hearts to stop. Some of these efforts were part of the Stargate Project, which after its declassification became best known for its experiments with *remote viewing* or targeted clairvoyance.

[49] Farwell, Matt, "Tom DeLonge's Warped UFO Tour." *The New Republic*, August 10, 2023 (www.newrepublic.com).

[50] The anonymously authored 177-page "Anonymous Public Domain UAP Timeline" laying out a detailed, case-by-case history of UFO/UAP encounters as told through public domain documents was "leaked" to the UFO-centric news agency News Nation prior to the 2023 Congressional UFO hearing. As of this writing in June of 2024, the full document may be found online at *Internet Archive* (archive.org).

[51] Ibid.

[52] See Thomas, Gordon, *Secrets and Lies: A History of CIA Mind Control and Germ Warfare*.

[53] Michael Heiser asked this question during his review of Nick Redfern's *Final Events* his blog at www.drmsh.org, November 27, 2010.

CALLED

The primary source material is crucial for understanding the "Four Georges" of the classic Contactee era. See George Van Tassel's *Collected Proceedings of the College of Universal Wisdom*, Adamski's *The Flying Saucers Have Landed, Inside the Flying Saucers*, and other volumes, and George Hunt Williamson's *The Saucers Speak, Other Tongues, Other Flesh*, and other works. See references for details.

[54] Cultural historian and Fortean commentator Jason Colavito reminds us in his book, *The Cult of Alien Gods: H.P. Lovecraft and Extraterrestrial Pop Culture* that von Däniken lifted the material published in his blockbuster volume, *Chariots of the Gods* from the work of Jacques Bergier and Louis Pauwels, whose earlier publication, the 1960 cult classic *Morning of the Magicians*, presented a strange mashup of the pair's wild ideas on extraterrestrials, Theosophy, Nazis, and Lovecraft. In their book can be found the entire "ancient astronaut" theory, with all of its bizarre and unfounded nuances. Though that work is a difficult read, another author, Robert Charroux, included them in his own later writings—in a much easier to grasp style. Von Däniken used material from these authors' ideas for a 1964 magazine article, which attracted a publisher and a book deal for *Chariots of the Gods*, arguably one of the most unfortunately influential books of the twentieth century. The intellectual theft was just one of the many frauds and cons committed by von Däniken before and after his celebrity.

MEN IN THE NIGHT

For more on the "Men in Black" phenomenon and perspectives on it, see Rojcewicz, Peter M., "The 'Men in Black' Experience and Tradition: Analogues with the Traditional Devil Hypothesis." *Journal of American Folklore*, vol. 100, no. 396, Ray Boeche's "UFOs: Caught in a Web of Deception" (See Note 34), and Nick Redfern's book,

[55] See *They Knew Too Much About Flying Saucers* by Gray Barker

[56] Albert Bender detailed his extraterrestrial odyssey in the book, including encounters with the Men in Black and the story of "Contact Day" in *Flying Saucers and the Three Men*. Quoted material in this section is from his own account.

[57] Bender, Albert K. *Flying Saucers and the Three Men.*

[58] See Keel, John, *Operation Trojan Horse.*

A LITTLE TOO FAMILIAR (PART I)

I cannot more highly recommend Martin's blockbuster book, *Hostage to the Devil: The Possession and Exorcism of Five Contemporary Americans*, which includes Martin's extensive account of "Jamsie" and his possession by a familiar spirit.

[59] Martin, Malachi, *Hostage to the Devil*, p.301

[60] See *Hostage to the Devil*, 249-320 for the full account of Jamsie's possession and exorcism.

[61] Ibid.

[62] Ibid.

[63] Ibid.

[64] Ibid.

[65] Ibid.

[66] For the whole story of Valiant Thor, see *Stranger in the Pentagon* by Frank Stranges. "Val" and Frank wrote a number of other books together, but I found one to be enough.

[67] Martin, *Hostage to the Devil*.

[68] The story of Derenberger and Indrid Cold was first shared by John Keel in his book, *The Mothman Prophecies*. Degerberger wrote his own, extended version of his friendship with Cold in *Visitors from Lanulos*.

[69] In the documentary *Aliens and Demons*, Heiser rightfully scoffs at Adamski's "warmed over Gnosticism."

TAKEN

[70] For those not familiar with the "Missing 411" enigma, the phenomenon has been researched for decades by David Paulides, a former law enforcement officer who found that large numbers of people have been going missing in the National Parks for years, and that their cases contain eerie similarities and absurdities. His work has garnered an enormous following among those interested in the unexplained and in true crime. The story of the "robot grandma" is one of the most well-known of the thousands of accounts Paulides has collected, and you can read the whole account in the third of his book series: *Missing 411: North America and Beyond*.

[71] Of course, there are exceptions to this, such as the 1896 Lodi, California abduction attempt we discussed earlier. And there have been more recent contactees in the "classical" sense—even very notable ones such as Whitley

Strieber, Billy Meier, Chris Bledsoe and others that we will examine—that have come forward after the early Contactee era. These are individuals who have formed long and intimate relationships with their contactors. They've also had rides in "spacecraft," but the usual patterns of abduction cases are not, for the most part, present.

[72] Numerous books have been written addressing the events around the abduction of Betty and Barney Hill, including the classic by Stanton Friedman and Kathleen Marden , *Captured! The Betty and Barney Hill UFO Experience: The True Story of the World's First Documented Alien Abduction*. There are many takes on the Hill abduction by these various authors, including a recent volume that paints the whole affair as a study in racism, Matthew Bowman's *The Abduction of Betty and Barney Hill: Alien Encounters, Civil Rights, and the New Age in America*. The University of New Hampshire holds the Betty and Barney Hill Papers, consisting of seven boxes of documents and artifacts, including the dress Betty was wearing the night of the alleged abduction.
[73] For Budd Hopkins' account of the Linda Napolitano abduction events, see his book *Witnessed: The True Story of the Brooklyn Bridge UFO Abductions*. For a critical look at the case, see the work of George Hansen, et al. " A Critique of Budd Hopkins' Case of the UFO Abduction of Linda Napolitano" by Joseph J. Stefula, Richard D. Butler, and George P. Hansen, in *Third Eyes Only*, Issue No. 8, January, 1993; "'Torquemada' Responds to Jerome Clark" by George P. Hansen, in *Third Eyes Only*, Issue No. 7, 1992, and "Attempted Murder vs. The Politics of Ufology: A Question of Priorities in the Linda Napolitano Case" by George P. Hansen. 20 October 1992. (This paper was published in several periodicals including *The New Jersey Chronicle*, Vol. 3, Nos. 1/2, September-December, 1992.

[74] David Jacobs' first published work was *The UFO Controversy in America:* a book based on his doctoral dissertation for the University of Wisconsin at Madison. It was one of the first graduate theses to examine the UFO phenomenon, and the book based on it is still widely read, perhaps moreso because of the striking and disturbing developments in Jacobs' work and theories, of which many are highly critical. To explore that development yourself, review David Jacobs' cases, methodologies and analyses through his volumes listed in the references, in order of their publication: *Secret Life, Alien Encounters, The Threat* and *Walking Among Us*.

[75] David Jacobs has been a frequent guest on *Coast to Coast AM*, beginning with episodes hosted by the late Art Bell. All of Jacobs' appearances may be found and streamed on the program's website at coasttocoastam.com.

[76] If you are at all interested in the topics discussed in the book in your hands (or on your screen), do yourself a favor and procure for your own library Johsua Cutchin's mammoth collection of comparative strangeness, *An Ecology of Souls*, in which he demonstrates how every possible paranormal encounter and experience ultimately has to do with death and the human soul. In this section, I'm indebted to Cutchin's study of the connections between UFO experiences and visions of the dead.

THE DAYS OF NOAH

[77] Keel (1970).

[78] Whether you agree with his theories or not, Heiser's work has been deeply influential in bringing back the supernatural elements of the Bible and the reality of the spiritual war that still rages. See in particular *The Unseen Realm* and *Reversing Hermon*.

[79] The late Christian pastor Chuck Missler was also called a prophet by many of his followers. He wrote of his "Days of Noah" theory of UFOs in his book, *Return of the Nephilim* and elsewhere. Those interested in this cultural phenomenon can view many of Missler's presentations on YouTube as well. The late Tom Horn was also called a prophet by many. Among his works is *Nephilim Stargates: The Year 2012 and the Return of the Watchers*, in which he lays out his belief in the connection between biotechnology and the return of the Watcher angels in an extraterrestrial disguise.

[80] See Heiser's "An Imaginary Conversation with a Modern Nephilim Believer" on his blog a drmsh.com.

[81] Most who believe that the Watchers mated with human women also believe that, after their physical deaths, the Nephilim offspring of these unions became evil spirits and roamed the Earth; they are the beings known as "demons." These entities have manifested, theorists believe, as fairies, gnomes, sprites, djinn, bigfoot and other assorted characters throughout history. But none of that is true. The only spirits on Earth are good angels, fallen angels and, to a lesser extent, human souls. Yes, they have lots of disguises, but behind the masks you'll always find angels, and the bad ones are demons.

[82] For a Catholic take on the subject of human-angelic sexual relations, see Catholic historian Phillip Campbell's "Demonic Impregnation: Incubi and Succubi" on his blog at ww.unamsanctamcatholic.com.

[83] As we'll see, few Catholic scholars have warned against alien belief and the Nephilim hybrid theory. One of them, though a sedevacantist, is Brother Peter Dimond, who paints this particular deception as, accurately, one meant to target Christians, a view he shares with the late evangelical scholar Michael Heiser. (Dimond 2008). For Dimond's take on this idea, see the documentary film, *UFOs, Nephilim, Climate Change and the Devil.*

[84] See the *Missing 411* books by David Paulides.

[85] Greg Rinchich can be found on podcast recordings here and there. Though he hasn't published his claimed experiences, his stories of modern-day Nephilim sightings and claims of having to sign an agreement to not use the name of Jesus around them is well known among many ufology splinter groups interested in a biblical UFO connection.

[86] Stan Deyo collected his intricate, science-infused theory of everything in *The Cosmic Conspiracy.*

A LITTLE TOO FAMILIAR (PART 2)

Many books and scholarly articles have been written on the "Satanic Panic," a subject that is, I feel, still curiously misrepresented. Like Sagan's *The Demon-Haunted World,* most of commentaries on the topic are scathing critiques of Western Judeo-Christian culture, reducing the entire question of ritual abuse to "moral panic." Typically, the many verified cases of SRA around the world are ignored in such studies, and the phenomenon is reduced to just one more "great American witch hunt" in the tradition of the New England witch trials, the McCarthy hearings and so forth. As I think we can see, in just our very short look at it, there was much more to it. *Something* was going on, despite the flood of delusions and hoaxes surrounding some quieter truth.

[87] Bottoms, B. L., Shaver, P. R., & Goodman, G. S. (1996). An analysis of ritualistic and religion-related child abuse allegations. *Law and Human Behavior, 20*(1).

[88] See CA Raschke, "Satanic Ritual Abuse of Children is Widespread" from *Child Abuse: Opposing Viewpoints.*

[89] Goleman, Dan, "Proof Lacking for Ritual Abuse by Satanists." *The New York Times,* October 31, 1994.

[90]For the story of abortion-as-sacrament, see Drabiak, Katherine, "The Satanic Temple Asserts Medication Abortion is a Religious Right," for *Bill of Health*, the blog of the Petrie-Flom Center at Harvard Law School, February 9, 2024.

[91] See Dean, Gwen, "Comparisons of Abduction Accounts with Ritual Maltreatment" in *Alien Discussion: Proceedings of the Abduction Study Conference at MIT, Cambridge, Ma.*

[92] Michael Heiser in the film, *Aliens and Demons*.

AS ABOVE SO BELOW

The Shaver Mystery is available in five volumes. See references for details.

[93] See Note 54.

[94] Charles Hall's *Millennial Hospitality* series spans six books. All have been widely received as very well written and entertaining, and just as wide as the praise is the range of belief in Hall's accounts. Some adore him, some call him delusional, others believe he was brainwashed by the military. Still others call him a liar, hoaxer and thief. The first volume is highly recommended, as he Hall is, indeed, a great storyteller. If you want to read about, for example, how the Tall Whites go into Las Vegas at night to gamble (in disguise of course), read on through the series.

[95] For a thorough, excellent look at the tragic story of Paul Bennewitz, see Greg Bishop's *Project Beta: The Story of Paul Bennewitz, National Security, and the Creation of a Modern UFO Myth*.

[96] For more on Bennewitz's new computer, and the shady story behind it, see Bishop (2005).

[97] Bishop, 97.

[98] "UFO Base Found in New Mexico." *Weekly World News*, September 20, 1988, 1.

[99] While a guest on Curt Jaimungal's popular podcast, *Theories of Everything*, Howe now infamously lost her composure after being confronted with the fact that evidence of extraterrestrials she'd presented as real was, in fact, not.

[100] See UAMN TV's channel on YouTube for Alan Stainfeld's interview with Linda Howe entitled, "Linda Howe - Memories of My Life
in Ancient Egypt… Revelations," posted April 2024.

[101] George Knapp conducted a number of interviews with John Lear for channel 8 in Las Vegas. Recordings of these interviews may be found on the *8 News Now* channel on YouTube.

[102] As with so many "references" for this book, it's hard to send readers to source materials to verify information, because as Linda Howe has said, it's all a "fractured hall of mirrors with a quicksand floor," so I send readers with a grain of salt to read more about Phil Schneider in a book by two authors who choose to remain anonymous because they are in fear of the "New World Order:" The book is called *The Dulce Wars: Underground Alien Bases and the Battle for Planet Earth: This is Not Science Fiction. . . A True-To-Life "War of The Worlds* by "Branton" with a forward by "Commander X." Readers may also want to seek out the recorded lecture given by Schneider in 1995 at the Dulce UFO Conference, which may be found on YouTube.

SKINWALKERS, SPIRITUALISTS AND SPACE X

For more on black money and paranormal research, including UFOs, see (with a grain of salt) the book *Skinwalkers at the Pentagon*.

[103] For an expose on the relationship between "well-funded UFO obsessives" and the U.S. government, see Jason Colavito's "How Washington Got Hooked on Flying Saucers" in *The New Republic* (newrepublic.com), My 21, 2021.

A LITTLE TOO FAMIIAR (PART III)

The towering UFO researchers John Keel and Jacques Vallée both published their highly influential works on this chapter's subject at essentially the same time. See Keel's *Operation Trojan Horse* and Vallée's *Passport to Magonia*. See also Timothy Good's *Earth: An Alien Enterprise* and Joshua Cutchin's *An Ecology of Souls* and *A Trojan Feast*.

[105] See Silver's book, *Strange and Secret Peoples* for this and other fascinating accounts in this line of study.

[106] See Ed Walters' books in references.

[107] Interestingly, it was also revealed that the family were what have been called "holy jumpers" or "holy rollers." Reporters shared that the family was known for the rollicking religious meetings they held in their apartment. Presumably, they were members of a church involved in the Wesleyan-Holiness movement. Protestants including Free Methodists and Wesleyan Methodists services often included dancing, shaking or other physical outbursts by members supposed to be under the power of the Holy Spirit. Of course, many fellow Protestants accused such faithful of being, rather, under demonic influence: an interesting assertion for our purposes. Today, many Protestants—and Catholics—frown on the so-called "charismatic" movements of their respective faiths, calling them diabolically influenced. Such movements also include shaking, convulsing and even audible phenomena like "holy laughter."

[108] Josiffe, Christopher, "Gef the Talking Mongosse." *Fortean Times*, December 2016.

[109] See Holzer, Hans, "The Devil in Texas,´ *Ghosts*.

[110] On June 2, 2022, journalist Shi Li Bartov reported for *Newsweek* that "a survey of 120 Italian exorcists by the Pontifical Athenaeum Regina Apostolorum, a Vatican-approved university in Rome, found that they were overwhelmed by a growing number of "possessed" people. Researcher Giuseppe Frau shared that some exorcists were seeing 30 to 50 cases a day.

THE SUMMONERS

[111] Rogan, Tom, "Did Steven Greer Fake a UFO with Flares?" *Washington Examiner*, July 31, 2020 (www.washingtonexaminer.com).

[112] Boeche, Ray, "ÚFOs: Caught in a Web of Deception," a paper originally delivered at the Gulf Breeze UFO Conference in Gulf Breeze Florida on February 12, 1994.via Academia (www.academia.edu).

[113] See Bledsoe's *UFO of God* for his full story from his own perspective.

[114] Chris Bledsoe's son, Ryan, appeared on Danny Jones' podcast (S1 E215) in early 2024. The episode is available on podcast platforms and to watch on Jones' YouTube channel.

115 Tsakanikas, Matthew, "Rosicrucian Principles Infiltrating Christianity: A Theological Advisory Against *UFO of God*" on his blog at Catholic460.substack.com (February 20, 2024).

116 Diana Pasulka on *The Joe Rogan Experience* podcast (Episode 2091), January 24, 2024

117 Ryan Bledsoe on the Danny Jones (Konkrete) podcast (Episode 215), December 28, 2023.

118 Ellwood, Robert, "Contact, Religion, and the Human Future." *Encyclopaedic Sourcebook of UFO Religions*, 378.

119 See Partridge's discussion of Theosophical principles and themes in his book, *UFO Religions*.

120 See references for details of Adamski's books, *The Flying Saucers Have Landed* (co-written with Desmond Leslie), *Inside the Space Ships*, and *Flying Saucers Farewell.*

121 Peebles, Curtis, *Watch the Skies*, 113.

122 Williamson's books include *Other Tongues—Other Flesh* (1957), *Secret Places of the Lion* (1958), *UFOs Confidential* with John McCoy (1958), *Road in the Sky* (1959) and *Secret of the Andes* (1961). If you look into them you'll find, I think, that they are largely mashups of biblical reinterpretation and Theosophy.

123 In the cult classic, *The Secret Life of Puppets*, see the section on Scientology in particular.

125 See references for details on the *Urantia Book.*

126 Gardner complied the details of his expose of Sadler and the "secret sleeper" into a book, *Urantia: The Great Cult Mystery.*

127 See Valverde, Raul, "Alien Encounters, the Theology of the Urantia Book, and the Origins of Human Consciousness," *Journal of Consciousness Studies*, 11(4):232-252, July 2020.

[128] A number of books have been published detailing the origins of Heaven's Gate—and the tragedy its leaders engineered—, but I recommend for a very good overview see Robinson, Wendy Gale, "Heaven's Gate: The End." *Journal of Computer-Mediated Communication*, Volume 3, Issue 3, December 1, 1997.

[129] See the work of sociologist Susan J. Palmer, who devoted more than a decade of her career studying Raëlism up close and personal, publishing her findings in a number of articles and a book, *Aliens Adored: Raël's UFO Religion.*

[130] See Gregg, Stephen, "Poking Fun at the Pope: Anti-Catholic Dialogue, Performance and the 'Symbolic Construction' of Identity in the International Raëlian Movement." *International Journal for the Study of New Religions* 3(1). August 2022.

AWOL FOR THE ANTICHRIST

See Vance Davis' *Unbroken Promises* for his personal account of the Gulf Breeze Six saga. See also Craig R. Meyers' *War of the Words: The True But Strange Story of the Gulf Breeze UFO* for a look at the sheer absurdity of the entire Gulf Breeze chapter in the already absurd saga of ufology, including the bizarre tale of Ed Walters and the arrival of the AWOL soldiers.

[131] "Soldiers Were to Expose UFO Scam, Sister Says." *Pensacola News Journal.* July 20, 1990, 1.

[132] See Ed Walters' *The Gulf Breeze Sightings: The Most Astounding Multiple Sightings of UFOs in U.S. History* for the first-hand account of the Gulf Breeze odyssey from the controversial man himself.

[133] "AWOL Soldier's Excuse: Ouija Board Made us do it," *Tampa Bay Times*, July 28, 1992, 4.

JUST HERE FOR THE SOULS

See Bob Lazar's *Dreamland: An Autobiography* for Bob Lazar's testimony of his alleged experiences at Area 51 in his own words. For more on John Lear, see

George Knapp's interviews with Lear available on YouTube via the 8 News Now channel. Also listen to archived episodes of *Coast to Coast AM* featuring John Lear and hosted by the late Art Bell, which can be found at the *Coast to Coast AM* website (www.coasttocoastam.com).

[134] See the Farsight Institute website (www.Farsight.org).

[135] From the CE4 website (www.ce4research.com).

[136] Gary Nolan to Tucker Carlson on *Tucker Carlson Today*, March 8, 2022.

[137] Whiteside, Steph, "Whistleblower David Grusch Refused to Meet with Pentagon UFO Office." *News Nation*, May 3, 2024 (www.newsnationnow.com).

[138] Simkins, Jon, "Army Partners with Former Blink-182 founder's UFO Research Company to Study Alien Technology." *Military Times*, October 25, 2019. See also Banias, MJ, "Tom De Longe's UFO Research Company Paid $35,000 for 'Exotic' Metals that Might Actually Just be Slag." *Vice* at www.vice.com, October 2019. See also Banias, M. J., "UFO Researcher Explains why she Sold 'Exotic' Metal to Tom DeLonge." *Vice* at www.vice.com, November 2019. See also Berhaus, Daniel, "Tom DeLonge's UFO Organization has a $37.4 Million Deficit," *Vice* at ww.vice.com, October 2019. See also Letzter, Ralph, "The Truth About those 'Alien Alloys' in the *New York Times* UFO story." *Scientific American* (sceintificamerican.com), December 22, 2017.

[139] On Gary Nolan, see Diana Pasulka's *American Cosmic* and interviews with Nolan by Tucker Carlson (March 8, 2022) and Ross Coulthart (June 2022), the recordings of which can be found on YouTube on numerous channels.

[141] Parry, Emma, "X-Files: Pentagon Releases 1,500 Pages of Secret Documents About Shadowy UFO Programme After Four-Year Battle." The *Sun* (www.the-sun.com), April 5, 2022.

[142] See Byron Lacy's *Chosen: Chronicles of an Alien Abductee*, as well as an interview with Lacy which aired on *Coast to Coast AM* July 30, 2023, available at the *Coast to Coast* website (coasttocoastam.com).

[143] On the case of Katie, the "Gold Leaf Lady," see Stephen Braude's *The Gold Leaf Lady and Other Parapsychological Investigations*.

[144] See Jule Eisenbud's *The World of Ted Serios*. Also see Braude's *The Gold Leaf Lady* for Braude's experience with Serios during and after the Eisenbud research.

145 For a popular overview of the seances at Scole, see Grant and Jane Solomon's *The Scole Experiment: Scientific Evidence for Life After Death* and the Scole Experiment website at thescoleexperiment.com. For a skeptical look at the Scole phenomena, see Hyman, Ray, "How Not to Test Mediums: Critiquing the Afterlife Experiments." *Skeptical Inquirer.* 27 (1), 20-30.

146 Keel, John (1996) *Operation Trojan Horse*, 192.

147 For more on these talking poltergeists and what I call "letters from Hell" cases described in this section, see references for works by Kishbucher, Moffitt, Holzer, Taylor and Fitzhugh. See also the account of the "Demon of Lemont" in my *Haunts of the White City*.

148 See Holzer, Hans, "The Devil in Texas." *Ghosts.*

149 See Bielski, Ursula "The Demon of Lemont." *Haunts of the White City.*

150 Rossetti, Msgr. Stephen, "Why Demons Text." On the blog *Exorcist's Diary* at www.catholicexorcism.org, July 22, 2021.

151 Quote by Gary Nolan to Ross Coulthart in an interview in June of 2022, available to view on the YouTube channel 7NEWS Spotlight.

152 See Demobly Kokota, "Episodes of Mass Hysteria in African Schools: A Study of Literature." *Malawi Medical Journal* , 2011 Sep; 23(3).

153 Prostak, Sergio, "Scientists Suggest Turin Shroud Authentic" in *Sci News* (www.scinews.com), December 21, 2011.

154 Keel, John, "On Ultraterrestrials and the Superspectrum," *The Eighth Tower.*

155 For more on Robert Goddard's rocketry experiments, see David Clary's *Rocket Man: Robert L. Goddard and the Birth of the Space Age.*

156 In a post on his *Final Events* blog on February 8, 2012 Redfern discussed von Karman, Parsons, Goddard and the golem association and quotes Rene Druks' statement from Nat Freedland's *The Occult Explosion* (www.eventsfinal.blogspot.com_.

[157] See Fowler, Raymond E., *The Andreasson Affair: The Documented Investigation of a Woman's Abduction Aboard a UFO.*

[158] Musgrave, JB and Houran, J. "Flight and Abduction in Witchcraft and UFO Lore." *Psychological Reports* 86(2), 669-88.

[159] For a full account of the experiences of "Claudia," see Jacobs, David, *The Threat.*

[160] See Leir's *The Aliens and the Scalpel : Scientific Proof of Extraterrestrial Implants in Humans.*

[161] See Patrick Huyghe, "Alien Implant—or Human Underwear?" *Omni*, vol. 17, no. 7, Apr. 1995, 46.

THE POSTER CHILD

It's always uncomfortable to recommend books that you really don't want people to buy, adding to the wealth and popularity of the authors. That is the case with many of the books referenced in this work, I'm afraid. At the top of that list are Strieber's books. I hate to recommend them, but it's crucial that you do read them, because few other poor souls demonstrate just how evil, influential, all-possessing and anti-Catholic the UFO phenomenon can be. And so, to learn more about Strieber, see his *Communion, The Key, The Afterlife Revolution, Jesus,* and *A New World* (details in references).

[162] Strieber, Whitley, "My Catholic Struggle." On his blog, *Unknown Country*, December 10, 2011 (www.unknowncountry.com).

[163] Ibid.

[165] Strieber, Whitley, *The Afterlife Revolution.*

OF UNKNOWN ORIGIN

[166] Information about Mark Macy and World ITC in this section of the chapter is summarized and quoted from the World ITC website at www.worlditc.org.

[168] For the full story of George Meek and the Spiricom, see Fuller, John G., *The Ghost of 29 Megacycles.*

[169] I've been familiar with this quote for decades but haven't been able to track down the source of it or the journal *Astra*. I do, however, include it because all of the other documented evidence of the incidents discussed point to it being authentic.

[170] See Bander, Peter (1973), *Voices from the Tapes: Recording from the Other World*, 123.

[171] Ibid., 10.

[172] Ibid., 139.

[173] Ibid., 93.

[174] Ibid., 133.

TREKKIES IN THE VATICAN

[175] Martin, Malachi, *The Jesuits*, 27.

[176] Spencer, Kyle, "A rainbow over Catholic colleges," *New York Times* (www.nytimes.com), July 30, 2013.

[177] See Maier, Francis X. "The Jesuits: What Went Wrong," *The Catholic Thing* (www.thecatholicthing.org), November 2022.

[178] Pullella, Philip, " Vatican Scientists Say Belief in Aliens is Ok," *Reuters* (Reuters.com), May 14, 2008.

[180] Consolmagno, Guy, "A Jesuit Astronomer's Guide to Avoiding Awful Science Fiction," *U.S.* Catholic (www.uscatholic.org), March 18, 2015.

[181] Grossman, Samantha, "Pope Francis Says he Would Baptize Martians if They Asked," *Time* (www.time.com), May 13, 2014.

[183] For Thigpen's full testimony, see "His Open Arms Welcomed Me—the Story of a Former Evangelical Pastor" via the Coming Home Network (www.chnetwork.org), January 13, 2011.

[184] Thigpen's answer is quoted from "Catholic Q&A" on the Catherine of Sienna website (www.stcatherinercc.org).

185 Daniel O'Connor, in a video entitled, "Padre Pio Believed in Aliens? (NO. And neither did St. John Chrysostom or the others!)" on the *Daniel O'Connor* YouTube channel, 2023.

186 Akin's full testimony may be found in Patrick Madrid's *Surprised by Truth: 11 Converts Give the Biblical and Historical Reasons for Becoming Catholic.*

187 Material in this section references and quotes from Matt Fradd's interview with Jimmy Akin on Fradd's podcast, *Pints with Aquinas* in the Spring of 2024. See www.pintswithaquinas.com for details and to listen to or watch the full episode.

188 See O'Connor, Daniel, *Only Man Bears His Image*, for scores of biblical, theological and magisterial arguments against alien belief.

189 In his book, *Only Man Bears His Image,*" Daniel O'Connor quotes the work, *Ireland and the Antipodes: The Heterodoxy of Virgil of Salzburg*, by John Carey, in which Carey recounts the story of Pope Zachary's denouncement.

190 Material in this section references and quotes from Akin's podcast, *Jimmy Akin's Mysterious World*, episode numbers 269 and 270 (See Audible listing to listen to full episodes).

191 Material in this section references and quotes from Irene Weinberg's interview with Fr. Nathan Castle on Weinberg's podcast, *Grief and Rebirth: Finding the Joy in Life, episode entitled* "Father Nathan Castle: A Catholic Priest Who Has Helped 'Stuck Souls' Who Died Suddenly And Traumatically Adjust To The Afterlife, Including Patrick Swayze's Deceased Sister!," available via Weinberg's website (www.ireneweinberg.com).

192 Material in this section references and quotes from episodes 306 and 307 of *Jimmy Akin's Mysterious World*, available on Audible and YouTube.

193 Chapter commentary on Pasulka is based on Pasulka's books, *American Cosmic and Encounters*, which I have frequently referenced in this book, as well as her statements during some of her many podcast appearances since her explosion of popularity a few years ago. I make reference to and quote from a number of them in this section. These podcasts are very long, but I really encourage readers to listen to or watch them in order to experience just how damaging to and misrepresentative of the Catholic faith are many of Pasulka's statements, only a fraction of which I have referenced in my discussion. I have relied most heavily on the most popular of these, as these reach the largest and most diverse

audiences. These include Pasulka's interviews by Joe Rogan (*The Joe Rogan Experience*, episode #2091, January 2024), Danny Jones (The *Danny Jones Podcast*, episode #188, June 2023), Curt Jaimungal (*Theories of Everything*, episode #42, May 2022), Jesse Michels (*Jesse Michels*, December 2023), Whitley Strieber (*Dreamland* podcast, 2024) and the popular Christian podcast, *Blurry Creatures* (episode #126, October 2023). All are readily available online at various audio and visual streaming platforms such as Audible, Spotify, Apple Podcasts and YouTube.

[195] Bledsoe, Chris, *UFO of God.*

[196] Hay, Donald, "On Being a Christian Academic,": a lecture given at Oxford GCU on October 13, 2008. Transcript at www.dcmoxford.org.

[197] Tsakanikas, Matthew, "Rosicrucian Principles Infiltrating Christianity: A Theological Advisory Against *UFO of God*" on his blog at Catholic460.substack.com (February 20, 2024).

[198] Material in this section references and quotes from the recorded video lecture listed on YouTube as "Paul & Ben Eno: Aliens and Exorcism: Why Do UFOs Turn Up in 'Possession' Cases?" and found on the *Exeter TV* YouTube channel.

EPILOGUE

[199] O'Connor, Daniel, *Only Man Bears His Image.*

[200] The full text of the *Catechism of the Catholic Church* (CCC) §358 reads "God created everything for man, but man in turn was created to serve and love God and to offer all creation back to him: What is it that is about to be created, that enjoys such honor? It is man that great and wonderful living creature, more precious in the eyes of God than all other creatures! For him the heavens and the earth, the sea and all the rest of creation exist. God attached so much importance to his salvation that he did not spare his own Son for the sake of man. Nor does he ever cease to work, trying every possible means, until he has raised man up to himself and made him sit at his right hand."

202 On Blake Lemoine, see "The AI Ouija Board: Is Artificial Intelligence Only Seeming to be Human—or Channelling Intelligent Spirits?" on the blog *Rod Dreher's Diary*, November 3, 2023. From Blake Lemoine himself see: "I Worked on AI at Google: My Worst Fears are Coming True" for *Newsweek* (www.newsweek.com), February 27, 2023. Also watch Lemoine interviewed on *Michael Sandler's Inspire Nation* YouTube channel in the episode entitled, "Is AI a "Catastrophic" Danger to Humanity? Whistleblower and Google LaMDA Engineer Blake Lemoine," October 2023.

203 Daly, Alan, "*Endeavor* Voyage: Kamay—Botany Bay" for the National Museum of Australia (www.nma.gov.au).

REFERENCES AND FURTHER READING

Adamski, George. *Inside the Flying Saucers*. CreateSpace, 2014.
—————— and Desmond Leslie. *The Flying Saucers Have Landed*. Createspace Independent Publishing Platform, 2017.
Barker, Gray. *They Knew Too Much about Flying Saucers*. Illuminet Press, 1996.
Bell, Art and Whitley Strieber. *The Coming Global Superstorm*. Simon & Schuster, 2004.
Bender, Albert, and Gray Barker. *Flying Saucers and the Three Men*. 2014.
Berliner, Don, and Stanton T Friedman. *Crash at Corona*. Cosimo, Inc., 2004.
Bielski, Ursula. *Haunted Bachelors Grove*. Arcadia Publishing, 2016.
—————. *Haunts of the White City : Ghost Stories from the World's Fair, the Great Fire, and Victorian Chicago*. History Press, 2019.
Bishop, Greg. *Project Beta : The Story of Paul Bennewitz, National Security, and the Creation of a Modern UFO Myth*. New York: Paraview Pocket Books, 2005.
Blavatsky, H P. *Isis Unveiled : A Master Key to the Mysteries of Ancient and Modern Science and Theology*. Pantianos Classics, 2018.
—————. *The Secret Doctrine : The Synthesis of Science, Religion, and Philosophy*. Pasadena, California: Theosophical University Press, 2014.
Bowman, Matthew. *The Abduction of Betty and Barney Hill*. Yale University Press, 2023.
Carter, John. *Sex and Rockets : The Occult World of Jack Parsons*. London: Feral House, 2005.
Charles James Hall. *Millennial Hospitality*. Author House, 2003.
Charles Webster Leadbeater. *Man Visible and Invisible*. 1903.
Churton, Tobias. *Aleister Crowley : The Biography*. London: Watkins, 2012.
—————. *Aleister Crowley in America*. Simon and Schuster, 2017.
Clarke, Arthur C. *Childhoods End*. Pan Macmillan, 2017.
Colavito, Jason. *The Cult of Alien Gods*. Prometheus Books, 2010.
Corso, Philip J, and William J Birnes. *The Day after Roswell*. New York: Gallery Books, 2017.
Cutchin, Joshua. *A Trojan Feast*. 2015.
—————. *An Ecology of Souls*.
David Michael Jacobs. *UFOs and Abductions*. 2000.
DeKoster, Katie. *Child Abuse: Opposing Viewpoints*.1994.
Derenberger, Woodrow W, and Harold W Hubbard. *Visitors from Lanulos : My Contact with Indrid Cold*. Point Pleasant, West Virginia: New Saucerian Books, 2014.

Deyo, Stan. *The Cosmic Conspiracy*. 2010.

Ellwood, Robert S, and Gregory D Alles. *The Encyclopedia of World Religions*. New Delhi: Viva Books, 2010.

----------------------, and Harry B Partin. *Religious and Spiritual Groups in Modern America*. London: Routledge, 2017.

Fitzhugh, Pat. *The Bell Witch*. The Armand Press, 2009.

Friedman, Stanton T, and Kathleen Marden. *Captured! The Betty and Barney Hill UFO Experience (60th Anniversary Edition)*. Red Wheel/Weiser, 2021.

Gerdes, Louise I. *Child Abuse : Opposing Viewpoints*. Farmington Hills, Michigan: Greenhaven Press, 2003.

Gorightly, Adam. *The Beast of Adam Gorightly*. Virtualbookworm Publishing, 2005.

Heiser, Michael S. *Reversing Hermon : Enoch, the Watchers & the Forgotten Mission of Jesus Christ*. Crane, Missouri: Defender Publishing, 2017.

——————————. *The Unseen Realm: Recovering the Supernatural Worldview of the Bible*. Saint Louis: Lexham Press, 2019.

Holzer, Hans. *Ghosts*. Open Road Media, 2012.

Hopkins, Budd. *Intruders*. August Night Press, 2021.

——————————. *Missing Time*. August Night Press, 2021.

—————————— and Phyllis Halldorson. *Witnessed*. Simon and Schuster, 1997.

Horn, Thomas R. *Nephilim Stargates : The Year 2012 and the Return of the Watchers*. Crane, Missouri: Anomalos Publishing House, 2007.

Jacobs, David M. *Secret Life*. Touchstone, 1993.

——————————. *The Threat : Revealing the Secret Alien Agenda*. Fireside, 2011.

——————————. *Walking Among Us : The Alien Plan to Control Humanity*. San Francisco, Ca, Disinformation Books, 2015.

Jacobsen, Annie. *Area 51 : An Uncensored History of America's Top Secret Military Base*. New York: Little, Brown and Co, 2011.

——————————. *Phenomena*. New York, Little, Brown, 28 Mar. 2017.

Keel, John. *Operation Trojan Horse*. 2015.

——————————. *The Mothman Prophecies*. New York: Godalming, 2013.

Kenneth Albert Arnold, and Ray Palmer. *The Coming of the Saucers*. 1952.

Kishbucher, Michael. *The Appalachian Legend of the Wizard Clip*. Arcadia Publishing, 2023.

Lachman, Gary. *Aleister Crowley*. Penguin, 2014.

Lazar, Bob. *Dreamland*. Interstellar, 2019.

Leadbeater, Charles. *Clairvoyance*. Createspace Independent Publishing Platform, 12 July 2016.

Lewis, James R, and Jere Paul Surber. *Encyclopedic Sourcebook of UFO Religions*. Humanity Books, 1 June 1998.

Mack. *Abduction: Human Encounters with Aliens*. Simon and Schuster, 15 Dec. 2009.

Martin, Malachi. *Hostage to the Devil: The Possession and Exorcism of Five Contemporary Americans*. New York, Quality Paperback Book Club, 2000.

Mcandrew, James, and United States. Department Of The Air Force. *The Roswell Report : Case Closed*. Washington, D.C., Headquarters United States Air Force, 1997.

Moffitt, Deborah. *Unwelcomed*. 12 Sept. 2015.

Nadis, Fred. *The Man from Mars : Ray Palmer's Amazing Pulp Journey*. New York, Jeremy P. Tarcher/Penguin, 2014.

Nelson, Victoria. *The Secret Life of Puppets*. Cambridge, Mass. ; London, Harvard University Press, 2003.

O'Connor, Daniel. *Only Man Bears His Image*. Oct. 2023.

Palmer, Susan. *Aliens Adored : Raël's UFO Religion*. New Brunswick Etc., Rutgers University Press, 2004.

Parsons, Jack W. *Freedom Is a Two Edged Sword*. 1990.

Partridge, Christopher. *UFO Religions*. Routledge, 2012.

Pasulka, Diana. *American Cosmic*. Oxford University Press, 2019.

——————. *Encounters*. St. Martin's Essentials, Nov. 2023.

Paulides, David. *Missing 411. North America and Beyond*. North Charleston, S.C., Createspace, 2012.

Pauwels, Louis, et al. *The Morning of the Magicians*. London Souvenir, 2007.

Pendle, George. *Strange Angel : The Otherworldly Life of Rocket Scientist John Whiteside Parsons*. Orlando: Harcourt, Inc, 2006.

Polidoro, Massimo. *Final Seance*. Prometheus Books, 2010.

Pritchard, Andrea. *Alien Discussions : Proceedings of the Abduction Study Conference*. Cambridge, Mass., North Cambridge Press, 1994.

Randle, Kevin D, and Donald R Schmitt. *UFO Crash at Roswell*. New York, Avon Books, 1991.

Redfern, Nick. *Final Events and the Secret Government Group on Demonic UFOs and the Afterlife*. San Antonio, Tx, Anomalist Books, 2010.

——————. *The Real Men in Black*. Red Wheel/Weiser, 2011.

Ronson, Jon. *Men Who Stare at Goats The*. W.F. Howes Ltd, 2010.

Ross, Hugh, et al. *Lights in the Sky & Little Green Men : A Rational Christian Look at UFOs and Extraterrestrials*. Colorado Springs: Navpress, 2002.

Sagan, Carl. *Demon-Haunted World: Science as a Candle in the Dark*. Ballantine Books, 2011.

Shaver, Richard S. *The Shaver Mystery*. Armchair Fiction & Music, 2011.

Sinnett, Alfred Percy. *Incidents in the Life of Madame Blavatsky*. 1886.

Solomon, Grant. *The Scole Experiment*. Campion Books, 2012.

Stranges, Frank E. *Stranger at the Pentagon*. New York: Universe Publishing, 1997.

Strieber, Whitley. *Communion*. Avon, 1987.

——————. *Jesus: A New Vision*. Walker & Collier, 2021.

——————. *The Key*. Penguin Random House, 2011.

——————. *The Afterlife Revolution*. Beyond Words, 2020.

Swedenborg, Emanuel. *Things Heard and Seen.* 1875.

Taylor, Jason R. *You Can't See Me, but I'm Here.* AuthorHouse, 2005.

Thigpen, Paul. *Extraterrestrial Intelligence and the Catholic Faith : Are We Alone in the Universe with God and the Angels?* Gastonia, North Carolina:, Tan Books, 2022.

Thomas, Gordon. *Secrets and Lies.* Konecky, William S. Associates, Inc., 2007.

Urantia Foundation. *The Urantia Book.* Chicago, Illinois: Urantia Foundation, 2015.

Vallee, Jaques. *Passport to Magonia.* Daily Grail Publishing, 2014.

————. *UFO Chronicles of the Soviet Union.* Ballantine, 1992.

Wells, H G. *The Outline of History.* Middleton, Delaware: Okitoks Press, 2017.

————. *War of the Worlds.* William Heinemann, 1898.

Williamson, George Hunt. *Other Tongues - Other Flesh.* Library of Alexandria, 1953.

————. *The Saucers Speak.* Health Research Books, 1996.

ABOUT THE AUTHOR

Historian, folklorist, and parapsychologist Ursula Bielski has been investigating the paranormal for nearly four decades. A native Chicagoan, Ursula is the author of more than a dozen popular and critically acclaimed books, including the groundbreaking *Chicago Haunts* series, one of the pioneering works of the ghostlore genre. She has appeared on scores of television and radio programs and hosted *The Hauntings of Chicago* for PBS, also serving as the program's executive producer. Bielski has also authored or contributed to a number of academic articles on parapsychological subjects, and she teaches courses in supernatural folklore and cemetery history at Chicago-area colleges. In 2018 she received the Chicago Public Library Foundation award for significant contributions to the city's literary culture..

Ursula has gone on to found worldofthesupernatural.com, a creative hub and community featuring books, podcasts, online courses and more. She hosts the weekly program, *Uncanny Catholici* on the World of the Supernatural, as well as *The Ghostlorist* podcast, featuring readings of haunted histories with Catholic analysis.

In 2021, Ursula co-founded Little Flowers mission and school in Pakistan, which teaches reading, writing and the Gospel to enslaved children and their families and raises funds to free them from brick slavery.

A lifelong Catholic, Ursula attended St. Benedict Elementary and High Schools in Chicago and received her Bachelor's in History from Benedictine University and a Masters in Cultural and Intellectual American History from Northeastern Illinois University. Today, she still lives in Chicago with her husband, where she writes, cooks, makes stuff for her Etsy shops, watches old thrillers and film noirs, and obsessively texts her two grown daughters.

OTHER BOOOKS FROM THIS AUTHOR

Chicago Haunts: Ghostlore of the Windy City
More Chicago Haunts: Scenes from Myth & Memory
Chicago Haunts 3
Graveyards of Chicago
There's Something Under the Bed
Creepy Chicago (for kids)
Haunted Gary
Haunted Bachelors Grove
Haunts of the White City
The Haunting of Joliet Prison
A Year With the Holy Souls
The Devil in Dreamland
Catholic Kids' Prayer Journal
Chicago Haunts: The Ultimate Collection (2024)
And the Shadows Flee Away (2024)
Catholic Ghosts (2025)
Extraordinary Activity of the Devil (2025)
The Haunting of Twentynine Palms (2025)
The Paranormal Minefield (2025)